SYMBOLIC COMPUTATION

Artificial Intelligence

Springer Series
SYMBOLIC COMPUTATION - *Artificial Intelligence*

N.J. Nilsson: *Principles of Artificial Intelligence*. XV, 476 pages, 139 figs., 1982

J.H. Siekmann, G. Wrightson (Eds.): *Automation of Reasoning 1. Classical Papers on Computational Logic 1957–1966*. XII, 525 pages, 1983

J.H. Siekmann, G. Wrightson (Eds.): *Automation of Reasoning 2. Classical Papers on Computational Logic 1967–1970*. XII, 637 pages, 1983

L. Bolc (Ed.): *The Design of Interpreters, Compilers, and Editors for Augmented Transition Networks*. XI, 214 pages, 72 figs., 1983

M.M. Botvinnik: *Computers in Chess. Solving Inexact Search Problems*. XIV, 158 pages, 48 figs., 1984

L. Bolc (Ed.): *Natural Language Communication with Pictorial Information Systems*. VII, 327 pages, 67 figs., 1984

R.S. Michalski, J.G. Carbonell, T.M. Mitchell (Eds.): *Machine Learning. An Artificial Intelligence Approach*. XI, 572 pages, 1984

A. Bundy (Ed.): *Catalogue of Artificial Intelligence Tools. Second, Revised Edition*. XVII, 168 pages, 1986

C. Blume, W. Jakob: *Programming Languages for Industrial Robots*. XIII, 376 pages, 145 figs., 1986

J.W. Lloyd: *Foundations of Logic Programming. Second, Extended Edition*. XII, 212 pages, 1987

L. Bolc (Ed.): *Computational Models of Learning*. IX, 208 pages, 34 figs., 1987

L. Bolc (Ed.): *Natural Language Parsing Systems*. XVIII, 367 pages, 151 figs., 1987

N. Cercone, G. McCalla (Eds.): *The Knowledge Frontier, Essays in the Representation of Knowledge*. XXXV, 512 pages, 93 figs., 1987

continued after index

Yun Peng   James A. Reggia

Abductive Inference Models for Diagnostic Problem-Solving

With 25 Illustrations

Springer-Verlag
New York   Berlin   Heidelberg
London   Paris   Tokyo   Hong Kong

Yun Peng
University of Maryland
Department of Computer Science
College Park, Maryland 20742, USA
The Institute of Software
Academia Sinica
Beijing, China

James A. Reggia
University of Maryland
Department of Computer Science
College Park, Maryland 20742
USA

Library of Congress Cataloging-in-Publication Data
Peng, Yun.
   Abductive inference models for diagnostic problem-solving / Yun
Peng, James A. Reggia.
      p.   cm.—(Symbolic computation. Artificial intelligence)
   Includes bibliographical references and index.
   1. Problem solving.   2. Artificial intelligence.   3. Problem
solving.   4. Abduction (Logic)   5. Reasoning.   I. Reggia, James A.
II. Title.   III. Series.
Q335.P414   1990
006.3—dc20   90-36687

Printed on acid-free paper

Camera-ready copy provided by the authors using troff on UNIX.
Printed and bound by R.R. Donnelly & Sons, Harrisonburg, Virginia.
Printed in the United States of America.

9 8 7 6 5 4 3 2 1

ISBN 0-387-97343-5 Springer-Verlag New York Berlin Heidelberg
ISBN 3-540-97343-5 Springer-Verlag Berlin Heidelberg New York

Preface

Making a diagnosis when something goes wrong with a natural or man-made system can be difficult. In many fields, such as medicine or electronics, a long training period and apprenticeship are required to become a skilled diagnostician. During this time a novice diagnostician is asked to assimilate a large amount of knowledge about the class of systems to be diagnosed. In contrast, the novice is not really taught how to reason with this knowledge in arriving at a conclusion or a diagnosis, except perhaps implicitly through case examples. This would seem to indicate that many of the essential aspects of diagnostic reasoning are a type of intuition-based, common sense reasoning.

More precisely, diagnostic reasoning can be classified as a type of inference known as *abductive reasoning* or *abduction*. Abduction is defined to be a process of generating a plausible explanation for a given set of observations or facts. Although mentioned in Aristotle's work, the study of formal aspects of abduction did not really start until about a century ago. The emergence of computational models for various abductive inference applications in artificial intelligence (AI) and cognitive science is even more recent, having begun little more than a decade ago. Considering the importance of abductive inference and how widely it is used in everyday life and in numerous special fields, the late emergence of formal and computational models of abduction is somewhat surprising. This is particularly true when contrasted with the maturity of some deductive inference models, such as first order predicate calculus.

This book is about reasoning with causal associations during diagnostic problem–solving. It is an attempt to formalize the currently vague notions of abductive inference in the context of diagnosis. The material brings together and synthesizes the efforts of a ten year period of research by the authors and others. The core results were initially developed as a formal theory of diagnostic inference called *parsimonious covering theory*, and were then extended to incorporate probability theory. Within parsimonious covering theory, various diagnostic problems are formally defined, properties of diagnostic problem–solving are identified and analyzed, and algorithms for finding plausible explanations in different situations are given along with proofs of their correctness.

Parsimonious covering theory captures in a precise form many of the important features of the imprecise, intuitive concept of abduction. It not only forms a good theoretical foundation for automated diagnostic problem–solving, but also provides a useful framework for examining other non–diagnostic applications characterized as abductive problems. Practically, this theory may provide important guiding principles for constructing various diagnostic knowledge–based systems capable of handling a broad range of problems. Of course, the theory developed in this book does *not* represent a complete theory of abduction, even for diagnostic problem–solving. Nevertheless, we believe it represents a substantial step forward in formalizing some aspects of diagnostic reasoning in a general, application–independent fashion.

This book is intended for readers with a background in artificial intelligence or cognitive science. While some of the material involves mathematical derivations, only basic knowledge of elementary set theory, logic and probability theory is assumed. Our emphasis is on developing an intuitive understanding rather than on mathematical rigor. Thus, the intuitions behind the results presented in this book are explained and stressed in the text, while their formal proofs are given in appendices at the ends of appropriate chapters. These appendices can be skipped by those whose primary interests are the methods of parsimonious covering theory and how to apply them to various problems rather than the mathematical development of the theory. This book is not only suitable for self–study, but could also be used as a text for graduate courses in AI, knowledge engineering, or cognitive science that include material on abductive inference. This book could also be used as a reference source for professionals in these and other related areas.

The material in this book is organized as follows. Chapters 1 and 2 informally introduce the reader to the basic characteristics of abductive inference and diagnostic problem–solving. Some computational diagnostic problem–solving systems based on parsimonious covering theory and examples of problem–solving with these systems are presented. This approach is contrasted to other existing computational models of diagnostic reasoning, both to motivate the intuitions behind the theory and to demonstrate its basic features.

Chapter 3 presents the basic model of parsimonious covering theory. Diagnostic problems and their solutions are defined in unambiguous mathematical terms, and formal algorithms for finding problem solutions are then developed. This formulation, although based on very simple causal networks, is seen to capture the essence of abductive diagnostic reasoning and can provide a theoretical foundation for a variety of real–world applications.

The basic framework of parsimonious covering theory can be extended in various ways to accommodate different types of information. Some of these theoretical extensions are presented in Chapters 4 and 5 where probability theory is incorporated into basic parsimonious covering theory, capturing information about the uncertainty of causal relations. Other extensions are given in Chapter 6 where more general causal networks involving intermediate states and "causal chaining" are used. These

extensions greatly enhance the breadth and power of parsimonious covering theory and its potential practical applications.

One difficulty that arises in developing parsimonious covering theory
and other models of abductive diagnosis is the computational complexity
involved. For example, in some situations, finding the most probable
causative hypothesis for a given set of symptoms/manifestations may take
time exponential to the size of the causal network if multiple disorders
may occur simultaneously. To circumvent this potentially formidable
difficulty, an approximation algorithm based on connectionist modeling is
presented in Chapter 7. This model, taking advantage of highly parallel
computations, requires a more or less constant amount of time for
problem–solving, yet yields very accurate results. It offers an attractive
alternative to traditional AI sequential search in diagnostic problem-
solving. Finally, Chapter 8 closes the book with concluding remarks about
non–diagnostic abduction and future research directions.

The development of parsimonious covering theory has benefited from
contributions from a number of individuals. These contributions are referenced in the text, including those from Sanjeev Ahuja, Bill Chu, Venu
Dasigi, C. Lynne D'Autrechy, Sharon Goodall, Dana Nau, Barry Perricone,
Srinivasan Sekar, Malle Tagamets, Stanley Tuhrim, and Pearl Wang. We
have been very fortunate in working with such talented collaborators.
Finally, we wish to express our thanks to the staff at Springer-Verlag,
especially Gerhard Rossbach and Donna Moore, for their help in bringing
this book to completion.

Yun Peng
James A. Reggia

College Park, Maryland
January, 1990

Contents

1
Abduction and Diagnostic Inference

> "Ah, my dear Watson, there we come to the
> realms of conjecture where the most logical mind
> may be at fault. Each may form his own
> hypothesis upon the present evidence, and yours is
> as likely to be correct as mine."
>
> Arthur C. Doyle, *The Empty House*

Abduction is a type of logic or reasoning which derives plausible explanations for the data at hand. In this book, formal and computational models of the abductive reasoning process that underlies diagnostic problem-solving are considered. The core material presented is that of "parsimonious covering theory" and various extensions to it. Among other things, this theory provides a theoretical foundation for the recent and continuing efforts to automate abductive reasoning in diagnostic problem-solving.

Before getting into parsimonious covering theory itself, in this chapter we briefly discuss some prerequisite issues of importance, such as the nature of abductive reasoning and its characteristics, why it is important to understand and to formalize abduction, and the fact that diagnostic problem-solving is a type of abductive inference. Our aim is to provide motivation, terminology, and background for the development of the formal theory found in later chapters of this book.

1.1. Abductive Inference

In informal terms, *abduction* or *abductive inference* is generally taken to mean "inferring the best or most plausible explanations for a given set of facts" [Pople73, Thargard78, Josephson82,84, Encyclopedia Britannica]. Abduction, deduction, and induction are three fundamental logics of scientific inquiry and reasoning. Capturing abductive inference in artificial intelligence (AI) systems has proven to be a very difficult task, and even defining and characterizing abduction in precise terms remains to be fully achieved.

The origin of the term "abduction" can be traced back to ancient Greece. In *Prior Analytics*, Aristotle mentioned a process for manipulating syllogisms that he called "apagoge". What Aristotle meant by apagoge is the process of looking for premises to make the desired conclusion become more plausible, suggesting hypothesis testing. The Greek prefix *apo* suggests motion away, making "abduction" an appropriate translation. The actual term "abduction" was first introduced into modern philosophy and science by the renowned American philosopher Charles S. Peirce [Peirce31,55]. In this view, abduction, though positively related to deduction and induction, is a distinguished fundamental logic in its own right.

Abduction is more frequently used in everyday "common sense" reasoning and in expert–level problem–solving than is generally recognized. In fact, superficial examination of conclusions reached using abductive reasoning are often viewed as deductive inference. "Elementary, my dear Watson," says Sherlock Holmes, the master of "deduction", as he makes one of his brilliant abductive inferences. From time to time, the authors have encountered statements suggesting that conclusions reached using abductive reasoning were actually reached deductively. For example, "I deduced that the car's battery was dead because the engine would not start and the headlights did not come on." While the battery may indeed be dead and this is certainly a plausible explanation for the facts at hand, one cannot *deduce* such a conclusion in this situation. The reality might be that both headlights have burned out simultaneously and that the fuel line is blocked (another possible explanation for the observations). It may seem that the former *hypothesis* or *explanation* is more plausible, consisting as it does of one fault (dead battery) rather than three (two headlights plus fuel line), but the point here is that one cannot *deduce* anything with certainty in this situation. The most one can do is to consider a dead battery to be a plausible hypothesis among other possible hypotheses, to be subsequently tested and validated ("see, when I put my finger across the terminals, nothing happens ... OUCH!"). Abduction involves not only making hypotheses, but also discriminating among them based on their plausibility.

To the authors' knowledge, the term "abduction" was first introduced into the AI literature around 1973 [Pople73]. However, abductive reasoning has received surprisingly little attention from the AI community until very recently. This is unfortunate considering that many AI systems are actually trying to solve abductive tasks (as one of the few AI texts that even mentions this topic rightfully points out [Charniak85]). However, it is now becoming more widely realized that, although very difficult, capturing abductive inference in AI systems is a task with tremendous potential payoff. For this reason, AI researchers have recently devoted increasing attention to developing abductive inference methods in a wide range of applications.

Prominent among these applications is diagnostic problem–solving, which we will consider more fully below. Other applications exist in machine vision, natural language processing, legal reasoning, plan interpretation, and learning. For example, natural language understanding models that abductively construct plausible interpretations of stories have been developed (see Chapter 10, [Charniak85]). These and related models involve "motivational analysis", by which is meant recognition of the intention of others, and "plan recognition" [Litman87, Josephson87b, Kautz86]. Legal situations, with opposing lawyers offering alternative explanatory hypotheses and arguing for their plausibility, are a rich source of abductive inference, and some work has been done on modeling such inference [Thagard89]. Other work has focused on general purpose abductive models for interpreting novel events (e.g., MGR, for Model Generative Reasoning [Coombs87]), and on applying abductive inference methods during learning [O'Rorke89].

In these different application fields the details of the abductive inference process used may vary. Some of these fields are sufficiently complex and the knowledge involved is so ill–structured that it has not seemed useful to even try to mimic them by computer programs using present techniques. Some others, particularly diagnostic inference, are relatively structured, and their basic characteristics are better understood, due to work on computer–aided diagnostic systems and studies done in cognitive science during the last few decades. This is one reason that we have chosen abductive diagnostic inference, which directly utilizes those important features of abduction mentioned above, as the focus of our work and this book. The work on diagnostic inference described in this book serves as a case study of basic features of general abduction. Further, the work described here should also contribute to the development of automated diagnostic systems by establishing a theoretical foundation for them.

1.2. Abduction as a Class of Logic

To further demonstrate the characteristics of abductive inference, we next compare it with deduction and induction through simple but instructive syllogisms. *Deductive* reasoning consists of a general Rule (the major premise) and a specific Case (minor premise) from which a specific Result (conclusion) can be deduced:

> *Given Rule* – All the balls in the box are black.
> + *Case* – These balls are from the box.
> _____
> *Conclude Result* – These balls are black.

Inductive reasoning consists of a specific case and specific result from which a general rule can be hypothesized:

> *Given Case* – These balls are from the box.
> + *Result* – These balls are black.
> _____

Hypothesize Rule – All balls in the box are black.

In contrast to deduction and induction, *abductive* reasoning consists of a general rule and a specific result from which a specific case can be hypothesized:

> *Given Rule* – All balls in the box are black.
> + *Result* – These balls are black.

> *Hypothesize Case* – These balls are from the box.

Induction, like abduction, involves making and testing hypotheses. In fact the term "induction" is sometimes used to describe an inference process which includes abductive inference. The difference between these two terms should be clear from the above examples, at least as we use them in this book. In induction, what is being hypothesized is the general rule, while in abduction it is the specific case. Moreover, an inductive hypothesis is usually drawn not from a single situation but from a large number of situations that collectively support the plausibility of the hypothesized general rule. In contrast, abductive inference can be and usually is conducted with information about a single situation.

Deductive inference, on the other hand, is similar to abduction in that a result is produced for a specific case. In deduction, however, the result is a logical consequence of the general rule and the case that is held to be true. If both rule and case are true, then the result is also true. In contrast, with abduction even if both the general rule (general knowledge) and the specific result (observed facts) are true, the inferred specific case is only a possibility; it is not definitely true. In the abductive syllogism above, the observed black balls might actually come from some other place.

Moreover, if the general rule is not an absolute implication, but some less certain assertion like "Almost all balls in the box are black", then even the deductive syllogism no longer holds. One cannot even infer by pure deduction from the case "These balls are from the box" the conclusion "These balls are black". This is why many "rule-based" systems in AI have adopted various measures of uncertainty, even when they are largely deductive in nature (see next chapter). On the other hand, in abduction, even though the general rule is not an absolute implication, "These balls are from the box" is still a possible explanation of the observed fact "These balls are black".

Frequently, more than one possible explanation exists during abductive inference, so a disambiguation process is often needed to discriminate between alternative explanations. For example, if both *a* and *b* can independently cause *fact-1*, and *fact-1* is observed to be present, then both *a* and *b* are possible explanations for *fact-1*. If a second fact is known, say *fact-2* is also present, and we know that *a* is capable of causing *fact-2* but

b is not, then we might presume that a would be more likely than b, or that a is more *plausible* as an explanation of both *fact-1* and *fact-2* than b. The *plausibility* of competing alternative explanations is an important and difficult issue in abduction and is examined in detail later in this book.

In the contrasts above, a comparison is made between "pure" deductive and abductive inferences to emphasize their distinguished features as two different inference methods. The reader should, however, appreciate the fact that some computer models based directly on deductive methods that are used to solve abductive problems often incorporate uncertainty measures and other meta–deductive features. Such rule–based systems are no longer purely deductive. The point is that a more direct, non–deductive formulation of abductive inference is needed which, if it captures appropriate features of abduction in a natural way, should be more suitable for abductive problems than formulations starting with direct deductive methods [Nau84].

1.3. Diagnostic Problem–Solving

A diagnostic problem is a problem in which one is given a set of *manifestations* (findings, symptoms) and must explain why they are present by using one's knowledge about the world. Diagnostic problems can be found in various areas, for example, diagnosis in clinical medicine, computer program debugging, and fault localization in electronics, to mention just a few. Because of the limitations of human memory and the complexity of many diagnostic problems, knowledge–based systems for diagnostic problem solving have great potential for practical applications. They are being used in industry and are an active research area in AI. Just as important, diagnosis provides a useful "case study" of abductive reasoning.

It is widely accepted that human diagnostic inference falls naturally into the category of abduction [Pople73,82, Reggia83a,85a,b, Charniak85, Elstein78] and it is perhaps the most typical and best understood class of abductive problem–solving applications. Consider medical diagnosis as an example. Medical textbooks present associations between diseases and manifestations in the form of "disease d_i may cause symptoms (manifestations) $m_1, m_2, \ldots, m_k$". Usually, some rough estimates of uncertainty are attached to the causal associations. If a set of symptoms or manifestations are found to be present, a doctor tries to identify a set of one or more diseases (hypothesis generation) which is capable of causing all of the patient's present manifestations (or at least the most significant ones), and thus to account for or "explain" these findings. Informal estimates of plausibility or probability, the parsimony principle (Occam's razor), and contextual information (e.g., the patient's age; inter–relations between diseases) are used to disambiguate among possible hypotheses to select the most plausible ones. If the resulting hypothesis is not sufficiently convincing or further disambiguation of existing hypotheses is needed, questions may be asked or laboratory data obtained to discover additional information and permit hypothesis revision.

Researchers from various fields have conducted a number of empirical studies of human diagnostic reasoning or of how human diagnosticians perform abductive inference to reach their conclusions [Elstein78, Kassirer78, Rubin75]. Based on these studies, it can be concluded that human diagnostic reasoning often involves "hypothesis generation" (forming candidate explanations), "hypothesis updating" (updating existing hypotheses or generating new hypotheses based on newly available information), and "hypothesis testing" (disambiguating existing hypotheses). *Hypothesize-and-test cycles* continue until the plausibility of one or more hypotheses pass some given criteria and they are accepted as reasonable explanations (diagnoses) for the given findings. It is convenient to view the sequential, repetitive hypothesize–and–test process (sometimes also called the *hypothetico–deductive* process) involved as consisting of cycles having three steps (see Figure 1.1):

(1) *disorder evocation*, in which a set of individual hypothesis elements (disorders) are evoked through associations with a newly given manifestation;

(2) *hypothesis formation*, in which the hypothesis elements so generated are combined with previously formed hypotheses to form a set of new hypotheses such that each hypothesis can account for both old and new manifestations; and

(3) *question generation* or *hypothesis testing*, in which a new "question" is generated whose answer may be used to test and to further disambiguate existing hypotheses.

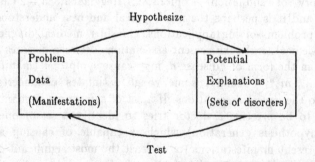

Figure 1.1. The cycle of hypothesize–and–test reasoning during diagnostic problem–solving.

Disorder evocation is the retrieval from long–term memory of causative disorders as the diagnostician detects a new manifestation in the information available about a problem. This evoking of potential causes for the manifestation begins very early in the diagnostic process and draws on the diagnostician's memory of causal associations between disorders and their manifestations. Ideally, the diagnostician's knowledge base or long–term memory includes the set of all possible causative disorders for each manifestation and the set of all possible manifestations for each disorder. Usually, a *single* manifestation (rather than combinations of manifestations) is responsible for evoking new disorders for incorporation into the evolving hypotheses [Kassirer78].

The second phase of the hypothesize–and–test cycle, hypothesis evaluation or formation, involves the incorporation of possible causes of the new manifestation into the hypotheses under consideration. This may require attributing the manifestation to some disorder already assumed to be present (i.e., already in some existing hypotheses), or adding new disorders evoked by the manifestation to form new hypotheses. In other words, the set of plausible hypotheses is continuously changing during this process. It is in this sense that abduction is considered to be a non–monotonic logic [Reggia84a]. The evolved hypothesis at times may become relatively complex. Not only may it contain a great deal of uncertainty about which of several disorders account for a certain manifestation, but it also might presume the simultaneous presence of multiple disorders (*multiple disorder hypothesis*). Another point worth noticing is that during this dynamic process, human diagnosticians tend to focus their attention on only a few most promising hypotheses while the rest are put aside but not completely forgotten. Later, if some new unexpected findings become available, these deferred hypotheses may be reconsidered. In other words, human diagnosticians adopt some form of a best–first search strategy to narrow their search space.

Empirical evidence suggests that hypothesis formation can best be viewed as a resolution of two conflicting goals:

Covering goal: The goal of explaining all of the manifestations that are present.
Parsimony goal: The goal of minimizing the complexity of the explanation.

The second goal, sometimes referred to as "Occam's razor", can be viewed as an attempt to focus the reasoning process and therefore restrict searching, as a reflection of human memory limitations, or as a "common sense" heuristic that is correct most of the time.

It is important to appreciate the sequential nature of diagnostic reasoning. As the diagnostician gradually learns information about a problem, his or her hypothesis(es) changes to reflect this new information. For example, if a patient complains of sudden onset of chest pain, a physician's initial hypotheses might be something like:

HYPOTHESIS H1: "Heart attack, *or* pulmonary embolus, *or* ..."

Although multiple disorders are under consideration, they are alternatives here: the presence of a *single* disorder of uncertain identity is being postulated. As further details become available, some of these initially considered disorders might be eliminated. If it was then learned that the patient also had a chronic cough, the hypotheses might change to:

HYPOTHESIS H2: "Heart attack, *or* pulmonary embolus, *or* ... "
and
"bronchitis, *or* asthma, *or* ... "

reflecting the physician's belief that at least two diseases must be present to account for this patient's symptoms. Note that at this point, there is both uncertainty (indicated by *or*) and the presumption that multiple simultaneous disorders are present (indicated by *and*). The possible presence of multiple simultaneous disorders (two in this case, more in others) is one of the features of general diagnostic problem–solving that has proven difficult to capture in primarily deductive computer systems (see Chapter 2).

Another aspect of hypothesis evaluation is the ranking of the likelihood of competing disorders. The term *competing disorders* refers to hypothesized alternatives which can account for the same or similar manifestations, such as heart attack and pulmonary embolus in hypothesis H1 or H2. This term arises because these disorders can be viewed as "competing" with one another to be in an explanation for the observed manifestations (in contrast to, say, heart attack and bronchitis, which can be viewed as "cooperating" to form explanations). Perhaps surprisingly, human diagnosticians in medicine appear to use only a three point weighting scheme to rank competing disorders: a particular finding may be "positive, noncontributory or negative with respect to a particular hypothesis" [Elstein78]. At the end of a problem–solving session, human diagnosticians are thus able to rank competing disorders only in very coarse fashion (e.g., disorder *d* is definitely present, *d* is very likely to be present, *d* may be present, *d* is possible but not probable). Most of this ranking can be accounted for by either of two rules: (a) weighting based on counting the number of positive findings, or (b) weighting based on counting the number of positive findings minus the number of expected findings found to be absent [Elstein78].

The third phase of the hypothesize–and–test cycle, question generation, represents the "test" phase. The word "question" here is being used in a general sense to indicate any type of information–gathering activity. Investigators studying human diagnostic problem–solving often divide such questions into two categories: *protocol-driven* and *hypothesis-driven*. Protocol-driven questions are those a diagnostician generally asks as a routine during a diagnostic session. In contrast, hypothesis-driven questions seek information that is specifically needed to modify the evolving hypothesis. Investigators who observe diagnosticians sometimes attribute each hypothesis-driven question to a specific problem-solving strategy: attempting to confirm a hypothesis, attempting to eliminate a hypothesis, or attempting to discriminate between two or more hypotheses [Kassirer78, Elstein78].

Many aspects of the diagnostic reasoning process are incompletely understood at the present time. For example, it is unclear how a diagnostician reasons effectively about multiple simultaneous disorders. In such situations each manifestation must be attributed to an appropriate disorder, and competing disorders must be ranked in the context of other disorders assumed to be present. It is also unclear exactly how diagnosticians decide to terminate the diagnostic process because a "solution" has been reached.

1.4. Overview of What Follows

This chapter has provided a brief but essential introduction to abductive inference in general and to diagnostic reasoning as a special type of abductive inference. This material will provide the reader with a useful framework within which to fit what follows. Chapter 2 builds on this introductory framework in describing a number of computational models of diagnostic problem-solving. It informally introduces the reader to the basic ideas and flavor of parsimonious covering theory which forms the core material in the rest of the book.

The basic formulation of parsimonious covering theory, which deals with the simplest type of diagnostic problems (i.e., problems without intermediate states), is presented in Chapters 3 – 5. Chapter 3 gives the central concepts of the theory, including diagnostic problem formulation and knowledge representation, operations for hypothesis formation and updating, and various problem-solving algorithms. Chapters 4 and 5 describe the integration of parsimonious covering theory and probability theory. Chapter 4 treats the formal aspects of this integration, and develops a probability calculus for the integrated model. Chapter 5 concentrates on developing a best-first search strategy and algorithms which are capable of deriving the most probable explanation(s) for a given set of manifestations. Issues concerning the quality of problem solutions are also addressed in this chapter.

Chapter 6 extends the basic model developed in Chapter 3 to more general problems with intermediate states and with causal chaining. Chapter 7 addresses another issue: instead of deriving problem solutions using traditional algorithmic methods, a parallel processing approach for diagnosis based on "neural network" or "connectionist" techniques is discussed. A diagnostic problem is viewed as a non–linear optimization problem, and the underlying causal network as a neural/connectionist network. The solution, i.e., the most probable explanation, is obtained as an emergent property of collective parallel local interactions between nodes in the network.

Parsimonious covering theory is a substantial step forward in formalizing some aspects of diagnostic reasoning in a general, application-independent fashion. However, this theory and its extensions as presented in this book do not represent a complete theory of abduction, even for diagnostic problem–solving. The limitations of parsimonious covering theory are addressed in Chapter 8. Chapter 8 also briefly discusses potential applications of parsimonious covering theory, including some non-diagnostic ones (natural language processing, learning). Research directions within the domain of diagnostic problem–solving as well as for abductive logic in general are also discussed.

2
Computational Models for Diagnostic Problem Solving

> "Find out the cause of this effect, or rather say, the cause of this defect, for this effect defective comes by cause."
> Shakespeare

We now turn to the issue of automating diagnostic problem–solving and briefly survey representative previous work in this area. Such work is substantial, going back to almost the advent of electronic stored–program computers [Reggia85f], and for this reason the material that follows must unfortunately be quite selective. It is organized into three sections. The first section describes some basic concepts of knowledge–based systems. Two important methods that have been used widely to implement knowledge–based diagnostic systems, statistical pattern classification and rule–based deduction, are briefly described. The second section describes another class of systems which we will refer to as *association–based abductive systems*. These latter models capture the spirit of abductive reasoning in computer models. Two substantial examples of such systems are given and used to introduce the basic terminology of parsimonious covering theory in an informal, intuitive fashion. The third and the final section briefly addresses some practical issues that arise in implementing computational models for diagnosis.

2.1. Knowledge–Based Problem–Solving Systems

The design and use of knowledge–based (expert) systems has been an important and very fruitful part of AI. As problem–solving programs, their performance has reached the level of human experts in some specialized problem domains where considerable precision or expertise is needed. The most distinguishing feature of knowledge–based systems, besides their high performance, is the separation of the knowledge from the inference mechanism. The program's "knowledge", abstracted from human expertise about the problem domain, is contained in the *knowledge base*. The *inference mechanism* uses the information in the knowledge base to draw conclusions about input data. This is illustrated by the simple model in

Figure 2.1 below.

There are a number of fundamental problems which must be solved in developing a knowledge–based system. These include the problems of knowledge representation (what kind of representation is best for storing knowledge in the knowledge base), knowledge acquisition (how to acquire expertise from human experts), reasoning models (what kind of inference mechanism to use), and answer justification (how and to what extent to justify the system's conclusions in a way understandable to users). Solutions to these problems are interdependent and have varied from application to application [Addis85, Coombs84, Ramsey86, Reggia85f, Torasso89, Weiss84].

2.1.1. Structural (Symbolic) and Probabilistic (Numeric) Knowledge

At least two kinds of knowledge are used by human diagnosticians as well as by most advanced AI diagnostic systems. They are referred to here as *structural* and *probabilistic* knowledge. Structural knowledge (usually in symbolic form in knowledge–based diagnostic systems) specifies what the entities of interest are in an application domain and which entities are associated by what kind of association(s). Among these different kinds of associations, cause–effect relations are probably the most important in diagnostic problems–solving. For example, in medical diagnosis, the statements "disorder d_i may be a cause of manifestation m_j", or "m_j may be a manifestation of d_i" associate d_i and m_j together. This association comes from either the compilation of so–called deeper knowledge of *underlying mechanisms* (e.g., in medicine, for certain physiological reasons, d_i and m_j are causally associated) or from the *extraction of regularities* from past experience (e.g., d_j and m_j are causally associated because symptom m_j has

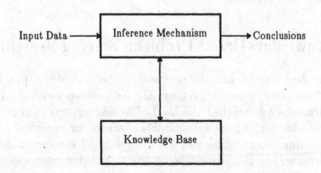

Figure 2.1. A simple model of a knowledge–based system.

been found in certain cases of patients having disorder d_i).

Probabilistic knowledge, on the other hand, reflects the uncertain aspects of such associations that people have in mind. Probabilistic knowledge (usually in numeric form in knowledge–based diagnostic systems) specifies the strength of associations and prior probabilities of individual entities. Here the term "numeric" is used loosely to mean at least ordinal information so that magnitudes can be compared. Thus probabilities may be represented as actual numbers (0.5, 0.01, etc.) or in non–numeric symbolic form ("very common", "moderate", "very rare", etc.). We use the term "probabilistic knowledge" here regardless of whether a probability estimate or some other measure ("belief", "certainty factor", etc.) is used.

During problem solving, the focus of attention can be narrowed to some extent solely through the use of structural knowledge. For example, d_i might be categorically excluded from any hypothesis because it is not a cause of any present manifestations. However, this approach in general could result in the consideration of a large number of unlikely hypotheses. On the other hand, completely relying on probabilistic knowledge usually requires a large amount of data and many numerical computations, and results in a system which is very sensitive to the correctness of the data obtained. Furthermore, statistical pattern classification techniques which use only probabilistic knowledge are mainly concerned with *selection* from predefined categories rather than construction of those categories as required by abductive diagnostic inference. For example, a Bayesian classification system (see below) may be able to calculate the posterior probability of a given multiple disorder hypothesis, but by itself is not able to *construct* such a hypothesis from individual disorders. Therefore, for a high performance diagnostic system, both structural and probabilistic knowledge appear indispensable.

Most people developing knowledge–based diagnostic systems using AI techniques have realized that incorporating probabilistic measurements or other weighting schemes into symbolic systems is a necessity for good system performance. Unfortunately, in many AI systems this is done in an informal and heuristic fashion, and thus may not be justified rigorously or trusted in general situations. A consistent and unified model that incorporates the use of both kinds of knowledge is very desirable in developing a formal abductive logic in general, and in developing high performance knowledge–based diagnostic systems in particular.

A great variety of computer–aided diagnostic systems have been developed during the past few decades [Addis85, Coombs84, Ramsey86, Reggia85f, Torasso89, Weiss84]. Although many of these systems have achieved expert–level performance in various applications, all have some serious limitations. These limitations become more acute when they are applied to problems in which multiple disorders can be present simultaneously. The knowledge representation and inference mechanisms used in many systems are not well suited for capturing the abductive nature of diagnostic problem–solving in this situation.

We now briefly consider two previous approaches to automating diagnostic problem–solving techniques. A critical appraisal of them is given to motivate the need for abductive models of diagnostic reasoning. In addition, we introduce some basic statistical pattern classification concepts and terminology that will be used later in this book (Chapters 4, 5, and 7). For a more thorough comparison of different methods of knowledge–based systems, see [Ramsey86].

2.1.2. Statistical Pattern Classification

There are many widely used statistical pattern classification techniques [Duda73, Rogers79, deDombal75]. We focus on one of them, Bayesian classification. Bayesian classification has been applied to various diagnostic problems almost since the advent of the electronic digital computer [Ledley59] and has sometimes achieved quite remarkable results. For example, in medicine high performance Bayesian diagnostic systems have been developed for diagnosing the cause of acute abdominal pain [deDombal75], congenital heart disease [Warner64], stroke [Zagoria83], and solitary pulmonary nodules [Templeton67], to mention just a few, as well as for related non–diagnostic problems such as identification of potential suicides [Gustafson77].

In diagnostic systems using Bayesian classification, knowledge is represented as prior probabilities of disorders and conditional probabilities between disorders and manifestations. For example, in medicine there are situations where each of n diseases may individually be a cause for a patient's symptoms. If d_i is the ith disease, then $P(d_i)$ is the prior probability of d_i, i.e., how commonly d_i occurs in general. Let M_J represent the set of all known manifestations for a particular patient, and let $P(M_J|d_i)$ represent the conditional probability of M_J given the presence of d_i, i.e., how commonly the manifestations M_J would occur in the presence of d_i. Suppose we know $P(d_i)$ for all n diseases and $P(M_J|d_i)$ for all possible combinations of manifestations for each d_i. Then, assuming that the disorders are mutually exclusive and exhaustive, Bayes' theorem can be directly applied to obtain $P(d_i|M_J)$, i.e., the *posterior probability* of each d_i for a given patient, using

$$P(d_i|M_J) = \frac{P(M_J|d_i) \cdot P(d_i)}{P(M_J)} = \frac{P(M_J|d_i) \cdot P(d_i)}{\sum_{k=1}^{n} P(M_J|d_k) \cdot P(d_k)} \tag{2.1}$$

The posterior probability $P(d_i|M_J)$ gives the probability that disorder d_i would occur, given the presence of manifestations M_J. The disorder with highest calculated posterior probability may then be chosen as the diagnosis. Intuitively, this application of Bayes' Theorem makes sense. Ignoring the normalization factor (i.e., the denominator in the above formulas), it says that the likelihood of the ith disorder is proportional to the two factors in the numerator of Equation 2.1: how much the pattern of the present manifestations "looks like" or matches the pattern of those manifestations expected when d_i is present (i.e., $P(M_J|d_i)$), and how common d_i is in general (i.e., $P(d_i)$).

There are several problems with the direct application of Bayesian classification as described above. This and other statistical techniques require that one either measure the needed probabilities (a time–consuming and costly task [Reggia82a]) or that they be estimated by domain experts (repeatedly shown to be unsatisfactory [Leaper72, Tversky74, Shapiro77]). The amount of data required to estimate the necessary probabilities can be extremely large. If D is the set of all disorders and M is the set of all possible manifestations, then one needs $|D|$ prior probabilities and $2^{|M|} \times |D|$ conditional probabilities (here the vertical bars indicate set cardinality, i.e., $|D|$ and $|M|$ represent the total number of disorders and manifestations in D and M, respectively). For many real world problems where M is quite large, acquiring the data needed to estimate these probabilities is difficult, if not impossible.

Some systems reduce the demand for a large portion of conditional probabilities by assuming that all manifestations are independent in general as well as in the sub–populations of each disorder. Under this assumption, $P(M_J) = \prod_{m_j \in M_J} P(m_j)$ and $P(M_J|d_i) = \prod_{m_j \in M_J} P(m_j|d_i)$, where "$\prod$" means "product" (e.g., $\prod_{m_j \in M_J} P(m_j) = P(m_1) \cdot P(m_2) \cdots$ where m_1, m_2, etc. are in M_J). Thus, the posterior probability

$$P(d_i|M_J) = \frac{P(M_J|d_i) \cdot P(d_i)}{P(M_J)} = P(d_i) \cdot \prod_{m_j \in M_J} \frac{P(m_j|d_i)}{P(m_j)}. \qquad (2.2)$$

This formula only requires binary conditional probabilities $P(m_j|d_i)$ and individual prior probabilities $P(d_i)$ and $P(m_j)$ and thus the total number of probabilities is reduced to around $|M| \times |D|$. This manifestation independence assumption is, however, usually unrealistic. For example, any manifestations which are findings of the same disorder are not independent but are potentially strongly correlated. Moreover, when multiple simultaneous disorders exist, the correlations between manifestations are even more complicated. Some proposals have been made to handle this difficulty, but none are very satisfactory [Davies72, Fryback78, Norusis75, Ben–Bassat80, Charniak83]. In Chapter 4, we will show how the causal relations between disorders and manifestations can be used to address this problem, at least in part. In Chapter 5, similar attempts by others are also presented and discussed.

Another difficulty with traditional Bayesian classification is the assumption that all disorders are mutually exclusive. However, as was discussed in Chapter 1, it is not uncommon for diagnostic problems to have more than one disorder occur at the same time. These simultaneous disorders may be correlated to varying degrees and such correlations are often dependent on the given input (the present manifestation set). The few previous attempts to apply Bayesian classification to handle diagnostic problems where multiple simultaneous disorders occur have not been too successful (see Chapter 4). It should be immediately evident that considering all possible sets of disorders (although these sets themselves compose a mutually exclusive and exhaustive set) is not practically viable because as many as $2^{|M|} \times 2^{|D|}$ conditional probabilities $P(D_I | M_J)$ plus $2^{|D|}$ prior probabilities $P(D_I)$ would be required.

Finally, the traditional version of Bayes' theorem works only in a "concurrent" mode (i.e., all present findings are given in advance, and then the ranking of all predefined hypotheses occurs based on their posterior probabilities). There are no means for constructing hypotheses and generating questions to obtain further information unless the inference mechanism is greatly enhanced (as in [Gorry68]).

One major reason for these deficiencies of traditional Bayesian classification (and statistical pattern classification in general) is that they abandon much of the structural knowledge human diagnosticians use in practice. In purely probabilistic models the regularities and associations are implicitly embedded in the statistical data. If, by experience or deeper knowledge of mechanisms, one can extract and represent causal associations in symbolic form and use them in the inference process, then probabilistic knowledge will not play as critical a role. When both kinds of knowledge are used together, unrealistic assumptions for simplifying probabilistic calculations would have less impact on the accuracy of diagnoses. This is probably one reason that some AI diagnostic systems, e.g., MYCIN, INTERNIST–1, etc., have a performance level comparable to human experts even though they only use heuristic weighting schemes to handle uncertainty.

2.1.3. Production (Rule–Based) Systems

Unlike the methods mentioned above, production systems in AI involve primarily symbolic (non–numeric) inference, although diagnostic systems using this approach typically have a mechanism for representing and propagating "certainty measures". The diagnostic knowledge in these systems is represented as a set of *rules* or *productions*. Although the exact syntax used varies, a rule/production in general has the basic form

IF antecedents **THEN** consequents,

meaning that if the antecedents are true, then it logically follows that the consequents are also true. Rules are not branching points in a program, but instead are non–procedural statements of fact that typically serve as the basis for deductive inferences. A measure of certainty (probabilistic knowledge about the truth of the consequents given that the antecedents are true) can be attached to each rule when the deduction involved is not absolutely certain. The inference mechanism of a rule–based system consists of a rule interpreter that applies rules from the knowledge base to a problem's features in order to reach conclusions about the case. The inference method is basically direct deduction, perhaps augmented by the propagation of certainty factors.

Some rule–based diagnostic systems have produced impressive results in the last decade. For example, in medicine these include MYCIN for infectious diseases [Shortliffe76], CASNET/GLAUCOMA for glaucoma [Weiss78], TIA for assessment of transient ischemic attacks [Reggia84b], and MDX, a prototype of general medical diagnosis [Chandrasekaran79, Mittal79]. Rule–based expert systems are also widely used in various non-medical fields, e.g., PROSPECTOR for assisting geologists in mineral exploration [Duda78], DENDRAL for analyzing molecular structures of organic chemicals, HEARSAY–II for speech understanding [Erman80], and DART for computer fault diagnosis [Bennett81]. Some of these systems involve hypothesis generation and refinement as well as deductive inference. Because of extensive research and experimentation, techniques for rule–based systems are relatively mature, allowing people to build various systems for different applications with great flexibility.

When used in diagnostic problem–solving, however, rule–based systems face a number of serious problems. One of the major problems is that it is often difficult to represent domain knowledge in terms of rules, especially if one already has available descriptive information, such as knowledge from text–books or domain experts [Reggia78, Shortliffe76, Buchanan70]. One reason for this difficulty is the "directionality" of production rules. Rules in diagnostic rule–based systems are typically of the form "**IF** <manifestations> **THEN** <cause>". However, much of the knowledge familiar to domain experts that is used to create such rules is descriptive and goes in the opposite direction: if some disorder is present, then certain manifestations will typically occur [Nau84]. As a result, it is sometimes claimed that one is "thinking backward" when using rules [Davis77].

Another source of difficulty with rule development is that one must include all of the necessary context for a rule's application in its antecedent clauses [Davis77, Reggia85a]. Since all of the relevant factors for applying a rule are not always obvious or even known, this can result in errors of omission in the antecedents of rules and consequently affect system performance. For example, suppose that a disorder d_1 is capable of causing manifestations m_1, m_2 and m_3. In a rule–based system, one might represent this piece of knowledge by the rule R_1 given below

R_1: **IF** m_1, m_2, and m_3
      THEN CONCLUSION d_1 (with some measure of certainty).

Suppose also that disorder d_2 is capable of causing m_1, m_2, m_3 and m_4, represented in an analogous rule R_2:

R_2: **IF** m_1, m_2, m_3, and m_4
      THEN CONCLUSION d_2 (with some measure of certainty).

If a specific diagnostic problem occurred involving the presence of m_1, m_2 and m_3, then a diagnostician would normally consider d_1 and d_2 as alternative hypotheses because both of these two disorders are capable of causing the given present manifestations. In contrast, the use of rule R_1 and R_2 would lead to considerations of only d_1 as a hypothesis because the antecedents of R_2 are not satisfied. Although this problem could easily be handled by the use of an additional rule associating d_2 with m_1, m_2 and m_3 (perhaps with a different certainty measure), such an approach can rapidly result in creation of many rules.

The following difficulty is even more serious. If a specific problem occurred having the presence of m_1, m_2, m_3 *and* m_4, a human diagnostician would normally discard d_1 as a hypothesis because it cannot explain all of the observed manifestations while d_2 can. The use of R_1 and R_2 as written, however, would still result in d_1 and d_2 as alternative hypotheses. One might be tempted to solve this problem by modifying R_1 to be

R_1': **IF** m_1, m_2, m_3 and $\overline{m_4}$
      THEN CONCLUSION d_1 (with some measure of certainty).

Alternatively, one might add a new rule to the original set $\{R_1, R_2\}$ written as

R_3: **IF** m_4 **THEN** CONCLUSION $\overline{d_1}$ (with some measure of certainty).

If all such contextual knowledge is obvious (which is generally not the case), incorporating it into rules, as shown in the above examples, would again cause a proliferation of the antecedents of each rule, and would potentially cause a combinatorial explosion in the total number of rules for the knowledge base. Further, in diagnostic problems where m_4 is present, using m_4 as evidence against d_1 as in rule R_3 may be inappropriate, as when some other disorder that may cause m_4 is also present simultaneously.

It has generally proven difficult for rule–based systems to construct hypotheses containing multiple disorders. Part of the reason for this difficulty is that rule–based systems typically do not distinguish between alternative and complementary disorders resulting from firing of rules and generally have no systematic means of composing, from those individually deduced disorders, multiple disorder hypotheses capable of accounting for all present manifestations. For example, suppose a given set of present manifestations M_J triggers three rules to fire which respectively deduce three different disorders d_1, d_2, and d_3, none of which alone are capable of accounting for all manifestations $m_j \in M_J$. However, some combinations of them, say, $\{d_1, d_3\}$ or $\{d_2, d_3\}$, *can*. A human diagnostician may naturally conclude that these two combinations are the only reasonable hypotheses that need to be looked at because he can make the distinction that d_1 and d_3 are complementary to each other (so are d_2 and d_3), while d_1 and d_2 are alternatives to each other. However, typical rule–based systems list only the three disorders and leave the work of constructing any hypotheses to the user.

There are, of course, ways to address this problem within the framework of rule–based systems. For example, one might enlarge the consequents part of rules to specify the presence/absence of each disorder in D. This could cause a proliferation of the necessary consequents parts and thus potentially result in a combinatorial explosion in the number of rules. One might keep only those rules which capture typical and important relations between various groups of manifestations and groups of disorders. By doing so, however, one may generate a system that fails to work when the common patterns of manifestations do not appear.

Finally, the problem of how to select certainty factors and manipulate them during the inference process and hypothesis construction in a way that is consistent with probability theory is not satisfactorily solved. The schemes that have been proposed previously for this are, more or less, heuristic. Rule–based systems require conditional probabilities of disorders given a present manifestation set, while in many cases domain experts are more familiar with conditional probabilities of manifestations given the presence of certain disorders, i.e., probabilities for the opposite "direction" [Charniak85, Pearl86b]. The transformation from the latter to the former is in general very difficult unless either much more information is available or a set of very restrictive assumptions are made (see Chapter 4). Even if the required conditional probabilities are available for all rules, the problems of probability propagation and probability synthesis for multi-disorder hypotheses still remains [Shortliffe76, Adams76, Charniak83].

Many of the difficulties discussed above, as well as others such as the limited answer justification abilities of rule–based systems, can be viewed as arising from trying to solve abductive problems starting from a deductive framework. In order to cope with these problems, most real world rule–based diagnostic systems use control strategies that are much more complex than simple rule–based deduction. The techniques used to enhance control are sometimes domain–dependent and in general lack theoretical foundations. The heavy burden of designing control is left on the shoulders of system designers. This damages the generality of the rule–based system technique as a general model for knowledge–based system construction, especially for constructing knowledge–based diagnostic systems.

2.2. Association–Based Abductive Models

Associative (or semantic) networks have long been studied as a knowledge representation method in AI [Quillian68, Findler79]. An associative network usually consists of *nodes*, representing entities such as objects, concepts, and events, and *links* between the nodes, representing the interrelations or associations between nodes. This is in contrast to statistical or rule–based models where relationships between individual entities are often implicitly embedded in conditional probabilities or conditional rules and often interwoven. Their expressive power makes associative networks particularly suitable for representing the causal associations between disorders and manifestations in many diagnostic applications.

2.2.1. Basic Concepts

The characteristics of association–based abductive models for diagnostic problem-solving are the use of symbolic cause–effect associations between individual entities, and a repetitive hypothesize–and–test process as the basic inference mechanism. A number of computer–aided diagnostic systems can be classified in this category, e.g., INTERNIST–1 for internal medicine [Pople75, Miller82], NEUROLOGIST for neurology [Catanzarite79], PIP for edema [Pauker76], IDT for fault diagnosis of computer hardware [Shubin82], and domain–independent systems such as KMS.HT [Reggia81], MGR [Coombs87], PEIRCE [Punch86], and others. Because the causal relationship is represented by pair–wise associations between individual entities in association–based systems, the problem of context can be handled by the control strategy, namely, the "hypothesis formation" part of the hypothesize–and–test process. Therefore the need for using contextual information (like in the antecedents of rules) can be largely avoided while creating the knowledge base. This makes the knowledge base easier to create but places a greater burden on the inference mechanism.

Given one or more initial problem features, the inference mechanism generates a set of potential plausible hypotheses or "causes" which can explain the given problem features. These hypotheses are then tested by (1) the use of various procedures which measure their ability to account for the known features, and (2) the generation of new questions whose answers will help to discriminate or disambiguate among the most likely hypotheses. This hypothesize–and–test cycle is then repeated with the additional information so acquired. The previous hypotheses now may be updated and new hypotheses formed. Since this inference mechanism is a direct model of the human diagnostic reasoning process described in Chapter 1, the processing done by these systems is relatively understandable to users.

Association–based abductive models using cause–effect associative knowledge have some potential advantages over other existing techniques and thus this method seems to be very promising. However, this approach is still in an early stage of development relative to statistical pattern classification and rule–based systems. Many of the abductive models developed so far are domain–dependent, e.g., INTERNIST–1 [Pople75], PIP [Pauker76], and IDT [Shubin82]. Their knowledge representation is tailored to specific applications, and their inference mechanisms rely heavily on heuristics extracted from the characteristics of these specific domains. Being successful in their respective applications, these domain–specific models helped to clarify the basic ideas of the abductive nature of diagnostic inference and inspired a departure from the more traditional statistical pattern classification and rule–based approaches. On the other hand, the domain–specific nature of these models limits their generality and their applicability to other problems.

More recent models in this category have included application–independent systems, such as KMS.HT [Reggia81], MGR [Coombs87], and PEIRCE [Punch86]. Clearly separating the domain–independent aspects of knowledge representation and the inference process from specific application information, these systems enjoy higher generality, but stop short of forming theoretical frameworks of abductive reasoning: the code itself is the model in these systems. Some representative models of both domain–specific and domain–independent systems of association–based abduction and their limitations will be further discussed in Chapter 3 to compare them with parsimonious covering theory.

In summary, unlike statistical pattern classification and rule–based systems which have firmly established underlying theories (i.e., probability theory and deductive logic, respectively), association–based abductive

Table 2.1. Three models for constructing automated diagnostic systems.

Model	Representation	Inference Mechanism	Theoretical Basis
statistical pattern classification (often Bayesian)	*a priori* and conditional probabilities	calculation of posterior probabilities	probability theory
rule–based deduction	conditional rules (productions)	deduction (with enhancements)	first order predicate logic
association–based abduction	frames, semantic networks	hypothesize–and–test	?

models have lacked such a theoretical base to support them until recently (see rightmost column of Table 2.1).

2.2.2. Parsimonious Covering Theory: An Informal Preview

Parsimonious covering theory is aimed at providing a theoretical foundation for association–based abductive models by formalizing the abductive nature of the diagnostic reasoning process. In other words, it represents an attempt to remove the question mark in Table 2.1, at least in part. The theory was originated by Reggia et al. [Reggia83a,85a], and then substantially expanded by Peng and Reggia [Peng85,86,87a,b,c] as well as others over the last several years. While parsimonious covering theory was the first application–independent theoretical model of abductive diagnostic inference, other related models are evolving and we will discuss some of them at appropriate places in later chapters. Before turning to the formal treatment of the theory in forthcoming chapters, we first illustrate its basic ideas about what knowledge is used, how it is organized, how inference is conducted, etc., through some abductive problem–solving systems based on this theory.

Recall the simple example of car trouble–shooting in the last chapter. There we encountered two kinds of entities. Some entities, such as "engine does not start" and "headlights do not come on", are directly observable. They are called *manifestations* in parsimonious covering theory and denoted by the set M. Individual manifestations are denoted by a subscripted lower case m, e.g., m_j. Some other entities, such as "battery is dead" and "fuel line is blocked", can be considered as causes of manifestations. They are called *disorders*, denoted by the set D, and their presence must be inferred. Individual disorders are denoted by a subscripted lower case d, e.g., d_i. Manifestations and disorders are connected through causal associations to form a causal network, representing domain–specific knowledge. A portion of a simple causal network for car trouble–shooting is illustrated in Figure 2.2 below. For a more complete car trouble–shooting knowledge base, there would be many more manifestations and disorders, and they would be interrelated in a much more complicated way. But to illustrate the basic ideas, we will use this simple network as an example.

The causal associations shown by arrows in Figure 2.2 are pair–wise, and take the direction from disorders to manifestations. Each disorder is thus associated with all manifestations it may cause. The presence of a manifestation can *evoke* all of its causative disorders through the causal network. The word "evoke" here means "suggest as possibilities". For example, "engine does not start" evokes two possible disorders "battery dead" and "fuel line blocked", while "left headlight does not come on" evokes "battery dead" and "left headlight burned out". A set of evoked disorders can be considered as composing a differential diagnosis (set of

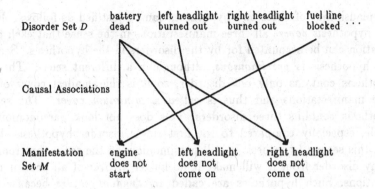

Figure 2.2. A portion of the causal network for a simple automotive trouble–shooting system.

explanatory alternatives) for the manifestation that evokes them in each case.

When the first manifestation "engine does not start" is detected during diagnostic problem–solving, the initial hypotheses would be the two disorders it evokes:

"battery dead" *or* "fuel line blocked".

Each of these two hypotheses consists of a single disorder. Each of these disorders is capable of causing the engine not to start and they are the only possible disorders, as far as this small knowledge base is concerned, that can do so. To further discriminate between these two hypotheses, questions about the presence of other manifestations might be asked, such as

"Do the headlights come on?"

If both lights do not come on, then we have two new manifestations (involving the left and right headlights, respectively) which will each evoke a set of disorders, their respective causes. The inference mechanism in the parsimonious covering theory successively incorporates these sets of evoked disorders into the set of existing hypotheses. In this specific example, parsimonious covering theory would come up with two alternative *hypotheses* or *explanations* for the three manifestations:

"battery dead"
        or
"fuel line blocked" *and*
"left headlight burned out" *and*

"right headlight burned out".

The plausibility of these two hypotheses can be justified as follows. First, each hypothesis *covers* all three manifestations in the sense that each manifestation can be accounted for by the disorders in the hypothesis. Second, each hypothesis is *parsimonious*, although in a different sense. The first hypothesis contains only one disorder, so it is the smallest cover of the three manifestations and thus is called a *minimum cover*. The second hypothesis contains three disorders. This does not look parsimonious or simple, especially compared to the first single–disorder hypothesis. However, this second hypothesis is still parsimonious in the sense that removal of any disorder from it will make it no longer a cover of all present manifestations. Such hypotheses are called *irredundant covers* because they contain no redundant or extraneous disorders.

The inference process used in parsimonious covering theory can be considered as a model of the sequential hypothesize–and–test cycle of human diagnostic reasoning discussed in Chapter 1. The "hypothesize phase" of the cycle is realized by disorder evocation through the causal associations of Figure 2.2, and by hypothesis updating to obtain parsimonious covers for all known manifestations. The "test phase" is realized by a question–answering process to explore for more manifestations for hypothesis discrimination. This cycle continues, taking one new manifestation at a time, until all relevant questions are asked and all manifestations are processed. In many real–world situations there may not be a single disorder capable of covering or accounting for all present manifestations. Therefore, the final hypotheses are not restricted to be single disorders, as shown by the second hypothesis involving three disorders in the example above.

2.2.3. An Example: Chemical Spill!

As a first example of a computerized diagnostic system based on parsimonious covering theory, we consider the Chemical Spill System. This system is for a "toy problem" involving diagnosing the cause(s) of a chemical spill contaminating a creek. It was built using KMS.HT, a domain–independent software program for constructing knowledge–based systems based on parsimonious covering theory. KMS.HT is, to the authors' knowledge, the first domain–independent software environment for creating and studying abductive diagnostic problem–solving systems [Reggia82a]. To use KMS.HT one creates a file containing a description for each relevant disorder in terms of the manifestations it causes. KMS.HT reads these descriptions and constructs a causal network from them. This network is then combined by KMS.HT with programs for parsimonious covering and interfacing to users; the resultant software is thus a complete expert system for diagnostic problem–solving. Although KMS.HT is no longer in active use today, systems modeled after it have been used in a variety of industrial, governmental and academic applications.

For the Chemical Spill System, there are a total of 14 different types of chemical spills capable of contaminating the water: *Sulfuric acid* (H_2SO_4), *Hydrochloric acid* (HCl), *Carbonic acid*, *Benzene*, *Petroleum*, *Thioacetamide*, *Cesmium*, etc. They form the set of all possible disorders D. The type of spill which has occurred is determined based on six monitoring station measurements: pH of the creek water (acidic, normal, or alkaline), water color (normal color is green or brown; color is red or black when discolored), water appearance (clear or oily), radioactivity, spectrometry results (the water may abnormally contain carbon, sulfur, or metal), and specific gravity of the water. Abnormal values of these measurements form the set of all possible manifestations M. When a spill occurs, an alarm goes off and the system starts to collect manifestation data such as the acidity of the creek water or its color. The goal of the system is to identify the chemical(s) involved in the spill (more than one chemical could simultaneously be present).

The knowledge base for the system is originally given in a natural descriptive format. Each type of spill which could occur is listed with the manifestations it might produce, thus specifying the cause–effect relationships between individual disorders and individual manifestations. A few such descriptions are given below. The first, for example, describes the "disorder" sulfuric acid in terms of its manifestations (water acidic, sulfur detected by spectrometry, etc.).

Sulfuric acid (H_2SO_4): This can contaminate the river at any time, but is especially likely in May and June (i.e., months of heavy use in manufacturing). This is a very strong acid, so it can be expected to usually make the water acidic. Spectrometry will always detect sulfur.

Benzene: This gives water an oily appearance that may be detected by photometry. Spectrometry may detect carbon.

Petroleum. This is used constantly, but most heavily in the months of July, August and September. It may turn the water black and give it an oily appearance and may decrease the specific gravity of the water. Spectrometry usually detects carbon.

A complete description of the knowledge used in this system can be found in [Ramsey86]. These natural–language descriptions of causal associations can easily be encoded in an appropriate knowledge representation language. Here are the above three examples taken from the Chemical Spill knowledge base encoded using KMS.HT:

Sulfuric Acid
   [Description:
      Month of Year = May <h>, June <h>;

                pH = Acidic <h>;
                Spectrometry Results = Sulfur <a>],
    Benzene
       [Description:
                Spectrometry Results = Carbon <m>;
                Appearance = Oily <m>],
    Petroleum
       [Description:
                Month of Year = July <h>, Aug <h>, Sept <h>;
                Water Color = Black <m>;
                Appearance = Oily <m>;
                Spectrometry Results = Carbon <h>;
                Specific Gravity of Water = Decreased <m>].

To understand this descriptive knowledge representation more fully, it is necessary to know about some KMS.HT conventions used here: symbolic probabilities and the separation of causal and non-causal associations. Symbolic probabilities, indicated in angular brackets in each disorder's description above, are subjective, non-numeric estimates of how frequently an event may occur. The five possible estimates used in KMS.HT are:

                a = always,
                h = high likelihood,
                m = medium likelihood,
                l = low likelihood,
                n = never.

Thus, "<h>" following pH = Acidic in the description of Sulfuric Acid indicates that this disorder is highly likely to cause the water to be acidic, and "<m>" following Appearance = Oily in Benzene's description indicates that Benzene may cause this manifestation with medium likelihood.

    The second KMS.HT convention used here is the separation of causal and non-causal associations. Certain features of a disorder can be viewed as being caused by the disorder being described (i.e., they are manifestations in parsimonious covering theory terminology). For example, Sulfuric Acid has two manifestations: pH = Acidic and Spectrometer Results = Sulfur; and Petroleum has four. In contrast, other features of a disorder are not causally associated with it. For example, the months that a chemical is used and how frequently it is used during those months may provide very significant information about the likelihood of that chemical being present, but they are *not caused* by the spill of that chemical. Features such as these are referred to as *setting factors* in KMS.HT parlance. Which features in the knowledge base are manifestations and which are setting factors are indicated in the database scheme specified by the knowledge base author (see [Reggia81,82b]). In the descriptions of the Chemical Spill knowledge base, the only setting factor is the months of use of a chemical, while all of the other assertions specify manifestations.

Based on the above conventions, the reader should be able to appreciate that the descriptions above are a fairly accurate representation of the information given in natural–language form. Note that unlike rules in rule–based systems, the disorders and manifestations in this knowledge base are associated by a direct causal relation, having direction from causes (disorders) to effects (manifestations). These causal relations are between *individual* entities, not groups of entities as occurs with rules. This representation is very natural for describing the underlying causal knowledge in many diagnostic domains, and may greatly facilitate knowledge base construction and management.

Also note that if a specific manifestation m_j is in the description of a disorder d_i, this only means that d_i *may* cause m_j to be present, e.g., this causal association is not categorical. This uncertainty is captured by the symbolic probabilities $<h>$, $<m>$, or $<l>$ attached to causal associations. Exceptional situations where an association is categorical, i.e., it always or never holds, are indicated by symbolic probabilities $<a>$ and $<n>$, respectively.

Since the causal associations are between individual disorders and manifestations, not only are all manifestations which may be caused by a disorder readily available in that disorder's description, but also the construction of the set of all causes of a specific manifestation becomes fairly easy. For example, since manifestation "pH = Acidic" only appears under disorders Benzenesulfonic Acid, Carbonic Acid, Hydrochloric Acid, and Sulfuric Acid, they are thus the only causes of pH = Acidic. In other words, these causes form the "differential diagnosis" of the manifestation pH = Acidic and can be evoked by its presence. This process of retrieving the precompiled set of causative disorders of a manifestation from the knowledge base is the process of *hypothesis evocation* described in Chapter 1. In parsimonious covering theory, the notion of $effects(d_i)$ is used to denote the set of all manifestations that may be caused by disorder d_i, and $causes(m_j)$ is used to denote the set of all disorders that may cause manifestation m_j (the formal definitions of these and related sets are given in Chapter 3). Thus, $effects$(Sulfuric Acid) = {pH = Acidic, Spectrometry Results = Sulfur}, and $causes$(pH = Acidic) = {Benzenesulfonic Acid, Carbonic Acid, Hydrochloric Acid, Sulfuric Acid}.

During problem–solving with the Chemical Spill System, the manifestations (abnormalities) which are present are detected and processed one by one, mimicking the sequential diagnostic process occurring during human diagnostic problem–solving. Postulating the presence of one or more chemicals forms a hypothesis for the given present manifestations. Since there are 14 disorders in this simple example, there are 2^{14} possible different sets of disorders, i.e., 2^{14} possible hypotheses, but the Chemical Spill System only considers those sets of disorders which are "parsimonious". For the sake of illustration, we will adopt minimum cardinality as the criterion for parsimony, i.e., a valid hypothesis must be a minimum size cover of all present manifestations. The goal of the inference process is then to find all minimum covers as the final solution.

When a manifestation m_j is detected as present, it evokes all its causative disorders (i.e., the set $causes(m_j)$) from the causal associative knowledge base. The evoked disorders are then combined with existing hypotheses (minimum covers of previously known manifestations) to form new hypotheses capable of explaining all the known manifestations, including the new one. This process of hypothesis evocation and hypothesis updating continues until no new manifestations are available.

Rather than representing the solution (all minimum covers) as an explicit list of all possible hypotheses, parsimonious covering theory (and KMS.HT) organizes the disorders involved in these hypotheses into a more compact structure called a *generator*. A generator is a collection of several groups of different disorders that implicitly represent a set of hypotheses in the solution and can be used to generate them. If A, B, and C are disjoint sets of different disorders, a generator $\{A, B, C\}$ means all hypotheses are made by taking one disorder from set A, one from set B, and one from set C. It thus implicitly represents all hypotheses of the form $\{d_A, d_B, d_C\}$ where $d_A \in A$, $d_B \in B$, and $d_C \in C$. For example, a generator

$$\{\{d_1, d_2, d_3\} \{d_4, d_5, d_6, d_7\}\}$$

compactly represents the twelve hypotheses

$$\{\{d_1, d_4\} \{d_2, d_4\} \{d_3, d_4\} \{d_1, d_5\} \{d_2, d_5\} \{d_3, d_5\}$$
$$\{d_1, d_6\} \{d_2, d_6\} \{d_3, d_6\} \{d_1, d_7\} \{d_2, d_7\} \{d_3, d_7\} \}.$$

In general, if the ith set in a generator contains n_i disorders, then that generator represents $\prod_i n_i$ hypotheses, usually a great savings over representing them separately. Moreover, as will be shown later, the disorders in a single set in a generator (e.g., $\{d_1, d_2, d_3\}$ in the above example) typically cover the same or a similar set of manifestations, facilitating problem-solving. Representing hypotheses as a generator is also closer to human diagnosticians' organization of possibilities (competing disorders) during problem-solving.

In what follows, an example case is run on the Chemical Spill System where the system collects information by asking multiple choice questions. User typing is italicized and appears only on lines immediately below question marks. Periodically the generator representing the current hypotheses or other information about problem-solving is displayed (indicated by enclosure in a box). Explanatory comments are inserted where appropriate, right-justified within parentheses.

(The problem–solving system is activated when a chemical spill occurs.)

Month of Year:
  (1) April
  (2) May
  (3) June
  (4) July
  (5) August
  (6) September
= ?
3.

> possibilities now being categorically rejected:
>   Carbon Isotope

(The question–answering sequence starts. The first question is about the time at which the spill occurred, i.e., a question about a setting factor. Since it occurred in June and the knowledge base indicates that Carbon Isotope is never used in June, this disorder is removed from consideration in this problem. The system then proceeds to ask the next question.)

pH:
  (1) Acidic
  (2) Normal
  (3) Alkaline
= ?
1.

> Hypotheses:
>   Generator:
>   Competing possibilities:
>   Benzenesulfonic Acid
>   Carbonic Acid
>   Hydrochloric Acid
>   Sulfuric Acid

(The first manifestation, pH = Acidic, evokes the four possible chemical contaminants which can make the water acidic. Any of these four alone is a reasonable hypothesis (i.e., a minimum cover), so one generator containing a single set of the four alternative disorders is formed to represent these four single–disorder hypotheses.)

Spectrometry:
  (1) Metal
  (2) Carbon
  (3) Sulfur
= ? (multiple answers permitted)
1 & 2

Possibilities now being categorically rejected:
  Sulfuric Acid.

(Sulfuric Acid is rejected and removed from the set of existing hypotheses because a spill of Sulfuric Acid will *always* causes Sulfur to be detected by the spectrometer but it is not detected in this case.

The presence of metal evokes four disorders: Hydroxyaluminum, Cesmium, Rubidium, and Radium. None of them is in the current generator. Thus, to cover the old manifestation (acidic pH) and this new manifestation, new hypotheses including at least two disorders must be formed.

On the other hand, the presence of carbon evokes six disorders: Carbonic Acid, Benzene, Petroleum, Benzenesulfonic Acid, Thioacetamide, and Chromogen. Two of them, Carbonic Acid and Benzenesulfonic Acid, are already in the current generator. They thus cover both pH = Acidic and Spectrometry = Carbon. Successively incorporating these two sets of evoked disorders into the set of four existing hypotheses, the system now obtains eight minimum covers for the three existing manifestations. These eight hypotheses are organized into the following generator consisting of two sets of disorders (two competing groups). Note that each disorder in the first competing group covers both pH = Acidic and Spectrometry = Carbon, while each of those in the second group covers Spectrometry = Metal.)

Hypotheses:
  Generator:
    Competing possibilities:
      Carbonic Acid
      Benzenesulfonic Acid
    Competing possibilities:
      Radium
      Rubidium
      Cesmium
      Hydroxyaluminum

(As an example, one of the eight hypotheses or explanations represented by this generator is "Carbonic Acid *and* Radium are present". Note how naturally the system recognizes that multiple disorders must be present, and sorts them into two groups of disorders that "compete" to account for the observed manifestations. The system inspects this generator and, since some of the disorders considered are radioactive, dynamically selects the following question.)

Radioactivity:
  (1) Present
  (2) Absent
= ?
1.

Hypotheses:
  Generator:
    Competing possibilities:
      Carbonic Acid
      Benzenesulfonic Acid
    Competing possibilities:
      Radium
      Rubidium
      Cesmium

(The presence of radioactivity evokes four disorders: Sulfur Isotope, Cesmium, Rubidium, and Radium. Note that every existing hypothesis involves one of these newly evoked disorders, except for those hypotheses involving Hydroxyaluminum which is not radioactive. The system thus removes Hydroxyaluminum from the current generator, resulting in a new generator representing six minimum covers for the current present manifestations.)

Specific Gravity:
   (1) Increased
   (2) Normal
   (3) Decreased
= ?
1.

(The manifestation "increased specific gravity" again evokes the four disorders: Hydroxyaluminum, Cesmium, Rubidium, and Radium, the same as those caused by "radioactivity". Therefore, this new manifestation does not cause any changes to the current hypotheses, so the final solution is represented by the generator in the last box above.)

•   •   •

In the foregoing example, there are a total of five manifestations: pH = Acidic, Spectrometry = Metal & Carbon (two manifestations), Radioactivity = Present, and Specific Gravity = Increased. A total of six hypotheses, all with cardinality of two, are generated. Each is a minimum cover of the five present manifestations. To check that they are indeed minimum covers, first note that no single chemical is capable of causing all five manifestations. Thus, any minimum cover must contain at least two chemicals. It is also easy to check that each hypothesis generated is a cover. For example, consider the hypothesis

Radium *and* Benzenesulfonic Acid

whose two disorders are taken from different competing groups of the generator. Radium covers Spectrometry = Metal, Radioactivity = Present, and Specific Gravity = Increased; while Benzenesulfonic Acid covers pH = Acidic and Spectrometry = Carbon. Also note that both chemicals are used in the month of June. Thus these six hypotheses can be concluded to be minimum covers. It turns out that these are the only minimum covers for the given manifestations in this example.

As noted earlier, even in this small system, there are total of 2^{14} = 16,384 different sets of disorders. Among them, 91 sets have two disorders. The problem–solving system demonstrated above manages to identify all six plausible hypotheses (taking only minimum covers to be "plausible") from this large search space and thus shows the computational effectiveness of applying parsimonious covering theory. In real–world problems this ability to focus on plausible inferences is much more impressive because of the enormous search space involved (e.g., 2^{50} and above typically).

2.2.4. A More Substantial Example of Medical Diagnosis

Through the example of the Chemical Spill System, we have informally introduced many of the basic ideas of parsimonious covering theory, including the knowledge representation (disorder set D, manifestation set M, and how the causal relationship between disorders and manifestations is organized); the set of present manifestations M^+, the important concepts such as parsimonious covers, explanations, problem solution, and generators; and the sequential hypothesize–and–test inference process.

As a general theoretical model, parsimonious covering theory is intentionally kept simple and abstract, and it does not explicitly address some important issues concerning a functioning diagnostic system, e.g., how to generate questions in the "test" phase of the hypothesize–and–test process, when the inference process should stop, etc. In this subsection, another more substantial example of a medical diagnostic system for dizziness, also based on parsimonious covering theory and implemented through KMS.HT, is used to illustrate that this theory is capable of supporting more complex knowledge and various solutions to these important practical issues.

The patient who complains of dizziness is generally a very difficult diagnostic problem for the physician. The term "dizziness" is often used to describe a variety of different sensations, such as vertigo (a sensation of rotation or movement), imbalance (a sensation of impending falling and dysequilibrium), lightheadedness (a sensation of impending fainting), etc. These nonspecific manifestations can be caused by numerous medical diseases that are distributed across multiple medical specialties. Examples of possible diagnoses of a patient with dizziness include:

orthostatic hypotension secondary to drugs (orthostatic hypotension is a
   fall in blood pressure upon standing up, and can be a side effect of certain medications, among other things);
heart disease, such as an irregular heart beat or an abnormal heart valve;
basilar migraine: headache due to painfully dilated blood vessels which
   supply blood to the balance centers of the brain;
inner ear diseases: these interfere with the balance mechanisms of the inner
   ear, and include viral labyrinthitis, Meniere's disease, and otosclerosis;
hyperventilation: overbreathing, typically secondary to anxiety.

It is entirely possible that more than one cause of dizziness can be present simultaneously in a patient.

2.2.4.1. Description of the System

The dizziness diagnosis system DDx is a fairly substantial medical knowledge–based system for diagnosing dizziness. It was the first problem–solving system implemented based on parsimonious covering theory [Reggia81]. Its purpose was simply to see whether the basic ideas of parsimonious covering theory would produce both computationally tractable as well as medically reasonable problem solutions when applied to a challenging albeit circumscribed medical problem. The knowledge base for DDx is derived from numerous medical references and contains information about 50 causes of dizziness (set D), and was built using KMS.HT. We now describe its components in detail.

Describing a patient to system DDx involves providing a collection of assertions that describe the patient and the patient's manifestations. For example,

> Age = 50;
> Dizziness = Present
>   [Type = Vertigo; Course = Episodic];
> Neurological Symptoms = Diplopia

represent three such assertions. Each assertion is of the form

$$<attribute> <relation> <value [elaboration]>,$$

so the three statements here mean: "This is a 50 year old individual with episodic vertigo (a type of dizziness where one feels a sensation of motion) and double vision (diplopia)." During a problem–solving session this case–specific information is acquired in a sequential fashion, generally in response to questions generated dynamically by the diagnostic system (just as with the Chemical Spill System). The legitimate attributes and their possible values are predefined in a data schema. This case–specific data provides, among other things, the set of all present manifestations M^+.

Similar to the Chemical Spill System described in the last section, information in the knowledge base in DDx is also organized into "descriptions". Each description provides a textbook–like summary of the disorder with which it is associated. An example of a description for Meniere's disease taken from DDx's knowledge base is illustrated in Figure 2.3.

Symbolic probabilities are again used as estimates of the frequency of event occurrence, e.g., the "$<l>$" following Meniere's disease indicates that this disorder is relatively uncommon, and the "$<h>$" on the last line of the description indicates that Meniere's disease often causes impaired hearing. The descriptions also includes "setting factors", e.g., the age of

```
Meniere's Disease <l>
[Description:
    Age = From 20 to 30 <l>;
    Dizziness = Present
        [Type = Vertigo <m>;
        Course = Acute and Persistent <m>,
        Episodic [Episode Duration = Minutes <l>, Hours <h>;
                Occurrence = Positional <h>, Orthostatic <m>,
                            Non–Specific <l>] ];
    Head Pain = Present <l>
        [Predominant Location = Periaural <m>];
    Neurological Symptoms = Hearing Loss By History <h>,
                        Tinnitus <h>;
    Pulse During Dizziness = Marked Tachycardia <l>;
    Neurological Signs = Nystagmus <m>
        [Type = Horizontal <m>, Rotatory],
    Impaired Hearing <h>            ]
```

Figure 2.3. The description of Meniere's Disease in Dizziness Diagnosis
System DDx. See the text for an explanation.

the patient. Furthermore, instead of simply providing a list of all manifestations for a disorder in its description, DDx adopts another convention
called "elaborations". Elaboration provides further details about a manifestation and is indicated as part of an assertion inside square brackets.
For example, in the description in Figure 2.3,

```
Dizziness = Present
    [Type = Vertigo <m>;
    Course = Acute and Persistent <m>,
    Episodic . . . ]
```

elaborates on the type of dizziness manifested by Meniere's disease by indicating that it is vertiginous in nature and that it occurs either in an acute,
persistent fashion or in episodes.

With this information the description of Meniere's disease given in Figure 2.3 should be relatively understandable. It indicates that Meniere's
disease is a relatively uncommon disease and is a cause of dizziness. The
dizziness it causes is vertiginous in nature and either acute and persistent
or episodic. When episodic, the episodes usually last for hours and are
especially produced by positional changes of the head. Meniere's disease
occasionally causes periaural headache (headache near the ear), frequently
causes hearing loss and tinnitus (ringing in the ear), and so forth.

The knowledge base of DDx contains 50 descriptions, one for each
disease that may cause dizziness (i.e., the set D). Manifestations listed in
all of these descriptions form the set M. As discussed in the last section,
not only can all manifestations caused by a specific disease d_i (i.e.,

$effects(d_i)$) be easily obtained through d_i's description, but also all causes of a specific manifestation m_j (i.e., $causes(m_j)$) can be obtained. Thus, the descriptions of all the 50 disorders completely define a knowledge base for dizziness diagnosis.

As with the Chemical Spill System, the minimum cardinality condition was adopted as the parsimony criterion for DDx, and the inference process is a sequential hypothesize–and–test process to find all minimum covers for the given M^+ for a case. The present manifestations are made known gradually through the answering of the questions. The question generation in DDx is more complicated than in Chemical Spill System where only six possible manifestations need to be considered. Instead of inquiring about every manifestation, DDx dynamically generates the next question based on the current tentative hypotheses. At any moment during the inference process, the set of all tentative or working hypotheses is organized as one or more generators.

2.2.4.2. An Example Solution

In what follows, a portion of the problem–solving process of DDx for an example case is presented (the interaction with the user is similar to that of the Chemical Spill System but larger so we omit it for brevity). After learning that two manifestations

>Dizziness
>[Type = Sensation of Impending Faint,
>   Ill–Defined Light–Headedness;
> Course = Episodic]

and

>Orthostatic Hypotension,

are present, DDx generates 13 single–disorder hypotheses (minimum covers of these manifestations), organized in the following generator:

>Multiple System Atrophy
>Idiopathic Orthostatic Hypotension
>Sympathotonic Orthostatic Hypotension
>Automatic Neuropathy
>Orthostatic Hypotension Secondary To Phenothiazines
>Orthostatic Hypotension Secondary To Antidepressants
>Orthostatic Hypotension Secondary To L–Dopa
>Orthostatic Hypotension Secondary To Antihypertensive
>   Medications
>Orthostatic Hypotension Secondary To Diuretics
>Hyperbradykinism

Orthostatic Hypotension Secondary To Parkinsonism
Orthostatic Hypotension Secondary To Previous Sympathectomy
Orthostatic Hypotension Secondary To Prolonged Recumbency

Any one of these 13 disorders can account for (cause) the two manifestations present .

Through a question–answering process, DDx then obtains the following new information (the tentative hypotheses generated after each new manifestation are omitted):

Neurological symptoms =
    Scintillating Scotomas,
    Syncope.
Current medications =
    Large Amounts of Quinine,
    Phenothiazines,
    Antihypertensive Agents.
Neurological examination =
    Homonymous Field Cut
        [Type = Rotatory;
            Duration = Transient During Dizziness],
    Nystagmus,
    Impaired Hearing.

This new information represents five manifestations (Scintillating Scotomas, Syncope, Homonymous Field Cut, Nystagmus, and Impaired Hearing) as well as relevant contextual information (medications). The final solution, represented by a single generator having three sets of disorders, is then obtained and illustrated below. Each explanation now consists of three disorders, one from each competing group of disorders in the generator. There are total 1 × 4 × 6 = 24 potential explanations for this given example case.

Basilar Migraine <a>
    &
Ototoxicity Secondary to Quinine <h>
Otosclerosis <m>
Labyrinthine Fistula <l>
Meniere's Disease <l>
    &
Orthostatic Hypotension Secondary to Antihypertensive
        Medications <h>
Orthostatic Hypotension Secondary to Phenothiazines <h>
Idiopathic Orthostatic Hypotension <m>
Automatic Neuropathy <m>

Multiple System Atrophy <1>
Orthostatic Hypotension Secondary to Parkinsonism <1>

Moreover, this final diagnosis offered by DDx includes a ranking of alternative disorders within each group of competing disorders. Using the symbolic probability convention given earlier, this diagnosis can be verbally
interpreted to mean: "This patient has basilar migraine. In addition, the
patient also probably has ototoxicity secondary to the quinine he is taking,
although he could have otosclerosis or even one of the other unlikely inner
ear disorders listed. Finally, the patient also has orthostatic hypotension
which is probably due to his medications, but might be due to one of the
other listed causes." This final diagnostic account of the patient's complex
set of signs and symptoms is fairly plausible. Note that in this example
case, the final solution is represented by a single generator. In general,
however, more than one generator may be needed to represent all explanations.

2.3. Some Issues

The two examples in the last section raise a number of important issues
that must be addressed when one is building a functioning real–world diagnostic system. We now discuss how parsimonious covering theory supports
the solutions of these issues.

2.3.1. What is Parsimony?

To determine what characteristics make a set of disorders a plausible or
"best" or "simplest" explanation for a given set of manifestations is a very
important issue for automated diagnostic systems as well as for other
abductive inference applications. This problem has not been resolved satisfactorily. In both the Chemical Spill System and Dizziness Diagnostic System examples above, minimum cardinality was used as the criterion for
parsimony. In other words, these systems adopt the notion that smaller
hypotheses (containing fewer disorders) are better or more plausible than
larger ones, an approach advocated by other frameworks for abduction
[Pople82, Thagard89]. The minimality condition is actually only one of the
several possible parsimony criteria. As mentioned before, another often
used criterion of parsimony is *irredundancy*, i.e., a hypothesis is plausible
if it does not contain any extraneous disorders. Stated otherwise, irredundancy means that one cannot remove any of the disorders from the
hypothesis and still have that hypothesis cover all of the present manifestations.

The advantage of minimality is that it is more focused, thus resulting in
a smaller number of hypotheses to consider in the final diagnosis.

Irredundancy, on the other hand, is more inclusive: a minimum cover is also irredundant but not vice versa. Thus, the irredundancy condition usually results in more, sometimes many more, final hypotheses (explanations) than the minimality condition. For example, at the end of the diagnostic session, the Chemical Spill System produced a single generator representing only six minimum covers for the given manifestations. If, instead, the irredundancy condition had been used, then the system would have returned the following solution:

Generator:
    Competing possibilities:
        Carbonic Acid
        Benzenesulfonic Acid
    Competing possibilities:
        Radium
        Rubidium
        Cesium
Generator:
    Competing possibilities:
        Hydroxyaluminum
    Competing possibilities:
        Carbonic Acid
        Benzenesulfonic Acid
    Competing possibilities:
        Sulfur Isotope
Generator:
    Competing possibilities:
        Benzene
        Petroleum
        Thioacetamide
        Chromogen R23
    Competing possibilities:
        Radium
        Rubidium
        Cesium
    Competing possibilities:
        Hydrochloric Acid
Generator:
    Competing possibilities:
        Benzene
        Petroleum
        Thioacetamide
        Chromogen R23
    Competing possibilities:
        Sulfur Isotope

Competing possibilities:
Hydrochloric Acid
Competing possibilities:
Hydroxyaluminum

The four generators here represents 24 irredundant covers, including all six minimum covers. Some of the irredundant covers contain three disorders, some others contain four. Similarly, the example case involving dizziness diagnosis would have generated 24 irredundant covers in addition to the 24 minimum ones. Such final diagnoses often seem to contain too many alternative hypotheses. On the other hand, the minimum cardinality condition has its own problems. Among other things, the real diagnosis may be an irredundant cover but not a minimum cover in some situations. Thus this minimum cardinality condition might fail to identify the real causes, leading to erroneous results.

Minimum cardinality, irredundancy, along with some other parsimony conditions are formally defined in Chapter 3. Both of these conditions are supported by the generator operations developed in parsimonious covering theory (actually, these operations are concentrated on finding all irredundant covers, but minimum covers can be selected from the irredundant ones by checking their cardinalities). In Chapter 4, after probability theory is incorporated into parsimonious covering theory, a more objective criterion of hypothesis plausibility, namely the likelihood or posterior probability of hypotheses, is introduced. Various subjective conditions such as minimum cardinality and irredundancy are then analyzed to show in what situations a specific parsimony criterion is or is not justifiable.

2.3.2. Question Generation and Termination Criteria

The vast majority of questions generated by the two example diagnostic systems fall into the category of hypothesis–driven questions (see Chapter 1). They are generated based on the disorders in the hypotheses being considered at that point during problem–solving. Parsimonious covering theory does not address the issue of how to generate such questions, nor the issue of when question generation should stop and the diagnostic process thus terminate. However, these issues can be resolved in the framework of the theory, and we discuss here how this was done in KMS.HT.

Let us say that a disorder is *active* if it is in one of the current hypotheses. Then to select its next question KMS.HT simply extracts from the description of each active disorder the first attribute in an assertion whose current value is not yet known (recall that assertions, attributes, and values were described in Section 2.2.4). From these candidate attributes, the one which appears in the largest number of descriptions of active disorders is then selected to form the basis of the next question.

This simple, heuristic approach to question generation makes no claim to optimality. However, it does have certain properties that make it a useful strategy to follow. Since it selects one of the most commonly referenced attributes of active disorders, it usually produces questions that help to discriminate among the competing explanations in the current hypotheses. In addition, since it selects candidate questions from the *first* unknown attributes remaining in the descriptions, it allows the knowledge base author to exert partial control over the order in which questions are generated (i.e., by consistently ordering the assertions in descriptions in a similar fashion). Finally, this approach to question generation has the advantage of being computationally inexpensive when compared with more sophisticated optimization schemes that might be used.

Once a new question has been answered by the user, another hypothesize–and–test cycle begins. This continues until none of the active disorders' descriptions contain assertions about attributes whose values have not been obtained from the user; at this point, no further questions can be generated. This termination condition is a somewhat arbitrary approach to deciding when sufficient information has been obtained. While it asks about all attributes relevant to ranking the competing explanations involved at termination time, it might leave some information unsought. For example, there are situations where some present manifestations are not included in the initial complaints, nor are they manifestations of any of the disorders in the current hypotheses. Such manifestations may be ignored by this question generation method. To permit the knowledge base author to insure the level of completeness of information collection that is desired from a knowledge–based system, protocol–driven questions that should always be asked may optionally be included as explicit instructions to a knowledge–based system built with KMS.HT at the time it is constructed.

2.3.3. Contextual Information and Ranking of Hypotheses

Before the termination condition is met, the hypothesize–and–test control cycles in the example systems above are only concerned with the construction of all possible explanations (parsimonious covers) without regard to their relative likelihood (with one exception, see below). Once the termination condition is satisfied, the systems enter a final scoring phase during which competing disorders are ranked relative to one another for the first time. For each active disorder at termination time two numeric scores are calculated: a *setting score* and a *match score*. The setting score involves setting factors. Although not causally associated with disorders, these factors provide information about the context within which the problem occurs (e.g., the month of the chemical spill, the age of a patient, etc.) that will affect the prior probabilities of disorders and thus are very important for assessing their likelihoods. The match score, involving causal relationships and the strengths of these relationships, measures how well a disorder's manifestation pattern matches the pattern of present manifestations. These two scores are calculated using the symbolic probabilities in the knowledge base as well as any symbolic probabilities incorporated in a user's response to questions. A simple weighting scheme (a = 4, h = 3, ..., n = 0) is used to convert symbolic probabilities to numbers in these calculations.

A final score is then calculated for each active disorder based on both its setting score and its match score. Since this final numerical weighting is intended to provide only a "ballpark" indication of how likely the disorder is, it is subsequently converted back into a symbolic probability to emphasize its imprecise and heuristic nature. This is illustrated in DDx's final diagnosis (see the end of Section 2.2.4) where competing disorders are listed in the order of their final scores, indicating the likelihood of their occurrences.

The exception mentioned earlier to the use of symbolic probabilities only after problem–solving terminates involves discarding disorders with zero likelihood *during* problem–solving. The symbolic probabilities "a" and "n" are used to determine when a disorder d_i should be *categorically rejected* by the inference mechanism. For example, the description of "Orthostatic Hypotension Secondary to L–Dopa" in the knowledge base of system DDx contains the categorical assertion

$$\text{Current Medications} = \text{L–Dopa} <a>.$$

Thus, if DDx discovered that a patient was not taking L–Dopa, the disorder "Orthostatic Hypotension Secondary to L–Dopa" would be immediately discarded from any further consideration by the inference mechanism. In effect, what occurs is that the set D is changed: the set of all possible disorders is modified by removing any disorders discovered to be categorically rejected during problem–solving.

With the exception of the elimination of disorders like this, however, ranking of hypotheses in KMS.HT occurs after the construction of parsimonious covers. This is not ideal: it means that substantial effort may be invested in keeping around very improbable explanations. Later in this book (Chapters 4 and 5) we will consider how probability theory and parsimonious covering can be integrated and used simultaneously during problem–solving.

2.3.4. Answer Justification

Answer justification refers to the ability of a knowledge–based system to explain or justify how and why it arrived at conclusions such as a diagnosis. There is a great deal of importance attached to developing methods for answer justification. For example, surveys of physicians' attitudes have revealed that some sort of answer justification ability is very important for physician acceptance of diagnostic systems in medicine [Bernstein78]. In addition, answer justification abilities are useful for analyzing errors made by an evolving knowledge–based system and for teaching students problem–solving concepts with completed knowledge–based systems. For these and other reasons, AI researchers have designated answer justification one of the key research topics in developing knowledge–based systems in general and diagnostic systems in particular [SIGART85].

Previous work on methods for answer justification can be divided into various categories [Reggia85d]. The approach most relevant here involves having a system describe the general inference method that was used (e.g., the procedure that was followed, calculations performed, or saying that deduction was used) and/or the application–specific knowledge that was applied by the program in making decisions. Examples of programs adopting this approach include those which cite a procedurally oriented goal stack [Winograd73], state a procedure followed to accomplish a task [Swartout77], analyze the probabilities of clinical associations in a statistically oriented knowledge base [Reggia85e], and maintain a trace of the chain of deductions made during problem–solving so that appropriate rules can be produced [Davis76]. With this approach the domain knowledge is used for both problem–solving and answer justification, assuring that changes to this information are automatically and consistently reflected in both of these activities.

Systems built on parsimonious covering theory such as Chemical Spill System and DDx can also support answer justification in this fashion. Answer justification is based on the causal relationships specified in the descriptions of disorders. It consists of two parts: *categorical justification*, which explains why a disorder is or is not included in the final differential diagnosis, and *probabilistic justification*, which explains why those disorders included in the differential diagnosis are ranked as they are. To illustrate how this is done, consider the example case with DDx above (see Section 2.2.4).

The inference process stops when no additional relevant manifestations are available. The final 24 hypotheses are represented by a single generator having three competing groups of disorders. Each hypothesis contains Basilar Migraine, an inner ear disorder (the second group of competing disorders), and a cause of Orthostatic Hypotension (the third group of competing disorders):

Basilar Migraine <a>
               &
Ototoxicity Secondary to Quinine <h>
Otosclerosis <m>
Labyrinthine Fistula <l>
Meniere's Disease <l>

&
Orthostatic Hypotension Secondary to Antihypertensive
          Medications <h>
Orthostatic Hypotension Secondary to Phenothiazines <h>
Idiopathic Orthostatic Hypotension <m>
Automatic Neuropathy <m>
Multiple System Atrophy <l>
Orthostatic Hypotension Secondary to Parkinsonism <l>

First, consider how the system categorically justifies this final diagnosis
based on the coverage of present manifestations by disorders. It will be
shown in the next chapter that for a generator like this, disorders in each
group of competing disorders exclusively cover some present manifestations
that are not covered by any other disorder in the same generator. Thus,
listing all present manifestations that are solely covered by this group of
disorders provides a reason for why at least one of these disorders must be
present in an explanation: it is necessary to account for those manifestations. In the following, upon the request of the user, system DDx categorically justifies why some disorders exist in its final diagnosis.

·   ·   ·

Ready For Command:
    justify diagnosis
                              (The user asks that the final diagnosis be
                              justified.)
The diagnosis is inferred by finding all plausible
    explanations (minimum covers) for the
    known manifestations.
The value "Basilar Migraine" is necessary to
    account for the following manifestations:
        Headache
            [Predominant Location = Occipital]
        Scintillating Scotomas
        Homonymous Field Cut
            [Duration = Transient During Dizziness.]
This value can also account for the following
    manifestations but not uniquely:
        Syncope
        Dizziness
            [Type = Sensation of Impending Faint;
                Course = Episodic;
                [Episode Duration = Hours]
                [Predominant Occurrence = Nonspecific]]
                              (DDx starts its justification by explaining

that basilar migraine is a plausible diagnosis because it is the only disorder that can explain the patient's Transient Field Cut, Occipital Headache, and Scintillating Scotomas. It also can explain the Syncope and Dizziness, but so do other disorders postulated to be present in the final diagnosis.)

One of the following values:

Ototoxicity Secondary to Quinine <h>
Otosclerosis <m>
Labyrinthine Fistula <l>
Meniere's Disease <l>

is necessary to account for the following manifestations:

Impaired Hearing,
Nystagmus
  [Type = Rotatory;
   Duration = Transient During Dizziness.].

(The system indicates that it is also necessary to postulate the presence of one of these inner ear disorders to account the patient's Impaired Hearing and Nystagmus (abnormal eye movements). The justification for disorders in the third group of competing disorders is similar so it is omitted for brevity.)

.   .   .

Now consider the justification of the ranking of competing disorders. In the generator for the final diagnosis, the first competing group contains only one disorder (Basilar Migraine), so its ranking of <a> (always) is self–explanatory. The second and third groups contain multiple competing disorders with different rankings. Justification of these rankings is done as follows, motivated by answer justification methods developed for use with Bayesian classification [Reggia85e]. For a disorder ranked <h> (highly likely), justification is given by listing only those present manifestations which *favor* its presence (i.e., are causally related to that disorder). Thus, to justify the disorder

Ototoxicity Secondary to Quinine <h>,

in the second competing group, the system gives the following message:

For Ototoxicity Secondary to Quinine, factors which favor
   this disorder include the following:
       Large Amounts of Quinine.
This disorder is more likely to cause the following present
   manifestations than some of its competitors:
       Impaired Hearing.

For disorders of intermediate likelihood $<m>$, such as Otosclerosis in the
second group, factors that *favor* as well as are *against* (expected but absent
manifestations) are listed as the justification of their ranking. For the
lowest ranked disorders $(<l>)$, only factors which are *against* each
disorder are cited.

   Moreover, why some disorders are absent can also be explained by the
system. A disorder is not in the final diagnosis for one of the two reasons:
either it is not in any parsimonious cover for the given M^+, or its
occurrence is categorically ruled out by the symbolic probabilities in the
knowledge base (e.g., the disorder is expected to always cause a manifestation but this manifestation is found absent in the given case). The
justification of the absence of disorders by DDx is illustrated for the example above as follows:

. .   .

Ready For Command:
   justify diagnosis ≠ hypoglycemia.
                           (The user wishes to know why Hypogly-
                           cemia is not a reasonable part of the dif-
                           ferential diagnosis.)
Hypoglycemia can explain some of the
   known manifestations but is not in
   any minimum set of disorders that
   explains all present manifestations.
Do you wish to see a list of the manifestations
   it does not cover?
   no.
Ready For Command:
   justify diagnosis ≠ Cogan's Syndrome.
                           (Again, the user asks "why not", this
                           time for Cogan's Syndrome.)
Cogan's Syndrome was first categorically
   rejected when the following statement
   in its description was found to be false:
       Hyperemic Conjunctiva = Present $<a>$.

. .   .

In summary, this section has shown that diagnostic systems based on parsimonious covering theory can support relatively reasonable answer justifications. A great deal of the naturalness of these explanations comes from the fact that the knowledge representation methods used in parsimonious covering theory directly model those of the human diagnostician.

3
Basics of Parsimonious Covering Theory

"And where a Mathematical Reasoning can be had, it is as great a Folly to make use of any other, as to grope for a Thing in the Dark, when you have a Candle standing by you."

John Arbuthnot, *On the Laws of Chance*

In this chapter we start the task of formalizing abductive diagnostic problem–solving. As revealed by examples in Chapter 2, such formalization will involve diagnostic entities (disorders, manifestations, intermediate states), the causal associations relating these entities, the notion of diagnostic explanation, and very importantly, the process of hypothesize–and–test reasoning. Our ultimate goal is to derive a formal model that captures a significant part of the causal knowledge and inference method described in the previous chapters.

In parsimonious covering theory, diagnostic knowledge is represented as an associative network of causal relationships (see Figure 3.1). Disorders, indicated by nodes in set D, are causally related to intermediate pathological states (set S), and ultimately to measurable manifestations (set M). For example, in medicine, "heart attack" would be a disorder, "shock" a pathological state, and "confused" a manifestation. A heart attack may cause shock, which in turn may cause someone to be confused. The state of being confused is considered to be a directly observable abnormality, making it a manifestation, while shock and heart attack are not considered to be directly observable (their presence must be inferred). As another example, the Chemical Spill System presented in Chapter 2 has specific chemicals as disorders (e.g., Sulfuric acid, Hydrochloric acid, etc.) and various measurements of the properties of the water as manifestations (e.g., pH, color, radioactivity of the water, etc.).

The associative knowledge used in general diagnostic problem–solving applications, where intermediate states and chains of causal links are involved, is usually very large and complex. One approach to formalizing the structure and usage of this knowledge is to examine directly the most general case possible. While this is obviously the ultimate goal to be achieved, as a starting point in presenting the parsimonious covering theory it introduces a large amount of complexity and details that may obscure the central ideas of the theory. Thus, we will initially consider in

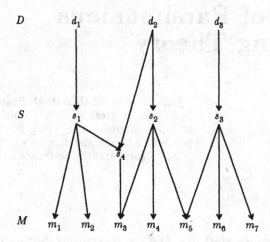

Figure 3.1. Causal associative network of a general diagnostic
problem where nodes represent diagnostic elements and
links represent causal relationships (e.g., d_1 may cause s_1
in this illustration).

this chapter only the simplest version of parsimonious covering theory and
discuss its implications. In this simplest version, a diagnostic problem is
restricted to only two kinds of entities or elements, namely disorders and
manifestations, and the causal associations between them. The intermediate states in S are *not* considered. Not only conceptually clearer and easier
to understand, this simplified model itself as an approximation may be
very powerful in many real–world applications. The chemical spill and dizziness systems in the previous chapter are examples of this kind of causal
structure. In Chapters 4 and 5 we will consider associating probabilities
with disorders and causal associations, but for now we simply ignore this
issue. In Chapter 6 this simplified model is also extended to a more general
form to capture intermediate states and causal chaining. It will be seen
then that this simplified model is just a special or restricted case of the
general model. Until then, when we speak about a diagnostic problem, we
refer to a simplified problem without intermediate states.

The rest of this chapter starts by formulating diagnostic problems and
their solutions in Section 3.1, and analyzing the properties of this formulation in Section 3.2. A considerable part of the chapter is devoted to the
development of an algebra for generators in Section 3.3. This algebra will
provide basic operations for problem–solving algorithms. In Section 3.4, a
problem–solving algorithm is presented and its correctness is established.
The formulation of diagnostic problems together with this problem–solving
algorithm presented in this chapter capture the central concepts of parsimonious covering theory. Finally, comparisons to existing abductive diagnostic systems and to some other formalisms are given in Sections 3.5 and

3.6. Section 3.7 provides a summary. The material in this chapter makes heavy use of set notation and set operations. The Appendix in Section 3.8 provides a list of set notation used in this and subsequent chapters. Proofs of all lemmas and theorems are given in the Appendix in Section 3.9.

3.1. Problem Formulation

3.1.1. Diagnostic Problems

In the simplest version of parsimonious covering theory, we use two discrete finite sets to define the scope of diagnostic problems (see Figure 3.2). They are the set D, representing all possible disorders d_i that can occur, and the set M, representing all possible manifestations m_j that may occur when one or more disorders are present. For example, in medicine, D represents all known diseases (or some relevant subset of all diseases, such as the 50 or so diseases in the Dizziness Diagnosis System in the last Chapter), and M represents all possible measurable symptoms, examination findings, and abnormal laboratory results that can be caused by diseases in D. We will assume that D and M have no elements in common, and that the presence of any d_i is not directly measurable.

To capture the intuitive notion of causation, we use a relation C, from D to M, to associate individual disorders and manifestations. An association $<d_i,m_j>$ in C means d_i may directly cause m_j. Note that this does *not* mean that d_i *necessarily* causes m_j, but only that it *might*. In other words, the probability associated with a causal association is presumed to be neither zero (no causal association in this case) nor one (necessary causation) but somewhere in between. This reflects the real world situation in many cases. Further, it should be clear that the causal associations pictured here are *not* logical implications. For example, not all patients having the flu

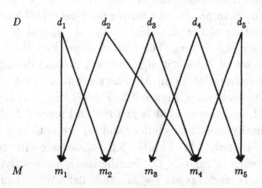

Figure 3.2. Causal network of a diagnostic problem $<D,M,C,!>$.

have the same symptoms. Some may have fever, sore throat, cough, running nose, and so forth, while others may only have some of these symptoms. Having the flu does not imply that any specific one of these manifestations is present. Also note that, by restricting relation C from D to M, this model does not allow any element of M to cause some element of D, nor elements within one set to cause each other.

To complete the problem formulation, we use M^+, a subset of M to denote the set of manifestations known to be present. Note that M^+ does not necessarily have to be specified all at once at the beginning of problem–solving; it can be gradually obtained from the answers of questions posted during the sequential hypothesize–and–test process as illustrated with the examples in Chapter 2. At termination time (i.e., when problem–solving ends), all manifestations not in M^+ are assumed to be absent. We will return to this issue in Chapter 6, as well as situations where not only the present manifestations are given, but certain disorders may also be given to be present. Such disorders, referred to as a *volunteered partial solution*, can be viewed as an extension of M^+.

Now we gather these ideas into a formal definition of a diagnostic problem.

definition 3.1: A *diagnostic problem* P is a 4–tuple $< D,M,C,M^+ >$ where:
$D = \{d_1, d_2, \ldots, d_n\}$ is a finite, non–empty set of objects, called disorders;
$M = \{m_1, m_2, \ldots, m_k\}$ is a finite, non–empty set of objects, called manifestations;
$C \subseteq D \times M$ is a relation with $domain(C) = D$ and $range(C) = M$, called causation; and
$M^+ \subseteq M$ is a distinguished subset of M which is said to be present.

By this definition, the sets D, M, and C together specify the problem environment wherein the diagnostic process is conducted, and they correspond to the knowledge base in a knowledge–based system for a class of problems. For example, for the simple diagnostic problem in Figure 3.2, D is a set consisting of five disorders $d_1, d_2, \ldots, d_5$ and M consists of five manifestations $m_1, m_2, \ldots, m_5$. The Cartesian product $D \times M$ in Definition 3.1 represents a set of pairs $< d_i, m_j >$ for each distinct disorder d_i in D and each distinct manifestation m_j in M. There are total $5 \times 5 = 25$ such pairs in $D \times M$ for the problem in Figure 3.2. The relation C is typically a small subset of $D \times M$, and this is what is pictured in Figure 3.2. For example, d_1 and m_1 are causally associated, but d_1 and m_3 are not, so $< d_1, m_1 >$ is in C but $< d_1, m_3 >$ is not. In Figure 3.2, there are 10 such disorder–manifestation pairs in relation C. Furthermore, by restricting relation C to $domain(C) = D$ and $range(C) = M$, this definition requires that any disorder d_i be causally associated with some manifestation m_j, and vice versa.

The set M^+ represents the features which are taken to be present in a specific given problem (unlike the general knowledge in D, M and C, M^+ is knowledge about a specific case or instance). It corresponds to the input in a knowledge–based system. In situations like in Figure 3.2 where one is not concerned with a specific diagnostic problem but is interested only in the underlying causal associative network, the notation $<D,M,C,?>$ will be used to designate the network under consideration. One thing worth noticing about the above problem definition is that there is no further restriction on the causal relation C and the problem input M^+: any disorder can potentially be associated with any manifestation, and any manifestation can be a member of M^+. This gives the formulation great generality. As noted above, C is generally a proper subset of $D \times M$, i.e., usually not every pair of disorder and manifestation is causally associated.

For a diagnostic problem P, it is convenient and useful to define the following sets or functions based on relation C:

definition 3.2: For any $d_i \in D$ and $m_j \in M$ in a diagnostic problem $P = <D,M,C,M^+>$,
$effects(d_i) = \{m_j | <d_i,m_j> \in C\}$, the set of objects directly caused by d_i; and
$causes(m_j) = \{d_i | <d_i,m_j> \in C\}$, the set of objects which can directly cause m_j.

The sets $effects(d_i)$ and $causes(m_j)$ are illustrated in Figure 3.3. As discussed in Chapter 2, these concepts are intuitively familiar to human diagnosticians. For example, medical textbooks often have descriptions of diseases which include, among other facts, the set $effects(d_i)$, the manifestations

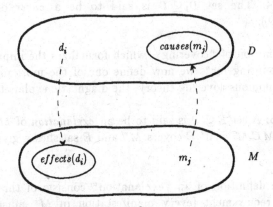

Figure 3.3. The sets $effects(d_i)$ and $causes(m_j)$ defined by parsimonious covering theory.

caused by each disease d_i. Physicians often refer to the "differential diagnosis" of a manifestation m_j, which corresponds to the set $causes(m_j)$. These sets as defined above can easily be generalized from individual disorders and manifestations to sets of disorders and manifestations as follows.

definition 3.3: For any $D_I \subseteq D$ and $M_J \subseteq M$ in a diagnostic problem $P = <D,M,C,M^+>$,
$$effects(D_I) = \bigcup_{d_i \in D_I} effects(d_i), \text{ and}$$
$$causes(M_J) = \bigcup_{m_j \in M_J} causes(m_j).$$

Thus, for example, the effects of a set of disorders are just the union ("sum") of effects of individual disorders in the set.

example: For the diagnostic problem in Figure 3.2,
$effects(d_1) = \{m_1, m_2\}$,
$causes(m_2) = \{d_1, d_3\}$,
$effects(\{d_1, d_4\}) = \{m_1, m_2, m_3, m_5\}$, and
$causes(\{m_4, m_5\}) = \{d_2, d_3, d_4, d_5\}$.   □

3.1.2. Solutions for Diagnostic Problems

Having characterized diagnostic problems, we now characterize solving them. This involves formally defining the notion "cover" based on the causal relation C, deciding the criterion for parsimony, and formally defining the concept of an explanation (explanatory hypothesis).

definition 3.4: The set $D_I \subseteq D$ is said to be a *cover* of $M_J \subseteq M$ if $M_J \subseteq effects(D_I)$.

Based on the notion of "covering", which formalizes the imprecise term of "causally accounting for", we now define one of the most important concepts of parsimonious covering theory, the diagnostic explanation.

definition 3.5: A set $E \subseteq D$ is said to be an *explanation* of M^+ for a problem $P = <D,M,C,M^+>$ iff E covers M^+ and E satisfies a given parsimony criterion.

Note that the definition of an "explanation" consists of three conditions: the covering requirement (every manifestation in M^+ must be causally associated with some of E's members), the parsimony requirement (the covering must be parsimonious), and the requirement that an explanation must consist of disorders only. The covering condition captures what one intuitively expects from an "explanation", i.e., it must be able to causally account for all manifestations said to be present. An explanation must also be a subset of D, for otherwise (if it contains some non–disorders) the diagnostic process is considered incomplete. Among all such covers, parsimonious ones are considered more plausible than others. It is from the above definition of explanation that "parsimonious covering theory" received its name.

Based on Definition 3.5, a central question in this theory is thus: What is the nature of "parsimony" or "simplicity"? Put otherwise, what makes one cover of M^+ more plausible than another? As noted in Chapter 2, there are a number of different criteria for the imprecise notion of parsimony, minimum cardinality and irredundancy being just two of them.

definition 3.6:
(1). A cover D_I of M_J is said to be *minimum* if its cardinality is smallest among all covers of M_J.
(2). A cover D_I of M_J is said to be *irredundant* if none of its proper subsets is also a cover of M_J; it is *redundant* otherwise.
(3). A cover D_I of M^+ is said to be *relevant* if it is a subset of *causes*(M^+); it is *irrelevant* otherwise.

We have seen examples of minimum and irredundant covers in Chapter 2. Figure 3.4 graphically illustrates an irredundant cover of two disorders for a given M^+.

The third parsimony criterion above, *relevancy*, is looser than irredundancy. Covers of this type are called relevant because each disorder in such

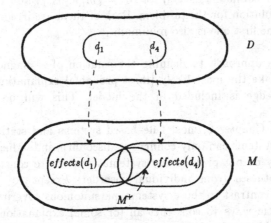

Figure 3.4. Pictorial representation of an irredundant cover $\{d_1, d_4\}$ for M^+ where M^+ is not contained in either *effects*(d_1) or *effects*(d_4).

a cover is causally associated (i.e., relevant) to some given present feature (i.e., the disorder is in the set of $causes(M^+)$). This reflects real world situations where a diagnosis usually consists of only those disorders which are evoked from a given set of present features. A disorder with none of its manifestations present is usually considered not a possible component for a diagnosis, although it is possible to imagine presumably rare situations where an irrelevant cover might be of interest.[*]

There are some other possible parsimony criteria. However, for various computational and conceptual reasons which will become clear later, irredundancy is a preferable choice among these and the above three criteria in the absence of other information. Thus, unless noted otherwise, when we talk about a parsimonious cover or an explanation in the following, we always mean an irredundant cover. Further discussion about these criteria is given in the next section, and a more detailed analysis and the justification for favoring the use of irredundancy are given in Chapters 4 and 6.

In many diagnostic problems, such as those occurring in medicine, the diagnostician is generally interested in knowing all plausible explanations for a case rather than a single explanation because they, as alternatives, can affect the course of actions taken by the diagnostician. This leads to the following definition of the problem solution:

definition 3.7: The *solution* of a diagnostic problem $P = \,<D,M,C,M^+>$, designated $Sol(P)$, is the set of all explanations of M^+.

example: In Figure 3.2, $\{d_1,d_4\}$ and $\{d_2,d_3,d_4\}$ are the only plausible explanations (i.e., irredundant covers) for $M^+ = \{m_1,m_2,m_3\}$, and therefore they compose the solution for the problem. Both of them are irredundant covers of M^+ while the first one is also minimum.   □

An alternative approach to defining the solution of a diagnostic problem would be to take the most likely (most probable) explanation(s) if probabilistic knowledge is included in the model. This will be discussed in Chapter 4.

As noted in Chapter 2, most rule–based systems and statistical pattern classification systems can only confirm or disconfirm individual disorders in isolation. They do not provide any systematic means to construct multiple disorder hypotheses from individual disorders except for some simple heuristics. In contrast to those systems, parsimonious covering theory provides systematic ways to construct all (or some) explanations for various diagnostic problems. In these problem–solving methods, *sets* of disorders

---

(*) For example, if d_i has a prior probability of 0.99, then even though none of its manifestations are present an otherwise relevant cover including d_i might be a viable possibility. This situation is handled by the probabilistic model in Chapters 4 and 5.

are formed and checked for confirmation based on covering and parsimony principles. The constructive nature of problem–solving is one of the distinctive features of this theory as well as some other abductive models. Before we proceed to formulate the problem–solving aspect of the theory, some of its properties are analyzed first.

3.2. Properties of Diagnostic Problems

The following propositions describe certain basic properties of diagnostic problems defined in parsimonious covering theory. They will be used repeatedly both explicitly and implicitly in subsequent development of the theory in this book. First, some very elementary properties are stated that follow directly from the definitions above.

lemma 3.1: Let $P = <D,M,C,?>$ be the causal network for a diagnostic problem, and $d_i \in D$, $m_j \in M$, D_I, $D_K \subseteq D$, and $M_J \subseteq M$. Then
(a) $effects(d_i) \neq \varnothing$, $causes(m_j) \neq \varnothing$;
(b) $d_i \in causes(effects(d_i))$, $m_j \in effects(causes(m_j))$;
(c) $D_I \subseteq causes(effects(D_I))$, $M_J \subseteq effects(causes(M_J))$;
(d) $M = effects(D)$, $D = causes(M)$;
(e) $d_i \in causes(m_j)$ iff $m_j \in effects(d_i)$;
(f) $effects(D_I) - effects(D_K) \subseteq effects(D_I - D_K)$.

lemma 3.2: If $P = <D,M,C,?>$ is the causal network for a diagnostic problem with $D_I \subseteq D$ and $M_J \subseteq M$, then $D_I \cap causes(M_J) = \varnothing$ iff $M_J \cap effects(D_I) = \varnothing$.

We can now proceed to characterize the concept of explanation in the following lemmas. From the definition of irredundant cover, it is clear that

lemma 3.3: If D_K is a cover of M_J in a diagnostic problem, then there exists a $D_I \subseteq D_K$ which is an irredundant cover of M_J.

Lemmas 3.1 (d) and 3.3 immediately lead to the following result which holds for all three criteria in Definition 3.5.

theorem 3.4 (Explanation Existence Theorem): There exists at least one explanation for M^+ for any diagnostic problem $P = <D,M,C,M^+>$.

For any cover D_I of M^+, if every $m_j \in M^+$ covered by some $d_i \in D_I$ is also covered by some other disorder(s) in D_I, then d_i is "redundant" in the sense that $D_I - \{d_i\}$ still covers M^+. This can be stated more precisely as follows.

lemma 3.5: A cover D_I of M_J is irredundant iff for every $d_i \in D_I$, there exists some $m_j \in M_J$ which is uniquely covered by d_i, i.e., $m_j \in effects(d_i)$ but $m_j \notin effects(D_I - \{ d_i \})$.

This lemma is very useful when one is to establish the irredundancy of a cover. And it immediately leads to the following lemmas.

lemma 3.6: If D_I is an irredundant cover of M_J, then $|D_I| \leq |M_J|$. More specifically, if E is an explanation of M^+ for a diagnostic problem, then $|E| \leq |M^+|$.

lemma 3.7: $E = \emptyset$ is the only explanation for $M^+ = \emptyset$.

These results lead to an important observation which we will later relate to various diagnostic problem–solving systems:

theorem 3.8 (Competing Disorders Theorem): Let E be an explanation for M^+, and let $M^+ \cap effects(d_1) \subseteq M^+ \cap effects(d_2)$ for some $d_1, d_2 \in D$. Then,
(a) d_1 and d_2 are not both in E; and
(b) if $d_1 \in E$, then there is another explanation E' for M^+ containing d_2 but not d_1 of equal or smaller cardinality.

This theorem formalizes the notion of "competing disorders" in diagnostic problems that can be viewed as alternatives to one another (they "compete" with each other to explain certain manifestations). If all manifestations in M^+ covered by one disorder are also covered by another disorder, these two disorders are alternatives to each other, so only one of them needs to appear in an explanation, and they are competing with each other to be recognized as more plausible (in this sense, they form a differential diagnosis and may need to be discriminated in the subsequent diagnostic process). We will see later that, after the formal introduction of generator–sets (sets of generators), the notion of competing disorders can be extended with respect to other disorders, e.g., disorders d_1 and d_2 are competitors if d_3 is occurring. Further, we will return to the notion of competition in discussing parallel versions of parsimonious covering (see Chapter 7).

We now consider the relationship between the different parsimony criteria described earlier, and illustrate this relationship in Figure 3.5.

lemma 3.9: Let 2^D be the power set of D, and let $S_{mc}, S_{ic}, S_{rc},$ and S_c be sets of all minimum covers, all irredundant covers, all relevant covers, and all covers of M^+ for a given diagnostic problem $P = <D,M,C,M^+>$, respectively. Then $\emptyset \subseteq S_{mc} \subseteq S_{ic} \subseteq S_{rc} \subseteq S_c \subseteq 2^D$.

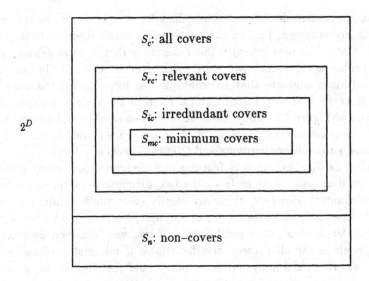

Figure 3.5. A taxonomy of covers where $S_{mc} \subseteq S_{ic} \subseteq S_{rc}$ $\subseteq S_c \subseteq 2^D = S_c \cup S_n$.

The next lemma shows that the *set* of all irredundant covers of M^+ of a diagnostic problem as a whole has a kind of optimality property.

lemma 3.10 (Subsumption Property): For a diagnostic problem $P = <D,M,C,M^+>$, let S_{ic} be the set of all irredundant covers of M^+. Then S_{ic} is the smallest set of covers such that for any $D_K \subseteq D$ covering M^+, there is a D_I in that set of covers with $D_I \subseteq D_K$.

By this lemma, S_{ic}, the set of explanations of M^+, is the smallest set of covers which implies (or implicitly represents) all covers of M^+. Thus, any cover is either in this set S_{ic} or can be systematically generated by adding extra disorders into one of S_{ic}'s member (i.e., all covers of M^+ are in S_{ic} or are supersets of some set in S_{ic}). This property of S_{ic} is not only theoretically interesting, but also computationally important, as will be seen later.

example: Lemma 3.9 can easily be checked for the example problem in Figure 3.2. There is only one minimum cover, $\{d_1,d_4\}$, of $M^+ = \{m_1,m_2,m_3\}$. This plus $\{d_2,d_3,d_4\}$ are the only irredundant covers of M^+. Besides these two, there are 3 more relevant covers $\{d_1,d_4,d_2\}$, $\{d_1,d_4,d_3\}$, and $\{d_1,d_2,d_3,d_4\}$, generated by adding extra relevant disorders to the irredundant covers. Since disorder d_5 is causally irrelevant to M^+, adding d_5 to each relevant cover results in an irrelevant cover. Thus there are a total of 10 covers, 5 of which are irrelevant. All other 22 subsets of D are not covers (examples of non–covers are $\varnothing$, $\{d_1\}$, $\{d_2, d_4\}$, etc.).   □

In some application domains, a single–disorder restriction has been used as a parsimony criterion, i.e., an explanation is a single disorder that covers the given M^+. The problem with this criterion is that in most general diagnostic problems there may not exist single disorder covers. On the other hand, intuition suggests that relevancy is too loose as a parsimony criterion in many real world applications. Even in the simple example problem given in Figure 3.2, where there are only two irredundant covers, there are five relevant covers. Because of their limited usefulness, we will not considered single–disorder covers and relevant covers any further.

Minimal cardinality captures features and assumptions of many previous abductive diagnostic systems (e.g., the two diagnostic system examples in the last chapter). However, there are clearly cases where minimum covers are not necessarily the best ones. For example, suppose that either a very rare disorder d_1 alone, or a combination of two very common disorders d_2 and d_3 could cover all present manifestations. If minimal cardinality was chosen as the parsimony criterion, d_1 would be chosen as a viable hypothesis (explanation) while $\{d_2, d_3\}$ would be discarded. A human diagnostician, however, may prefer $\{d_2, d_3\}$, or at least consider it as a possible alternative. Therefore, solely on an intuitive basis, irredundancy has been chosen by us as well as others as the criterion of parsimony [Peng85,87c, Reiter87, deKleer87]. Later, after the introduction of probability theory into parsimonious covering theory (see Chapter 4), it will be shown in a more objective fashion that irredundancy is really a much more realistic criterion than minimum cardinality. The subsumption property of irredundancy (Lemma 3.10) also gives it some computational advantages over minimum cardinality in more general situations where intermediate states are explicitly represented in diagnostic problem formulation (this will be shown in Chapter 6). Moreover, whenever the user prefers minimum covers, they can simply be retrieved from all irredundant covers.

3.3. An Algebra of Generator–Sets

In this section we start the development of problem–solving techniques with the simplest type of diagnostic problems as defined in Section 3.1. An abductive problem–solving process should be *constructive*. Based on the associative knowledge stored in relation C, it should construct plausible explanations for a given M^+ rather than test every member of the power set 2^D. The main reason for this is that $|2^D|$ is in general very large and most of the members of 2^D are irrelevant to the given problem, while the number of explanations of a particular problem is relatively small. Also, to mimic the "hypothesize–and–test" cycling, the problem–solving process should be *sequential*, i.e., the present features of a problem (M^+) are given and processed one at a time. The constructive and sequential nature is one of the distinctive features of this model and of abductive reasoning in general.

In Chapter 2, we informally introduced a structure called a generator and used generators to represent the tentative and final solutions (sets of all explanations) during problem–solving for the Chemical Spill System and the Dizziness Diagnosis System. How these generator–sets evolved along with the discovery and processing of new manifestations was kept in a black box there. In what follows we will formalize this compact and convenient form of representation, and, by defining a set of operations over generators, show how it can be used in the problem–solving process. Generators will be used in algorithms for problem–solving here and in Chapter 6 (for more general causal networks). By setting up an algebra for manipulating generators here, specifying these algorithms becomes far easier. First, we formally define generators and generator–sets.

definition 3.8: Let $g_1, g_2, \ldots, g_n$ be non–empty pairwise–disjoint subsets of D. Then $G_I = \{g_1, g_2, \ldots, g_n\}$ is a *generator*. The *class generated by* G_I, designated, as $[G_I]$, is defined to be $[G_I] = \{\{d_1, d_2, \ldots, d_n\} \mid d_i \in g_i, 1 \leq i \leq n\}$.

A generator can be interpreted from two perspectives. By definition, a generator G_I is simply a set of $n \geq 0$ disjoint sets of disorders. However, from another perspective $[G_I]$ is analogous to a Cartesian set product, the difference being that $[G_I]$ consists of unordered sets rather than ordered tuples. In particular, $[G_I]$ contains precisely all possible sets of n elements which can be formed by taking one element from each $g_i \in G_I$. To remind the reader of these special purposes of generator G_I, we subsequently write $G_I = (g_1, g_2, \ldots, g_n)$ rather than $G_I = \{g_1, g_2, \ldots, g_n\}$ for generators. Recall that all tentative and final diagnoses in the Chemical Spill and Dizziness Diagnosis systems in Chapter 2 were represented by generators according to this definition. Also note that, from the definition, if $G_I = \emptyset$ then $[G_I] = \{\emptyset\}$.

It is useful to be able to talk about sets of generators when it is not possible to represent all explanations for a given problem by a single generator. For example, in Chapter 2 the Chemical Spill System organized its solution consisting of 24 irredundant covers into four generators.

definition 3.9: $G = \{G_1, G_2, \ldots, G_N\}$ is a *generator–set* if each $G_I \in G$ is a generator and $[G_I] \cap [G_J] = \emptyset$ for $I \neq J$. The *class generated by* G is $[G] = \bigcup_{I=1}^{N} [G_I]$.

Note that by this definition if generator–set $G = \varnothing$, then $[G] = \varnothing$; if $G = \{\varnothing\}$, then $[G] = \{\varnothing\}$. A generator–set is not simply a set of sets. It is a set of generators where the classes generated by each of its member generators do not overlap.

To help the reader to understand the generator–set operations developed below, an abstract diagnostic problem P_1 is given in Figure 3.6 and will be used as an example throughout the rest of this chapter.

example: In the diagnostic problem in Figure 3.6, if $M^+ = \{m_1, m_4, m_5\}$, then the set of all eight of its irredundant covers can be represented as $[G]$ where $G = \{G_1, G_2\}$ is a generator–set with $G_1 = (\{d_3,d_4\} \{d_8\})$ and $G_2 = (\{d_1,d_2\} \{d_7,d_8,d_9\})$. Note that G_2 compactly represents six explanations. (Incidently, $[G]$ is also the set of all minimum covers of M^+ in this case, a coincidence which is not true in general). If no other manifestations are present, then G represents the solution of this problem.   □

The form of generators offers more than just an effective representation. By grouping disorders together through operations to be defined shortly, it provides a natural way to compute and represent competing disorders (differential diagnoses) during problem–solving. If a generator G_I represents a set of explanations for a given M^+, then each $g_i \in G_I$ is a set of competing disorders. The competing disorders theorem (Theorem 3.8) is based on coverage of portions of M^+ by individual disorders in isolation. In contrast, generators group competing disorders in the context of the presence of other disorders in irredundant covers of all of M^+. For instance, in the foregoing example, to irredundantly cover $\{m_1,m_4,m_5\}$, d_3 and d_4 are competitors in the context of d_8 in generator G_1, and d_1 and d_2 are competitors in the context of any one of d_7, d_8, and d_9 in G_2. Later, in Section 3.5.1, an example demonstrates that generator operations can group competing disorders together in situations where Theorem 3.8 fails to do so.

Next we turn to defining division and remainder operations over generator–sets, creating an algebra of generator–sets. These operations are defined in such a way that they can be used in algorithms to properly update existing hypotheses (represented as a generator–set) using a set of disorders evoked by a newly discovered manifestation. In other words, they are used to mechanize the "hypothesis formation" process during problem–solving. These operations are purely mechanical in nature, and at times it is somewhat tedious to follow the details of these operations and the proofs of the properties they possess. The reader unconcerned with the mechanical details of these operations can skip directly to the summary in the last two paragraphs of this section and read that summary in the context of Figure 3.6.

The first operations to be introduced are various *division* operations. Using the disorders evoked by a newly discovered manifestation, a division operation selects from existing hypotheses those which cover both the old

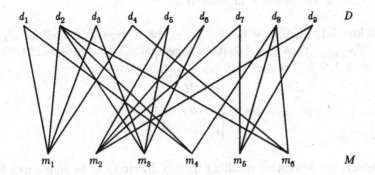

$causes(m_1) = \{d_1, d_2, d_3, d_4\}$ $causes(m_2) = \{d_5, d_6, d_7, d_9\}$
$causes(m_3) = \{d_2, d_3, d_5, d_6\}$ $causes(m_4) = \{d_1, d_2, d_8\}$
$causes(m_5) = \{d_7, d_8, d_9\}$ $causes(m_6) = \{d_2, d_4, d_8\}$

$G = \{G_1, G_2\}$ is a generator–set representing the set of all
    irredundant covers of $M^+ = \{m_1, m_4, m_5\}$
    where $G_1 = (\{d_3, d_4\} \{d_8\})$ and $G_2 = (\{d_1, d_2\} \{d_7, d_8, d_9\})$

$H_1 = causes(m_3) = \{d_2, d_3, d_5, d_6\}$

$Q^J = div(G, H_1) = Q^{J_1} \cup Q^{J_2}$ represents all irredundant covers of
    $\{m_1, m_4, m_5\}$ that also cover m_3
    where $Q^{J_1} = div(G_1, H_1) = \{(\{d_3\} \{d_8\})\}$
    and $Q^{J_2} = div(G_2, H_1) = \{(\{d_2\} \{d_7, d_8, d_9\})\}$

$Q^K = res(G, H_1) = Q^{K_1} \cup Q^{K_2}$ represents all irredundant covers of
    $\{m_1, m_4, m_5\}$ that do not cover m_3
    where $Q^{K_1} = res(G_1, H_1) = \{(\{d_4\} \{d_8\})\}$
    and $Q^{K_2} = res(G_2, H_1) = \{(\{d_1\} \{d_7, d_8, d_9\})\}$

$Q^L = augres(G, H_1) = Q^{L_1} \cup Q^{L_2}$
    where $Q^{L_1} = augres(G_1, H_1) = \{(\{d_4\} \{d_8\} \{d_2, d_5, d_6\})\}$
    and $Q^{L_2} = augres(G_2, H_1) = \{(\{d_1\} \{d_7, d_8, d_9\} \{d_3, d_5, d_6\})\}$

$Q^R = res(Q^L, Q^J) = \{(\{d_4\} \{d_8\} \{d_5, d_6\})(\{d_1\} \{d_7, d_8, d_9\} \{d_5, d_6\}) (\{d_1\} \{d_7, d_9\} \{d_3\})\}$
  represents all irredundant covers of $\{m_1, m_4, m_5, m_3\}$ that are
  redundant covers of $\{m_1, m_4, m_5\}$

$G^{rev} = Q^J \cup Q^R$ is a generator–set representing the set of
    all 14 irredundant covers of $\{m_1, m_4, m_5, m_3\}$

Figure 3.6. A diagnostic problem $P_1 = \, <D, M, C, ?>$

manifestations and the new manifestation.

definition 3.10: Let $G_I = (g_1, g_2, \ldots, g_n)$ be a generator and let $H_1 \subseteq D$ where $H_1 \neq \emptyset$. Then $Q = \{ Q_k \,|\, Q_k$ is a generator $\}$ is a *division* of G_I by H_1 if for all k, $1 \leq k \leq n$, $Q_k = (q_{k1}, q_{k2}, \ldots, q_{kn})$ where

$$q_{kj} = \begin{cases} g_j - H_1 & \text{if } j < k, \\ g_j \cap H_1 & \text{if } j = k, \\ g_j & \text{if } j > k. \end{cases}$$

Informally, all generators resulting from a division can be considered to be calculated as follows. For any given order of g_j's in G_I, the first generator in the division of G_I by H_1 is the same as G_I except that g_1 is replaced by $g_1 \cap H_1$. In the second generator, g_1 is replaced by $g_1 - H_1$, g_2 is replaced by $g_2 \cap H_1$, other g_j's are not changed, and so on. In the kth generator, all g_j's prior to g_k are replaced by $g_j - H_1$, g_k is replaced by $g_k \cap H_1$, and all g_j's after g_k are unchanged. It is clear from the foregoing definition that for any generator Q_k resulting from division of G_I by H_1, one set it contains, namely q_{kk}, is a subset of H_1. Thus, by Definition 3.8, for all $E \in [Q_k]$, $E \cap H_1 \neq \emptyset$. The set difference operations $q_{kj} - H_1$ for all $j < k$ are to ensure $[Q_k]$ and $[Q_{k'}]$ are disjoint for different generators resulting from the division and thus to ensure that the division Q is a generator–set. To see this informally, take the first and the second generators Q_1 and Q_2. By the foregoing definition, $Q_1 = (q_{11}, g_2, g_3, \ldots)$ and $Q_2 = (q_{21}, q_{22}, g_3, \ldots)$. Since $q_{11} = g_1 \cap H_1$ and $q_{21} = g_1 - H_1$, q_{11} and q_{21} are disjoint. Thus, intuitively, any members of $[Q_1]$ and $[Q_2]$ would differ on their first elements. The implication and usage of these properties of the division operation will be formally stated and proven in Lemma 3.11.

Note that during the division operation, if some empty set results from the set intersection or difference operation, e.g., $g_j \cap H_1 = \emptyset$ for some j, then $(\ldots, \emptyset, \ldots)$ is produced which, by Definition 3.8, is not a generator, and therefore by Definition 3.10 is not to be included in the result of the division. Thus, if $|G_I| = n$, we can have at most n generators in a division of G_I by H_1, and usually much less than n.

example: For problem P_1 in Figure 3.6, consider division of generator $G_1 = (\{ d_3, d_4 \} \{ d_8 \})$ of G by $H_1 = causes(m_3) = \{ d_2, d_3, d_5, d_6 \}$. Following Definition 3.10, $Q_1 = (\{ d_3 \} \{ d_8 \})$ is a generator, but Q_2 is not since $\{ d_8 \} \cap H_1 = \emptyset$. Therefore, the generator–set $Q^J_1 = \{ Q_1 \}$ is a division of G_1 by H_1. Similarly, the generator–set $Q^J_2 = \{ (\{ d_2 \} \{ d_7, d_8, d_9 \}) \}$ is a division of $G_2 = (\{ d_1, d_2 \} \{ d_7, d_8, d_9 \})$ by H_1.   □

It is clear that since generator G_I is an unordered set of sets, if we change the ordering of members in G_I, a different generator–set may result from the operation of division. Fortunately, it can be shown that, for any two distinct divisions Q^J and Q^K that result from different orderings of the g_i's in G_I, $[Q^J] = [Q^K]$, i.e., all possible divisions of G_I by H_1 for all possible orderings of G_I will generate the same class regardless of the orderings of the components in G_I [Reggia85a]. Therefore, we will use $div(G_I, H_1)$ to refer to the division of G_I by H_1 resulting from a particular but arbitrary ordering in which $g_1, g_2, \ldots, g_n$ in G_I are given during the operation. Next, the division operation is generalized to the division of a generator–set by a set of disorders.

definition 3.11: Let G be a generator–set and $H_1 \subseteq D$ where $H_1 \neq \emptyset$. A division of G by H_1 is

$$div(G, H_1) = \bigcup_{G_I \in G} div(G_I, H_1).$$

From the foregoing definitions, a division of a generator/generator–set will produce a new generator–set. Now we present important results about what this new generator–set represents.

lemma 3.11: Let G_I be a generator, G be a generator–set and $H_1 \subseteq D$ where $H_1 \neq \emptyset$. Then
(a) $div(G_I, H_1)$ is a generator–set with
   $[div(G_I, H_1)] = \{ E \in [G_I] \mid E \cap H_1 \neq \emptyset \}$; and
(b) $div(G, H_1)$ is a generator–set with
   $[div(G, H_1)] = \{ E \in [G] \mid E \cap H_1 \neq \emptyset \}$.

This lemma provides an intuitive meaning for generator/generator–set division. The class generated by a division of G_I by H_1, $[div(G_I, H_1)]$, is a subset of $[G_I]$. Members (sets of disorders) in that class are those of $[G_I]$ which contain at least one element of H_1. This is also the case for $div(G, H_1)$, a division of a generator–set G by H_1. Divisions being generator–sets guarantees that no duplicates exist in the class they generate. This property makes division very useful in sequential diagnostic problem–solving. For example, given a problem, the set of all explanations of currently known manifestations M_J can be represented by $[G]$ where G is some generator–set. When a new manifestation, say $m_j \notin M_J$, is confirmed as also being present, then $div(G, causes(m_j))$ represents those explanations of M_J which also cover the new manifestation m_j because each of them contains a disorder in $causes(m_j)$. Thus, $div(G_1, causes(m_j))$ represents an updated set of explanations for $M^+ \cup \{m_j\}$. This is demonstrated in the following example.

example: For the problem P_1 in Figure 3.6, suppose knowing that $M^+ = \{m_1, m_4, m_5\}$ had led to a tentative solution represented by $G = \{G_1, G_2\}$. Suppose m_3 is then also discovered to be present. It can easily be checked that some of the members of $[G]$, say $\{d_3, d_8\}$, also cover m_3, but some others, say $\{d_4, d_8\}$, do not. By Lemma 3.11, the division operation $Q^J = div(G, causes(m_8)) = Q^{J_1} \cup Q^{J_2}$ can be used to find the former, i.e., all members in $[G]$ that also cover m_8. As illustrated in Figure 3.6, Q^J would thus represent part of the revised solution for the enlarged manifestation set $\{m_1, m_4, m_5, m_3\}$.   □

To represent those members of $[G]$ which cannot cover the newly discovered m_j, a remainder operation called the *residual* of a division is introduced. Recall from Definition 3.10 that the generators resulting from a division of $G_I = (g_1, g_2, \ldots, g_n)$ by H_1 are

$$(g_1 \cap H_1, g_2, \ldots, g_{n-1}, g_n)$$
$$(g_1 - H_1, g_2 \cap H_1, \ldots, g_{n-1}, g_n)$$

$$(g_1 - H_1, g_2 - H_1, \ldots, g_{n-1} \cap H_1, g_n)$$
$$(g_1 - H_1, g_2 - H_1, \ldots, g_{n-1} - H_1, g_n \cap H_1).$$

Carrying this one more step, it naturally leads to the conjecture that the remaining members of $[G_I]$ after the division, i.e., those who do not share common elements with H_1, could be represented by a generator

$$(g_1 - H_1, g_2 - H_1, \ldots, g_{n-1} - H_1, g_n - H_1).$$

This observation leads to the definition of the residual operation below. It will be seen that the residual operation is complementary to the division operation in terms of the explanations it represents.

definition 3.12: Let $G_I = (g_1, g_2, \ldots, g_n)$ be a generator, G a generator-set, and $H_1 \subseteq D$ where $H_1 \neq \varnothing$. Then the *residual of a division of G_I by H_1* is

$res(G_I, H_1) =$

$$\begin{cases} \{(g_1 - H_1, \ldots, g_n - H_1)\} & \text{if } g_i - H_1 \neq \varnothing \text{ for all } i, 1 \leq i \leq n, \\ \varnothing & \text{otherwise;} \end{cases} \quad \text{(a)}$$

and the *residual of a division of G by H_I* is

$$res(G, H_1) = \bigcup_{G_I \in G} res(G_I, H_1). \quad \text{(b)}$$

The basic idea of operation *res* is to remove from G_I all elements of H_1, and thus the resulting generator-set will not generate anything which shares some element with H_1. This is formalized in the next lemma.

lemma 3.12: For G_I, G and H_1 as defined in Definition 3.12,
(a) $res(G_I, H_1)$ is a generator-set with
$[res(G_I, H_1)] = \{E \in [G_I] \mid E \cap H_1 = \varnothing\}$; and

(b) $res(G, H_1)$ is a generator–set with

$$[res(G, H_1)] = \{ E \in [G] \mid E \cap H_1 = \varnothing \}.$$

From Lemmas 3.11 and 3.12, it immediately follows that $[div(G_I, H_1)]$ and $[res(G_I, H_1)]$ partition $[G_I]$, and $[div(G, H_1)]$ and $[res(G, H_1)]$ partition $[G]$.

example: For problem P_1 in Figure 3.6, we have, by Definition 3.12,

$$Q^K = res(G, H_1) = Q^{K_1} \cup Q^{K_2} \text{ where}$$
$$Q^{K_1} = res(G_1, H_1) = \{(\{ d_4 \} \{ d_8 \})\}, \text{ and}$$
$$Q^{K_2} = res(G_2, H_1) = \{(\{ d_1 \} \{ d_7, d_8, d_9 \})\}.$$

It can be seen that $[Q^K] = [res(G, H_1)]$ contains all members of $[G]$ which do not contain any cause of m_3, and that this class and $[Q^J] = [div(G, H_1)]$ partition the class $[G]$.   □

So far, all division and residual operations are defined for a single set of elements $H_1 \subseteq D$ as the divisor. Now these operations are generalized to allow generators and generator–sets themselves to be the divisors.

definition 3.13: Let G and Q be generator–sets, $G_I \in G$ and $Q_J \in Q$ be generators, and $q_j \in Q_J$. Then a division of G_I by Q_J is

$$div(G_I, Q_J) = \begin{cases} \{G_I\} & \text{if } Q_J = \varnothing, \\ div(div(G_I, q_j), Q_J - (q_j)) & \text{otherwise;} \end{cases} \tag{a}$$

a division of G by Q_J is

$$div(G, Q_J) = \bigcup_{G_I \in G} div(G_I, Q_J). \tag{b}$$

Recall that generator Q_J is a collection of disorder sets q_j. Basically what $div(G_I, Q_J)$ does, as recursively defined above, is to successively divide G_I by every disorder set q_j in Q_J. This is illustrated by the following example.

example: If $G_I = (\{ d_3, d_4 \} \{ d_5 \} \{ d_7, d_9 \} \{ d_2, d_8 \})$ and $Q_J = (\{ d_2 \} \{ d_7, d_8 \})$, then

$$div(G_I, Q_J) = div(div(G_I, \{ d_2 \}), (\{ d_7, d_8 \})) \qquad \text{(by def. 3.13a)}$$
$$= div(\{(\{ d_3, d_4 \} \{ d_5 \} \{ d_7, d_9 \} \{ d_2 \})\}, (\{ d_7, d_8 \})) \qquad \text{(by def. 3.10)}$$
$$= div((\{ d_3, d_4 \} \{ d_5 \} \{ d_7, d_9 \} \{ d_2 \}), (\{ d_7, d_8 \})) \qquad \text{(by def. 3.13b)}$$
$$= div(div((\{ d_3, d_4 \} \{ d_5 \} \{ d_7, d_9 \} \{ d_2 \}), \{ d_7, d_8 \}), \varnothing) \qquad \text{(by def. 3.13a)}$$
$$= \{ (\{ d_3, d_4 \} \{ d_5 \} \{ d_7 \} \{ d_2 \}) \}. \qquad \text{(by defs. 3.10 \& 3.13a)}$$

□

Recall that in Lemma 3.11, for $H_1 \subseteq D$, $[div(G_I, H_1)]$ contains only those sets of elements in $[G_I]$, each of which has at least one element of H_1. Then, by successively dividing G_I by *every* $q_j \in Q_J$, the result would be members of $[G_I]$ which contain at least one element of *each* q_j in Q_J. By the definition of generators, this is equivalent to saying that $div(G_I, Q_J)$ represents those members of $[G_I]$ that contain a member of $[Q_J]$ as a subset. This is observed in the foregoing example where $[div(G_I, Q_J)] = \{\{d_3, d_5, d_7, d_2\}, \{d_4, d_5, d_7, d_2\}\}$, both sets here being supersets of some member of $[Q_J]$ (namely $\{d_2, d_7\}$), and both being the only members of $[G_I]$ having this property. An analogous observation also holds for $div(G, Q_J)$, a division of generator-set by a generator. This property is formally stated in the following lemma.

lemma 3.13: Let G, G_I, Q_J, and q_j be defined as in Definition 3.13. Then:
(a) $div(G_I, Q_J)$ is a generator-set with
   $[div(G_I, Q_J)] = \{E \in [G_I] \mid$ there exists $E' \in [Q_J]$ where $E' \subseteq E\}$;
(b) $div(G, Q_J)$ is a generator-set with
   $[div(G, Q_J)] = \{E \in [G] \mid$ there exists $E' \in [Q_J]$ where $E' \subseteq E\}$.

Residual operations can be analogously generalized to represent members of $[G_I]$ or $[G]$ remaining from the divisions. The properties of the residual operation (Lemma 3.12) are also preserved in a more general form.

definition 3.14: Let G and Q be generator-sets, $G_I \in G$ and $Q_J \in Q$ be generators, $q_j \in Q_J$. Then a *residual of division of G_I by Q_J* is

$$res(G_I, Q_J) = \begin{cases} \emptyset & \text{if } Q_J = \emptyset, \\ res(G_I, q_j) \cup res(div(G_I, q_j), Q_J - (q_j)) & \text{otherwise;} \end{cases} \quad \text{(a)}$$

a *residual of division of G by Q_J* is

$$res(G, Q_J) = \bigcup_{G_I \in G} res(G_I, Q_J); \quad \text{(b)}$$

and a *residual of division of G by Q* is

$$res(G, Q) = \begin{cases} G & \text{if } Q = \emptyset, \\ res(res(G, Q_J), Q - \{Q_J\}) & \text{otherwise.} \end{cases} \quad \text{(c)}$$

The idea behind the recursive definition 3.14a is that, to obtain all $E \in [G_I]$ which are not a supersets of some $E' \in [Q_J]$, we first partition them into two classes against an arbitrary $q_j \in Q_J$: $res(G_I, q_j)$ and $div(G_I, q_j)$. All of those $E \in [G_I]$ which do not intersect with q_j are in the first class. For those which share some common elements with q_j (i.e., those in the second class), they must differ from $E' \in [G_I]$ based on some other q_k, and thus they can be recursively obtained by residual operations over the rest of $q_k \in Q_J$.

example: If G_I and Q_J are as given in the preceding example, then

$$res(G_I, Q_J) = res(G_I, \{d_2\}) \cup res(div(G_I, \{d_2\}), (\{d_7, d_8\})) \qquad \text{(by def. 3.14a)}$$

$$= \{(\{d_3, d_4\} \{d_5\} \{d_7, d_9\} \{d_8\})\} \qquad \text{(by def. 3.12a)}$$

$$\cup\ res(\{(\{d_3, d_4\} \{d_5\} \{d_7, d_9\} \{d_2\})\}, (\{d_7, d_8\})) \qquad \text{(by def. 3.10)}$$

$$= \{(\{d_3, d_4\} \{d_5\} \{d_7, d_9\} \{d_8\})\}$$

$$\cup\ res((\{d_3, d_4\} \{d_5\} \{d_7, d_9\} \{d_2\}), (\{d_7, d_8\})) \qquad \text{(by def. 3.14b)}$$

$$= \{(\{d_3, d_4\} \{d_5\} \{d_7, d_9\} \{d_8\})\}$$

$$\cup\ res((\{d_3, d_4\} \{d_5\} \{d_7, d_9\} \{d_2\}), \{d_7, d_8\}) \qquad \text{(by def. 3.14a)}$$

$$\cup\ res(div((\{d_3, d_4\} \{d_5\} \{d_7, d_9\} \{d_2\}), \{d_7, d_8\}), \varnothing)$$

$$= \{(\{d_3, d_4\} \{d_5\} \{d_7, d_9\} \{d_8\})$$

$$(\{d_3, d_4\} \{d_5\} \{d_9\} \{d_2\})\}. \qquad \text{(by defs. 3.12a \& 3.14a)}$$

$\square$

Complementary to Lemma 3.13, we have the following results about the properties of residual operations.

lemma 3.14: Let G, Q, G_I, Q_J and q_j be defined as in Definition 3.14. Then:
(a) $res(G_I, Q_J)$ is a generator–set with
$[res(G_I, Q_J)] = \{E \in [G_I] \mid$ there does not exist $E' \in [Q_J]$ where $E' \subseteq E\}$;
(b) $res(G, Q_J)$ is a generator–set with
$[res(G, Q_J)] = \{E \in [G] \mid$ there does not exist $E' \in [Q_J]$ where $E' \subseteq E\}$;
(c) $res(G, Q)$ is a generator–set with
$[res(G, Q)] = \{E \in [G] \mid$ there does not exist $E' \in [Q]$ where $E' \subseteq E\}$.

From Lemmas 3.13 and 3.14, it immediately follows that $[G_I]$ is partitioned by $[div(G_I, Q_J)]$ and $[res(G_I, Q_J)]$. Similarly, $[G]$ is partitioned by $[div(G, Q_J)]$ and $[res(G, Q_J)]$. This can easily be checked for the two preceding examples. The eight members of $[G_I]$ in these examples are now partitioned into two classes: two of these eight containing some members of $[Q_J]$ are in $[div(G_I, G_J)]$, and the remaining six of them are in $[res(G_I, Q_J)]$.

To make the algebra complete and symmetric, a division of a generator–set G by a generator–set Q can be defined as

$$div(G, Q) = \begin{cases} \varnothing & \text{if } Q = \varnothing, \\ div(G, Q_J) \cup div(res(G, Q_J), Q - \{Q_J\}) & \text{otherwise;} \end{cases}$$

and it can be proven that $div(G, Q)$ is a generator–set and $[div(G, Q)] = \{E \in [G] \mid$ there exists $E' \in [Q]$ where $E' \subseteq E\}$. Since division by a generator–set is not used in subsequent problem–solving algorithms, the formal proof is omitted.

The final operation introduced here for diagnostic problem–solving with generators is called the *augmented residual*, designated *augres*. This constructive operation is a minor extension of the residual operation. Recall that if $[G]$ is the set of all explanations of M^+ in a diagnostic problem, and $m_j \notin M^+$ is a new manifestation, then any $E \in [G]$ is either in $[div(G, causes(m_j)]$ and thus covers both M^+ and m_j, or in $[res(G, causes(m_j)]$ and thus covers M^+ but not m_j. The basic idea of the operation *augres* is to augment the residual by adding appropriate disorders from $causes(m_j)$ so that all set of disorders generated by the augmented residual will then cover m_j as well as M^+. To avoid duplicates, we choose those disorders in $causes(m_j)$ which do not appear in the original generator G_I to augment $res(G_I, causes(m_j))$. Then, by combining operations *div* and *augres*, all explanations of $M^+ \cup \{m_j\}$ can be constructed from all explanations of M^+ and from the disorders in $causes(m_j)$.

definition 3.15: Let $G_I = (g_1, g_2, \ldots, g_n)$ be a generator, G a generator-set, and $H_1 \subseteq D$ where $H_1 \neq \varnothing$. Then the *augmented residual* of division G_I by H_1 is

$$augres(G_I, H_1) =$$

$$\begin{cases} \{(g_1 - H_1, \ldots, g_n - H_1, A)\} & \text{if } g_i - H_1 \neq \varnothing, \ 1 \leq i \leq n, \ A \neq \varnothing, \\ \varnothing & \text{otherwise;} \end{cases} \tag{a}$$

where $A = H_1 - \bigcup_{i=1}^{n} g_i$.

The augmented residual of division G by H_1 is

$$augres(G, H_1) = \bigcup_{G_I \in G} augres(G_I, H_1). \tag{b}$$

lemma 3.15: Let G_I, G, and H_1 be as defined in Definition 3.15. Then $augres(G_I, H_1)$ and $augres(G, H_1)$ are generator–sets.

example: For problem P_1 in Figure 3.6,

$$Q^{L_1} = augres(G_1, H_1) = \{(\{d_4\} \ \{d_8\} \ \{d_2, d_5, d_6\})\}, \text{ and}$$
$$Q^{L_2} = augres(G_2, H_1) = \{(\{d_1\} \ \{d_7, d_8, d_9\} \ \{d_3, d_5, d_6\})\}.$$

Both of them are generator–sets and the classes they generate are disjoint. Thus, $Q^L = Q^{L_1} \cup Q^{L_2} = augres(G, H_1)$ is a generator–set. ☐

In summary, this section has introduced the concept of using a generator-set to represent the solution of a diagnostic problem, and the operations of division, residual, and augmented residual with which to manipulate these generator–sets during problem–solving. Suppose that at some point during problem–solving, a set of manifestations M_1 are known to be present and generator–set G^1 represents a tentative solution (i.e., all explanations of M_1). If an additional manifestation m_j not in M_1 is discovered, then manifestations $M_2 = M_1 \cup \{m_j\}$ are known to be present. Then the division

$$div(G^1, \, causes(m_j))$$

results in a generator–set representing all explanations in $[G^1]$ that also cover m_j and hence M_2. Also,

$$res(G^1, \, causes(m_j))$$

is a generator–set representing all explanations in $[G^1]$ that do not cover m_j. However, by adding appropriate elements of $causes(m_j)$ to each set in $res(G^1, \, causes(m_j))$ to form an augmented residual,

$$augres(G^1, \, causes(m_j)),$$

we can convert each of the explanations for M_1 in $[G^1]$ that does not cover M_2 into a cover of M_2. The set of explanations represented by $div(G^1, \, causes(m_j))$ plus the covers represented by $augres(G^1, \, causes(m_j))$ come close to representing a revised solution or hypothesis for M_2. (A few redundant covers may result from $augres(G^1, \, causes(m_j))$. This problem will be dealt with in the next section.) Thus, the value of the operations defined in this section is that they concisely define how to revise incrementally the existing generator–set when a new manifestation is discovered during sequential problem–solving.

It should be appreciated that the division operation is a generalization of set intersection. In fact, abductive diagnostic systems assuming a single disorder is present and relying on intersection search to discover the disorder can be shown to be a special case of methods used in parsimonious covering theory (see Section 3.5.2 for one such example). To the extent that intersection is of fundamental importance in many knowledge–related areas of AI, it seems useful to explore any generalization of this concept and anticipate more widespread applications to non–diagnostic problems. Further, the constructive nature of the augmented residual operation may also prove very useful in other non–diagnostic domains, in the sense that constructive inference appears to be fundamental component of abductive reasoning in general.

3.4. Problem–Solving

Based on the generator operations developed in the previous section, we now present an algorithm for sequential problem–solving and establish its correctness. Important related issues such as answer justification and problem decomposition are also discussed.

3.4.1. Algorithmic Solution

The underlying causal networks of the simplest type of diagnostic problems with which we are now dealing can be viewed as bipartite graphs in graph–theoretic terms. Therefore, the algorithm presented here is called *BIPARTITE*. This algorithm works in a sequential and constructive manner. It takes one present manifestation m_j at a time, either from the set of given present manifestations M^+ or through an interactive question–answering process, and then incorporates $causes(m_j)$ into the existing hypotheses. This continues until all present manifestations are processed. The basic ideas of algorithm *BIPARTITE* are important not only in themselves but also because they will subsequently be extended and applied to more general problems in Chapter 6.

Algorithm *BIPARTITE* represents tentative hypotheses (explanations) and the final solution in generator–set form, and is based on the operations of generator division, residual, and augmented residual developed in the preceding section. For brevity, a function called "*revise*" is defined which can be used to construct new hypotheses from the existing hypotheses using disorders evoked by a newly arrived manifestation:

$$revise(G, H_1) = F \cup res(Q, F)$$
$$\text{where } F = div(G, H_1), \text{ and } Q = augres(G, H_1),$$

where $res(Q, F)$, as will be seen later, is used to remove all duplicate and redundant covers from $[Q]$. The function *revise* is the core of algorithm *BIPARTITE*, which is given below. In this and all other algorithms in this book, entries between "{*" and "*}" are comments; symbols in bold are keywords.

1. **function** $BIPARTITE(D,M,C)$
2.   **variables** m_{new} **manifestation,** H_1 **set of manifestations,**
         hypothesis **generator–set;**
3.   **begin**
4.   *hypothesis* = $\{\emptyset\}$;   {* initially no manifestations present *}
5.   **while** *Moremanifs* **do** {* while another manifestation exists *}
6. $m_{new} := Nextman$; {* obtain the new manifestation *}
7.   *hypothesis* := $revise(hypothesis, causes(m_{new}))$
                  {* update *hypothesis* by $causes(m_{new})$ *}
8.   **endwhile;**
9.   **return** *hypothesis*   {* generator–set for $Sol(P)$ *}
10.   **end.**

Algorithm *BIPARTITE* takes D, M, and C as a knowledge base, and keeps a generator–set called the *hypothesis* such that $[hypothesis]$ is the set of all irredundant covers of all manifestations known to be present so far. Each time a new manifestation m_{new} is discovered, it "evokes" all causes of m_{new}

and incorporates them into the current *hypothesis* to construct a new *hypothesis* using function *revise*. The newly constructed *hypothesis* then represents the set of all irredundant covers of all known manifestations including m_{new}. This process continues until all present manifestations are made known and processed. Then the generator–set *hypothesis* is returned as the solution of the problem $P = <D,M,C,M^+>$. The order in which manifestations are presented to the algorithm does not affect the explanations in the final solution (although the form of the final generator–set might be different for different manifestation orderings).

A brief example should clarify the process used in algorithm *BIPARTITE*. Recall the abstract diagnostic problem P_1 in Figure 3.6. Suppose manifestations m_1, m_4, m_5 and m_3 are discovered and processed in that order (they form the set M^+). A trace of problem–solving by *BIPARTITE* is given in Table 3.1. Here the first column is the list of newly discovered manifestations m_{new}, the second column is $causes(m_{new})$, and the third column is the set of all irredundant covers of all present manifestations known so far, in generator–set form. Each of these generator–sets is obtained by revising the previous generator–set using $causes(m_{new})$ of the current m_{new}. At line 5 of *BIPARTITE*, *Moremanifs* is an external boolean function which is assumed to return "true" if there are more manifestations left to be processed and "false" otherwise. *Nextman* is a non-deterministic external function which returns a new manifestation. The *only* assumption made here is that when *Moremanifs* returns false, all present manifestations have been discovered and returned by *Nextman*

Table 3.1. A trace of problem–solving by algorithm *BIPARTITE*.

m_{new}	$causes(m_{new})$	hypothesis
m_1	$\{d_1,d_2,d_3,d_4\}$	$\{(\{d_1,d_2,d_3,d_4\})\}$
m_4	$\{d_1,d_2,d_8\}$	$\{(\{d_1,d_2\}),(\{d_3,d_4\}\ \{d_8\})\}$
m_5	$\{d_7,d_8,d_9\}$	$\{(\{d_1,d_2\}\ \{d_7,d_8,d_9\})$ $(\{d_3,d_4\}\ \{d_8\})\}$
m_3	$\{d_2,d_3,d_5,d_6\}$	$\{(\{d_3\}\ \{d_8\})$ $(\{d_2\}\ \{d_7,d_8,d_9\})$ $(\{d_4\}\ \{d_8\}\ \{d_5,d_6\})$ $(\{d_1\}\ \{d_7,d_8,d_9\}\ \{d_5,d_6\})$ $(\{d_1\}\ \{d_7,d_9\}\ \{d_3\})\}$

(and all other manifestations in M are considered as being absent). Note that these two external functions may be application specific (i.e., their implementation depends on the application domain) and thus they are not formalized in the theory.

To establish the correctness of algorithm $BIPARTITE$, properties of generator operations are first established in the context of the hypothesis–updating process. From Lemma 3.11, we immediately have

lemma 3.16: Let G be a generator–set where $[G] = \{$ all irredundant covers of $M^+\}$, and let $m_j \in M - M^+$. Let $F = \{E \subseteq D \mid E$ is an irredundant cover of both M^+ and $M^+ \cup \{m_j\}\}$. Then $F = [div(G, causes(m_j))]$.

Irredundant covers of $M^+ \cup \{m_j\}$ other than those in $[div(G, causes(m_j))]$ must then cover M^+ alone redundantly. Next we indicate that these latter covers can be obtained by $augres(G, causes(m_j))$.

lemma 3.17: Let G and m_j be defined as in Lemma 3.16. Then any $E \subseteq D$ which is an irredundant cover of $M^+ \cup \{m_j\}$ but a redundant cover of M^+ must be in $[augres(G, causes(m_j))]$.

Combining Lemmas 3.16 and 3.17, if the set of all irredundant covers of M^+ is represented by a generator–set G and $m_j \in M - M^+$, then for any explanation E of $M^+ \cup \{m_j\}$, $E \in [div(G, causes(m_j))] \cup [augres(G, causes(m_j))]$. However, not every member of $[augres(G, causes(m_j))]$ is necessarily an irredundant cover of $M^+ \cup \{m_j\}$; some may be redundant covers. This problem leads to the next lemma which shows that all duplicate and redundant covers of $M^+ \cup \{m_j\}$ in $[augres(G, causes(m_j))]$ can be removed by a residual operation.

lemma 3.18: Let G and m_j be defined as in Lemma 3.16, $F = div(G, causes(m_j))$, and $Q = augres(G, causes(m_j))$. Let $S = \{E \subseteq D \mid E$ is an irredundant cover of $M^+ \cup \{m_j\}$ but a redundant cover of $M^+\}$. Then $S = [res(Q, F)]$.

example: For problem P_1 in Figure 3.6, $[G]$ is the set of all irredundant covers of $M^+ = \{m_1, m_4, m_5\}$. A division of G by $causes(m_3)$, Q^J, represents all irredundant covers of M^+ which also cover m_3. An augmented residual of G, Q^L, contains all other irredundant covers of $M^+ \cup \{m_3\}$. However, not every member of $[Q^L]$ is an irredundant cover of $M^+ \cup \{m_3\}$. For instance, $\{d_4, d_8, d_2\} \in [Q^L]$ is not such a cover since one of its proper subsets $\{d_2, d_8\}$ belonging to $[Q^J]$ is also a cover of $M^+ \cup \{m_3\}$. This is the same for $\{d_1, d_3, d_8\} \in [Q^L]$. The way to remove these redundant covers from Q^L, is to take the residual of Q^L by Q^J. One such residual is

$Q^R = res(Q^L, Q^J)$

$= \{(\{d_4\}\ \{d_8\}\ \{d_5,d_6\})$

$(\{d_1\}\ \{d_7,d_8,d_9\}\ \{d_5,d_6\})$

$(\{d_1\}\ \{d_7,d_9\}\ \{d_3\})\}$

Then by De Morgan's law, $[G^{rev} = Q^J \cup Q^R]$ is the set of all irredundant covers of $\{m_1,m_4,m_5,m_3\}$. Incidently, $[Q^J]$ contains all explanations of cardinality 2 while $[Q^R]$ contains those of cardinality 3.   □

It follows from Lemmas 3.16 and 3.18 that if $[G] = \{$explanations of $M^+\}$, then $[revise(G, causes(m_j)] = \{$explanations of $M^+ \cup \{m_j\}\}$. The correctness of algorithm $BIPARTITE$ can now be stated using the results above, as given in the next theorem.

theorem 3.19: Let $P = <D,M,C,M^+>$ be a diagnostic problem. Then $Sol(P) = [BIPARTITE(D,M,C)]$.

The development of an algorithm for finding all explanations (defined as irredundant covers) of the given M^+ is now complete. Problem–solving algorithms for directly finding all *minimum covers* for the given M^+ have also been developed and reported in detail elsewhere [Reggia85a]. They include algorithm SOLVE which applies in situations where all manifestations in M^+ are given *a priori*, and algorithm HT which applies in situations where present manifestations are given one at a time through a question–answering process similar to $BIPARTITE$. Both of these algorithms use generator–sets to organize the set of all minimum covers in the same way as $BIPARTITE$ does for irredundant covers. Thus, for people only interested in finding all minimum covers, it can be done by either directly using SOLVE or HT, or by first using $BIPARTITE$ and then retaining only all those covers which have minimum cardinality.

3.4.2. Answer Justification in Parsimonious Covering Theory

As discussed in Chapter 2, a good theory of inference must not only be able to provide a basis for solving problems, but also for justifying a solution derived. In this subsection, we investigate how the parsimonious covering theory supports a system's ability for answer justification. Primarily, the rationale for a diagnostic explanation can be provided by citing cause–effect associations based on the underlying causal network. Since the knowledge representation and problem–solving methods in parsimonious covering theory are very natural and patterned after human information processing methods, this framework may provide a relatively intuitive rationale for a differential diagnosis from the viewpoint of the human diagnostician.

To explain why a disorder is or is not in the solution to a problem, answer justification based on parsimonious covering theory can go further than just citing all present manifestations that can be caused by the disorder. Recall that in Chapter 2, after reaching a final diagnosis (organized in a generator–set form), DDx justifies a competing group of disorders by citing all present manifestations *exclusively* covered by that group. In other words, without the occurrence of at least one member of that group, all those cited manifestations cannot be causally accounted for. To add more support to this justification, DDx also cites all present manifestations covered by this competing group but not uniquely, because these manifestations can also be accounted for by this group.

To understand why this works, it is useful to consider a single explanation in the solution. The key concept is that, as revealed by Lemma 3.5, for every disorder d_i in an explanation (an irredundant cover of the given M^+), there is a manifestation $m_j \in M^+$ which is uniquely covered by d_i among all disorders in that explanation. Thus, disorders in an explanation divide M^+ into nonempty subsets. Manifestations that lie in a region of M^+ which is covered solely by one disorder in the explanation provide a reason for why that disorder must be present: it is necessary to account for those manifestations. This is also true for generators, as illustrated by the following definitions and lemmas.

definition 3.16: Let $G_I = (g_1, g_2, \ldots, g_n)$ be a generator in the solution $Sol(P)$ of a problem $P = <D,M,C,M^+>$. Then, for $g_i \in G_I$, define

(a) $common(g_i) = \bigcap_{d_i \in g_i} effects(d_i)$, and

(b) $common^+(g_i) = common(g_i) \cap M^+$.

The set $common(g_i)$ represents manifestations causally associated with *all* disorders in g_i. The set $common^+(g_i)$ represents present manifestations having this property, which thus can be accounted for by any one of the disorders in g_i. Figure 3.7 illustrates this concept for a generator $G_J = (g_1, g_2)$, where $common^+(g_1)$ is indicated by regions 2 and 3.

From the definition of explanation (Definition 3.5), the following results are readily established.

lemma 3.20: Let G_I be a generator in $Sol(P)$ where $P = <D,M,C,M^+>$ is a diagnostic problem. Then

(a) $M^+ = \bigcup_{g_i \in G_I} common^+(g_i)$; and

(b) for all $g_i \in G_I$, $common^+(g_i) \neq \emptyset$.

As illustrated in Figure 3.7, it may be that for distinct g_i and g_j in G_I $common^+(g_i) \cap common^+(g_j) \neq \emptyset$. It is, therefore, convenient to partition $common^+(g_i)$'s accordingly.

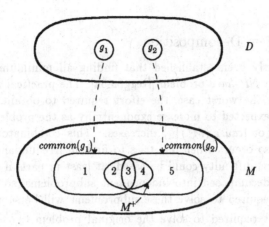

Figure 3.7. The sets in a generator $G_J = (g_1, g_2)$ divide M^+ into *common*, *owned*, and *shared* regions (see text for details).

definition 3.17: Let $common^+(g_i)$ be as in definition 3.16. Then
$$owned^+(g_i) = common^+(g_i) - \bigcup_{g_i \neq g_j} common^+(g_j);$$
$$shared^+(g_i) = common^+(g_i) - owned^+(g_i).$$

In Figure 3.7, $owned^+(g_1)$ is indicated by region 2 and $shared^+(g_1)$ by region 3. While it is possible that $shared^+(g_i) = \varnothing$, it is always the case that the following is true.

lemma 3.21: Let P and G_I be as in Lemma 3.20. Then for all $g_i \in G_I$, $owned^+(g_i) \neq \varnothing$.

The property that $owned^+(g_i) \neq \varnothing$ for each $g_i \in G_I$ is essential for the answer justification method described below. In the parsimonious covering theory framework, a categorical justification can be provided for the presence of disorders in a generator forming a part of the problem solution by stating the following.

(1). The presence of one of the disorders in $g_i \in G_I$ is necessary to account for the manifestations in $owned^+(g_i)$, which, as shown above, is never empty.
(2). Any disorders in g_i could account for the manifestations in $shared^+(g_i)$, although other disorders in G_I not in g_i may also account for these manifestations.

This is how categorical justification of a solution was done by DDx in Chapter 2.

3.4.3. Problem Decomposition

It has previously been established that finding all minimum covers for a given M^+ is an *NP-hard* problem [Reggia85a]. The practical implication of this is that in the worst case, the effort required to obtain all minimum covers can be expected to increase exponentially as the problem size (measured by $|M^+|$ or $|causes(M^+)|$) increases. This combinatorial explosion presumably also occurs when one tries to find all irredundant covers for a given M^+. This difficulty could be eased, at least in part, if a given problem could be decomposed into independent subproblems, so that the sum of the effort required to solve these subproblems will be substantially less than the effort required to solve the original problem ($2^{n_1 + n_2} \gg 2^{n_1} + 2^{n_2}$ usually).

Next, we present two example situations where diagnostic problems can be decomposed or split to smaller subproblems. The first of these conditions is based on the concept of *pathognomonic manifestations*.

definition 3.18: A manifestation $m_j \in M$ is pathognomonic for disorder $d_i \in D$ if $causes(m_j) = \{ d_i \}$.

The concept of a pathognomonic manifestation is a familiar one in several fields. For example, physicians use this name for findings that uniquely characterize a disease (e.g., Kayser–Fleischer rings are said to be a pathognomonic sign for hepatolenticular degeneration). Also, the concept of an essential prime implicant in boolean minimization problems is analogous to a disorder which is the sole cause of a pathognomonic manifestation. When present, pathognomonic manifestations can be used to simplify solving diagnostic problems as shown below.

lemma 3.22: Let $P = <D,M,C,M^+>$ be a diagnostic problem where $m_j \in M$ is a pathognomonic manifestation for $d_i \in D$. Then
(a) every cover of M^+ contains d_i,
(b) $D_I \subseteq D$ covers $M^+ - effects(d_i)$ iff $D_I \cup \{ d_i \}$ covers M^+, and
(c) D_I is an explanation for $M^+ - effects(d_i)$ iff $D_I \cup \{ d_i \}$ is an explanation of M^+.

The following decomposition theorem immediately follows:

theorem 3.23: Let $P = <D,M,C,M^+>$ be a diagnostic problem where $m_j \in M^+$ is a pathognomonic manifestation for $d_i \in D$, and let $Q = \{Q_1, \ldots, Q_n\}$ be a generator-set for $Sol(P')$, where $P' = <D,M,C,M^+ - effects(d_i) >$. Then $G = \{ G_1, \ldots, G_n \}$, where $G_I = Q_I \cup (\{ d_i \})$

for $1 \leq I \leq n$, is a generator–set for $Sol(P)$.

The second example of a situation where a diagnostic problem can be conveniently decomposed into subproblems is based on a concept of "connectedness" of manifestations. Connectedness is defined recursively in the following definition:

definition 3.19: Manifestations m_a and m_b in M are *connected* to each other if either
(a) $causes(m_a) \cap causes(m_b) \neq \emptyset$, or
(b) there exits $\{m_1, \ldots, m_n\} \subseteq M$ such that $m_a = m_1$, $m_b = m_n$ and each m_j is connected to m_{j+1} for all j, $1 \leq j \leq n - 1$.
Otherwise m_a and m_b are *unconnected* to each other.

This concept can be extended to sets of manifestations and pairs of sets of manifestations in a natural way. For example, $M_J \subseteq M$ is a connected set if for all $m_a, m_b \in M_J$, m_a is connected to m_b. However, the key concept we will need is the following:

definition 3.20: Two sets of manifestations M_1 and M_2 are *unconnected* to each other if for all $m_1 \in M_1$ and $m_2 \in M_2$, $causes(m_1) \cap causes(m_2) = \emptyset$.

Using the concept of unconnectedness, we can immediately show the following.

lemma 3.24: Let $P = <D,M,C,M^+>$ be a diagnostic problem with $M_1^+ \cup M_2^+ = M^+$ where M_1^+ and M_2^+ are unconnected to each other. Then
(a) $causes(M_1^+) \cap causes(M_2^+) = \emptyset$; and
(b) $E \subseteq D$ is an explanation for M^+ iff there are explanations E_1 and E_2 for M_1^+ and M_2^+ such that $E = E_1 \cup E_2$.

theorem 3.25: Let $P = <D,M,C,M^+>$ be a diagnostic problem, and let $M^+ = M_1^+ \cup M_2^+$ where M_1^+ and M_2^+ are unconnected to each other. If $G = \{G_1, \ldots, G_K\}$ is a generator–set for $Sol(P_1)$ where $P_1 = <D,M,C,M_1^+>$ and $Q = \{Q_1, \ldots, Q_L\}$ is a generator–set for $Sol(P_2)$ where $P_2 = <D,M,C,M_2^+>$, then

$$R = \{G_I \cup Q_J | 1 \leq I \leq K, 1 \leq J \leq L\}$$

is a generator–set for $Sol(P)$.

This theorem establishes that if M^+ can be partitioned into N unconnected subsets, then the original problem can be partitioned into N independent subproblems. The generator–set for the solution to the original problem is then easily constructed by composing the generators from the solutions to the subproblems. Note that since G_I and Q_J have no disorders in common, the "union" operation here is really just appending G_I and Q_J together (a similar observation holds for Theorem 3.23).

3.5. Relevance to Abductive Diagnostic Systems

One of the purposes of parsimonious covering theory is to provide a formal, application–independent framework that captures the basic ideas of abduction as used in recent abductive diagnostic systems. This section therefore briefly illustrates the relationship between some of these computational models and the formal parsimonious covering theory presented here.

Many knowledge–based diagnostic systems which use a hypothesize–and–test inference mechanism or which might reasonably be considered as models of human diagnostic reasoning depend heavily upon the use of production rules. These systems use a hypothesis–driven approach to guide the invocation of rules, which in turn modify the hypothesis. While a rule–based hypothesize–and–test approach may produce good performance, such a process does not provide a convincing model of what has been learned about human diagnostic reasoning in the empirical studies cited earlier in Chapter 1. Furthermore, invocation of rules to make deductions or perform actions does not capture in a general sense such "abductive" concepts as coverage, parsimony, or explanation as defined earlier.

In contrast to these rule–based systems, several recent computational models of diagnostic reasoning are more "purely abductive" in nature. Three of these systems, namely, INTERNIST–1 [Pople75, Miller82], KMS.HT [Reggia81,82b], and IDT [Shubin82], will be considered further here as representative examples. The goal is to illustrate how parsimonious covering theory formalizes the basic abductive aspects of inference used in these application–oriented systems, and to mention some of their limitations from the viewpoint of parsimonious covering theory.

3.5.1. Multiple Simultaneous Disorders Assumption

A number of abductive diagnostic systems assume that multiple disorders may occur simultaneously, and we consider two of them here: INTERNIST–1 and KMS.HT. INTERNIST–1 is a large medical knowledge–based system developed and evaluated earlier by others on an intuitive basis [Pople75, Miller82]. It uses diagnostic knowledge organized in a descriptive fashion similar to that of parsimonious covering theory (i.e., based on causal associations between individual entities) and does not rely on production rules to guide its hypothesize–and–test process. It is based on roughly the same principles as the parsimonious covering theory: it attempts to account for M^+ with as few disorders as possible during problem–solving. Among the set of disorders evoked by the initial known

manifestations, INTERNIST-1 selects one with the highest score according
to a heuristic weighting scheme. It then constructs a differential diagnosis
consisting of competing disorders of the highest scored disorder, and
further discriminates among them using a question–answering process with
the goal of obtaining a single disorder to be a component in the final diagnosis. By doing so, INTERNIST-1 apparently makes the assumption that
the equivalent of a single generator is sufficient to represent the solution of
a diagnostic problem. As we have seen, this is not always the case, even
when minimum cardinality is used as a parsimony criterion, thus raising
the possibility that INTERNIST-1 might at times omit some relevant
explanations. Furthermore, unlike the more parallel or breadth–first
approach in parsimonious covering theory, the heuristic scoring procedure
used by INTERNIST-1's inference mechanism that guides the construction
and modification of the single generator is essentially serial or depth–first.
It first attempts to establish the presence of one disorder among its competitors, and then proceeds to establish the next one, etc. This roughly
corresponds to constructing and completing a single explanation in parsimonious covering theory. This serial approach used by INTERNIST-1
proved to be a significant limitation when dealing with real–world diagnostic problems [Miller82], reflecting its "inability to perceive the multiplicity
of problems in a case all at once" [Pople77].

In addition, using parsimonious covering theory to analyze the
INTERNIST-1 approach to grouping together competing disorders (those
disorders forming a differential diagnosis, or a set in the generator as in
parsimonious covering theory terms) shows that even in some situations
where a single generator *could* generate the entire solution, INTERNIST-1
would apparently fail to group competing disorders properly. This is
explained below.

INTERNIST-1 uses the following simple but clever heuristic to group
competing disorders together: "Two diseases are competitors if the items
not explained by one disease are a subset of the items not explained by the
other; otherwise, they are alternatives (and may possibly coexist in the
patient)" [Miller82]. In terms of parsimonious covering theory, this
corresponds to stating that d_1 and d_2 are competitors if $M^+ - effects(d_1)$
contains or is contained in $M^+ - effects(d_2)$. Suppose $M^+ - effects(d_1) \subseteq$
$M^+ - effects(d_2)$. Then it follows that $effects(d_2) \cap M^+ \subseteq effects(d_1) \cap M^+$,
so the competing–disorder theorem (Theorem 3.8) applied to d_1 and d_2.
This makes it quite reasonable to intuitively view d_1 and d_2 as "competitors" in parsimonious covering theory, and to group them together as is
done in INTERNIST-1. On the other hand, parsimonious covering theory
also shows that there are situations where the INTERNIST-1 heuristic
would fail to group together disorders as competitors which should clearly
be considered as such if one is using a generator to represent the solution
to a diagnostic problem.

For example, suppose that $M^+ = \{m_1, m_2, \ldots, m_8\}$ and $causes(M^+) = \{d_1, d_2, d_3\}$. Suppose further $M^+ \cap effects(d_1) = \{m_2, m_4, m_5, m_6, m_7, m_8\}$, $M^+ \cap effects(d_2) = \{m_3, m_4, m_5, m_6, m_7, m_8\}$, $M^+ \cap effects(d_3) = \{m_1, m_2, m_3\}$. In parsimonious covering theory, $Sol(P) = \{\{d_1, d_3\}, \{d_2, d_3\}\}$. This solution can be represented by the single generator $(\{d_1, d_2\}, \{d_3\})$ constructed using generator operations if algorithm *BIPARTITE* is applied to successive manifestations $m_1, m_2, m_3, m_4, \ldots$, where d_1 and d_2 are grouped together as competitors. However, suppose that d_1 were ranked highest by the INTERNIST-1 heuristic scoring procedure. Then $M^+ - effects(d_1) = \{m_1, m_3\}$, and $M^+ - effects(d_2) = \{m_1, m_2\}$, neither of which is contained in the other. Thus, in this situation where a single generator *could* correctly represent the solution, INTERNIST-1 would apparently fail to group d_1 and d_2 together as competitors.

INTERNIST-1 has introduced many innovative and influential concepts for building knowledge–based diagnostic systems. Our comments above should not be viewed as a criticism of the pioneering effort which it represents. Rather, our comments are intended to reinforce the validity of the formal parsimonious covering theory by showing that its results in part correspond to those arrived at independently by others on an intuitive basis. In addition, the comments above illustrate the utility of a theoretical foundation for analyzing current computational models, so that a careful assessment of their limitations can be made.

The second computational model of diagnostic reasoning considered here that also assumes the possibility of multiple simultaneous disorders is the domain–independent system KMS.HT discussed in Chapter 2 [Reggia81]. As was seen with the two example diagnostic systems in Chapter 2 which were developed using KMS.HT, the inference mechanism is essentially a sequential parsimonious covering theory–like hypothesize–and–test approach with a variety of enhancements designed to make this approach more robust in the real–world. Both minimum cardinality and irredundancy have been adopted by KMS.HT as the parsimony criterion to define the notion of "explanation". KMS.HT antedated by years and in part motivated the development of the formalization of parsimonious covering theory. It provides a domain–independent *program* rather than a domain–independent *theory* as described in this book. Moreover, as illustrated by the example systems developed through KMS–HT in Chapter 2, it addresses and resolves issues important for real–world applications such as question generation methods, termination criteria, ranking of competing disorders in problem solutions, and adjustment of the hypothesis in the context of information about non–manifestations (i.e., setting factors). Generally, a heuristic approach was taken to resolving each of these issues in KMS.HT.

3.5.2. Single Disorder Assumption

In some diagnostic problems of more limited scope it proves convenient and appropriate to make the single–disorder assumption: only one disorder can occur at a time. IDT (Intelligent Diagnostic Tool), is a knowledge–based system for diagnosing faults in PDP 11/03 computers that makes this assumption [Shubin82]. In IDT a computer is viewed as composed of a number of "atomic units" (controllers, interfaces, disk drivers, etc.). A disorder d_i represents the hypothesis that the ith atomic unit is broken. Diagnostic knowledge is represented as deductive formulas associated with test results, e.g., "$\overline{d_1} \rightarrow d_2 \vee d_3$" or "$d_3 \rightarrow \overline{d_6}$". These formulae are not restricted to be Horn clauses (i.e., the right hand side can be a disjunction). The goal of the diagnostic process is to prove a formula of the form "$d_i \vee d_j \vee \cdots \vee d_k$", where the members of the set $\{d_i, d_j, \ldots, d_k\}$ are all inside of a single replaceable computer module. The developers of IDT prove that if one makes the "extralogical single–fault assumption", then *any* formula E associated with a test result can be transformed into a disjunctive formula (a clause) containing only positive literals (nonnegated d_i) that is equivalent to E. Furthermore, if one represents each such clause "$d_1, d_2, \ldots, d_n$" by its corresponding set of literals $\{d_1, d_2, \ldots, d_n\}$, then it can be shown that set intersection is the only operation necessary for combining test results.

From the perspective of parsimonious covering theory, each IDT test result corresponds to a manifestation m_j, and the set of positive literals $\{d_1, \ldots, d_n\}$ associated with it corresponds to $causes(m_j)$. Furthermore, the inference mechanism used in IDT, namely set intersection, can be shown to be a special case of generator division that occurs when the single–disorder assumption is made. Stating it more precisely, if $P = <D, M, C, M^+>$ is a diagnostic problem in which single disorder covers of M^+ exist, then the following steps

    1. *hypothesis* $:= \{(D)\}$;
    2. **for** $m_j \in M^+$ **do** *hypothesis* $:= div(hypothesis, causes(m_j))$;

will produce a generator–set $\{(D')\}$, where D' is equal to $\bigcap\limits_{m_j \in M^+} causes(m_j)$, the set of all single disorders that can cover all manifestations in M^+.

3.6. Comparison to Other Formalisms

Recently, several models of diagnostic inference were independently developed by others which are also aimed at developing abstractions of the key concepts of abductive diagnostic problem–solving. We now briefly discuss three of them: R. Reiter's "Theory of Diagnosis from First Principles" [Reiter87], J. de Kleer and B. C. Williams' "GDE (General Diagnostic

Engine)" model [deKleer87], and J. R. Josephson et al's model of "Assembly of Composite Explanatory Hypotheses" [Josephson87]. All three coincide to our parsimonious covering theory to some extent but differ from it on some important issues.

3.6.1. Reiter's Theory of Diagnosis from First Principles

In this model, the diagnostic process begins with a description of a system together with an observation of the system's behavior. If the observation conflicts with the way the system is meant to behave, then one is confronted with a diagnostic problem. The model is a first-order logic system. A system under investigation is represented as a pair $< SD, COMPONENTS>$ where $COMPONENTS$ is the set of all components of the system while SD is a set of first-order sentences representing the system description. In other words, SD specifies logical relationships of inputs-outputs of members of $COMPONENTS$. Reiter's theory uses McCarthy's $AB[\ ]$ predicate, meaning abnormal, in the system description. If no component is abnormal, then the system will behave in the way as specified by SD. For example, let x be a logical "and gate" with two inputs and one output. The normal behavior of this component can be described by the following first-order sentence:

$$ANDG(x) \wedge \overline{AB}(x) \rightarrow out(x) = and(in1(x),\ in2(x)),$$

meaning that if x is not abnormal (indicated by $\overline{AB}(x)$), then its output should be the logical and of its two input.

An observation of the system, OBS, is also a set of first-order sentences. A diagnostic problem is a discrepancy between an observed behavior OBS and the behavior predicted by SD, and thus is formalized as the inconsistency of

$$SD \cup \{\ \overline{AB}(c_i)\ |c_i \in COMPONENTS\} \cup OBS.$$

By adopting the principle of parsimony, a *diagnosis* of the problem is defined to be a *minimal* set $\Delta \subseteq COMPONENTS$ such that the failure of all members in Δ but not any member in $COMPONENTS - \Delta$ can account for the detected discrepancy. In first-order language, such a Δ should make

$$SD \cup OBS \cup \{\ AB(c_i)\ |c_i \in \Delta\ \} \cup \{\ \overline{AB}(c_i)\ |c_i \in COMPONENTS - \Delta\ \}$$

consistent. In this definition, the term "minimal set" means "irredundant set" in terms of parsimonious covering theory. To avoid possible confusion with the term "minimum cardinality", "irredundant" instead of "minimal" is used to denote such sets in parsimonious covering theory.

For solving diagnostic problems, the notion of *conflict set* is defined to be a subset of *COMPONENTS* such that at least one of its members must be abnormal in order to account for the discrepancy. That is, for a conflict set $\{c_1, \ldots, c_k\} \subseteq COMPONENTS$,

$$SD \cup OBS \cup \{\overline{AB}(c_1), \ldots, \overline{AB}(c_k)\}$$

is inconsistent. A conflict set is minimal if none of its subsets is also a conflict set for the given *OBS*. It is obvious that there may be many different minimal conflict sets for a problem, each of which may be related to a special feature in the discrepancy. Thus the notion of *hitting set* is defined to be a subset of *COMPONENTS* such that it intersects with every conflict set (it therefore, of course, intersects with each minimal conflict set). Reiter proves that a diagnosis for the $< SD, COMPONENTS, OBS>$ is a minimal hitting set.

In comparison to parsimonious covering theory, the set *COMPONENTS* corresponds to the disorder set D; a measurable behavior discrepancy corresponds to a manifestation m_j, and the set *OBS* corresponds to the set of given present manifestations M^+. The causal associations between disorders and manifestations are not explicitly given, but are instead embedded in the logical relationships specified by logical sentences in *SD*. Thus, the causal relationships must be inferred. Similarly, whether a measure reflects a normal behavior or a component failure must also be logically determined by *SD*. A "conflict set" corresponds to a superset of $causes(m_j)$ for some discrepancy m_j since the causes of m_j cannot all be normal in order to account for m_j's presence, and a "minimal conflict set" is equivalent to the set $causes(m_j)$. A "hitting set" is equivalent to a cover because it contains at least one element from $causes(m_j)$ for every $m_j \in M^+$, and a "minimal hitting set" is equivalent to our irredundant cover.

Reiter's theory requires one to find all diagnoses (all minimal hitting sets, or irredundant covers in our terminology) for a given *OBS*. The algorithmic approach is basically a breadth–first search of the space of size $2^{COMPONENTS}$. A frontier node in the tree generated during the search represents a partial diagnosis. At each step, a sound and complete theorem prover is called to generate a suitable conflict set which does not contain any member of the partial diagnosis represented by the node selected for expansion. Some pruning techniques are incorporated to remove duplicates and irredundancy. This process is shown to find all diagnoses. Reiter's search process is different from our algorithm *BIPARTITE* essentially in the following two aspects. First, the problem solution is obtained and organized as individual diagnoses rather than as generators, and thus competing disorders are not explicitly represented. Secondly, and more importantly, Reiter's theory does not include a mechanism to update tentative diagnoses when a new discrepancy is discovered, i.e., it does not implement the sequential, iterative hypothesize–and–test process which is crucial for many diagnostic applications. It also does not address the issue of probabilistic reasoning which we will turn to in the next chapter.

In summary, Reiter's and our theories strongly resemble each other in many important ways concerning diagnostic reasoning, e.g., multiple disorders (faults) may be present simultaneously; a diagnosis must be able to account for all present manifestations (or observed discrepancies) and should do so irredundantly (the principle of parsimony); not using rule–like heuristic knowledge directed from observations to diagnosis, but logical or causal knowledge directed from disorders to observable entities, etc. The major difference in problem formulation is that Reiter's theory takes a more general knowledge representation and thus can potentially be applied to a wider range of problem domains. It is especially suitable for problems such as electronic circuit fault localization where logical relationships among elements are easy to obtain. In contrast our theory concentrates on a more specific representation, the causal network, and thus is especially suitable for problems such as medical diagnosis where the primary associations are causal relations. One significant cost of the generality of Reiter's theory is the construction of conflict sets through a theorem prover, usually a computationally very time consuming process.

3.6.2. De Kleer and Williams' GDE Model

Reiter's theory of diagnosis was influenced by the work of de Kleer and others and can be considered as a formal account of "intuitive" techniques in the GDE (General Diagnostic Engine) model [deKleer87]. In the GDE model, a system's behavior is specified by a set of assumptions, and the difference between the system's predicted and observed behaviors must be accounted for by violations of some prespecified assumptions. Notions of conflict and minimal conflict, as well as candidate and minimal candidate, are defined. They are in essence equivalent to conflict set, minimal conflict set, hitting set ánd minimal hitting set, respectively, of Reiter's theory. Similar to Reiter's model, a predictive mechanism is used to generate conflict sets and a search of a superset–subset lattice is used to find all minimal candidates.

The major difference between Reiter's and de Kleer and Williams' models are in problem–solving. First, although the major effort of problem–solving is in finding all minimal candidates, de Kleer's model considers the problem solution to include not only all minimal candidates but also all supersets of them, i.e., all covers in parsimonious covering theory terminology. Secondly, the GDE model allows sequential diagnosis, i.e., it can update tentative candidates upon the arrival of newly discovered evidence. Finally, the GDE model includes a mechanism to determine what measurement (test) should be taken in order to further discriminate among existing candidates. The criterion for measurement selection is to minimize the entropy of candidate probabilities.

3.6.3. Josephson et al's Assembly of Composite Hypotheses

Josephson et al proposed a framework for assembling small hypotheses, each of which is capable of explaining part of the given findings for a diagnostic problem, into a best composite hypothesis which is self–consistent and capable of explaining all of the findings of the problem [Josephson87]. Based on this framework, a workable prototype system called RED was implemented for use in blood banks as a red–cell antibody identification consultant [Smith85]. The model consists of two modules: a classification machine and a means–ends machine. A diagnostic problem is first decomposed into subproblems. The classification machine is then used for selecting plausible small hypotheses for each subproblem by instantiating pre-stored explanatory "concepts" together with a symbolic likelihood for each hypothesis. The set of such small local hypotheses for each subproblem roughly corresponds to the set $causes(m_j)$ for a present manifestation m_j in parsimonious covering theory. This decomposition permits establishing separate problem–specific methods (representation and inference methods) for the distinct subproblems.

A specialized means–ends machine is then used for assembling these plausible small hypotheses of subproblems into a "best" composite explanation for the given problem as a whole. At any time during the assembly process, the means–ends machine detects the differences between the goal state (everything explained) and the present state (the tentative composite which does not explain everything), and focuses on a salient difference (a most significant unexplained finding based on domain knowledge). Then the most plausible hypothesis (with highest symbolic likelihood) of this unexplained salient finding is selected and integrated into the tentative composite. When so doing, the means–ends machine takes into account various hypothesis interactions. For example, explanatory interaction due to overlapping in what the component hypotheses can account for may result in superfluous (redundant) parts in the composite; substantive interactions due to incompatibility of two hypotheses may result in an inconsistent composite; one hypothesis may be a subtype of the other; etc.

The assembled composite explanation is then used as a starting point by an *overview critic* procedure to explore the space of alternative composites. This procedure repeatedly does the following: identify all indispensable parts in the current composite (where an indispensable part of a explanation is one without which no complete composite explanation can be found in the whole hypothesis space); remove all nonindispensable parts from the composite; reassemble a complete composite from the remaining indispensable parts.

The final composite explanation is complete since all findings are accounted for by one or more hypotheses in the composite, and it is parsimonious since all superfluous parts have been identified and removed. It is also maximally plausible (best) in the sense that all hypothesis parts in the composite are most plausible in their respective subtasks in the context of interactions.

Both Josephson's and our models explicitly consider the diagnostic process as an explanation–constructing abductive process. Parsimonious covering theory is a formal model, however, while Josephson's model is an informal, more application–oriented framework. A major difference between these two models is that in parsimonious covering theory the goal is typically to find all irredundant covers, while in the composite hypothesis assembly one concentrates on finding one of the "best" covers. The heuristic approach they take to discriminate between alternatives is computationally efficient and may be plausible in many applications. However, as a local optimization technique, this approach is not guaranteed to work in all cases because a globally optimal composite hypothesis is not necessarily composed of the best local results. This issue will be dealt with in Chapter 4 where the posterior probability (likelihood) of a composite explanation will be seen not to be a simple sum or product of the likelihoods of its individual explanation components. The interactions between likelihoods of these individual components can be more complex and can lead to situations where the explanation having the highest likelihood contains some components which are not the best in their local context.

3.7. Conclusions

In this chapter, we have presented the basic ideas of parsimonious covering theory. These basics include the definitions of a diagnostic problem, an explanation, and a solution to a problem. Within this formulation, an algebra of generator–sets and algorithm *BIPARTITE* were developed to capture the hypothesize–and–test process during problem–solving. As a formalization of the basic abductive reasoning for diagnostic problem–solving, parsimonious covering theory is consistent with many features of human diagnostic reasoning as revealed by empirical studies (see discussion in Chapter 1). It also captures in a domain independent and abstract fashion many features of existing abductive diagnostic systems such as INTERNIST–1, KMS.HT, and IDT. Although this was done within the scope of the simplest causal networks for diagnostic problems, it will be seen that these basic ideas are readily applicable to more general situations where intermediate states and causal chaining exist (Chapter 6).

So far, the parsimonious covering theory only formalizes the representation and utilization of one kind of knowledge used in diagnostic problem–solving, namely the categorical or structural knowledge. In the next two chapters, parsimonious covering theory is extended to incorporate another kind of equally important knowledge, probabilistic knowledge, in the same formal and domain–independent fashion. The integration of parsimonious covering theory and probability theory results in a more general and reasonable problem–solving strategy.

3.8. Appendix Summarizing Set Notation

Symbol	Meaning
$\in$	Element of
$\subseteq$	Subset of
$\subset$	Proper subset of
$\supseteq$	Superset of
$\supset$	Proper superset of
$\emptyset$	Empty set
$\cup$	Set union
$\cap$	Set intersection
$-$	Set difference
$\times$	Cartesian product
2^A	Power set of set A
$\vert\ \vert$	Set cardinality
$\{\ \}$	Set
$<\ >$	Ordered tuple
$(\ )$	Generator
$[\ ]$	Class generated by a generator

3.9. Mathematical Appendix

proof of Lemma 3.1.

(a) Since by Definition 3.1, $domain(C) = D$ and $range(C) = M$. The proposition then follows immediately from Definition 3.2.

(b) By (a) there must exist $m_j \in effects(d_i)$ such that $<d_i, m_j> \in C$. Thus $d_i \in causes(m_j) \subseteq \bigcup\limits_{m_k \in effects(d_i)} causes(m_k) = causes(effects(d_i))$. The proof of $m_j \in effects(causes(m_j))$ is analogous.

(c) Immediately from (b) by Definition 3.3.

(d) Since $domain(C) = D$ and $range(C) = M$, then $effects(D) \subseteq M$. Conversely, for any $m_j \in M$, $m_j \in effects(causes(m_j)) \subseteq effects(D)$ by (b). Thus $M \subseteq effects(D)$. The proof of $D = causes(M)$ is analogous.

(e) $d_i \in causes(m_j)$ iff $<d_i, m_j> \in C$ iff $m_j \in effects(d_i)$, all by definition of relation C.

(f) For any $m_j \in effects(D_I) - effects(D_K)$, $m_j \in effects(D_I)$, i.e., there exists some $d_i \in D_I$ such that $<d_i, m_j> \in C$. Since $m_j \notin effects(D_K)$, it follows that $d_i \notin D_K$. So $d_i \in D_I - D_K$. Thus $m_j \in effects(d_i) \subseteq effects(D_I - D_K)$. □

proof of Lemma 3.2.

By Definition 3.3, $D_I \cap causes(M_J) = \emptyset$ iff for all $d_i \in D_I$, $m_j \in M_J$: $<d_i, m_j> \notin C$ iff $M_J \cap effects(D_I) = \emptyset$.   □

proof of Lemma 3.3.

Assume that D_K is not an irredundant cover of M_J. Then there exists some $d_1 \in D_K$ such that $D_K^{(1)} = D_K - \{d_1\}$ covers M_J by the definition of irredundant cover. If $D_K^{(1)}$ is still not an irredundant cover of M_J, then there exists some d_2 such that $D_K^{(2)} = D_K^{(1)} - \{d_2\}$ covers M_J. Since the size of D_K is finite, after k steps of such removals for some finite number k, we will have $D_K^{(k)} \subset D_K^{(k-1)} \subset \cdots \subset D_K^{(2)} \subset D_K^{(1)} \subset D_K$ such that $D_K^{(k)}$ covers M_J and none of proper subsets of $D_K^{(k)}$ is also a cover of M_J, i.e., $D_K^{(k)} \subset D_K$ is an irredundant cover of M_J.   □

proof of Theorem 3.4.

By Lemma 3.1d, $M^+ \subseteq M = effects(D)$, i.e., there is always a cover, namely D, of M^+. Then the theorem follows immediately from Lemma 3.3.   □

proof of Lemma 3.5.

Let D_I be an irredundant cover of M^+. If there exists some $d_i \in D_I$ such that for all $m_j \in M_J$, $m_j \in effects(D_I - \{d_i\})$, then $M_J \subseteq effects(D_I - \{d_i\})$, i.e., $D_I - \{d_i\}$ is also a cover of M^+, which contradicts that D_I is an irredundant cover of M^+.

Conversely, if every $d_i \in D_I$ uniquely covers some $m_j \in M_J$, then removal of any d_i from D_I makes it a non–cover of M_J, thus, D_I is an irredundant cover of M_J.   □

proof of Lemma 3.6.

Immediately from Lemma 3.5.   □

proof of Lemma 3.7.

Immediately from Theorem 3.4 and Lemma 3.6.   □

proof of Theorem 3.8.

(a) Suppose that both d_1 and d_2 are in E. Since $M^+ \cap effects(d_1) \subseteq M^+ \cap effects(d_2)$, then for any $m_k \in M^+$, if $m_k \in effects(d_1)$, then $m_k \in effects(d_2)$. Therefore, $E - \{d_1\}$ is also a cover of M^+. This contradicts the irredundancy of E.

(b) By the same argument as in (a), if $d_1 \in E$, then $E' = (E - \{d_1\}) \cup \{d_2\}$ is also a cover of M^+. Then by Lemma 3.3, there exists some $E_1 \subseteq E'$ which is an irredundant cover of M^+, and $|E_1| \le |E'| = |E|$. It remains to show that $d_2 \in E_1$. This is done by showing that any subset of E' must contain d_2 if it is a cover of M^+. Since E is an irredundant cover of M^+, there exists some $m_j \in M^+$ such that m_j is in $effects(d_1)$ but not in $effects(E - \{d_1\})$ by Lemma 3.5. Therefore, the same m_j must be in $effects(d_2)$ but not in

$effects(E' - \{d_2\})$, which implies that any subset of E' covering M^+ must contain d_2.   □

proof Lemma 3.9.
(1) For any $D_I \in S_{mc}$, none of its proper subsets is also a cover of M^+, for otherwise it is not a minimum cover. Thus, $D_I \in S_{ic}$.
(2) Let $D_I \in S_{ic}$. Then by Lemma 3.5 and Definition 3.6, for every $d_i \in D_I$, $d_i \in causes(m_j)$ for some $m_j \in M^+$. Thus, $D_I \subseteq causes(M^+)$, i.e., $D_I \in S_{rc}$.
(3) The rest of the lemma, $S_{rc} \subseteq S_c \subseteq 2^D$, is obvious from the definitions.   □

proof of Lemma 3.10.
By Lemma 3.3, for any $D_K \subseteq D$ covering M^+, there exists some $D_I \subseteq D_K$ such that $D_I \in S_{ic}$. Also, any set of covers having this property must contain S_{ic} because for each irredundant cover there is no subset of it which is also a cover of M^+ except itself. Therefore, S_{ic} is the smallest set of covers having such a property.   □

proof of Lemma 3.11.
(a) By the definition of generator division, every $Q_k \in div(G_I, H_1)$ is a generator. Now for any two distinct $Q_j = \{q_{j1}, q_{j2}, \ldots, q_{jm}\}$ and $Q_k = \{q_{k1}, q_{k2}, \ldots, q_{kn}\}$ in $div(G_I, H_1)$, we show that $[Q_j] \cap [Q_k] = \varnothing$, and thus prove $div(G_I, H_1)$ is a generator-set. Without loss of generality, assume $j < k$. Then it suffices to show that $q_{jj} \cap q_{kr} = \varnothing$ for all r. For the case where $r = j$, we have $q_{jj} = g_j \cap H_1$ and $q_{kr} = g_j - H_1$, so $q_{jj} \cap q_{kj} = \varnothing$. For the case where $r \neq j$, we have $g_j \cap g_r = \varnothing$, and thus since $q_{jj} \subseteq g_j$ and $q_{kr} \subseteq g_r$, we have $q_{jj} \cap q_{kr} = \varnothing$.
Now we show that $[div(G_I, H_1)] = \{E \in [G_I] \mid E \cap H_1 \neq \varnothing\}$. For any $d_i \in E = \{d_1, d_2, \ldots, d_n\} \in [div(G_I, H_1)]$, $d_i \in q_{ki} \subseteq g_i$, thus $E \in [G_I]$, and $d_k \in q_{kk} = g_k \cap H_1$ for some k, whence $E \cap H_1 \neq \varnothing$. Thus $[div(G_I, H_1)] \subseteq \{E \in [G_I] \mid E \cap H_1 \neq \varnothing\}$.
Conversely, let $E = \{d_1, d_2, \ldots, d_n\} \in [G_I]$ such that $E \cap H_1 \neq \varnothing$. Then $d_i \in g_i$ for all i, and E contains at least one $d_i \in H_1$. Let k be the smallest i such that $d_i \in H_1$. Then from the definition of Q_k,

for all $i < k$, $q_{ki} = g_i - H_1 \neq \varnothing$, so $d_i \in q_{ki}$,
for $i = k$, $q_{kk} = g_k \cap H_1 \neq \varnothing$, so $d_k \in q_{kk}$, and
for all $i > k$, $q_{ki} = g_i \neq \varnothing$, so $d_i \in q_{ki}$.

Thus, $E \in [(q_{k1}, q_{k2}, \ldots, q_{kn})] = [Q_k] \subseteq [div(G_I, H_1)]$.
(b) By (a) $div(G_I, H_1)$ is a generator-set in $div(G, H_1) = \bigcup_{G_I \in G} div(G_I, H_1)$. Now consider any two distinct generators Q_1 and Q_2 where $Q_1 \in div(G_I, H_1)$ and $Q_2 \in div(G_J, H_1)$ for G_I and G_J in G. If $G_I = G_J$ (i.e., they are in the division of a same generator G_I), then by (a) $[Q_1] \cap [Q_2] = \varnothing$. Otherwise, since $[Q_1] \subseteq [G_I]$ and $[Q_2] \subseteq [G_J]$, and $[G_I] \cap [G_J] = \varnothing$, so $[Q_1] \cap [Q_2] = \varnothing$. Thus $div(G, H_1)$ is a generator-set.
Also note that by (a) and Definition 3.11,

$$E \in [div(G, H_1)] \text{ iff } E \in [div(G_I, H_1)] \text{ for some } G_I \in G,$$
$$\text{iff } E \in \{E \in [G_I] \mid E \cap H_1 \neq \varnothing\} \text{ for some } G_I \in G,$$
$$\text{iff } E \in \{E \in [G] \mid E \cap H_1 \neq \varnothing\}.$$

Thus, $[div(G, H_1)] = \{E \in [G] \mid E \cap H_1 \neq \varnothing\}$. □

proof of Lemma 3.12.

(a) If $g_i - H_1 = \varnothing$ for some $g_i \in G_I$, then $res(G_I, H_1) = \varnothing$ is a generator–set which implies $[res(G_I, H_1)] = \varnothing$. On the other hand, $g_i - H_1 = \varnothing$ implies that $g_i \subseteq H_1$, and by the definition of generators, all $E \in [G_I]$ thus must contain some element in H_1. Therefore $\{E \in [G_I] \mid E \cap H_1 = \varnothing\} = \varnothing = [res(G_I, H_1)]$.

If $g_i - H_1 \neq \varnothing$ for all $g_i \in G_I$, then $(g_1 - H_1, g_2 - H_1, \ldots, g_n - H_1)$ is a generator, thus $\{(g_1 - H_1, g_2 - H_1, \ldots, g_n - H_1)\}$ is a generator–set, and

$$[res(G_I, H_1)] = [\{(g_1 - H_1, g_2 - H_1, \ldots, g_n - H_1)\}]$$
$$= \{(h_1, h_2, \ldots, h_n) \in [G_I] \mid h_i \in g_i - H_1 \text{ for all } g_i \in G_I\}$$
$$= \{E \in [G_I] \mid E \cap H_1 = \varnothing\}.$$

(b) By the definition of generator–sets, for any two distinct G_I, G_J in G, $[G_I] \cap [G_J] = \varnothing$. Also, since $[res(G_K, H_1)] \subseteq [G_K]$ for all $G_K \in G$, it follows that $[res(G_I, H_1)] \cap [res(G_J, H_1)] = \varnothing$, i.e., $res(G, H_1)$ is a generator–set. The rest of part (b) follows immediately from part (a). □

proof of Lemma 3.13.

(a) and (b) are proved together by induction on $|Q_J|$.

base case: $|Q_J| = 0$, then $Q_J = \varnothing$.

(a) $div(G_I, Q_J) = \{G_I\}$ is a generator–set and $[div(G_I, Q_J)] = [\{G_I\}] = [G_I]$. On the other hand, $\{E \in [G_I] \mid \text{ there exists } E' \in [Q_J] \text{ where } E' \subseteq E\} = [G_I]$ because $[Q_J] = [\varnothing] = \{\varnothing\}$ and for any $E \in [G_I], \varnothing \subseteq E$.

(b) By (a), $div(G, Q_J) = \bigcup_{G_I \in G} \{G_I\} = G$ is a generator–set. By arguments

similar to (a), $[div(G, Q_J)] = [G] = \{E \in [G] \mid \text{ there exists } E' \in [Q_J] \text{ where } E' \subseteq E\} = [G]$.

induction step: Assume that (a) and (b) hold for all Q_J where $0 \leq |Q_J| < n$ for some n. Now show that they hold for any Q_J with $|Q_J| = n$.

(a) Let $G^1 = div(G_I, q_j)$, then by Lemma 3.11, G^1 is a generator–set. By the inductive hypothesis, since $|Q_J - (q_j)| < n$, $div(G_I, Q_J) = div(G^1, Q_J - (q_j))$ is also a generator–set and

$$[div(G_I, Q_J)] = \{E \in [G^1] \mid \text{ there exists } E' \in [Q_J - (q_j)] \text{ where } E' \subseteq E\}$$
$$= \{E \in [G_I] \mid E \cap q_j \neq \varnothing \text{ and there exists } E' \in [Q_J - (q_j)]$$
$$\text{where } E' \subseteq E\}$$
$$= \{E \in [G_I] \mid \text{ there exists } E' \in [Q_J] \text{ where } E' \subseteq E\}.$$

(b) Note that for any distinct G_S and G_R in G, $[G_S] \cap [G_R] = \varnothing$. By (a) $[div(G_S, Q_J)] \subseteq [G_S]$ and $[div(G_R, Q_J)] \subseteq [G_R]$. Therefore, $[div(G_S, Q_J)] \cap [div(G_R, Q_J)] = \varnothing$. Thus $div(G, Q_J) = \bigcup_{G_I \in G} div(G_I, Q_J)$ is a generator–set, and

$$[div(G, Q_J)] = \bigcup_{G_I \in G} \{E \in [G_I] \mid \text{there exists } E' \in [Q_J] \text{ where } E' \subseteq E\}$$

$$= \{E \in [G] \mid \text{there exists } E' \in [Q_J] \text{ where } E' \subseteq E\}. \qquad \Box$$

proof of Lemma 3.14.

(a) and (b) are proved together by induction on $|Q_J|$.

base cases: $|Q_J| = 0$, then $Q_J = \emptyset$.

(a) Then $res(G_I, Q_J) = \emptyset$ is a generator–set and $[res(G_I, Q_J)] = \emptyset$. Also, since $[Q_J] = [\emptyset] = \{\emptyset\}$ and $\emptyset \subseteq E$ for all $E \in [G_I]$, it follows that $\{E \in [G_I] \mid \text{there does not exist } E' \in [Q_J] \text{ where } E' \subseteq E\} = \emptyset = [res(G_I, Q_J)]$.

(b) Also $res(G, Q_J) = \bigcup_{G_I \in G} res(G_I, Q_J) = \bigcup_{G_I \in G} \emptyset = \emptyset$ is a generator–set with $[res(G, Q_J)] = [\emptyset] = \emptyset$. Similar as in (a), $[res(G, Q_J)] = \{E \in [G] \mid \text{there does not exist } E' \in [Q_J] \text{ where } E' \subseteq E\}$.

induction step: Assume (a) and (b) hold for all Q_J with $0 \leq |Q_J| < n$ for some n. Now show that they hold for any Q_J with $|Q_J| = n$.

(a) Since $Q_J \neq \emptyset$, by the definition, $res(G_I, Q_J) = res(G_I, q_j) \cup res(div(G_I, q_j), Q_J - (q_j))$ where $q_j \in Q_J$. $res(G_I, q_j)$ is a generator–set by Lemma 3.12, $div(G_I, q_j)$ is a generator–set by Lemma 3.11, classes generated by them partition the class $[G_I]$. It follows, by the inductive hypothesis, that $res(div(G_I, q_j), Q_J - (q_j))$ is also a generator–set and the class it generates is a subset of $[div(G_I, q_j)]$, therefore is disjoint to $[res(G_I, q_j)]$, so $res(G_I, Q_J)$ is a generator–set. Note

$$[res(G_I, q_j)] = \{E \in [G_I] \mid E \cap q_j = \emptyset\}$$
$$= \{E \in [G_I] \mid E \cap q_j = \emptyset \text{ and there does not exist } E' \in [Q_J]$$
$$\text{where } E' \subseteq E\}$$

because $E \cap q_j = \emptyset$ implies that there does not exist any $E' \in [Q_J]$ with $E' \subseteq E$; while

$$[res(div(G_I, q_j), Q_J - (q_j))]$$
$$= \{E \in [div(G_I, q_j)] \mid \text{there does not exist } E' \in [Q_J - (q_j)]$$
$$\text{where } E' \subseteq E\}$$
$$= \{E \in [G_I] \mid E \cap q_j \neq \emptyset \text{ and there does not exist } E' \in [Q_J]$$
$$\text{where } E' \subseteq E\}.$$

Union them together, by De Morgan's law, it follows that

$$[res(G_I, Q_J)] = \{E \in [G_I] \mid \text{there does not exist } E' \in [Q_J] \text{ where } E' \subseteq E\}.$$

(b) For all G_I in G, $res(G_I, Q_J)$ are generator–sets, and classes they generate are disjoint to each other because these classes are subsets of classes generated by G_I's which are disjoint to each other, so $res(G, Q_J)$ is a generator–set. Since $[G] = \bigcup_{G_I \in G} [res(G_I, Q_J)]$, and all $[res(G_I, Q_J)]$ are disjoint to each other,

$$[res(G, Q_J)] = \bigcup_{G_I \in G} \{E \in [G_I] \mid \text{ there does not exist } E' \in [Q_J]$$
$$\text{where } E' \subseteq E\}$$
$$= \{E \in G \mid \text{ there does not exist } E' \in [Q_J] \text{ where } E' \subseteq E\}.$$

(c) By induction on $|Q|$.

base case: Since $|Q| = 0$, $Q = \emptyset$ and $[Q] = \emptyset$. Then $res(G, Q) = G$ is a generator–set, and $[res(G, Q)] = [G]$. Since $[Q] = \emptyset$ has no member, $\{E \in [G] \mid \text{ there does not exist } E' \in [Q] \text{ where } E' \subseteq E\} = [G]$.

induction step: Assume it holds for all Q with $0 \le |Q| < n$ for some n. Now show that it holds for any Q with $|Q| = n$. Let $G^1 = res(G, Q_J)$. G^1 is a generator–set by (b), $res(G, Q) = res(G^1, Q - \{Q_J\})$ is a generator–set by the inductive hypothesis. Since
$$[G^1] = \{E \in [G] \mid \text{ there does not exist } E' \in [Q_J] \text{ where } E' \subseteq E\},$$

$$[res(G, Q)] = [res(G^1, Q - \{Q_J\})]$$
$$= \{E \in [G^1] \mid \text{ there does not exist } E' \in [Q - \{Q_J\}]$$
$$\text{where } E' \subseteq E\}$$
$$= \{E \in [G] \mid \text{ there does not exist } E' \in [Q] \text{ where } E' \subseteq E\}. \quad \square$$

proof of Lemma 3.15.

(1) If $g_i - H_1 = \emptyset$ for some $g_i \in G_I$ or $A = H_1 - \bigcup_{g_i \in G_I} g_i = \emptyset$, then $augres(G_I, H_1) = \emptyset$ which is a generator–set. Otherwise, $A \ne \emptyset$, $g_i - H_1 \ne A$ for all $g_i \in G_I$, and $g_i - H_1 \ne g_j - H_1$ for all pairs of distinct g_i, g_j in G_I. It follows that $(g_1 - H_1, g_2 - H_1, \ldots, g_n - H_1, A)$ is a generator, therefore $augres(G_I, H_1)$ is a generator–set.

(2) To show that $augres(G, H_1)$ is a generator–set, it only needs to be shown that $[augres(G_I, H_1)] \cap [augres(G_J, H_1)] = \emptyset$ for all distinct pairs G_I, G_J in G. Assume the contrary that there exist $E_I \in [augres(G_I, H_1)]$ and $E_J \in [augres(G_J, H_1)]$ with $E_I = E_J$. By the definition of augmented residual, $E_I = E'_I \cup \{d_i\}$ and $E_J = E'_J \cup \{d_j\}$ where $E'_I \in [res(G_I, H_1)]$, $E'_J \in [res(G_J, H_1)]$, and d_i, d_j are in H_1. It is clear that $E'_I \ne E'_J$ by Lemma 3.14, and neither of them contains any element in H_1. Then it follows that $E_I \ne E_J$ which is a contradiction. $\quad \square$

proof of Lemma 3.16.

By Lemma 3.11, for all $E \in [div(G, causes(m_j))]$, E is in $[G]$ and $E \cap causes(m_j) \ne \emptyset$. Since E is an irredundant cover of M^+, it follows that E is also an irredundant cover of $M^+ \cup \{m_j\}$. Conversely, for any $E \subseteq D$ irredundantly covering both M^+ and $M^+ \cup \{m_j\}$, it must be in $[G]$ and $E \cap causes(\{m_j\}) \ne \emptyset$ must be true. Therefore, E belongs to $[div(G, causes(m_j))]$ by Lemma 3.11. $\quad \square$

proof of Lemma 3.17.

This proof consists of 3 steps.

(1) Prove that $E \cap causes(m_j) = \{d_i\}$ is a singleton.

Since E is an irredundant cover of $M^+ \cup \{m_j\}$, by Lemma 3.5, we claim that there exists some $d_i \in E$ which uniquely covers m_j, for otherwise all $d_i \in E$ would uniquely cover some manifestations in M^+, contradicting the fact that E is a redundant cover of M^+.

(2) Prove that $E' = E - causes(m_j)$ belongs to $[res(G, causes(m_j))]$.

By (1), $E' = E - \{d_i\}$ where $\{d_i\} = E \cap causes(m_j)$. If E' does not cover M^+, then any other proper subset of E which covers M^+ (there must exist such a subset because E is a redundant cover of M^+) must contain d_i, therefore cover $M^+ \cup \{m_j\}$ which contradicts that E is an irredundant cover of $M^+ \cup \{m_j\}$. Also by (1), every $d_k \in E'$ uniquely covers some manifestations in M^+, thus it follows from Lemma 3.5 that E' is an irredundant cover of M^+. Since none of $d_k \in E'$ covers m_j (it is uniquely covered by d_i), then by Lemma 3.12, E' belongs to $[res(G, causes(m_j))]$.

(3) Prove that E belongs to $[augres(G, causes(m_j))]$.

By (2), $E = E' \cup \{d_i\}$ where $E' \in [res(G, causes(m_j))]$ and $\{d_i\} = E \cap causes(m_j)$. Then $E' \in [res(G_J, causes(m_j))]$ for some G_J in G. Let

$$res(G_J, causes(m_j))$$
$$= \{(g_1 - causes(m_j), g_2 - causes(m_j), \ldots, g_n - causes(m_j))\}.$$

Then $E' = \{d_1, d_2, \ldots, d_{k-1}, d_k, d_{k+1}, \ldots, d_n\}$ where $d_k \in g_k - causes(m_j)$ for all g_k in G_J, and $E = \{d_1, d_2, \ldots, d_{k-1}, d_k, d_{k+1}, \ldots, d_n, d_i\}$. Now look at d_i. If it belongs to some g_k in G_J, then by replacing d_k by d_i, $\{d_1, d_2, \ldots, d_{k-1}, d_i, d_{k+1}, \ldots, d_n\} \in [div(G, causes(m_j))]$ covers $M^+ \cup \{m_j\}$ and is an proper subset of E which contradicts that E is an irredundant cover of $M^+ \cup \{m_j\}$. Thus d_i must be in $causes(m_j) - \bigcup_{g_k \in G_J} g_k$, i.e.,

$E \in [augres(G, causes(m_j))]$. □

proof of Lemma 3.18.

For any E in S, E is in $[Q]$ by Lemma 3.17. For any $E' \in [F]$, by Lemma 3.16, E' is an irredundant cover of both M^+ and $M^+ \cup \{m_j\}$. But E is a redundant cover of M^+, so $E \neq E'$. Also both E and E' are irredundant covers of $M^+ \cup \{m_j\}$, so E' cannot be a proper subset of E. Then by Lemma 3.14c, $E \in [res(Q, F)]$.

Conversely, for any E in $[res(Q, F)]$, E is in $[Q]$, thus covers $M^+ \cup \{m_j\}$ by the definition of $augres$. E is thus also a cover of M^+. Now we only need to show that E covers $M^+ \cup \{m_j\}$ irredundantly. Suppose the contrary that E is a redundant cover of $M^+ \cup \{m_j\}$. Then there is some $E_1 \subset E$ which is an irredundant cover of $M^+ \cup \{m_j\}$. Such E_1 must be in $[F]$ if it is also an irredundant cover of M^+. But this is impossible by the properties of operation res (Lemma 3.14c). Therefore, E_1 must be a redundant cover of M^+ and is in $[Q]$ by Lemma 3.17. Then, as shown in the proof of Lemma 3.17, both $E_1' = E_1 - causes(m_j)$ and $E' = E - causes(m_j)$ are irredundant covers of M^+, and $E_1' \subset E'$ which is a contradiction. Therefore E is an irredundant cover of $M^+ \cup \{m_j\}$. □

proof of Theorem 3.19.

By induction on $|M^+|$.

Base case: $|M^+| = 0$, i.e., $M^+ = \emptyset$. Then $Sol(P) = \{\emptyset\}$. On the other hand, in *BIPARTITE*, *hypothesis* $= \{\emptyset\}$ from the initialization at line 4. Since $|M^+| = 0$, *Moremanifs* $=$ false, no statement between line 5 and line 8 will be executed, and *BIPARTITE* returns $\{\emptyset\}$. But $[\{\emptyset\}] = \{\emptyset\}$, thus the theorem holds.

Induction step: Assume it holds for $0 \leq |M^+| < N$ for some N. Now consider a problem $P_N = \langle H,D,M,C,M_N \rangle$ where $M_N = \{m_1, m_2, \ldots, m_N\} \subseteq M$. After the first $N - 1$ manifestations, say $m_1, m_2, \ldots, m_{N-1}$ have been received and processed, by the inductive hypothesis, the function will have *hypothesis* with $[hypothesis] = \{E \subseteq D \mid E$ is an irredundant cover of $M_{N-1}\}$ at the end of the **while** loop (line 8) where $M_{N-1} = \{m_1, m_2, \ldots, m_{N-1}\}$. Since there is one more present manifestation left, *Moremanifs* $=$ true at line 5, the **while** loop has to be executed one more time. During this execution, the last present manifestation is obtained in m_{new} by calling *Nextman* function at line 6, and all its causes are obtained at line 7. By the definition of function *revise* and Lemmas 3.16 and 3.18 $[hypothesis]$ is the set of all irredundant covers of M_N at line 8, i.e., the solution of the problem P_N. The execution of the function *BIPARTITE* will then terminate and the value of *hypothesis* is returned since no more manifestation is left and *Moremanifs* $=$ false. Thus, $Sol(P_N) = [BIPARTITE(D,M,C)]$ holds. Since it holds for any problem with $|M^+| = N$, it follows that $Sol(P) = [BIPARTITE(D,M,C)]$ holds for all diagnostic problems $P = \langle D,M,C,M^+ \rangle$.   □

proof of Lemma 3.20.

(a) By the definition of $common^+(g_i)$, for any $g_i \in G_I$, we have $common^+(g_i) \subseteq M^+$. So $\bigcup_{g_i \in G_I} common^+(g_i) \subseteq M^+$. Conversely, assume that there exists an $m_j \in M^+$ such that $m_j \notin \bigcup_{g_i \in G_I} common^+(g_i)$. Then for all $g_i \in G_I$, $m_j \notin common^+(g_i)$ and $m_j \notin common(g_i)$, so it is possible to find a set $D_I = \{d_i \mid d_i \in g_i$ and $m_j \notin effects(d_i), 1 \leq i \leq n\}$ of n disorders, one from each g_i, and none of which cover m_j, so $m_j \notin effects(D_I)$. But this contradicts the fact that D_I is an explanation because $D_I \in [G_I] \subseteq Sol(P)$. Thus, $M^+ \subseteq \bigcup_{g_i \in G_I} common^+(g_i)$.

(b) Suppose $common^+(g_i) = \emptyset$ for some $g_i \in G_I$. Let $\hat{G}_I = G_I - \{g_i\}$, and let $E \in [\hat{G}_I]$. Since $common^+(g_i) = \emptyset$, for any $m_j \in M^+$ there is a $d_i \in g_i$ such that $m_j \notin effects(d_i)$. But since $E \cup \{d_i\} \in [G_I] \subseteq Sol(P)$ is an irredundant cover of M^+, there must be a $d_k \in E$ such that $m_j \in effects(d_k)$. Since it holds for every $m_j \in M^+$, it follows that $M^+ \subseteq effects(E)$, contradicting the irredundancy of $E \cup \{d_i\} \in [G_I] \subseteq Sol(P)$. Thus, $common^+(g_i) \neq \emptyset$ for all $g_i \in G_I$.   □

proof of Lemma 3.21.

By the definition of $owned^+(g_i)$, we must show that there is an $m_j \in common^+(g_i)$ such that for all $k \neq i$, $m_j \notin common^+(g_k)$. By Lemma 3.20b, we know that $common^+(g_i) \neq \varnothing$. Suppose that for all $m_j \in common(g_i)$, there is a $g_k \neq g_i$ such that $m_j \in common^+(g_k)$ also. Let $\hat{G}_I = G_I - (g_i)$ and let $E \in [\hat{G}_I]$. Then, for every $m_j \in M^+$, either of the following holds.

case 1: $m_j \in common^+(g_i)$, so by our supposition above there is a $g_k \in \hat{G}_I$ such that $m_j \in common^+(g_k)$.

case 2: $m_j \notin common^+(g_i)$, so by Lemma 3.20a, $m_j \in common^+(g_k)$ for some $g_k \in \hat{G}_I$.

Thus, in either case, $m_j \in common^+(g_k)$ for some $g_k \in \hat{G}_I$ and so $m_j \in effects(E)$. Since this holds for all $m_j \in M^+$, $M^+ \subseteq effects(E)$. On the other hand, since $[G_I] = Sol(P)$, $E \cup \{d_i\}$ for any $d_i \in g_i$ is an irredundant cover of M^+. This is a contradiction.   □

proof of Lemma 3.22.

(a) Since m_j is pathognomonic for d_i, $causes(m_j) = \{d_i\}$. By Lemma 3.1e, d_i is the only disorder such that $m_j \in effects(d_i)$. Let D_I be a cover of M^+. Then $m_j \in effects(D_I)$, so $d_i \in D_I$.

(b) Suppose D_I is a cover of $M^+ - effects(d_i)$. Then $M^+ - effects(d_i) \subseteq effects(D_I)$, so

$$M^+ \subseteq (M^+ - effects(d_i)) \cup effects(d_i)$$
$$\subseteq effects(D_I) \cup effects(d_i)$$
$$= effects(D_I \cup \{d_i\}),$$

making $D_I \cup \{d_i\}$ a cover for M^+. Conversely, suppose $D_I \cup \{d_i\}$ covers M^+. Then

$$M^+ \subseteq effects(D_I \cup \{d_i\})$$
$$= effects(D_I) \cup effects(d_i).$$

Therefore,

$$M^+ - effects(d_i) \subseteq (effects(D_I) \cup effects(d_i)) - effects(d_i)$$
$$\subseteq effects(D_I),$$

so D_I covers $M^+ - effects(d_i)$.

(c) Suppose $D_I \cup \{d_i\}$ is an explanation for M^+. Then by (b), D_I covers $M^+ - effects(d_i)$. If D_I is not an explanation of $M^+ - effects(d_i)$, then there must exist a $d_k \in D_I$ such that $D_I - \{d_k\}$ also covers $M^+ - effects(d_i)$. So again by (b), $D_I - \{d_k\} \cup \{d_i\}$ would also cover M^+. This contradicts the fact that $D_I \cup \{d_i\}$ irredundantly covers M^+ (since it is an explanation for M^+). Conversely, suppose D_I is an explanation for $M^+ - effects(d_i)$ but $D_I \cup \{d_i\}$ is not an explanation for M^+. Since $D_I \cup \{d_i\}$ covers M^+ by (b), so there must exist some $d_k \in D_I$ such that $D_I - \{d_k\} \cup \{d_i\}$ also covers M^+.

Then by (b) again, $D_I - \{d_k\}$ would cover $M^+ - effects(d_i)$, contradicting the fact that D_I is an irredundant cover of $M^+ - effects(d_i)$ □

proof of Theorem 3.23.

(1) Since Q is a generator–set for $M^+ - effects(d_i)$, d_i is irrelevant to $M^+ - effects(d_i)$. So d_i is not in any $q_i \in Q_I \in Q$. Therefore, $G_I = Q_I \cup (\{d_i\})$ are generators and $[G_I] \cap [G_J] = \varnothing$ for $I \neq J$ since $[Q_I] \cap [Q_J] = \varnothing$, i.e., G is a generator–set.

(2) By the definition of a generator–set and Lemma 3.22c,

$$[G] = \bigcup_{I=1}^{n} [G_I]$$

$$= \bigcup_{I=1}^{n} [Q_I \cup (\{d_i\})]$$

$$= \bigcup_{I=1}^{n} \{E \cup \{d_i\} | E \in [Q_I]\}$$

$$= \{E \cup \{d_i\} | E \in [Q]\}$$

$$= Sol(P).$$ □

proof of Lemma 3.24.

(a) Immediately from the definition of $causes(M_J)$ and set unconnectedness.

(b) Assume E_1 and E_2 are explanations for M_1^+ and M_2^+, respectively. Then it is obvious from the definition of covers that $E = E_1 \cup E_2$ is a cover of M^+. Moreover, by Lemma 3.5 each disorder in E_1 and in E_2 uniquely covers some manifestations in M_1^+ and M_2^+, respectively. So, every $d_k \in E$ uniquely covers some manifestation in M^+ (E_1 and E_2 are disjoint since $causes(M_1^+) \cap causes(M_2^+) = \varnothing$), and thus E is an explanation for M^+.

Conversely, assume E is an explanation for M^+. Let $E = E_1 \cup E_2$ where $E_1 = E \cap causes(M_1^+)$ and $E_2 = E - E_1$. Since $E \subseteq causes(M^+)$ and $causes(M_1^+) \cap causes(M_2^+) = \varnothing$, so $E_2 \subseteq causes(M_2^+)$ and thus $E_2 = E \cap causes(M_2^+)$. If E_1 does not cover M_1^+, then some disorder in E_2 must cover some manifestation in M_1^+ which is impossible since $E_2 \cap M_1^+ = \varnothing$. Therefore, E_1 and E_2 are covers for M_1^+ and M_2^+, respectively. The irredundancy of such covers immediately follows from the Lemma 3.5.   □

proof of Theorem 3.25.

Analogous to the proof of Theorem 3.23 and using Lemma 3.24.   □

4
Probabilistic Causal Model

> "The theory of probabilities is at bottom nothing
> but common sense reduced to calculus."
> Pierre Simon de Laplace

A limitation of parsimonious covering theory presented in the last chapter is that the solution $Sol(P)$ for a diagnostic problem $P = <D,M,C,M^+>$ may include a large number of alternative hypotheses. This occurs because $Sol(P)$ is defined to be the set of *all* irredundant covers of M^+. In order to further select from these potential explanations, some criteria other than parsimony are needed, and additional information must be integrated with the cause–effect associations in the knowledge base to support such disambiguation. As we reviewed in Section 2.1, besides symbolic causal knowledge, numeric probabilistic knowledge that captures the uncertain nature of causal relationships among diagnostic entities is also crucial for successful diagnosis. Therefore, one natural approach to cope with this problem would be to incorporate probabilistic knowledge into the model and to derive a computationally feasible likelihood measure as a means of ranking hypothesized explanations. Unfortunately, although a number of previous diagnostic expert systems have tried to do so, their approaches have been very limited and usually heuristic in nature [Shortliffe75, Duda76, Ben–Bassat80, Charniak83].

In what follows, probability theory and parsimonious covering theory are incorporated into an integrated formulation in a principled fashion. The resulting extended version of basic parsimonious covering theory will be referred to subsequently as a *probabilistic causal model*. We begin by deriving a *formal* probability calculus from probability theory in a rigorous fashion. Based on assumptions consistent with parsimonious covering theory, this calculus is capable of determining the relative likelihoods of multiple disorder hypotheses $D_I \subseteq D$ according to their posterior probabilities $P(D_I|M^+)$. Thus, the most probable hypotheses among all alternative hypotheses can be chosen as the problem solution. This calculus has several desirable features. First, it avoids the unrealistic probabilistic assumptions and huge amounts of statistical data required were one to use direct application of Bayes' theorem. Second, it is based on causal

associations between diagnostic entities rather than rules and thus facili-
tates knowledge acquisition. Third, since this calculus is consistent with
parsimonious covering theory, probabilistic and symbolic reasoning
processes can easily be integrated into a coherent inference mechanism to
achieve better diagnostic performance (presented in the next chapter). We
will see that this calculus has a number of other interesting properties
which are generally considered to be very desirable. For example, it treats
multiple simultaneous disorders in a more rigorous and convenient way
than previous approaches. This "multimembership" problem (i.e., multiple
simultaneous disorders) is generally recognized to be difficult to solve in
statistical pattern classification [Ben–Bassat80] as well as in AI.

Recall that in a diagnostic problem $P = <D,M,C,M^+>$, any $D_I \subseteq D$ for
which $M^+ \subseteq effects(D_I)$ is said to cover M^+. It is important to what follows
to note carefully the interpretation of this concept. Set D_I covering set M^+
means that all $m_j \in M^+$ alone can be caused by all disorders $d_i \in D_I$ alone.
In other words, the "set" M^+ represents the proposition that all $m_j \in M^+$
are present and all other manifestations are absent; the "set" D_I represents
the proposition that all $d_i \in D_I$ are present and all other disorders are
absent.[*]

Keeping this interpretation of set notation in mind, the *posterior proba-
bility* of D_I given M^+, $P(D_I|M^+)$, can be used to rank all covers D_I of M^+.
By Bayes' theorem,

$$P(D_I|M^+) = \frac{P(M^+|D_I)\,P(D_I)}{\sum\limits_{D_J \in 2^D} P(M^+|D_J)\,P(D_J)} = \frac{P(M^+|D_I)\,P(D_I)}{P(M^+)}$$

since all D_J's in 2^D consist of a mutually exclusive and exhaustive set of
events. As Charniak points out, $P(M^+)$ is a constant for the posterior probabilities of all $D_I \subseteq D$ [Charniak83]. Therefore, the *relative* rank of all
D_I's can be determined using only the numerator of the above equation,
i.e., by using just the corresponding values of conditional probabilities
$P(M^+|D_I)$ and prior probabilities $P(D_I)$ without considering the denomina-
tor $P(M^+)$. However, as discussed in Chapter 2, direct application of
Bayes' theorem even in this fashion would still require a huge amount of
statistical data (in the order of $2^{|M|} \times 2^{|D|}$). The goal of developing a proba-
bility calculus here is to make the task of computing $P(M^+|D_I)$ and $P(D_I)$
tractable while keeping it consistent with parsimonious covering theory so
that hypothesis formation and a hypothesize–and–test process can be conducted in a way similar to that described in the previous chapter.

(*) This interpretation of sets D_I and M^+ is also adopted by models of Reiter and of de
Kleer and Williams [Reiter87, deKleer87].

The development of a probability calculus that follows is based on these goals considered in the framework of the simplest two–layer (bipartite) causal networks. A set of assumptions are given first, based on which the formal probabilistic calculus is then developed to compute the relative likelihoods of hypotheses. A discussion of the properties of this probabilistic model and a brief comparison with other methods are also given in this chapter.

4.1. Definitions and Assumptions

In a bipartite diagnostic problem there are two classes of entities, D, representing all disorders, and M, representing all manifestations. There is also a relation C representing all cause–effect associations between these two classes of entities. Correspondingly, three types of *events* and related notations are defined in the probabilistic causal model as follows:

definition 4.1: Let $P = <D,M,C,M^+>$ be a diagnostic problem. We define the following.
(1). *Cause event*: $d_i \in D$ denotes the event that disorder d_i is present while saying nothing about the presence or absence of other disorders. Similarly, $\overline{d_i}$ denotes the absence of d_i.
(2). *Effect event*: $m_j \in M$ denotes the event that manifestation m_j is present while saying nothing about the presence or absence of other manifestations. Similarly, $\overline{m_j}$ denotes the absence of m_j.
(3). *Causation event*: for any $d_i \in D$ and $m_j \in M$, the single symbol $m_j{:}d_i$ denotes the event that d_i actually *causes* m_j. Causation event $m_j{:}d_i$ is true iff both d_i and m_j occur and m_j is actually being caused by d_i.

Cause events d_i and effect events m_j are commonly defined in most formulations of diagnostic problem–solving using Bayesian or other statistical pattern classification techniques. However, the third type of events, namely, causation events, whose definition is motivated by the symbolic causal relation C, is a significant innovation, which was independently proposed by Peng and Reggia [Peng86], and Cooper [Cooper84], although the latter was in an informal and less explicit form. The occurrence of causation event $m_j{:}d_i$ represents the realization or instantiation of the causal link $<d_i, m_j> \in C$. It is clearly related to events d_i and m_j but cannot be expressed by a boolean expression of events d_i and m_j because, in situations where both d_i and m_j occur, $m_j{:}d_i$ may still be false if m_j is not being caused by d_i (m_j may be caused by some other disorder in a multiple simultaneous disorder problem). Therefore, causation events are clearly a distinct type of basic event in a probabilistic causal world. A Venn diagram in Figure 4.1 illustrates the relationship between events d_i, m_j, and $m_j{:}d_i$. The advantage of explicitly defining a *causation event* rather than using conditional probability $P(m_j | d_i)$ (as was done by most existing models to capture the meaning of the cause–effect relation) will become evident shortly.

It should be clear from the foregoing definition that $m_j : d_i$ entails both d_i and m_j, i.e., $m_j : d_i \rightarrow d_i$ and $m_j : d_i \rightarrow m_j$ where " $\rightarrow$ " denotes logical implication. Conversely, $\overline{d_i}$ and $\overline{m_j}$ each entails $\overline{m_j : d_i}$. In other words, if " $\leftrightarrow$ " is used to denote logical equivalence, then

$$(m_j : d_i) \wedge d_i \leftrightarrow m_j : d_i \qquad (m_j : d_i) \wedge m_j \leftrightarrow m_j : d_i \qquad \text{(4.1a,1b)}$$

$$\overline{(m_j : d_i \wedge \overline{d_i})} \leftrightarrow \overline{d_i}, \qquad \overline{(m_j : d_i \wedge \overline{m_j})} \leftrightarrow \overline{m_j}. \; ^{(*)} \qquad \text{(4.1c,1d)}$$

One thing that defining causation events gives us is that like other types of events, it is valid to talk about conditional probabilities involving them.

definition 4.2: $P(m_j : d_i \,|\, d_i)$, the conditional probability of $m_j : d_i$ given d_i, is called the *conditional causal probability* of m_j as caused by d_i.

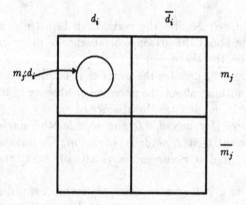

Figure 4.1. Relationship between a causation event $m_j : d_i$ and
a joint event $m_j \wedge d_i$. The circular area in the left upper
quadrant represents the causation event $m_j : d_i$, which entails $m_j \wedge d_i$ (the latter being represented by the entire left
upper quadrant). The left upper quadrant outside the cir-
cle represents event $m_j \wedge d_i \wedge \overline{m_j : d_i}$, i.e., the event that
both m_j and d_i are present but m_j is not caused by d_i.

(*) Following the same notations, $\overline{m_j} : d_i$ is the event that d_i causes the absence of m_j (i.e., d_i prevents m_j), $m_j : \overline{d_i}$ is the event that the absence of d_i causes m_j. Since these kinds of knowledge are not represented in the parsimonious covering theory developed in the preceding chapters, they will not be considered any further.

Since $P(m_j:d_i | d_i) = P((m_j:d_i) \wedge d_i) / P(d_i) = P(m_j:d_i) / P(d_i)$ by Equation 4.1a, the conditional causal probability reflects the average frequency with which a given d_i causes m_j. It is a better measurement of the strength of the causal association between d_i and m_j than the traditionally used conditional probability $P(m_j | d_i)$ in situations where multiple disorders may occur simultaneously. For example, suppose d_1 cannot cause m_1 but d_2 can. Then the causal association between d_1 and m_1 should be of strength 0. However, if d_1 and d_2 can be present at the same time, then the traditionally used value

$$P(m_1 | d_1) = \frac{P(m_1 \wedge d_1)}{P(d_1)}$$

$$= \frac{P(m_1 \wedge d_1 \wedge (d_2 \vee \overline{d_2}))}{P(d_1)}$$

$$= \frac{P(m_1 \wedge d_1 \wedge d_2) + P(m_1 \wedge d_1 \wedge \overline{d_2})}{P(d_1)}$$

$$> 0$$

because at least the first term of the numerator would be greater than 0 (since cases exist where both d_1 and d_2 are present simultaneously and m_1 is caused by d_2). On the other hand, using causation events, $P(m_1:d_1 | d_1) = 0$ because $m_1:d_1$ is always false. It is interesting to speculate that this may be one reason that "subjective probabilities" provided by domain experts are at times inaccurate estimates of measured conditional probabilities [Reggia82]: what the expert was really estimating might be the conditional causal probability between a disorder and a manifestation. Conditional causal probabilities $P(m_j:d_i | d_i)$ are a more accurate reflection than conditional probabilities $P(m_j | d_i)$ of the uncertainty of a cause–effect relationship. It is for this reason that $P(m_j:d_i | d_i)$ is referred to as a *causal strength* in this book. It is intuitively thought of as the numeric measure "attached" to the link $< d_i, m_j > \in C$ in the causal network representing the knowledge base of a diagnostic problem. Clearly, $P(m_j:d_i | d_i)$ is always less than or equal to $P(m_j | d_i)$ because $m_j:d_i$ entails $m_j \wedge d_i$, as illustrated in Figure 4.1.

Since a set of disorders D_I is interpreted to mean that all disorders in D_I are present *and all other disorders are absent*, the same set notation D_I is thus adopted to abbreviate the compound event $\bigwedge_{d_i \in D_I} d_i \bigwedge_{d_k \in D - D_I} \overline{d_k}$. Note that this is not the same as the event $\bigwedge_{d_i \in D_I} d_i$ which says nothing about the presence/absence of disorders not in D_I. Correspondingly, the set $M_J \subseteq M$ is the abbreviation of the event $\bigwedge_{m_j \in M_J} m_j \bigwedge_{m_l \in M - M_J} \overline{m_l}$.

Finally, it proves convenient to define the notion of a "context" of a causation event $m_j:d_i$. Intuitively, when the occurrence of a causation event $m_j:d_i$ for a particular case is being considered, it is possible that some other disorders and causations may actually be occurring simultaneously while still others may not be simultaneously present in that case. Thus, the occurrence/non–occurrence of other disorders and causations form a context for $m_j : d_i$. This context can be expressed as a conjunction of these other events. A causation event is not a part of its own context, and thus itself and its negation should not be included in any of its contexts. Formally, this notion is defined as follows.

definition 4.3: Let $m_j : d_i$ be a causation event. X is said to be a *context* of $m_j : d_i$ if X is a conjunction of any cause and causation events or their negations other than $m_j : d_i$ and $\overline{m_j : d_i}$.

Now the assumptions underlying the probabilistic causal model are formally stated.

1. *Knowledge assumptions*: For all cause events (disorders) $d_i \in D$, their prior probabilities $0 < P(d_i) < 1$ are given; for all causation events $m_j : d_i$, their causal strengths $0 \leq P(m_j : d_i | d_i) \leq 1$ are given, and $P(m_j : d_i | d_i) > 0$ iff $< d_i, m_j > \in C$. The notations p_i and c_{ij} will be used as abbreviations for $P(d_i)$ and $P(m_j : d_i | d_i)$, respectively.

2. *Independence assumptions*:

   2.1. *Disorder independence*: A cause event (disorder) $d_i \in D$ can occur independently of other cause events. That is, for $d_1 \in D$ and any distinct disorders $d_2, d_3, \ldots, d_k$ in D,

   $$P(d_1 \wedge d_2 \wedge \cdots \wedge d_k) = P(d_1) \, P(d_2 \wedge \cdots \wedge d_k). \tag{4.2a}$$

   2.2. *Causation independence*: If $d_i \in D$ occurs, causation event $m_j : d_i$ occurs independently of any of its contexts, i.e., if X is a context of $m_j : d_i$ and $P(X \wedge d_i) \neq 0$, then

   $$P(m_j : d_i | d_i \wedge X) = P(m_j : d_i | d_i) = c_{ij}. \tag{4.3a}$$

3. *Mandatory causation assumption*: No effect event (manifestation) $m_j \in M$ may occur without being caused by some disorder through some causation event. Combining this and the definition of causation event, it follows that for any $m_j \in M$,

$$m_j \leftrightarrow \bigvee_{d_i \in D} m_j : d_i. \tag{4.4a}$$

Assumption 1 presumes the availability of a prior probability p_i for each $d_i \in D$, and a causal strength c_{ij} for each $< d_i, m_j > \in C$. For $< d_i, m_j > \notin C$, c_{ij} is assumed to be zero. Thus, the knowledge base now includes numeric probabilistic knowledge as well as symbolic cause–effect knowledge. The total probabilities required are $|D| + |C|$ where $|D|$ is the number of disorders and $|C|$ is the number of nonzero strength causal links between individual disorders and manifestations. This is very much smaller than the infeasible exponential data requirement if Bayes' theorem were directly applied to the multimembership classification problems without any restrictive assumptions.

Contrary to the assumption that disorders are mutually exclusive and exhaustive which is made for many Bayesian classification models, disorder independence assumption 2.1 made here allows multiple disorders to occur simultaneously. One immediate consequence of this assumption is

$$P(d_1 \wedge d_2 \wedge \cdots \wedge d_k) = P(d_1) \, P(d_2) \cdots P(d_k) = \prod_{i=1}^{k} p_i \qquad (4.2b)$$

for distinct disorders $d_1, d_2, \ldots, d_k$ in D. Both Equations 4.2a and 2b can be applied to negations of cause events. For example,

$$P(d_1 \wedge d_2 \wedge \overline{d_3} \wedge \overline{d_4}) = P(d_1) \, P(d_2) \, P(\overline{d_3}) \, P(\overline{d_4}) = p_1 \, p_2 \, (1 - p_3) \, (1 - p_4).$$

Note that Assumption 2.1 assumes that d_i is not causally associated to d_k for all d_i and d_k in D.

Informally, Assumption 2.2 states that the causal strength, or tendency of d_i to cause m_j, does not change in the context of occurrence of other cause/causation events. That is, it is local to d_i and m_j only: whenever d_i is present, it always causes m_j with the fixed strength c_{ij} regardless of whether or not other disorders and causation events occur. This kind of causation invariance is quite different from and much preferable to the assumption of manifestation independence traditionally made when applying Bayesian classification. Intuitively, manifestations are generally not independent of one another if they have common causes. The manifestation conditional independence assumption (independence under each disorder) of [Charniak83] only partially solved this problem because manifestations may have more than one common disorder present. Assumptions similar to 2.2 were also made by Cooper and Pearl in different formulations in their work [Cooper84, Pearl86b]. This work will be discussed in Chapter 5.

Two useful results can be derived immediately from Equation 4.3a, causation independence. Let X be a context of $m_j : d_i$. First, from Equations 4.1a and 4.3a,

$$P((m_j : d_i) \wedge X \,|\, d_i) = P(m_j : d_i \,|\, d_i \wedge X) \, P(X \,|\, d_i)$$
$$= P(m_j : d_i \,|\, d_i) \, P(X \,|\, d_i)$$
$$= c_{ij} \, P(X \,|\, d_i). \qquad (4.3b)$$

Second, it follows from Equations 4.1a and 4.3b that,

$$P((m_j : d_i) \wedge X) = P((m_j : d_i) \wedge X \,|\, d_i) \, P(d_i)$$
$$= c_{ij} \, P(X \,|\, d_i) \, P(d_i)$$
$$= c_{ij} \, P(X \wedge d_i). \qquad (4.3c)$$

Note that both (4.3b) and (4.3c) hold even when $P(X \wedge d_i) = 0$. The three equations Equation 4.3a, b, and c will be used frequently as basic operations in deriving the probability calculus.

Finally, Assumption 3 is a very basic assumption in a diagnostic world. It combines the fact that any manifestation cannot be present unless it is caused by some disorder and the closed-world assumption that all possible causative disorders are explicitly listed in D. To the authors' knowledge, this cause–effect relationship assumption has not been made in the past. Note that from Assumption 1, if $< d_i, m_j > \notin C$ then $m_j : d_i$ is always false because d_i can never cause m_j. Using the "causes" function defined in Chapter 3, it follows from Assumption 3 that

$$m_j \leftrightarrow \bigvee_{d_i \in causes(m_j)} m_j : d_i \qquad (4.4b)$$

$$\overline{m_j} \leftrightarrow \bigwedge_{d_i \in causes(m_j)} \overline{m_j : d_i}. \qquad (4.4c)$$

Therefore,

$$P(m_j) = P(\bigvee_{d_i \in causes(m_j)} m_j : d_i),$$

which, if needed, can be computed from relevant p_i and c_{ij} values (see Theorem 4.15 later). This is why the prior probabilities $P(m_j)$ for $m_j \in M$ are not required as part of a knowledge base. This is intuitively justifiable because a manifestation m_j is the effect of its causes, and therefore, its probability should be able to be computed from the relevant p_i and c_{ij}.

In Figure 4.2, an example causal network is given where a prior probability is assigned to each disorder in D and a causal strength to each causal link in C. This example will be used throughout the rest of the chapter to provide illustrations of the results described.

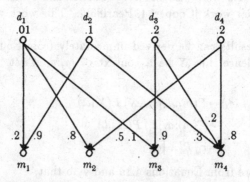

Figure 4.2. An example of a simple diagnostic problem where a prior probability is attached to each $d_i \in D$ and a causal strength to each $< d_i, m_j > \in C$.

4.2. A Probability Calculus

Based on the foregoing assumptions, our goal is to develop a calculus that is not only capable of calculating some measurement of likelihood of diagnostic hypothesis D_I given M^+, but to do so in a way that uses the prior probabilities and causal strengths involving just $d_i \in D_I$. This would usually only involve a tiny fraction of the probabilities in the knowledge base.

Recall that, by Bayes' theorem, to compare the posterior probabilities $P(D_1|M^+)$ and $P(D_2|M^+)$ for two hypotheses D_1 and D_2 for a given diagnostic problem $P = <D,M,C,M^+>$, we only need to compare the joint probabilities $P(M^+|D_1) P(D_1)$ and $P(M^+|D_2) P(D_2)$ because $P(M^+)$ is a constant. Also, by Assumption 2.1, the prior probabilities $P(D_1)$ and $P(D_2)$ can be readily computed by

$$P(D_I) = \prod_{d_i \in D_I} p_i \prod_{d_k \in D - D_I} (1 - p_k).$$

Thus the real issue, and the one we focus on in the rest of this section, is to derive a formula for the conditional probability $P(M^+|D_I)$ in terms of relevant causal strengths given in the knowledge base. This development first concerns the situations where only a single disorder occurs and is responsible for the presence of one or more manifestations; then it precedes to situations where multiple disorders occur. Finally, a likelihood measure for multiple disorder hypothesis is derived.

4.2.1. Single Disorder

Assumption 2.2 states that $m_j : d_i$ is independent of any of its contexts given that d_i is present. This kind of independence is now extended to a more general situation. Sometimes one needs to investigate the occurrence of a causation event $m_j : d_i$ in the situation where some effect events (manifestations) as well as some other cause and causation events are present or absent. By Assumption 3, an effect event can be expressed in an equivalent form as a disjunction of causation events (see Equations 4.4a, b, c). Therefore, a general boolean expression of cause and causation events can be used to represent contextual information about the presence/absence of manifestations as well as the occurrence of cause and causation events. This leads to the following definition.

definition 4.4: Y is said to be a *context set* of the causation event $m_j : d_i$ if Y is a boolean expression of cause and causation events other than $m_j : d_i$ itself.

example: Consider the causation event $m_3 : d_1$ in Figure 4.2. The situation that m_1 and d_2 are present and d_4 is absent and m_3 is caused by d_8 can be represented by $(m_1 : d_1 \lor m_1 : d_2) \land (d_2) \land (\overline{d_4}) \land (m_3 : d_8)$ which is a context set of causation event $m_3:d_1$. Note that the first disjunct $(m_1:d_1 \vee m_1:d_2) \leftrightarrow m_1$ by Equation 4.4b.   □

Note that since $\overline{m_j:d_i}$ is a boolean expression of $m_j:d_i$, the foregoing definition excludes the negation of $m_j:d_i$ from any of $m_j:d_i$'s context sets. Causation independence (Assumption 2.2 and related Equations 4.3a, b and c) can be generalized from single contexts to context sets, as stated in the following lemma.

lemma 4.1: If Y is a context set of $m_j:d_i$, then

$$P((m_j:d_i) \wedge Y | d_i) = c_{ij} P(Y|d_i). \tag{4.5a}$$

Multiplying both sides of Equation 4.5a by $P(d_i)$, and by Equation 4.1a, it follows that

$$P((m_j:d_i) \wedge Y) = c_{ij} P(Y \wedge d_i). \tag{4.5b}$$

Dividing both sides of Equation 4.5b by $P(Y \wedge d_i)$, assuming $P(Y \wedge d_i) \neq 0$, it follows that

$$P(m_j:d_i | Y \wedge d_i) = c_{ij} \tag{4.5c}$$

Equations 4.5a, b and c will be used frequently in the following.

The next lemma establishes the equivalence between the causal strength $P(m_j:d_i|d_i)$ and conditional probability $P(m_j|\{d_i\})$. Recall that individual d_i and the singleton set $\{d_i\}$ mean different things (the latter indicates all other disorders are absent, but the former says nothing about other disorders).

lemma 4.2: For any $d_i \in D$ and $m_j \in M$,

$$P(m_j|\{d_i\}) = P(m_j:d_i|d_i) = c_{ij}, \text{ and} \tag{4.6a}$$

$$P(\overline{m_j}|\{d_i\}) = P(\overline{m_j:d_i}|\{d_i\}) = 1 - c_{ij}. \tag{4.6b}$$

The equivalence of $P(m_j|\{d_i\})$ and $P(m_j:d_i|d_i)$ is an intuitively satisfying result to obtain because when only disorder d_i is present and all other disorders are absent, the presence of m_j can only be due to the presence of d_i alone. Thus, the probability of m_j being present in this situation is equal to how frequently m_j is caused by d_i, i.e., the causal strength c_{ij}. From Equations 4.6a and b, it immediately follows that if $< d_i, m_j > \notin C$, then $P(m_j|\{d_i\}) = 0$ and $P(\overline{m_j}|\{d_i\}) = 1$. Moreover, this lemma also shows one way to acquire c_{ij} from available statistical data: by Equation 4.6a one can measure the frequency of m_j when d_i occurs alone.

Next we show that $P(m_j|\{d_i\})$ has an invariance property similar to causation independence (Assumption 2.2) of causal strength $P(m_j:d_i|d_i)$.

lemma 4.3: If Y is a context set of the causation event $m_j : d_i$, then

$$P(m_j \wedge Y | \{d_i\}) = P(m_j | \{d_i\}) P(Y | \{d_i\}) \qquad (4.7a)$$

$$P(\overline{m_j} \wedge Y | \{d_i\}) = P(\overline{m_j} | \{d_i\}) P(Y | \{d_i\}). \qquad (4.7b)$$

Since different m_i and m_j can be considered context–sets to each other (they do not involve any common causation event), it immediately follows from Lemma 4.3 that

theorem 4.4 [Manifestation Conditional Independence I]: Let m_1, m_2 $, \ldots, m_k, m_{k+1}, \ldots, m_n$ be n distinct effect events (manifestations), and let d_i be any cause event (disorder). Then

$$P(m_1 \wedge m_2 \wedge \cdots \wedge m_k^{\rightarrow} \wedge \overline{m_{k+1}} \wedge \cdots \wedge \overline{m_n} | \{d_i\})$$

$$= \prod_{j=1}^{k} P(m_j | \{d_i\}) \prod_{l=k+1}^{n} P(\overline{m_l} | \{d_i\}) \qquad (4.8a)$$

$$= \prod_{j=1}^{k} c_{ij} \prod_{l=k+1}^{n} (1 - c_{il}). \qquad (4.8b)$$

Intuitively, when it is known that all but one disorder d_i is occurring, then d_i is the only possible cause for the presence of any manifestations. Thus it is very reasonable that manifestations are independent under $\{d_i\}$. This is quite different from the assumption of manifestation independence under d_i where the effects of other disorders on those manifestations are not completely excluded because d_i, unlike $\{d_i\}$, says nothing about other disorders.

4.2.2. Multiple Disorders

Now we turn to the situations where multiple disorders are occurring simultaneously, i.e., from $\{d_i\}$ to D_I, where D_I is a set of zero or more disorders. It will be seen that all results obtained in the previous subsection about singly occurring disorders can be generalized in multiple disorder situations. To do this, the definition of causation events and their corresponding context sets is extended from involving a single disorder to involving multiple disorders.

definition 4.5: For $m_j \in M$ and $d_1, d_2, \ldots, d_r \in D$, $m_j : (d_1 \wedge d_2 \wedge \cdots \wedge d_r)$ denotes the *joint–causation event* that m_j is caused by the set of disorders $d_1, d_2, \ldots, d_r$. It is true iff m_j and all d_i, $i = 1, 2, \ldots, r$, are present *and* m_j is actually being caused by *at least* one of these d_i's. In other words,

$$m_j : (d_1 \wedge d_2 \wedge \cdots \wedge d_r) \leftrightarrow \left[\bigvee_{i=1}^{r} (m_j : d_i) \right] \wedge d_1 \wedge d_2 \wedge \cdots \wedge d_r. \qquad (4.9)$$

The notion of joint–causation event $m_j:(d_1 \wedge \cdots \wedge d_r)$ is intended to represent the causal relationship between a group of present disorders (d_1 through d_r) and individual manifestations m_j. The definition is consistent with the intuition that a group of disorders causes a manifestation m_j if and only if one of the disorders in that group causes m_j. Note that this is different from the situation that m_j is caused by every disorder in that group. Where it is clear from the context that we are dealing with joint–causation events, $m_j:(d_1 \wedge \cdots \wedge d_r)$ will be abbreviated as $m_j:d_1 \wedge \cdots \wedge d_r$. It immediately follows that

$$P(m_j:d_1 \wedge d_2 \wedge \cdots \wedge d_r \mid d_1 \wedge d_2 \wedge \cdots \wedge d_r)$$
$$= P(m_j:d_1 \wedge d_2 \wedge \cdots \wedge d_r) \, / \, P(d_1 \wedge d_2 \wedge \cdots \wedge d_r)$$

is the conditional causal probability of the joint causation event $m_j:d_1 \wedge d_2 \wedge \cdots \wedge d_r$.

definition 4.6: A context set of joint–causation event $m_j:d_1 \wedge d_2 \wedge \cdots \wedge d_r$ is a boolean expression of cause and causation events other than $m_j:d_i$, $i = 1, 2, \ldots, r$.

Joint–causation events have invariance properties analogous to Equation 4.5 of single causation events, as shown in the next lemma.

lemma 4.5: Let $d_1, \ldots, d_r \in D$ be r distinct cause events, $m_j \in M$ be an effect event, and Y be a context set of the joint causation event $m_j:d_1 \wedge \cdots \wedge d_r$. Then

$$P((m_j:d_1 \wedge \cdots \wedge d_r) \wedge Y)$$
$$= P(m_j:d_1 \wedge \cdots d_r \mid d_1 \wedge \cdots \wedge d_r) \, P(Y \wedge d_1 \wedge \cdots \wedge d_r). \qquad (4.10a)$$

Dividing both sides of Equation 4.10a by $P(d_1 \wedge \cdots \wedge d_r)$, it then follows that

$$P((m_j:d_1 \wedge \cdots \wedge d_r) \wedge Y \mid d_1 \wedge \cdots \wedge d_r)$$
$$= P(m_j:d_1 \wedge \cdots d_r \mid d_1 \wedge d_2 \wedge \cdots d_r) \, P(Y \mid d_1 \wedge \cdots \wedge d_r). \qquad (4.10b)$$

From the disjunctive nature of joint–causation events, a result which computes the conditional causal probability of a joint–causation event can be established as in the following lemma.

lemma 4.6: Let $d_1, \ldots, d_r, d_{r+1} \in D$ be $r + 1$ distinct cause events, $m_j \in M$ be an effect event. Then

$$P(m_j:d_1 \wedge \cdots \wedge d_r \wedge d_{r+1} \mid d_1 \wedge \cdots \wedge d_r \wedge d_{r+1})$$
$$= P(m_j:d_1 \cdots \wedge d_r \mid d_1 \wedge \cdots \wedge d_r) + P(m_j:d_{r+1} \mid d_{r+1})$$

$$- P(m_j : d_1 \cdot \cdot \cdot \wedge d_r \,|\, d_1 \wedge \cdot \cdot \cdot \wedge d_r) \, P(m_j : d_{r+1} \,|\, d_{r+1}) \qquad (4.11a)$$

$$= 1 - \prod_{i=1}^{r+1} (1 - P(m_j : d_i \,|\, d_i)) $$

$$= 1 - \prod_{i=1}^{r+1} (1 - c_{ij}). \qquad (4.11b)$$

The next lemma, analogous to Lemma 4.3, establishes the equivalence of $P(m_j : d_1 \wedge \cdot \cdot \cdot \wedge d_r \,|\, d_1 \wedge \cdot \cdot \cdot \wedge d_r)$ and $P(m_j \,|\, \{ d_1, \dots, d_r \})$. Note again the different meaning of grouping disorders by logical "$\wedge$" and by set notation.

lemma 4.7: Let $D_I = \{ d_1, \dots, d_r \} \subseteq D$, $m_j \in M$. Then

$$P(m_j \,|\, D_I) = P(m_j : d_1 \wedge \cdot \cdot \cdot \wedge d_r \,|\, d_1 \wedge \cdot \cdot \cdot \wedge d_r), \qquad (4.12a)$$

$$P(\overline{m_j} \,|\, D_I) = P(\overline{m_j : d_1 \wedge \cdot \cdot \cdot \wedge d_r} \,|\, d_1 \wedge \cdot \cdot \cdot \wedge d_r). \qquad (4.12b)$$

Combining Equations 4.11 and 4.12, the next lemma gives the formula which explicitly represents $P(m_j \,|\, D_I)$ in terms of relevant c_{ij}.

lemma 4.8: If $D_I \subseteq D$ and $m_j \in M$, then

$$P(m_j \,|\, D_I) = 1 - \prod_{d_i \in D_I} (1 - c_{ij}), \quad \text{and} \qquad (4.13a)$$

$$P(\overline{m_j} \,|\, D_I) = \prod_{d_i \in D_I} (1 - c_{ij}). \qquad (4.13b)$$

Lemma 4.8 is an important and very reasonable result to obtain. If D_I is a hypothesis, this lemma allows us to calculate effectively the conditional probabilities of m_j and $\overline{m_j}$ given D_I using causal strengths only involving m_j and $d_i \in D_I$. Also, it implies that if none of $d_i \in D_I$ can cause m_j $(c_{ij} = 0)$, then $P(m_j \,|\, D_I) = 1 - \prod_{d_i \in D_I} (1 - 0) = 0$. On the other hand, as long as there exists some $d_i \in D_I$ which may cause m_j, then $P(m_j \,|\, D_I) \neq 0$. That is, in parsimonious covering theory terms, $P(m_j \,|\, D_I) \neq 0$ if and only if D_I covers m_j, or equivalently $m_j \in effects(D_I)$. Similarly, $P(\overline{m_j} \,|\, D_I) \neq 1$ if and only if $m_j \in effects(D_I)$.

Note that Equation 4.13a is a more general form of the well–known Bernoulli formula which says, for two independent events A and B, that $P(A \vee B) = P(A) + P(B) - P(A) \, P(B)$. The Bernoulli formula has been used in several previous diagnostic systems to combine support from multiple pieces of evidence (manifestations) to a conclusion (disorder) [Shortliffe75, Van Melle79, Kahn85]. Here, however, this formula is used to combine causal effects from multiple disorders to a manifestation that they may cause. The reason that it is inappropriate to use the Bernoulli formula to combine evidential support in many diagnostic applications will be presented in Section 4.3.3 where we discuss how multiple manifestations render their support to a disorder in this model.

From Equation 4.13a, it is clear that for two distinct disorders d_1, $d_2 \in D$,

$$P(m_j|\{d_1, d_2\}) = 1 - (1 - c_{1j})(1 - c_{2j}) = c_{1j} + c_{2j} - c_{1j} c_{2j},$$

and more generally, for $D_I \subseteq D$ and $d_i \in D - D_I$,

$$P(m_j|D_I \cup \{d_i\}) = P(m_j|D_I) + P(m_j|\{d_i\}) - P(m_j|D_I) P(m_j|\{d_i\})$$

$$= P(m_j|D_I) + c_{ij}(1 - P(m_j|D_I)). \tag{4.13c}$$

Equations 4.13a and c will be frequently used in forthcoming analysis and discussions.

Analogous to Lemma 4.5, the context invariance of $P(m_j|D_I)$ is also preserved in the multiple disorder situation. This is given in the next lemma.

lemma 4.9: Let $D_I = \{d_1, d_2, \ldots, d_r\} \subseteq D$, $m_j \in M$, and let Y be a context set of the joint causation event $m_j : d_1 \wedge d_2 \wedge \cdots \wedge d_r$. Then

$$P(m_j \wedge Y|D_I) = P(m_j|D_I) P(Y|D_I), \text{ and} \tag{4.14a}$$

$$P(\overline{m_j} \wedge Y|D_I) = P(\overline{m_j}|D_I) P(Y|D_I). \tag{4.14b}$$

Next, the most important theorem of this probability calculus, manifestation conditional independence under a given set of disorders D_I, is established. This theorem will directly lead to the main result we originally set out to derive.

theorem 4.10 [Manifestation Conditional Independence II]: Let m_1, m_2 $, \ldots, m_k, m_{k+1}, \ldots, m_n \in M$ be n distinct manifestations, $D_I = \{d_1, \ldots, d_r\} \subseteq D$. Then,

$$P(m_1 \wedge m_2 \wedge \cdots \wedge m_k \wedge \overline{m_{k+1}} \wedge \cdots \wedge \overline{m_n}|D_I)$$

$$= \prod_{j=1}^{k} P(m_j|D_I) \prod_{l=k+1}^{n} P(\overline{m_l}|D_I) \tag{4.15a}$$

$$= \prod_{j=1}^{k} \left(1 - \prod_{i=1}^{r}(1 - c_{ij})\right) \prod_{l=k+1}^{n} \prod_{i=1}^{r}(1 - c_{il}). \tag{4.15b}$$

For a "closed" diagnostic problem, i.e., a problem where all $m_j \in M^+$ are known to be present and all $m_l \in M - M^+$ are known to be absent, we have the following major result:

$$P(M^+|D_I) = \prod_{m_j \in M^+} P(m_j|D_I) \prod_{m_l \in M - M^+} P(\overline{m_l}|D_I)$$

$$= \prod_{m_j \in M^+} \left(1 - \prod_{d_i \in D_I}(1 - c_{ij})\right) \prod_{m_l \in M - M^+} \prod_{d_i \in D_I}(1 - c_{il}).$$

This is computationally reasonable except that the index for all absent manifestations $\overline{m_l}$ ranges over all $M - M^+$, thus involving some causal strengths not related to given manifestations in M^+ or disorders in D_I. Fortunately, this range can be constrained quite significantly. Since $c_{il} = 0$ for $<d_i, m_l> \notin C$, those absent manifestations which are not causally related to disorders in D_I can be removed from the calculation. Thus,

$$P(M^+|D_I)$$
$$= \prod_{m_j \in M^+} (1 - \prod_{d_i \in D_I} (1 - c_{ij})) \prod_{d_i \in D_I} \prod_{m_l \in effects(d_i) - M^+} (1 - c_{il}). \tag{4.16}$$

By Equation 4.16, $P(M^+|D_I)$ for any given M^+ and D_I can be completely expressed by c_{ij}'s which are in the knowledge base. Furthermore, only those c_{ij}'s are used in Equation 4.16 where $m_j \in M^+$ or $m_j \in effects(D_I)$. Thus, by taking advantage of the underlying causal relation C, we can compute $P(M^+|D_I)$ solely using causal strengths "local" or "relevant" to elements of M^+ and D_I. This is the goal we set out to achieve.

A similar kind of locality can also be achieved in computing $P(D_I)$. By Assumptions 1 and 2.1,

$$P(D_I) = P(\bigwedge_{d_i \in D_I} d_i \bigwedge_{d_k \in D - D_I} \overline{d_k})$$
$$= \prod_{d_i \in D_I} p_i \prod_{d_k \in D - D_I} (1 - p_k),$$
$$= \prod_{d_i \in D_I} \frac{p_i}{1 - p_i} \prod_{d_k \in D} (1 - p_k), \tag{4.17}$$

where $\prod_{d_k \in D} (1 - p_k)$ over all disorders is a constant for a given knowledge base and thus can be ignored if only the relative likelihood of $D_I \subseteq D$ is concerned.

4.2.3. Relative Likelihood Measures for Hypotheses

Recall that the relative likelihood of a diagnostic hypothesis D_I given M^+ can be determined by the numerator of Bayes' theorem, $P(M^+|D_I) P(D_I)$, because the denominator $P(M^+)$ is a constant for any given M^+. Equation 4.16 developed in the previous subsection provides a way to calculate $P(M^+|D_I)$ using only those causal strengths involving disorders in D_I and manifestations in $M^+ \cup effects(D_I)$; and by Equation 4.17 the relative prior probability of D_I can be represented by only those d_i's in D_I. These results lead to the definition of a *relative likelihood measure* $L(D_I, M^+)$ of D_I given M^+ which differs from the posterior probability $P(D_I|M^+)$ by only a constant factor.

definition 4.7: Let $P = <D,M,C,M^+>$ be a diagnostic problem, and let $D_I \subseteq D$. Then the relative likelihood of D_I given M^+, denoted as $L(D_I, M^+)$, is defined as

$$L(D_I, M^+)$$

$$= \prod_{m_j \in M^+} [1 - \prod_{d_i \in D_I} (1 - c_{ij})] \prod_{d_i \in D_I} \prod_{m_l \in effects(d_i) - M^+} (1 - c_{il}) \prod_{d_i \in D_I} \frac{p_i}{(1 - p_i)}. \quad (4.18a)$$

By Equations 4.16 and 4.17 and Bayes' theorem, $L(D_I, M^+)$ differs from the posterior probability $P(D_I|M^+)$ by only a constant factor $\prod_{d_k \in D} (1 - p_k) / P(M^+)$, so it is therefore an appropriate measure for ranking D_I relative to other hypotheses for any given M^+. Thus, among all $D_I \subseteq D$, those with the highest relative likelihood can be chosen as the problem solution. Note also that $L(D_I, M^+) \geq 0$, and $L(\varnothing, \varnothing) = 1$.

For clarity, we will consider $L(D_I, M^+)$ to consist of three components:

$$L(D_I, M^+) = L_1(D_I, M^+) \, L_2(D_I, M^+) \, L_3(D_I, M^+).$$

The first product

$$L_1(D_I, M^+) = \prod_{m_j \in M^+} P(m_j|D_I) = \prod_{m_j \in M^+} [1 - \prod_{d_i \in D_I} (1 - c_{ij})] \quad (4.18b)$$

informally can be thought of as a weight reflecting how likely D_I is to cause the presence of manifestations in the given M^+. The second product

$$L_2(D_I, M^+) = \prod_{m_l \in M - M^+} P(\overline{m_l}|D_I) = \prod_{d_i \in D_I} \prod_{m_l \in effects(d_i) - M^+} (1 - c_{il}) \quad (4.18c)$$

can be viewed as a weight based on manifestations expected with D_I but which are actually absent. The third product

$$L_3(D_I, M^+) = \prod_{d_i \in D_I} \frac{p_i}{(1 - p_i)} \quad (4.18d)$$

represents a weight based on prior probabilities of D_I. Again note that all of these products involve only probabilistic information local to $d_i \in D_I$ and $m_j \in M^+ \cup effects(d_i)$ instead of the entire knowledge base. In most cases, this results in a tremendous savings. Thus Equations 4.18 provide a computationally tractable means to rank hypotheses for a given M^+ in a diagnostic problem by computing and comparing their relative likelihood measures.

example: Let $M^+ = \{m_1, m_3\}$ for the problem in Figure 4.2. Then by Equations 4.18, the relative likelihoods of three covers of M^+, $\{d_1\}$, $\{d_2, d_3\}$, and $\{d_1, d_2, d_3\}$, are calculated as follows:

$$L_1(\{d_1\}, \{m_1, m_3\}) = c_{11} \, c_{13} = 0.2 \cdot 0.1 = 0.02$$
$$L_2(\{d_1\}, \{m_1, m_3\}) = (1 - c_{12}) = (1 - 0.8) = 0.2$$

$$L_3(\{d_1\}, \{m_1,m_3\}) = \frac{p_1}{1 - p_1} = \frac{0.01}{0.99} = 0.01.$$

Similarly,

$$L_1(\{d_2,d_3\}, \{m_1,m_3\}) = (1 - (1 - c_{21})(1 - c_{31}))(1 - (1 - c_{23})(1 - c_{33}))$$
$$= 0.9 \cdot 0.9 = 0.81$$

$$L_2(\{d_2,d_3\}, \{m_1,m_3\}) = (1 - c_{24})(1 - c_{34}) = 0.7 \cdot 0.8 = 0.56,$$

$$L_3(\{d_2,d_3\}, \{m_1,m_3\}) = \frac{p_2}{1 - p_2}\frac{p_3}{1 - p_3} = \frac{0.1}{0.9}\cdot\frac{0.2}{0.8} = 0.028.$$

And

$$L_1(\{d_1,d_2,d_3\}, \{m_1,m_3\})$$
$$= (1 - (1 - c_{11})(1 - c_{21})(1 - c_{31}))\ (1 - (1 - c_{13})(1 - c_{23})(1 - c_{33}))$$
$$= 0.92 \cdot 0.91 = 0.84$$

$$L_2(\{d_1,d_2,d_3\}, \{m_1,m_3\}) = (1 - c_{12})(1 - c_{24})(1 - c_{34})$$
$$= 0.2 \cdot 0.7 \cdot 0.8 = 0.11,$$

$$L_3(\{d_1,d_2,d_3\}, \{m_1,m_3\}) = \frac{p_1}{1 - p_1}\frac{p_2}{1 - p_2}\frac{p_3}{1 - p_3} = 0.00028.$$

Then, by Equation 4.18a,

$$L(\{d_1\}, \{m_1,m_3\}) = 0.00004,$$

$$L(\{d_2,d_3\}, \{m_1,m_3\}) = 0.013,$$

$$L(\{d_1,d_2,d_3\}, \{m_1,m_3\}) = 0.000026. \qquad \Box$$

The task of developing a formal probabilistic calculus for ranking the likelihood of D_I given M^+ is now completed. If a set of hypothesized disorders can be derived by any means, its relative likelihood can be computed in the way just described. This calculus, however, does not in itself provide a means to *generate* such hypotheses. Simply computing a relative likelihood for every hypothesis $D_I \subseteq D$ would require $2^{|D|}$ such computations and would be a very formidable task for large real–world applications. Fortunately, a way of constructing a much smaller yet sufficient set of hypotheses is possible. Since this formulation of the probabilistic causal model involves the same underlying framework as parsimonious covering theory, this calculus can be integrated into the theory to greatly restrict needed computations. The resulting diagnostic strategy, which is guaranteed to identify the most probable hypothesis, is given in the next chapter. This strategy uses symbolic knowledge and concepts from parsimonious covering theory to construct hypotheses, and it uses probabilistic knowledge to rank them and to focus the attention of the problem–solver during hypothesis construction. Before presenting this unified strategy, the next two sections are devoted to analyzing the properties of the probabilistic causal model developed here, and to comparing it with some other existing probabilistic models. Such analysis and comparison will further justify the rationale of this model.

4.3. Properties of the Probabilistic Causal Model

The probabilistic causal model developed in the previous section has a number of interesting properties which are well justified in some real world situations. Some of these properties are accepted by many people, but some others have not been recognized before.

4.3.1. Relationship to Basic Parsimonious Covering

In parsimonious covering theory, a basic definition states that a set of disorders $D_I \subseteq D$ is an explanation for M^+ if (1) D_I covers M^+, and (2) D_I is parsimonious (see Definition 3.5 in Section 3.1.2). First consider the covering principle: if a hypothesis $D_I \subseteq D$ is not a cover of M^+, then at least one present manifestation exists, say $m_j \in M^+$, that is not covered by D_I, i.e., for all $d_i \in D_I$, $<d_i, m_j> \notin C$ so $c_{ij} = 0$. Then by Equation 4.18a and b, $P(m_j | D_I) = 1 - \prod_{d_i \in D_I} (1 - c_{ij}) = 1 - 1 = 0$, and in turn $L(D_I, M^+) = 0$. That is, any $D_I \subseteq D$ which does not cover M^+ will have zero relative likelihood and in turn zero posterior probability $(P(D_I | M^+) = 0)$. The symbolic reasoning notion of "accounting for" in parsimonious covering theory is thus seen to be captured by the relative likelihood and posterior probability being nonzero only for covers in the probabilistic causal model. It thus follows that any most likely hypothesis D_I must be a cover of M^+ and that only covers need to be considered in searching for the most probable hypotheses (an important savings because usually a large majority of $D_K \subseteq D$ are not covers).

Moreover, the effects of absence of expected manifestations on the likelihood of an explanation is now also being taken into consideration, as indicated by $L_2(D_I, M^+)$, the second product of the relative likelihood (see Equation 4.18c). For example, if m_l is absent and for some $d_i \in D_I$ it is the case that $c_{il} = 1$, i.e., d_i always causes m_l, then $L_2(D_I, M^+) = 0$ and in turn $L(D_I, M^+) = 0$, so D_I is thus concluded not to be a likely hypothesis. On the other hand, were c_{il} very small (close to zero), the relative likelihood of D_I would not greatly be affected by the absence of m_l. In contrast, as discussed in Chapter 3, the absence of manifestations expected by evoked disorders is not addressed by basic parsimonious covering theory. This is because the causal link $<d_i, m_l>$ here is interpreted as d_i may cause m_l, i.e., the strength of the causal association is neither 1 nor 0 but somewhere in between. Thus, as long as d_i is evoked by some present manifestation $m_j \in M^+$, its expected but absent manifestations will not play any role in the future processing. By taking into consideration these absent manifestations and calculating the relative likelihood accordingly, the probabilistic causal model of this chapter is thus better able to further eliminate unlikely hypotheses or focus attention on the more probable ones. Of course, previous real–world applications of parsimonious covering theory adopted "scoring" of competing hypotheses for the same reason, but did so in an *ad hoc* fashion (see Chapter 2).

A difficult issue in abduction in general, and in parsimonious covering in particular, has been precisely defining what is meant by the "best" or "most parsimonious" or "most plausible" explanation for a given set of facts [deKleer87, Josephson87, Polya54, Pople73, Reggia83, Reiter87, Thagard78,89]. Previously conceived notions of parsimony or simplicity such as relevancy, minimum cardinality or irredundancy have been based on *subjective* criteria of hypothesis plausibility. The measure $L(D_I, M^+)$ derived in the last section now gives us an objective criterion of hypothesis plausibility: its relative likelihood. By examining previous subjective criteria of plausibility using $L(D_I, M^+)$ from the probability calculus, one can gain insight into the reasonableness of these criteria, and such an analysis is given next.

Let $D_I \subseteq D$ be a cover of M^+. For any $d_k \in D - D_I$, i.e., for any d_k not in D_I, it follows from Equations 4.13c and 4.18b that for the enlarged cover $D_I \cup \{d_k\}$

$$L_1(D_I \cup \{d_k\}, M^+)$$

$$= \prod_{m_j \in M^+} P(m_j | D_I \cup \{d_k\})$$

$$= \prod_{m_j \in M^+} [P(m_j | D_I) + P(m_j | \{d_k\}) - P(m_j | D_I) P(m_j | \{d_k\})]$$

$$= \prod_{m_j \in M^+} P(m_j | D_I) \left[1 + \frac{P(m_j | \{d_k\})}{P(m_j | D_I)} - P(m_j | \{d_k\}) \right]$$

$$= L_1(D_I, M^+) \prod_{m_j \in \mathit{effects}(d_k) \cap M^+} \left[1 + \frac{P(m_j | \{d_k\})}{P(m_j | D_I)} - P(m_j | \{d_k\}) \right] \quad (4.19a)$$

In the foregoing derivation, the range of the product's index is changed from $m_j \in M^+$ to $m_j \in \mathit{effects}(d_k) \cap M^+$. This is because for all m_j not in $\mathit{effects}(d_k)$, $c_{kj} = 0$ and in turn $P(m_j | \{d_k\}) = 0$. Also note that $P(m_j | D_I) \neq 0$ for all $m_j \in M^+$ since D_I covers M^+.

For $L_2(D_I \cup \{d_k\}, M^+)$ and $L_3(D_I \cup \{d_k\}, M^+)$, it is similarly the case that

$$L_2(D_I \cup \{d_k\}, M^+) = L_2(D_I, M^+) \prod_{m_l \in \mathit{effects}(d_k) - M^+} P(\overline{m_l} | \{d_k\}). \quad (4.19b)$$

$$L_3(D_I \cup \{d_k\}, M^+) = L_3(D_I, M^+) \frac{p_k}{1 - p_k}. \quad (4.19c)$$

Using these results (Equation 4.19), we can now proceed to examine the reasonableness of relevant, irredundant and minimum covers in the context of the probabilistic causal model.

Relevant Covers. Let D_I be a relevant cover of M^+, so by definition D_I covers M^+ and $D_I \subseteq causes(M^+)$. Let $d_k \notin causes(M^+)$, i.e., d_k is irrelevant to M^+, so $d_k \notin D_I$. Then $D_I \cup \{d_k\}$ is a irrelevant cover of M^+. For such a d_k, all of its manifestations are known to be absent, so it follows from Equations 4.19 that $L_1(D_I \cup \{d_k\}, M^+) = L_1(D_I, M^+)$, and thus

$$\frac{L(D_I \cup \{d_k\}, M^+)}{L(D_I, M^+)} = \left[\frac{p_k}{1 - p_k}\right] \prod_{m_l \in effects(d_k)} P(\overline{m_l} | \{d_k\})$$

$$= \left[\frac{p_k}{1 - p_k}\right] \prod_{m_l \in effects(d_k)} P(1 - c_{kl}).$$

In most real–world diagnostic problems, p_k is generally very small. For example, in medicine $p_k < 10^{-1}$ even for very common diseases in the general population, such as a cold or the flu, and is much much smaller (e.g., 10^{-6}) for rare diseases. Thus, $p_k / (1 - p_k) \ll 1$ usually. The product of $(1 - c_{kl})$ is also less than one and is often much less since it is a product of numbers less than one. Thus in most applications $L(D_I \cup \{d_k\}, M^+) \ll L(D_I, M^+)$, making an irrelevant cover much less likely than any relevant cover it contains. This effect is magnified as a cover becomes "more irrelevant", i.e., as additional irrelevant disorders d_l are included. Thus, it is generally only necessary to generate relevant covers as hypotheses for which $L(D_I, M^+)$ is calculated, and in most real–world problems this represents an enormous computational savings (typically, most covers are irrelevant covers).

The only exception would occur when p_k is fairly large, d_k is associated with very few manifestations, and all such associations are very weak. In particular, $L(D_I \cup \{d_k\}, M^+)$ would exceed $L(D_I, M^+)$ where d_k was a disorder irrelevant to M^+, only if

$$p_k > \frac{1}{1 + \prod_{m_l \in effects(d_k)} (1 - c_{kl})} > 0.5,$$

a distinctly atypical situation. An interesting consequence of this result is that if $M^+ = \varnothing$, since $\varnothing$ is the only relevant cover of such a M^+, the probabilistic causal model generally entails "no disorders are present" as the only reasonable explanation. This is consistent with parsimonious covering theory (see Lemma 3.7 in Section 3.2) and intuition.

Irredundant Covers. If D_I is an irredundant cover of M^+, then by definition no proper subset of D_I also covers M^+. For $d_k \notin D_I$ but $d_k \in causes(M^+)$, $D_I \cup \{d_k\}$ is a redundant but relevant cover of M^+. From Equations 4.19, it follows that

$$\frac{L_1(D_I \cup \{d_k\}, M^+)}{L_1(D_I, M^+)} = \prod_{m_j \in effects(d_k) \cap M_+} \left[1 + \frac{P(m_j|\{d_k\})}{P(m_j|D_I)} - P(m_j|\{d_k\})\right] \geq 1,$$

and

$$\frac{L_2(D_I \cup \{d_k\}, M^+)}{L_2(D_I, M^+)} = \prod_{m_l \in effect(d_k) - M^+} P(\overline{m_l}|\{d_k\}) \leq 1.$$

If $p_k \ll 1$, then

$$\frac{L_3(D_I \cup \{d_k\}, M^+)}{L_3(D_I, M^+)} = \frac{p_k}{1 - p_k} \ll 1.$$

In general, it is likely that the decrease in L_2 and L_3 caused by adding d_k will compensate for the increase in L_1 because p_k is typically small. Therefore, if the prior probabilities $p_i \ll 1$ for all $d_i \in D$ as in many applications, the most probable covers of M^+ are likely to be irredundant covers, consistent with intuitive arguments made in the past [deKleer87, Josephson87, Reggia84, Reggia85, Reiter87]. As the example at the end of the last section shows, although adding d_1 into irredundant cover $\{d_2, d_3\}$ increases L_1 from 0.81 to 0.84, it reduces L_2 from 0.56 to 0.11 and L_3 from 0.028 to 0.00028, thus making the redundant cover $\{d_1, d_2, d_3\}$ much less likely than the irredundant cover $\{d_2, d_3\}$ (0.000026 versus 0.013 relative likelihoods, respectively).

However, more care must be applied in restricting hypothesis generation to just irredundant covers. A careful analysis of Equations 4.19 should convince the reader that a redundant but relevant cover $D_I \cup \{d_k\}$ might on occasion be more probable than D_I if d_k is fairly common and $c_{kj} \gg P(m_j|D_I)$ for some $m_j \in M^+$. This represents a situation where a very frequent manifestation of a very common disorder is present. In this situation it is reasonable to include that disorder in some otherwise irredundant covers. This insight concerning the nature of parsimony was only recognized after the developing the probabilistic causal model. However, even in the situation where some redundant cover is more probable than an irredundant cover it contains, such a redundant cover might still be less probable than the most probable irredundant cover not contained in it. For instance, in the example at the end of the last section, a redundant cover $\{d_1, d_3\}$ has relative likelihood $L(\{d_1, d_3\}, \{m_1, m_3\}) = 0.000064$, which is greater than that of the irredundant cover $\{d_1\}$. However, the relative likelihood of $\{d_1, d_3\}$ is less than that of $\{d_2, d_3\}$, another irredundant cover which happens to be the most probable cover among all covers of $\{m_1, m_3\}$.

Minimum Covers. It is possible to identify situations where minimum cardinality of hypotheses is a reasonable criterion for hypothesis generation. For example, suppose that for all $d_i \in D$ the prior probabilities are $p_i \ll 1$ and are about equal, and for all $<d_i, m_j> \in C$ the causal strengths c_{ij} are fairly large in general. Let $\alpha \leq c_{ij} \leq \beta$ for all $<d_i, m_j> \in C$. Now consider two covers D_I and D_K of M^+ where $|D_I| < |D_K|$. It is evident from Equations 4.13a and 4.18 that $\alpha \leq L_1(D_I, M^+) \leq 1$, and thus

$$\frac{L_1(D_K, M^+)}{L_1(D_I, M^+)} \leq \frac{1}{\alpha}.$$

This ratio is not too much larger than 1 since c_{ij}'s are fairly large. On the average, a hypothesis consisting of more disorders would have more expected but absent manifestations. Therefore, it is usually the case that

$$\frac{L_2(D_K, M^+)}{L_2(D_I, M^+)} < 1.$$

Since p_i are very small and about equal, then

$$\frac{L_3(D_K, M^+)}{L_3(D_I, M^+)} \approx \left[\frac{p_i}{1 - p_i}\right]^{|D_K| - |D_I|} \ll 1.$$

Combining the above results for the ratios of L_1, L_2 and L_3 between D_I and D_K, it is clear that on the average

$$\frac{L(D_K, M^+)}{L(D_I, M^+)} \ll 1,$$

making the most probable covers of M^+ likely to be minimum covers. Unfortunately, however, in many real–world diagnostic situations the assumptions needed to make minimum cardinality a useful parsimony criterion are often violated. In medicine, for example, prior probabilities among diseases and causal strengths vary by as much as 10^6, and therefore, minimum cardinality would risk overlooking the most probable hypothesis and is generally not a reasonable criterion to adopt to limit hypothesis generation.

The above results indicate only that using irredundant or minimum covers is appropriate under certain conditions. These results do not represent a formal proof. It is for this reason that the problem solving strategy presented in the next chapter will consider 2^D to be the whole search space when looking for the most probable covers for M^+, rather than using only covers satisfying some parsimony criterion. However, as will become clear later, these parsimony principles are still useful heuristics for guiding the search process during problem solving.

4.3.2. Interdependence Among Disorders and Manifestations

In the context of cause–effect relationships, it is conceivable that individual manifestations are interrelated through common causative disorders, and individual disorders are interrelated through common manifestations. Different existing systems treat these interrelations differently, and most of these treatments are not wholly satisfactory for one reason or another. In this subsection, we discuss how the probabilistic causal model developed in this chapter addresses these issues. We start by establishing some preliminary results, and then precede to analyze various interrelations among diagnostic entities.

Preliminaries. From Assumption 2.2 (Equation 4.3c), for any distinct $<d_i, m_j>$ and $<d_k, m_l>$ in C,

$$P(m_j:d_i \wedge m_l:d_k) = P(m_j:d_i \,|\, d_i) \, P((m_l:d_k) \wedge d_i)$$
$$= P(m_j:d_i \,|\, d_i) \, P(m_l:d_k \,|\, d_k) \, P(d_i \wedge d_k).$$

Therefore, if $d_i \neq d_k$, then from Assumption 1 (Equation 4.2)

$$P(m_j:d_i \wedge m_l:d_k) = P(m_j:d_i \,|\, d_i) \, P(m_l:d_k \,|\, d_k) \, P(d_i) \, P(d_k)$$
$$= P(m_j:d_i) \, P(m_l:d_k),$$

i.e., two causation events involving different disorders are independent of each other. On the other hand, if $d_i = d_k$, then

$$P(m_j:d_i \wedge m_l:d_k) = P(m_j:d_i \,|\, d_i) \, P(m_l:d_k \,|\, d_k) \, P(d_i)$$
$$= P(m_j:d_i) \, P(m_l:d_k) \, \frac{1}{P(d_i)}$$
$$> P(m_j:d_i) \, P(m_l:d_k)$$

since $p_i < 1$. Similarly, we have $P((m_j:d_i) \wedge d_k) \geq P(m_j:d_i) \, P(d_k)$ where equality holds only if $d_i \neq d_k$. This can be generalized from two causation events to several disjuncts of disorders d_i and causation events $m_j:d_k$ (Theorem 4.14), but the following three lemmas are needed first to establish this result.

lemma 4.11: Let H be any positive boolean expression of cause/causation events (no negation is involved). Then for any $d_i \in D$,

$$P(H \wedge d_i) \geq P(H) \, P(d_i), \tag{4.20}$$

where the equality holds only if d_i does not appear in H.

lemma 4.12: Let H be any positive boolean expression of cause/causation events. Then for any $<d_i, m_j> \in C$,

$$P(H \wedge (m_j:d_i)) \geq P(H) \, P(m_j:d_i), \tag{4.21}$$

where the equality holds only if d_i does not appear in H.

Equations 4.20 and 4.21 are for relations between individual disorders and causations to H. Combining them together, it follows that:

lemma 4.13: Let H be any positive boolean expression of cause/causation events and h be a disjunct of cause/causation events. Then

$$P(H \wedge h) \geq P(H) \, P(h) \tag{4.22}$$

where the equality holds only if H and h do not involve a common cause event (disorder).

Applying Lemma 4.13 $n - 1$ times, it immediately follows that:

theorem 4.14: Let $h_1, \ldots, h_n$ be n distinct disjuncts of positive cause/causation events. Then

$$P(h_1 \wedge \cdots \wedge h_n) \geq \prod_{i=1}^{n} P(h_i), \tag{4.23}$$

where the equality holds only if no distinct pair h_i, h_j involves a common disorder.

Since any manifestation m_j can be expressed as a disjunction of causation events (see Equation 4.4b of Assumption 3), Theorem 4.14 can be used to study interrelationships between manifestations. We begin by deriving a formula computing the prior probability of any manifestation m_j. Recall that, by Assumption 3, a manifestation is an effect of its causative disorders and respective causation events; thus, its prior probability is a function of these events. By Equation 4.3b, for any $m_j \in M$, we have

$$P(m_j) = P(\bigvee_{d_i \in causes(m_j)} m_j : d_i).$$

Let $h \leftrightarrow \bigvee_{\substack{d_k \in causes(m_j) \\ d_k \neq d_i}} m_j : d_k$ for some $d_i \in causes(m_j)$. Then, $m_j = h \vee m_j : d_i$. Since

h is a context set of $m_j : d_i$, it then follows from Equation 4.21 that

$$
\begin{aligned}
P(m_j) &= P(h) + P(m_j : d_i) - P(h \wedge m_j : d_i) \\
&= P(h) + P(m_j : d_i) - P(h) \, P(m_j : d_i) \\
&= 1 - (1 - P(h)) \, (1 - c_{ij} \, p_i)
\end{aligned}
$$

where $P(m_j : d_i) = c_{ij} \, p_i$. This is again a Bernoulli formula. Applying the same derivation to $P(h)$, and so forth, it can be shown that

theorem 4.15: For any manifestation $m_j \in M$,

$$P(m_j) = 1 - \prod_{d_i \in causes(m_j)} (1 - c_{ij} \, p_i); \text{ and} \tag{4.24a}$$

$$P(m_j | d_i) = 1 - (1 - c_{ij}) \prod_{\substack{d_k \in causes(m_j) \\ d_k \neq d_i}} (1 - c_{kj} \, p_k). \tag{4.24b}$$

When the need arises, these formulas enable one to calculate the prior probability $P(m_j)$ and the conditional probability $P(m_j | d_i)$ easily from relevant causal strengths and disorder prior probabilities. This can be generalized to calculate conditional probabilities under multiple disorders such as

$$P(m_j|d_1 \wedge d_2) = 1 - (1 - c_{1j})(1 - c_{2j}) \prod_{\substack{d_k \in causes(m_j) \\ d_k \neq d_1, d_2}} (1 - c_{kj}\, p_k), \qquad (4.24c)$$

and to calculate prior probabilities of multiple manifestations such as $P(m_1 \wedge m_2)$, although the calculation for the latter may become quite complicated due to the interrelation between manifestations as revealed later.

Based on the above results it is possible to derive a number of interesting and important relationships among disorders and manifestations. These are cataloged in the rest of this section.

Causal Irrelevance and Probabilistic Independence. Recall that in Chapter 3, disorder $d_i \in D$ and manifestation $m_j \in M$ were said to be irrelevant to one another if $< d_i, m_j > \notin C$, i.e., d_i can never cause m_j. The presence/absence of one should not affect the likelihood of the presence of the other, i.e., in probability–theoretic terms, they should be independent of each other. This equivalence between the symbolic notion of causal irrelevance and the probability–theoretic notion of independence has also been suggested by others based on intuition [Charniak85] [Ben–Bassat80]. We now show that this intuitively reasonable property holds in this model. This is expressed in the following theorem which is an immediate consequent of Lemma 4.11.

theorem 4.16 [Disorder–Manifestation Interdependence Theorem]: Let $d_i \in D$ and $m_j \in M$. Then

$$P(m_j \wedge d_i) \geq P(m_j)\, P(d_i),$$

where the equality holds only if $< d_i, m_j > \notin C$.

The inequality $P(m_j \wedge d_i) > P(m_j)\, P(d_i)$ which holds if $d_i \in causes(m_j)$ implies $P(m_j|d_i) > P(m_j)$ and $P(d_i|m_j) > P(d_i)$. In words, if a disorder is present, then its causally related manifestations are more likely to appear, and if a manifestation is known to be present, the likelihoods of its causative disorders also increase. Both of these notions are well justified in real–world situations [Polya54].

Now consider an extreme case of strong disorder–manifestation correlation. Recall that when m_j has d_i as its only cause, m_j is called a *pathognomonic* manifestation of d_i. Whenever a pathognomonic manifestation m_j is present, parsimonious covering theory requires that d_i must also be present, regardless of the strength with which m_j is causally associated with d_i. In other words, in this situation m_j logically implies d_i, and thus the probability of d_i given m_j should be 1. The next theorem shows that this is also true in the probabilistic causal model.

theorem 4.17: If m_j is a pathognomonic manifestation of d_i in a diagnostic problem, then
(a) $P(d_i | m_j) = 1$, and
(b) $P(D_I | M_J) = 0$ if $m_j \in M_J$ and $d_i \notin D_I$.

Finally, the disorder–manifestation interdependence result (Theorem 4.16) can easily be generalized to cases with multiple disorders present simultaneously:

theorem 4.18: Let $d_1, d_2, \ldots, d_r$ be r distinct disorders in D and $m_j \in M$. Then

$$P(m_j \wedge (\bigwedge_{i=1}^{r} d_i)) \geq P(m_j) \prod_{i=1}^{r} P(d_i),$$

where equality holds only if $d_i \notin causes(m_j)$ for all $d_i \in D_I$.

Manifestation Interdependence. Manifestations are usually not independent of each other in real world problems. Therefore, the manifestation independence assumption, which is often used to reduce the data requirement and simplify the posterior probability computation in a number of existing Bayesian systems, is widely recognized to be a questionable assumption [Charniak83, Reggia85]. One important source of dependencies between manifestations arise because they share some of the same causes. For example, suppose m_1 and m_2 are two manifestations of disorder d_1. The presence of m_1 may make m_2 more likely to be present because m_1 increases the likelihood of d_1, which in turn affects the likelihood of m_2. This kind of dependence between manifestations through common causes is well captured in the probabilistic causal model.

theorem 4.19 [Manifestations Interdependence]: Let $m_1, m_2, \ldots, m_k$ be k distinct manifestations in M. Then

$$P\left[\bigwedge_{j=1}^{k} m_j\right] \geq \prod_{j=1}^{k} P(m_j), \qquad (4.25a)$$

where the equality holds only if none of these manifestations have common causes; and

$$P\left[\bigwedge_{j=1}^{k} m_j \mid d_k\right] \geq \prod_{j=1}^{k} P(m_j | d_k), \qquad (4.25b)$$

where the equality holds only if none of these manifestations have common causes other than d_k.

Part (a) of this theorem states that manifestations are independent of each other only if they do not have common causes. More interesting is that the converse, that two manifestations are interdependent if they do have some common causes, is also true in this model. This well–accepted and desirable property falls out of the initial assumptions of this model. Moreover, part (b) of the theorem states that manifestation conditional independence under disorder d_k, which is an assumption made in a number of Bayesian classification systems [Charniak83, Ben–Bassat80, Duda76], holds only if none of these manifestations have common causes other than d_k. Since this condition is not satisfied in most real–world applications, the manifestation conditional independence assumption only partially solves the problem of manifestation interdependence in Bayesian classification.

Disorder Interdependence Under Given Manifestations. Conversely, when two disorders have common manifestations they are correlated through the presence of such manifestations. That is, although disorders are assumed independent in the general population, they are dependent of one another in sub–populations of their common manifestations. This property also falls out of the initial assumptions of this model, as is proven in the next theorem.

theorem 4.20: [Disorder Interdependence]: Let d_1 and d_2 be two distinct disorders in D, and let $m_1 \in M$. Then

$$P(d_1 \wedge d_2 \,|\, m_1) \leq P(d_1 \,|\, m_1) \, P(d_2 \,|\, m_1),$$

where the equality holds only if either d_1 or d_2 does not cause m_1, i.e., only if c_{11} or c_{21} equals zero.

To understand Theorem 4.20 intuitively, note that it follows from probability theory that

$$P(d_1 \wedge d_2 \,|\, m_1) = P(d_1 \,|\, m_1) \, P(d_2 \,|\, d_1 \wedge m_1).$$

Therefore, Theorem 4.20 is equivalent to saying that $P(d_2 \,|\, m_1) \geq P(d_2 \,|\, d_1 \wedge m_1)$, where the equality holds only when m_1 is not a common manifestation of both d_1 and d_2. This is a very reasonable result from the viewpoint of parsimonious covering theory and intuition because when both m_1 and d_1 are known to be present and d_1 is in *causes*(m_1), m_1 will be largely accounted for by d_1, and thus any explanation is less likely to require d_2 as another cause of m_1 at the same time.

4.3.3. Non–Monotonic Evidence Accumulation

The probabilistic causal model has the desirable property that it leads to nonmonotonic evidence accumulation concerning hypothesis D_I. For example, new information (e.g., a previously unknown manifestation is discovered to be present) can *decrease* the likelihood of a previous hypothesis D_I significantly, even to zero, if D_I cannot cover the newly given manifestation. This can be shown easily from Theorem 4.10.

Naturally, a related question arises: How does a piece of new information affect the likelihood or belief of *individual* disorders? In the past, it has long been said that the belief in an individual disorder always increases when more of its evidence is revealed to be present [Polya54, Shortliffe76, Van Melle79, Kahn85]. Contrary to this common belief, in this subsection, we will see that nonmonotonicity also holds for individual disorders d_i. For example, $P(d_i|m_1 \wedge m_2)$ may be less than $P(d_i|m_1)$. New information stating that m_2 is present may reduce the likelihood of d_i even though no negative (preventive) cause–effect associations exist in the knowledge base. More strikingly, this nonmonotonicity holds even when both m_1 and m_2 are causally related to d_i and in isolation might therefore each be considered as evidence for d_i, and thus both manifestations support d_i when considered separately.

For simplicity, the theorem given below concerns only two manifestations, i.e., it compares the magnitude of $P(d_1|m_1 \wedge m_2)$ with that of $P(d_1|m_1)$ to see how the belief of the presence of d_1 changes when one more pieces of evidence is added. Since

$$P(d_1|m_1 \wedge m_2) = P(m_1 \wedge d_1|m_2) / P(m_1|m_2),$$

$P(d_1|m_1 \wedge m_2)$ can be viewed as a "double conditional probability", i.e., the conditional probability of d_1 given m_1 in the sub–population of m_2 instead of in the general population. Thus, unlike in single manifestation cases where $P(d_1|m_1)$ only depends on the correlation between d_1 and m_1, whether $P(d_i|m_1 \wedge m_2)$ is greater than, equal to, or less than $P(d_i|m_1)$ is determined not only by the causal associations between disorder d_i and each of the manifestations m_1 and m_2, but also by the interdependence of m_1 and m_2 as well.

theorem 4.21 [Evidence accumulation]: Let $d_1 \in D$, $m_1, m_2 \in M$, and $d_1 \in causes(m_1)$. Then
(a) $P(d_1|m_1 \wedge m_2) = P(d_1|m_1)$ if $causes(m_1) \cap causes(m_2) = \emptyset$;
(b) $P(d_1|m_1 \wedge m_2) < P(d_1|m_1)$ if $d_1 \notin causes(m_1) \cap causes(m_2) \neq \emptyset$;
(c) $P(d_1|m_1 \wedge m_2) > P(d_1|m_1)$ if $causes(m_1) \cap causes(m_2) = \{d_1\}$;
(d) $P(d_1|m_1 \wedge m_2) - P(d_1|m_1)$ is in $[-1, +1]$ otherwise.

An illustration of the theorem is given in Figure 4.3, and we informally consider the meaning of this theorem in the following.

In Figure 4.3a, m_2 is causally irrelevant to d_1 and does not share any common disorder with m_1. By Theorem 4.16 and 4.19, m_2 is independent of m_1 and d_1. Therefore, adding the presence of m_2 does not affect the posterior probability of d_1 given the presence of m_1. In Figure 4.3b, m_2 is causally irrelevant to d_1, so the probability of d_1 in the sub–population of m_2 is the same as in the general population. However, because m_1 and m_2 have some causes in common, their correlation through these common causes makes m_1 more likely in the sub–population of m_2 than in the

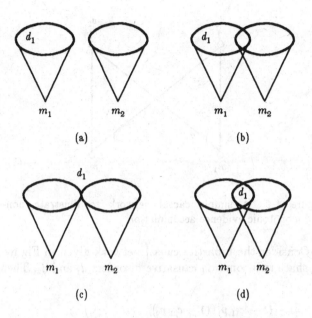

Figure 4.3. Non–monotonic evidence accumulation. When a
new manifestation is discovered, the posterior probability
of a disorder may increase, decrease, or stay unchanged.
(a) $causes(m_1) \cap causes(m_2) = \varnothing$: $P(d_1 | m_1 \wedge m_2) = P(d_1 | m_1)$
(b) $d_1 \not\subseteq causes(m_1) \cap causes(m_2) \neq \varnothing$: $P(d_1 | m_1 \wedge m_2) < P(d_1 | m_1)$
(c) $causes(m_1) \cap causes(m_2) = \{d_1\}$: $P(d_1 | m_1 \wedge m_2) > P(d_1 | m_1)$
(d) $\{d_1\} \subset causes(m_1) \cap causes(m_2)$: $P(d_1 | m_1 \wedge m_2) - P(d_1 | m_1)$ in
   $[-1, 1]$

general population (Theorem 4.19). The causal strength of d_1 to m_1, on the
other hand, is the same in both the general population and in the subpopulation of m_2 by the causation independence assumption. Thus the
presence of m_2 draws support of m_1 away from d_1 to disorders common to
both m_1 and m_2, resulting in a decrease in the posterior probability of d_1.
This is intuitively reasonable as we anticipate that some disorders in
$causes(m_1) \cap causes(m_2)$ will generally increase in likelihood when m_2 also
occurs. In Figure 4.3c, m_2 is relevant to d_1, and it therefore supports d_1.
Because d_1 is the only common cause of m_1 and m_2, intuitively the net
effect of adding m_2 should increase the belief of the presence of d_1. In Figure 4.3d, however, although both manifestations support d_1 individually,
m_2 may reduce the support of m_1 given to d_1 through some other causes
common to both m_1 and m_2. For example, if d_1 is weakly associated with
m_1 and m_2 while some other disorders are strongly associated with both of
these manifestations, then the net effect of adding m_2 could be to reduce
the posterior probability of d_1. The following example illustrates this case.

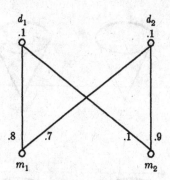

Figure 4.4. A simple causal network to illustrate non–monotonic evidence accumulation.

example: Consider the bipartite causal network given in Figure 4.4 where m_1 and m_2 share two common causative disorders d_1 and d_2. Then by Equations 4.24,

$$P(m_1) = [1 - (1 - c_{11}\, p_1)\, (1 - c_{21}\, p_2)]$$
$$= [1 - (1 - 0.08)\, (1 - 0.07)] = 0.1444,$$
$$P(m_1 \wedge d_1) = p_1\, [1 - (1 - c_{11})\, (1 - c_{21}\, p_2)]$$
$$= 0.1\, [1 - (1 - 0.8)\, (1 - 0.07)] = 0.0814,$$
$$P(m_1 \wedge d_2) = p_2\, [1 - (1 - c_{11}\, p_1)\, (1 - c_{21})]$$
$$= 0.1\, [1 - (1 - 0.08)\, (1 - 0.7)] = 0.0724,$$
$$P(d_1\,|\,m_1) = P(m_1 \wedge d_1)\, /\, P(m_1) = 0.5637,$$
$$P(d_2\,|\,m_1) = P(m_1 \wedge d_2)\, /\, P(m_1) = 0.5014.$$

That is, when only one manifestation m_1 is known, both d_1 and d_2 have about the same posterior probability (both are greater than 0.5) with d_1 being slightly more likely. Now consider their posterior probabilities when m_2 is also known. First, since $m_1 \leftrightarrow m_1\!:\!d_1 \vee m_1\!:\!d_2$ by Assumption 3, we can use Theorem 4.18 and Equation 4.24c to calculate

$$P(m_1 \wedge d_1 \wedge d_2) = P((m_1\!:\!d_1) \wedge d_2) + P((m_1\!:\!d_2) \wedge d_1) - P((m_1\!:\!d_1) \wedge (m_1\!:\!d_2))$$
$$= p_1\, p_2\, [1 - (1 - c_{11})\, (1 - c_{21})]$$
$$= 0.1 \cdot 0.1\, [1 - 0.2 \cdot 0.3] = 0.0094.$$

Then, substituting m_2 by $m_2\!:\!d_1 \vee m_2\!:\!d_2$ and using Equation 4.3c,

$$P(m_1 \wedge m_2) = c_{12}\, P(m_1 \wedge d_1) + c_{22}\, P(m_1 \wedge d_2) - c_{12}\, c_{22}\, P(m_1 \wedge d_1 \wedge d_2)$$
$$= 0.1 \cdot 0.0814 + 0.9 \cdot 0.0724 - 0.1 \cdot 0.9 \cdot 0.0094 = 0.072454,$$

$$P(m_1 \wedge m_2 \wedge d_1) = c_{12} P(m_1 \wedge d_1) + c_{22} P(m_1 \wedge d_1 \wedge d_2) - c_{12} c_{22} P(m_1 \wedge d_1 \wedge d_2)$$
$$= 0.1 \cdot 0.0814 + 0.9 \cdot 0.0094 - 0.1 \cdot 0.9 \cdot 0.0094 = 0.015754,$$

$$P(m_1 \wedge m_2 \wedge d_2) = c_{12} P(m_1 \wedge d_1 \wedge d_2) + c_{22} P(m_1 \wedge d_2) - c_{12} c_{22} P(m_1 \wedge d_1 \wedge d_2)$$
$$= 0.1 \cdot 0.0094 + 0.9 \cdot 0.0724 - 0.1 \cdot 0.9 \cdot 0.0094 = 0.065254,$$

$$P(d_1 | m_1 \wedge m_2) = P(m_1 \wedge m_2 \wedge d_1) \, / \, P(m_1 \wedge m_2) = 0.2174,$$

$$P(d_2 | m_1 \wedge m_2) = P(m_1 \wedge m_2 \wedge d_2) \, / \, P(m_1 \wedge m_2) = 0.9006.$$

Therefore,

$$P(d_1 | m_1 \wedge m_2) < P(d_1 | m_1),$$
$$P(d_2 | m_1 \wedge m_2) > P(d_2 | m_1).$$

That is, the belief of the presence of d_1 decreases after the second manifestation is added, while the belief of the presence of d_2 increases, and d_2 is now much more likely than d_1.   □

Cases (b) and (d) of Theorem 4.21 reveal a non–monotonic–like behavior of the probabilistic model. When new manifestations are discovered, belief in the presence of some disorders may actually decrease. This non–monotonic behavior can be intuitively justified in real world situations. For the foregoing example, since both d_1 and d_2 are causes of manifestation m_1 with fairly large strengths and both have the same prior probability, their posterior probabilities, given m_1, should be fairly great and not too much different from one another. They thus initially form a differential diagnosis "d_1 or d_2". When a new manifestation m_2 is discovered which is strongly associated with d_2 but very weakly associated with d_1, the belief of the presence of d_2 will naturally increase. For a human diagnostician in this case, belief in d_1 would be expected to go down and d_1 might thus even be "ruled out" from further consideration. That is, non–monotonicity does occur in the real–world during evidence accumulation.

This phenomenon has been modeled by some existing systems by the change of ratio of likelihoods or posterior probabilities of two disorders when new evidence appears (e.g., [Shortliffe76, Duda78]). In these systems, although a present manifestation never reduces the likelihood of a disorder, the relative ranking of disorders may change. For example, $P(d_i | m_1) \, / \, P(d_k | m_1) > 1$ for distinct d_i and d_k may change to $P(d_i | m_1 \wedge m_2) \, / \, P(d_k | m_1 \wedge m_2) < 1$ when a newly discovered manifestation m_2 is more strongly in favor of d_2 than d_1. However, such treatment can only handle mild changes of beliefs. It would fail to substantially rule out d_i by adding m_2 if both $P(d_i | m_1)$ and $P(d_k | m_1)$ are already very large, say greater than 0.5. In contrast, with the probabilistic causal model here, as illustrated by the foregoing example, a better modeling of non–monotonic behavior is achieved.

4.3.4. Relationship to Traditional Bayesian Classification Method

In this section we discuss the relationship between the probabilistic causal model and traditional Bayesian classification. Recall that Assumption 2.1 in the probabilistic causal model assumes that all disorders in D are independent of each other, and thus it allows multiple disorders to be present simultaneously. On the other hand, as we discussed in Chapter 2, in traditional Bayesian classification disorders are assumed to be mutually exclusive and thus at any time there is at most one disorder present. Furthermore, although in the general population there are some cases where no disorder occurs, Bayesian expert systems typically assume that a disorder *is* present, i.e., that normal cases with no manifestations are not under consideration [deDombal75, Zagoria83]. For such a subpopulation, exactly one disorder occurs in a given case, and thus disorder events d_i are not only mutually exclusive but also exhaustive. The assumption about disorders in this situation can be formally stated as follows:[*]

Assumption 2.1': All disorders in D compose a set of mutually exclusive and exhaustive events, i.e., $d_i \rightarrow \overline{d_j}$ for $i \neq j$, where $d_i, d_j \in D$, and $\sum_{d_i \in D} p_i = 1$.

If we replace Assumption 2.1 of the probabilistic causal model of this chapter by Assumption 2.1', keeping Assumptions 1, 2.2, and 3 unchanged, then the model reduces to traditional Bayesian classification. First, recall that the notation $\{d_i\}$ in the probabilistic causal model represents the event that d_i occurs and all other disorders do not. Then by Bayes' theorem,

$$P(\{d_i\} \mid M^+) = \frac{P(M^+|\{d_i\}) \, P(\{d_i\})}{P(M^+)} = \frac{P(M^+|\{d_i\}) \, P(\{d_i\})}{\sum_{D_I \subseteq D} P(M^+|D_I) \, P(D_I)}.$$

Since $d_i \rightarrow \overline{d_j}$ for all $j \neq i$ by Assumption 2.1', we have $d_i \leftrightarrow \{d_i\}$ and $P(D_I) = 0$ for all $D_I \subseteq D$ where $|D_I| \neq 1$ under this new assumption. Incorporating these into the above equation, we then have

$$P(d_i \mid M^+) = \frac{P(M^+|d_i) \, P(d_i)}{\sum_{d_i \in D} P(M^+|d_i) \, P(d_i)}$$

which is the formula used in traditional Bayesian classification. It is in this

---

(*) Here it is assumed that the prior probabilities p_i of all disorders are for the subpopulation where each individual case may have exactly one disorder occurring. If, instead, the prior probabilities of disorders are for the general population, these probabilities can easily be converted to their counterparts in the subpopulation by normalization. Thus, our treatment here about traditional Bayesian classification is more general than it appears.

sense that the probabilistic causal model developed in this chapter can be viewed as a generalization of traditional Bayesian classification.

Moreover, by disorder mutual exclusiveness of Assumption 2.1' and by Assumption 3 (mandatory causation), for any $m_j \in M$ and $d_i \in D$,

$$m_j \wedge d_i \leftrightarrow (\bigvee_{d_k \in causes(m_j)} m_j : d_k) \wedge d_i \leftrightarrow m_j : d_i.$$

Based on this fact, and dividing both sides of the equation $P(m_j \wedge d_i) = P(m_j : d_i)$ by $P(d_i) = p_i$, we immediately have the following:

theorem 4.22: If Assumption 2.1' replaces Assumption 2.1 in the probabilistic causal model, then

$$P(m_j | d_i) = P(m_j : d_i | d_i) = c_{ij}.$$

This theorem indicates that under Assumption 2.1', the notion of causal strength defined in the probabilistic causal model now becomes the conditional probability traditionally used in Bayesian classification. Subsequently, for absent manifestations $\overline{m_l}$, we have $P(\overline{m_l} | d_i) = (1 - c_{il})$. An immediate interesting consequence of this theorem is that $P(m_j | d_i) = 0$ if $d_i \notin causes(m_j)$ because $c_{ij} = 0$ in this situation. That is, if d_i and m_j are not causally related, then they cannot simultaneously be present. This is a very reasonable result to obtain from the assumptions of disorder mutual exclusiveness (Assumption 2.1') and mandatory causation of manifestations (Assumption 3) because the presence of such a d_i excludes all causative disorders of m_j (and therefore m_j itself) from occurring.

How m_j and d_i should be probabilistically correlated if they are *not* causally associated has been an actively debated question [Charniak85]. The combination of the above result and Theorem 4.16 may shed some light on this. They suggest that the correlation between such an m_j and d_i depends on the correlations between disorders. If disorders are mutually exclusive (Assumption 2.1'), then m_j and d_i prevent each other $(P(m_j \wedge d_i) = 0)$; if disorders are independent of each other (Assumption 2.1), then m_j and d_i are also independent of one another $(P(m_j \wedge d_i) = P(m_j) P(d_i)$, see Theorem 4.16).

Since D is a mutually exclusive and exhaustive set of events, applying Bayes' theorem, we have

$$P(m_j) = \sum_{d_k \in D} P(m_j | d_k) P(d_k) = \sum_{d_k \in causes(m_j)} c_{kj} p_k$$

because by Theorem 4.22 only those disorders $d_k \in causes(m_j)$ have $P(m_j | d_k) = c_{ik} \neq 0$; and

$$P(d_i | m_j) = \frac{P(m_j | d_i) P(d_i)}{\sum_{d_k \in D} P(m_j | d_k) P(d_k)} = \frac{c_{ij} p_i}{\sum_{d_k \in causes(m_j)} c_{kj} p_k}$$

for posterior probability of d_i given m_j.

Next we show that manifestation conditional independence, which has been used in a number of traditional Bayesian diagnostic systems, holds if Assumption 2.1 is replaced by Assumption 2.1$'$.

theorem 4.23: If Assumption 2.1$'$ replaces Assumption 2.1 in the probabilistic causal model, then

$$P(m_1 \wedge \cdots \wedge m_n \mid d_i) = \prod_{j=1}^{n} P(m_j \mid d_i).$$

Note that this property is not a separate assumption, as in some previous Bayesian systems, but is derived from other assumptions of the model. Also note that, because of the interdependencies between manifestations through some common disorder (see *Manifestation Interdependence* in Section 4.3.2), manifestations themselves are not independent of each other here.

Finally, $P(d_i \mid M^+)$, the posterior probability of individual disorder d_i given M^+ can now easily be computed based on Bayes' theorem and theorems 4.22 and 4.23:

$$
P(d_i \mid M^+) = \frac{P(M^+ \mid d_i)\, P(d_i)}{\sum_{d_k \in D} P(M^+ \mid d_k)\, P(d_k)}
$$

$$
= \frac{\prod_{m_j \in M^+} P(m_j \mid d_i) \prod_{m_l \in M - M^+} (1 - P(m_l \mid d_i))\, p_i}{\sum_{d_k \in D} \prod_{m_j \in M^+} P(m_j \mid d_k) \prod_{m_l \in M - M^+} (1 - P(m_l \mid d_k))\, p_k}
$$

$$
= \frac{\prod_{m_j \in M^+} c_{ij} \prod_{m_l \in M - M^+} (1 - c_{il})\, p_i}{\sum_{d_k \in D} \prod_{m_j \in M^+} c_{kj} \prod_{m_l \in M - M^+} (1 - c_{kl})\, p_k}.
$$

This is equivalent to the traditional Bayes' formula used in a number of Bayesian expert systems [deDombal75, Zagoria83].

Thus, replacing the disorder independence assumption with an assumption that disorders are mutually exclusive reduces the probabilistic causal model developed in this chapter to traditional Bayesian classification. In this sense, the essentials of the probabilistic causal model (causation events, causation independence, mandatory causation, etc.) can be viewed as a generalization of the traditional Bayesian approach in a causal world. On the other hand, Bayes' theorem, and probability theory in general, is not restricted only to cause–effect relations. In this sense, the probabilistic causal model is a special case of Bayes' theorem. It is only applicable to causal aspects of problem–solving, even in the domain of diagnosis. Some other aspects of diagnostic problem–solving, e.g., the treatment of setting factors such as a patient's age and sex, cannot be properly handled by this model, at least in its present form.

4.4. Comparison to Related Work

In general diagnostic problem–solving where more than one disorder d_i may occur simultaneously, a hypothesis for a given set of present manifestations M^+ is a set of disorders $D_I \subseteq D$. If the number of all possible disorders is $n = |D|$, this would involves 2^n potential diagnostic hypotheses, generally a very large number. Thus, calculating the posterior probabilities of all these hypotheses is a formidable if not computationally infeasible task. In addition, it has proven difficult in the past even to derive a computationally feasible method for computing the posterior probability $P(D_I | M^+)$ for each individual possible hypothesis D_I. Abductive diagnostic systems in AI have circumvented these difficulties by employing various heuristics to generate only a small number of most plausible hypotheses and using *ad hoc* scoring mechanisms to rank them [Catanzarite79, Josephson84,87, Miller82, Reggia83]. Systems relying mainly on statistical pattern classification methods have circumvented these difficulties primarily by viewing such problems as n independent binary classification problems (for each $d_i \in D$, classifying the problem as either d_i or $\overline{d_i}$) [Ben–Bassat80, Flehinger75]. These latter systems largely ignore the issues of how a manifestation $m_j \in M$ should be accounted for when more than one of its possible causes is hypothesized to be present, and how the interdependence between disorders in D_I given M^+ affects the posterior probability of D_I as whole.

The probabilistic causal model presented in this chapter has taken the domain–independent parsimonious covering theory of the underlying causal structure of diagnostic problems, and integrated the probability theory within that framework. The crucial innovation required to do this was the creation of a new class of events – causation events – to explicitly represent the uncertainty of the causal relationship between individual disorders and manifestations so that some assumptions (causal strength invariant in the respective contexts of causation events, no manifestation can be present without being caused by some disorder) can be formally laid out. While not without its limitations, these assumptions are far more reasonable than those often used in statistically oriented diagnostic systems, such as manifestation independence or conditional independence, formulation as n independent classification problems, etc. This point is further enhanced by the fact that this model has a number of properties concerning interrelationships among disorders and manifestations in various situations which are well justified in many real–world situations and are not possessed by other existing statistical systems.

Using just these assumptions, it was shown to be possible to rank any given hypotheses D_I and D_K relative to each other using $P(D_I|M^+)$ / $P(D_K|M^+) = L(D_I, M^+) / L(D_K, M^+)$, where the relative likelihood measure L is a function of the p_i and c_{ij} in the underlying causal network. Furthermore, this function is computationally tractable for comparing two hypotheses in the sense that it is based on calculations involving only $d_i \in D_I$ and $m_j \in M^+ \cup effects(D_I)$ and not on a more global computation over all possible disorders D and manifestations M. The relative ranking of diagnostic hypotheses D_I that results from this approach was demonstrated to be consistent with many of the concepts of symbolic parsimonious covering theory and intuition.

While this is an interesting result to obtain, by itself the ability to rank competing hypotheses does not solve the combinatorial problem of having 2^n diagnostic possibilities to rank relative to other another. Fortunately, it has been demonstrated that it is generally sufficient in this model to only consider a small fraction of the 2^n possible hypotheses. If a hypothesis D_I is not a cover of M^+, a priori it is known that $P(D_I|M^+) = 0$, so only hypotheses that are covers need to be considered. In many real–world diagnostic problems, such as those in medicine, this reduces the diagnostic possibilities to a tiny fraction of the 2^n that are possible. Furthermore, covers including $d_i \notin causes(M^+)$, i.e., irrelevant covers, are generally extremely impossible and for most domains can be safely ignored (see exception in the text). In fact, usually the set of all irredundant covers comes close to containing the "most probable explanations", although care must be exercised in considering exceptions where redundant but relevant covers are important. Thus it turns out that one does *not* actually need to consider all theoretically possible diagnostic hypotheses. Furthermore, in the next chapter it will be shown that this model can also support an effective search strategy which, by taking advantage of both symbolic and probabilistic knowledge, finds the probable hypothesis (or hypotheses if a tie of relative likelihood exists) after only generating or searching a tiny fraction of the hypothesis space 2^D.

To see further the merit of the probabilistic causal model introduced in this chapter, we compare it with two well–known models that incorporate uncertainty measurements with symbolic rule–based systems, namely, PROSPECTOR and MYCIN. Two other models, Cooper's NESTOR and Pearl's causal belief networks, are based on more general causal network with causal chaining, and will be discussed in Chapter 5.

PROSPECTOR is a rule–based computer consultation system for certain problems in "hard–rock" mineral exploration [Duda78]. Let $E = e_1 \wedge e_2 \wedge \cdots \wedge e_n$ be a pattern of evidence and H a hypothesis. In PROSPECTOR, each rule $E \rightarrow H$ is associated with two likelihood ratios $\lambda = P(E|H) / P(E|\overline{H})$ and $\overline{\lambda} = P(\overline{E}|H) / P(\overline{E}|\overline{H})$, representing the uncertainty of the truth of the rule, or the supporting strengths of E and $\overline{E}$ to H. The prior strength of H is required in terms of prior odds

$O(H) = P(H) / P(\overline{H})$. With this information the posterior odds of H is computed by $O(H | E) = \lambda\, O(H)$ when E is known to be true, and $O(H | \overline{E}) = \overline{\lambda}\, O(H)$ when E is known to be false [Duda76,78].

An immediately apparent problem with the rule–based formulation in PROSPECTOR is that it may require too many rules to adequately represent causal associations in diagnostic problem–solving, as was discussed in Chapter 2 for rule–based diagnostic systems in general. Also, the probability estimates of λ and especially of $\overline{\lambda}$ are difficult to obtain from domain experts, as the authors of PROSPECTOR stated [Duda76]. More severely, PROSPECTOR computes the combined support of $E_1, E_2, \ldots, E_r$ to H from r rules $E_i \rightarrow H$ by assuming that these E_i are conditionally independent under H. This assumption is less plausible than the causation invariance assumption (Assumption 2.2) of the probabilistic causal model because, in general, some other hypothesis may exist, say $\hat{H}$, which is also a common cause of some of these E_i. The interdependence among these E_i through $\hat{H}$ is ignored by this conditional independence assumption (see Theorem 4.19 and related discussion).

Moreover, in PROSPECTOR all hypotheses H are predefined. There is no coherent and theoretically justifiable means to form composite hypotheses and to rank them. This severely restricts the ability of the system to handle diagnostic situations where multiple disorders can occur simultaneously.

MYCIN, also a rule–based system, was designed to provide consultative advice on medical diagnosis and therapy for infectious diseases [Shortliffe76]. In MYCIN, a pair consisting of disorder d_i and manifestation m_j can be associated with two measures representing the supporting strengths of m_j to d_i, namely, the measurement of belief $MB[d_i, m_j]$ and the measurement of disbelief $MD[d_i, m_j]$. Simple incremental rules for adjusting MB and MD when new manifestations are discovered are also defined so that $MB[d_i, M_J]$ and $MD[d_i, M_J]$ for a set of present manifestations M_J can be computed from $MB[d_i, m_j]$ and $MD[d_i, m_j]$ of individual manifestations.

The authors of MYCIN state that these concepts and rules came from the theory of confirmation. But as Adams pointed out later, these rules could be identically derived from probability theory under the assumptions that manifestations are independent both in the general population and in sub–populations of disorders [Adams76]. Based on MB and MD, MYCIN defines certainty factor $CF[d_i, M_J] = MB[d_i, M_J] - MD[d_i, M_J]$ to rank every disorder given the presence of M_J (an *ad hoc* method of certainty factor propagation is also defined) [Shortliffe75]. The certainty factor definition and certainty factor propagation method do not obey probability theory unless a very strong assumption that disorders are independent and have equal prior probabilities is made (see pp. 183 in [Adams76]). As we analyzed earlier, these underlying assumptions are unrealistic and neglect the important interdependencies between manifestations, thus severely restricting the application of this method in general situations. (It is thus not difficult to find counter examples where MYCIN fails to deliver correct results, see pp. 182–183 in [Adams76]). More seriously, MYCIN apparently treats multiple simultaneous disorders rather poorly. In the final stage of problem–solving, a few disorders with the highest certainty factors are combined together as the diagnosis for therapy selection. In this diagnosis construction, MYCIN does not explicitly distinguish between alternative and complementary disorders and does not consider the interrelation between disorders. Simply choosing a few disorders with the highest certainty factors may not only lead to incorrect diagnosis, but it also does not guarantee that the final diagnosis will even cover all present manifestations. On the other hand, a good feature of MYCIN's uncertainty model is that the disbelief measurement MD allows preventive associations between disorders and manifestations to be represented in the knowledge base.

Finally, because of failing to take into consideration interrelations between disorders given M^+, belief measures in both PROSPECTOR and MYCIN are simply monotonically increasing (or non–decreasing) unless new evidence is specifically against a hypothesis. Thus, as analyzed in the discussion of Theorem 4.21, these systems do not directly model the non–monotonicity of evidence accumulation well.

Recently, others have developed various methods also aimed at including probabilistic inference in the framework of parsimonious covering theory. Interested readers are referred to [Yager85, Neapolitan87] for examples of such methods.

4.5. Mathematical Appendix

proof of Lemma 4.1.
Y can be represented in disjunctive normal form where each conjunct is a context of $m_j{:}d_i$. The proof is, therefore, by induction on the number of conjuncts in Y.
Base case: Y is a disjunction of one conjunct, i.e., Y is itself a context of $m_j{:}d_i$. The lemma holds trivially by Equation 4.3b (Assumption 2.2).
Induction step: Assume this lemma holds for all Y that are disjunctions of k contexts of $m_j{:}d_i$ for some $k \geq 1$. Now show that it holds for Y being a disjunction of $k+1$ contexts. Let $Y = Y_1 \vee X$ where Y_1 is a disjunction of k contexts and X is a single context of $m_j{:}d_i$. Also note that $Y_1 \wedge X$ itself is also a disjunction of k conjuncts, each of which is a context of $m_j{:}d_i$ by associative law. Then by Equation 4.3b and the inductive hypothesis,

$$P((m_j{:}d_i) \wedge Y | d_i)$$
$$= P((m_j{:}d_i) \wedge (Y_1 \vee X) | d_i)$$
$$= P((m_j{:}d_i) \wedge Y_1 | d_i) + P((m_j{:}d_i) \wedge X | d_i) - P((m_j{:}d_i) \wedge Y_1 \wedge X | d_i)$$
$$= c_{ij}[\, P(Y_1 | d_i) + P(X | d_i) - P(Y_1 \wedge X | d_i)\,]$$

$$= c_{ij} P(Y|d_i).$$ (4.5a)

Since it is true for all Y with $k + 1$ conjuncts, Equation 4.5a holds for all context sets of $m_j : d_i$.   □

proof of Lemma 4.2.

Let $X = \bigwedge_{d_k \in D - \{d_i\}} \overline{d_k}$, then $\{d_i\} = X \wedge d_i$. It then follows that $\{d_i\} \wedge (m_j : d_k)$ is false for all $k \neq i$, and by Equation 4.4b that $m_j \wedge \{d_i\} \leftrightarrow (m_j : d_i) \wedge \{d_i\}$. X is clearly a context of $m_j : d_i$, and $P(X \wedge d_i) \neq 0$ by Assumptions 1 and 2.1. Then by Equations 4.3a and 4.5c,

$$P(m_j|\{d_i\}) = P(m_j \wedge \{d_i\}) / P(\{d_i\})$$
$$= P((m_j : d_i) \wedge \{d_i\}) / P(\{d_i\})$$
$$= P(m_j : d_i | \{d_i\})$$
$$= P(m_j : d_i | X \wedge d_i)$$
$$= c_{ij}.$$ (4.6a)

From Equation 4.6a, 4.6b immediately follows.   □

proof of Lemma 4.3.

Note that $\{d_i\}$ is a context of $m_j : d_i$, so $Y \wedge \{d_i\}$ is a context set of $m_j : d_i$. From the proof of Lemma 4.2, $m_j \wedge \{d_i\} \leftrightarrow (m_j : d_i) \wedge \{d_i\}$, thus $m_j \wedge Y \wedge \{d_i\} \leftrightarrow (m_j : d_i) \wedge Y \wedge \{d_i\}$. Then by Equations 4.5b and 4.6a

$$P(m_j \wedge Y | \{d_i\}) = P(m_j \wedge Y \wedge \{d_i\}) / P(\{d_i\})$$
$$= P((m_j : d_i) \wedge Y \wedge \{d_i\}) / P(\{d_i\})$$
$$= c_{ij} P(Y \wedge \{d_i\}) / P(\{d_i\})$$
$$= P(m_j|\{d_i\}) P(Y|\{d_i\}).$$ (4.7a)

From Equation 4.7a, 4.7b immediately follows.   □

proof of Theorem 4.4.

By Equation 4.4b and 4.4c (Assumption 3) and Definition 4.4, $m_2 \wedge m_3 \wedge \cdots \overline{m_k} \wedge \overline{m_{k+1}} \wedge \cdots \overline{m_n}$ is a context set of $m_1 : d_i$, $m_3 \wedge \cdots \overline{m_k} \wedge \overline{m_{k+1}} \wedge \cdots \overline{m_n}$ is a context set of $m_2 : d_i$, and so forth. Then, applying Equation 4.7a k times and 4.7b $n - k$ times,

$$P(m_1 \wedge m_2 \wedge \cdots m_k \wedge \overline{m_{k+1}} \wedge \cdots \overline{m_n} | \{d_i\})$$
$$= P(m_1|\{d_i\}) P(m_2 \wedge \cdots m_k \wedge \overline{m_{k+1}} \wedge \cdots \overline{m_n} | \{d_i\})$$

.

.

.

$$= \prod_{j=1}^{k} P(m_j | \{d_i\}) \prod_{l=k+1}^{n} P(\overline{m_l} | \{d_i\}) \tag{4.8a}$$

$$= \prod_{j=1}^{k} c_{ij} \prod_{l=k+1}^{n} (1 - c_{il}). \tag{4.8b}$$

$\square$

proofs of Lemmas 4.5 and 4.6.

By induction on r, the number of disorders in the joint–causation event.

Base case: $r = 1$. Both lemmas hold trivially because Equation 4.10a is reduced to Equation 4.5b and $P(m_j : d_i | d_i) = c_{ij}$ by definition.

Induction step: Assume the lemmas hold for all joint–causation events with r disorders for some $r \geq 1$. Now show that it holds for joint–causation events of $r + 1$ disorders. Let Y be any context set of event $m_j : d_1 \wedge \cdots d_r \wedge d_{r+1}$. By Definition 4.6, it is obvious that Y is also a context set of $m_j : d_1 \wedge d_2 \wedge \cdots d_r$. Then by inductive hypothesis,

$$P((m_j : d_1 \wedge \cdots \wedge d_r) \wedge Y)$$
$$= P(m_j : d_1 \wedge \cdots \wedge d_r | d_1 \wedge \cdots \wedge d_r) P(Y \wedge d_1 \wedge \cdots \wedge d_r).$$

From Equations 4.9 and 4.1a we have

$$m_j : d_1 \wedge d_2 \wedge \cdots \wedge d_r \wedge d_{r+1}$$
$$\leftrightarrow \left[(\bigvee_{i=1}^{r} (m_j : d_i)) \wedge d_1 \wedge \cdots \wedge d_r \wedge d_{r+1} \right] \vee \left[(m_j : d_{r+1}) \wedge d_1 \wedge \cdots \wedge d_r \wedge d_{r+1} \right]$$
$$\leftrightarrow ((m_j : d_1 \wedge \cdots \wedge d_r) \wedge d_{r+1}) \vee ((m_j : d_{r+1}) \wedge d_1 \wedge \cdots \wedge d_r).$$

Because d_{r+1} and $m_j : d_{r+1}$ are contexts of $m_j : d_1 \wedge \cdots \wedge d_r$, and $d_1 \wedge \cdots \wedge d_r$ is a context of $m_j : d_{r+1}$, also noting that $m_j : d_1 \wedge \cdots \wedge d_r$ entails $d_1 \wedge \cdots \wedge d_r$ and $m_j : d_{r+1}$ entails d_{r+1}, it follows from the inductive hypothesis and Equation 4.5b that

$$P(m_j : d_1 \wedge \cdots \wedge d_r \wedge d_{r+1})$$
$$= P((m_j : d_1 \wedge \cdots \wedge d_r) \wedge d_{r+1}) + P((m_j : d_{r+1}) \wedge d_1 \wedge \cdots d_r)$$
$$\quad - P((m_j : d_1 \wedge \cdots \wedge d_r) \wedge (m_j : d_{r+1}))$$
$$= P(m_j : d_1 \wedge \cdots \wedge d_r | d_1 \wedge \cdots \wedge d_r) P(d_{r+1} \wedge d_1 \wedge \cdots \wedge d_r)$$
$$\quad + P(m_j : d_{r+1} | d_{r+1}) P(d_1 \wedge d_2 \wedge \cdots \wedge d_r \wedge d_{r+1})$$
$$\quad - P(m_j : d_1 \wedge \cdots \wedge d_r | d_1 \wedge \cdots \wedge d_r) P(m_j : d_{r+1} | d_{r+1}) P(d_1 \wedge \cdots^{l}h^{l}1p^{l} \cdot \wedge d_r \wedge d_{r+1}).$$

Dividing both sides of the foregoing equation by $P(d_1 \wedge \cdots \wedge d_r \wedge d_{r+1})$ and by inductive hypothesis, then Lemma 4.6 is proved as follows

$$P(m_j : d_1 \wedge \cdots \wedge d_r \wedge d_{r+1} | d_1 \wedge \cdots \wedge d_r \wedge d_{r+1})$$
$$= P(m_j : d_1 \wedge \cdots \wedge d_r | d_1 \wedge \cdots \wedge d_r) + P(m_j : d_{r+1} | d_{r+1})$$
$$\quad - P(m_j : d_1 \wedge \cdots \wedge d_r | d_1 \wedge \cdots \wedge d_r) P(m_j : d_{r+1} | d_{r+1}) \tag{4.11a}$$

$$= \left[1 - \prod_{i=1}^{r}(1 - c_{ij})\right] + c_{r+1,j} - \left[1 - \prod_{i=1}^{r}(1 - c_{ij})\right]c_{r+1,j}$$

$$= 1 - \prod_{i=1}^{r+1}(1 - c_{ij}). \tag{4.11b}$$

For Equation 4.10, since Y is a context set of $m_j:d_1\wedge\cdots\wedge d_r$ and $m_j:d_{r+1}$, similar to Equation 4.11 and using 4.11, it follows that

$$P((m_j:d_1\wedge\cdots\wedge d_r\wedge d_{r+1})\wedge Y)$$

$$= P((m_j:d_1\wedge\cdots\wedge d_r)\wedge d_{r+1}\wedge Y) + P((m_j:d_{r+1})\wedge d_1\wedge\cdots\wedge d_r\wedge Y)$$

$$- P((m_j:d_1\wedge\cdots\wedge d_r)\wedge(m_j:d_{r+1})\wedge Y)$$

$$= [\, P(m_j:d_1\wedge\cdots\wedge d_r\,|\,d_1\wedge\cdots\wedge d_r) + P(m_j:d_{r+1}\,|\,d_{r+1})$$

$$- P(m_j:d_1\wedge\cdots\wedge d_r)\,P(m_j:d_{r+1}\,|\,d_{r+1})\,]\,P(Y\wedge d_1\wedge\cdots\wedge d_r\wedge d_{r+1})$$

$$= P(m_j:d_1\wedge\cdots\wedge d_r\wedge d_{r+1}\,|\,d_1\wedge\cdots\wedge d_r\wedge d_{r+1})$$

$$P(Y\wedge d_1\wedge d_2\wedge\cdots\wedge d_r\wedge d_{r+1}). \tag{4.10a}$$

$\square$

proof of Lemma 4.7.

By Equations 4.4a and 4.9,

$$m_j\wedge D_I \leftrightarrow \left[\bigvee_{d_k\in D}m_j:d_k\right]\wedge\left[\bigwedge_{d_i\in D_I}d_i\right]\wedge\left[\bigwedge_{d_k\in D-D_I}\overline{d_k}\right]$$

$$\leftrightarrow \left[\bigvee_{d_i\in D_I}m_j:d_i\right]\wedge\left[\bigwedge_{d_i\in D_I}d_i\right]\wedge\left[\bigwedge_{d_k\in D-D_I}\overline{d_k}\right]$$

$$\leftrightarrow (m_j:d_1\wedge\cdots\wedge d_r)\wedge\left[\bigwedge_{d_k\in D-D_I}\overline{d_k}\right].$$

Since $\bigwedge_{d_k\in D-D_I}\overline{d_k}$ is a context set of $m_j:d_1\wedge\cdots\wedge d_r$, then by Lemma 4.5 (Equation 4.10a),

$$P(m_j\wedge D_I) = P\left[(m_j:d_1\wedge\cdots\wedge d_r)\wedge(\bigwedge_{d_k\in D-D_I}\overline{d_k})\right]$$

$$= P(m_j:d_1\wedge\cdots\wedge d_r\,|\,d_1\wedge\ldots\wedge d_r)\,P\left[d_1\wedge\cdots\wedge d_r\wedge(\bigwedge_{d_k\in D-D_I}\overline{d_k})\right]$$

$$= P(m_j:d_1\wedge\cdots\wedge d_r\,|\,d_1\wedge\cdots\wedge d_r)\,P(D_I).$$

Dividing both sides of the foregoing equation by $P(D_I)$ gives Equation 4.12a, and 4.12b follows immediately. $\square$

proof of Lemma 4.8.

Equations 4.13a and b follow immediately from Lemmas 4.7 and 4.6. $\square$

proof of Lemma 4.9.

As shown before (see the proof of Lemma 4.7), let $X = \underset{d_k \in D - D_I}{\wedge} \overline{d_k}$, then

$D_I \leftrightarrow X \wedge (\overset{r}{\underset{i=1}{\wedge}} d_i)$, $m_j \wedge D_I \leftrightarrow (m_j : d_1 \wedge \cdots \wedge d_r) \wedge X$,   and $m_j \wedge D_I \wedge Y$

$\leftrightarrow (m_j : d_1 \wedge \cdots \wedge d_r) \wedge X \wedge Y$. X is clearly a context set of $m_j : d_1 \wedge \cdots \wedge d_r$, and thus so is $Y \wedge X$. Then it follows from Lemmas 4.5 and 4.7 (Equations 4.10a and 4.12a) that

$P(m_j \wedge Y | D_I)$

$= P(m_j \wedge Y \wedge D_I) / P(D_I)$

$= P((m_j : d_1 \wedge \cdots \wedge d_r) \wedge Y \wedge X)) / P(D_I)$

$= P(m_j : d_1 \wedge \cdots \wedge d_r \mid d_1 \wedge \cdots \wedge d_r) \, P\left[Y \wedge X \wedge (\overset{r}{\underset{i=1}{\wedge}} d_i) \right] / P(D_I)$

$= P(m_j | D_I) \, P(Y \wedge D_I) / P(D_I)$

$= P(m_j | D_I) \, P(Y | D_I).$ (4.14a)

From 4.14a, 4.14b follows immediately.   □

proof of Theorem 4.10.

By Assumption 3 and Definition 4.6, $m_2 \wedge m_3 \wedge \cdots \wedge m_k \wedge \overline{m_{k+1}} \wedge \cdots \wedge \overline{m_n}$ is a context set of $m_1 : d_1 \wedge d_2 \wedge \cdots \wedge d_r$ and $m_3 \wedge \cdots \wedge m_k \wedge \overline{m_{k+1}} \wedge \cdots \wedge \overline{m_n}$ is a context set of $m_2 : d_1 \wedge d_2 \wedge \cdots \wedge d_r$, etc., and we will use these conjunctions of effect events here to designate the corresponding context sets. Equation 4.15a can be proven by successively applying Equation 4.14a k times on $m_1, \ldots, m_k$, then Equation 4.14b $n - k$ times on $\overline{m_{k+1}}, \ldots, \overline{m_n}$. By Equation 4.13a and 4.13b, Equation 4.15b then follows immediately from Equation 4.15a.   □

proof of Lemma 4.11.

Consider H to be in a disjunctive normal form. Based on Assumptions 2.1 and 2.2, it can easily be shown that since d_i is independent of any d_k and $m_j : d_k$ for $d_k \neq d_i$, it is independent of any boolean expression of d_k's and $m_j : d_k$'s. Therefore, we only need to show the case where d_i appears in H. The proof is then by induction on r, the number of conjuncts in H.

Base case: $r = 1$, i.e., $H = h_1$ where h_1 is a conjunct of cause/causation events. If d_i appears in h_1, then by Equation 4.1a $h_1 \wedge d_i \leftrightarrow h_1$. Thus we have

$$P(h_1 \wedge d_i) = P(h_i) > P(h_1) \, p_i$$

since $0 < p_i < 0$ by Assumption 1.

Inductive step: Assume that the lemma holds for some $r \geq 1$. Now show that it holds for $r + 1$. Let H be a disjunction of r conjuncts of cause/causation events, and h_1 a conjunct of positive cause/causation events, and $H \vee h_1 \neq H$ (i.e., h_1 is not entailed by H). For brevity, let

$\alpha = P((H \vee h_1) \wedge d_i) = P(H \wedge d_i) + P(h_1 \wedge d_i) - P(H \wedge h_1 \wedge d_i)$, and

$\beta = P(H \vee h_1) \, P(d_i)$.

Case 1: d_i appears in h_1 and may or may not appear in H.
Then by 4.1a, $h_1 \wedge d_i \leftrightarrow h_1$. Thus,

$$\alpha = P(H \wedge d_i) + P(h_1) - P(H \wedge h_1)$$
$$\beta = [P(H) + P(h_1) - P(H \wedge h_1)] \, p_i.$$

By inductive hypothesis, we have $P(H \wedge d_i) \geq P(H) \, p_i$, then

$$\alpha - \beta \geq [P(h_1) - P(H \wedge h_1)] \, (1 - p_i) > 0.$$

since $1 - P(d_i) > 0$ by Assumption 1 and $P(h_1) - P(H \wedge h_1) \geq 0$ because $H \wedge h_1$ entails h_1.

Case 2: d_i does not appear in h_1, but does in H.
Let H_1 be the disjunction of all conjuncts in H that involve d_i, and H_2 be the disjunction of all other conjuncts in H and h_1. Thus, $H \vee h_1 = H_1 \vee H_2$, d_i is independent of H_2 by inductive hypothesis, and $H_1 \wedge d_i \leftrightarrow H_1$. Then it follows that

$\alpha = P(H_1) + P(H_2) \, P(d_i) - P(H_1 \wedge H_2)$,

$\beta = p_i [P(H_1) + P(H_2) - P(H_1 \wedge H_2)]$, and

$\alpha - \beta = (1 - p_i) [P(H_1) - P(H_1 \wedge H_2)] > 0$

since $1 - p_i > 0$ and $P(H_1) - P(H_1 \wedge H_2) \geq 0$. Combining the above two cases, therefore, the lemma holds for all disjunctions of conjuncts of cause/causation events.   □

proof of Lemma 4.12.
Also consider H to be in a disjunctive normal form.
Case 1: $m_j : d_i$ does not appear in H.
Then by definition H is a context set of $m_j : d_i$. It then follows from Equation 4.5b and Lemma 4.11 that

$$P(H \wedge (m_j : d_i)) = c_{ij} \, P(H \wedge d_i) \geq c_{ij} \, P(H) \, p_i = P(m_j : d_i) \, P(H)$$

where the equality holds only if d_i does not appear in H by Lemma 4.11.
Case 2: $m_j : d_i$ does appear in H.
If every conjunct in H contains $m_j : d_i$, then $H \wedge m_j : d_i = H$ and in turn $P(H \wedge m_j : d_i) = P(H) > P(H) \, P(m_j : d_i)$ since $P(m_j : d_i) = c_{ij} \, p_i \neq 0$ by Assumption 1. Otherwise, let $H = H_1 \vee H_2$ where H_1 is a disjunct of all conjuncts in H involving $m_j : d_i$ and H_2 is a disjunct of all other conjuncts in H. Note that now $H \neq H_1$ and thus $P(H_1) > P(H_1 \wedge H_2)$. Then we have $H_1 \wedge m_j : d_i \leftrightarrow H_1$ and $H_1 \wedge H_2 \wedge m_j : d_i \leftrightarrow H_1 \wedge H_2$, and by Equation 4.5b, $P(H_2 \wedge m_j : d_i) = c_{ij} \, P(H_2 \wedge d_1)$. It then follows that

$$\alpha = P(H \wedge (m_j : d_i))$$

$$= P((H_1 \vee H_2) \wedge m_j : d_i)$$

$$= P(H_1) + c_{ij} P(H_2 \wedge d_i) - P(H_1 \wedge H_2).$$

$$\beta = P(H) \, P(m_j : d_i)$$

$$= [P(H_1) + P(H_2) - P(H_1 \wedge H_2)] \, P(m_j : d_i).$$

$$\alpha - \beta = (1 - P(m_j : d_i)) \, [P(H_1) - P(H_1 \wedge H_2)]$$

$$+ c_{ij} \, [P(H_2 \wedge d_i) - P(H_2) \, p_i] > 0$$

since both $[P(H_1) - P(H_1 \wedge H_2)]$ and $1 - P(m_j : d_i)$ are greater than zero, and by Lemma 4.11 $P(H_2 \wedge d_i) - P(H_2) \, P(d_i) \geq 0$. □

proof of Lemma 4.13.

The proof is by induction on the number of events in h. H is again considered to be in a disjunctive normal form.

Base case: h contain one event, i.e., $h = d_i$ or $h = m_j : d_i$. The lemma holds trivially by Lemmas 4.11 and 4.12.

Inductive step: Assume that the lemma holds for h containing $r \geq 1$ events. Now show that it also holds for $h \vee d_i$ and $h \vee m_j : d_i$.

(1) Show that $P((h \vee d_i) \wedge H) \geq P(h \vee d_i) \, P(H)$.

If d_i appears in h, then by Equation 4.1a, $h \vee d_i$ is a disjunct of r or fewer events since at least one cause or causation event in h involves d_i and thus it can be subsumed by d_i. In this situation the lemma holds by inductive hypothesis. Therefore, we only consider cases where d_i does not appear in h and thus h and d_i are independent of each other by Lemma 4.11. For brevity let $\alpha = P((h \vee d_i) \wedge H)$ and $\beta = P(h \vee d_i) \, P(H)$.

Case 1: d_i does not appear in H. Then H and d_i are independent of each other. It then follows that

$$\alpha = P(h \wedge H) + P(d_i \wedge H) - P(h \wedge d_i \wedge H)$$

$$= P(h \wedge H) + p_i \, P(H) - p_i \, P(h \wedge H),$$

$$\beta = P(h) \, P(H) + p_i \, P(H) - p_i \, P(h) \, P(H), \text{ and}$$

$$\alpha - \beta = [P(h \wedge H) - P(h) \, P(H)] \, (1 - p_i) \geq 0$$

where, by the inductive hypothesis, the equality holds only if h and H share some common disorder.

Case 2: d_i appears in H.

If d_i appears in every conjunct in H, then H entails d_i and in turn $h \vee d_i$. In this case it is obvious that $\alpha = P(H) > P(h \vee d_i) \, P(H)$. So we only consider cases where some conjuncts in H contain d_i, and some others do not. Let H_1 be the disjunction of all conjuncts in H containing d_i and H_2 be the disjunction of all other conjuncts in H. Then $H \leftrightarrow H_1 \vee H_2$. By boolean algebra, we have $d_i \wedge H_1 \leftrightarrow H_1$ and $(h \vee d_i) \wedge H_1 \leftrightarrow H_1$, and similarly $d_i \wedge H_1 \wedge H_2 \leftrightarrow H_1 \wedge H_2$ and $(h \vee d_i) \wedge H_1 \wedge H_2 \leftrightarrow H_1 \wedge H_2$. Then it follows that

$\alpha = P(H_1) + P((h \vee d_i) \wedge H_2) - P(H_1 \wedge H_2)$, and

$\beta = [P(H_1) + P(H_2) - P(H_1 \wedge H_2)] \, P(h \vee d_i).$

Since d_i does not appear in H_2, then by case **1** above, $P((h \vee d_i) \wedge H_2) \geq P(h \vee d_i) \, P(H_2)$. Therefore,

$$\alpha - \beta \geq [P(H_1) - P(H_1 \wedge H_2)] \, (1 - P(h \vee d_i)) > 0$$

since both $P(H_1) - P(H_1 \wedge H_2)$ and $(1 - P(h \vee d_i))$ are greater than zero.

(2) Show that $\alpha = P((h \vee m_j : d_i) \wedge H) \geq \beta = P(h \vee m_j : d_i) \, P(H)$.

Analogous to (1), we only consider cases where $m_j : d_i$ does not appear in h. Now using Lemma 4.12 instead of 4.11, it analogously follows that if $m_j : d_i$ does not appear in H, then

$$\alpha - \beta = [P(h \wedge H) - P(h) \, P(H)] \, (1 - P(m_j : d_i)) \geq 0$$

where equality holds only if h and H share some common disorders.
If $m_j : d_i$ appears in H, then

$$\alpha - \beta \geq [P(H_1) - P(H_1 \wedge H_2)] \, (1 - P(h \vee m_j : d_i)) > 0$$

where H_1 is the disjunction of all conjuncts in H which contain $m_j : d_i$ and H_2 is the disjunction of all other conjuncts of H.   □

proof of Theorem 4.14.
Equation 4.23 immediately follows after $n - 1$ successive applications of Lemma 4.13.   □

proof of Theorem 4.15.
Let $\{ d_1, \ldots, d_r \} \subseteq causes(m_j)$. Then, by Equation 4.4b, to prove Equation 4.24a is equivalent to proving $P(\bigvee_{i=1}^{r} m_j : d_i) = 1 - \prod_{i=1}^{r}(1 - c_{ij} \, p_i)$. Now prove the latter equation by induction on r.

Base case: $r = 1$. Holds trivially since $P(m_j : d_1) = c_{1j} \, p_1$ by definition.

Inductive step: Assume the equation holds for some $r - 1 \geq 0$. Now show that it holds for r. For brevity, let $X = \bigvee_{i=1}^{r-1} m_j : d_i$, then since d_r does not appear in X, by Lemma 4.12, $m_j : d_r$ and X are independent of each other. It then follows from inductive hypothesis that

$$P(\bigvee_{i=1}^{r} m_j : d_i) = P(X \vee m_j : d_r)$$

$$= P(X) + P(m_j : d_r) - P(X) \, P(m_j : d_r)$$

$$= 1 - (1 - c_{r,j} \, p_r)(1 - X)$$

$$= 1 - \prod_{i=1}^{r}(1 - c_{ij} \, p_i). \tag{4.24a}$$

To prove Equation 4.24b, let $X = \bigvee\limits_{\substack{d_k \in causes(m_j) \\ d_k \neq d_i}} m_j\!:\!d_k$, then $m_j \leftrightarrow X \vee m_j\!:\!d_i$. By

Lemmas 4.11 and 4.12, both d_i and $m_j\!:\!d_i$ are independent of X. It then follows that

$$P(m_j \wedge d_i) = P(X \wedge d_i) + P(m_j\!:\!d_i) - P(X \wedge m_j\!:\!d_i)$$

$$= [P(X) + c_{ij} - c_{ij}\,P(X)]\;p_i$$

$$= [1 - (1 - c_{ij})\,(1 - P(X))]\;p_i.$$

Dividing both sides by $P(d_i) = p_i$ and then substituting $P(X)$ by Equation 4.24a,

$$P(m_j\,|\,d_i) = 1 - (1 - c_{ij}) \prod_{\substack{d_k \in causes(m_j) \\ d_k \neq d_i}} (1 - c_{kj}\,p_k). \tag{4.24b}$$

$\square$

proof of Theorem 4.16.
By Equation 4.4b (Assumption 3),

$$m_j \leftrightarrow \bigvee_{d_k \in causes(m_j)} m_j\!:\!d_k.$$

Then the theorem is an immediate consequence of Equation 4.20 (Lemma 4.11). $\square$

proof of Theorem 4.17.
(a) Since d_i is the only cause of m_j, then by Equation 4.4b (Assumption 3), $m_j \leftrightarrow m_j\!:\!d_i$. It follows that $P(d_i\,|\,m_j) = P(d_i\,|\,m_j\!:\!d_i) = 1$ because by 4.1a m_jd_i entails d_i.
(b) Immediately follows from Equations 4.18 because D_I is not a cover of M_J. $\square$

proof of Theorem 4.18.
Analogous to the proof of Theorem 4.16. $\square$

proof of Theorem 4.19.
By Equation 4.4b (Assumption 3), $m_j \leftrightarrow \bigvee\limits_{d_i \in effects(m_j)} m_j\!:\!d_i$ for $j = 1, 2, \ldots, k$.

(a) Equation 4.25a is thus an immediate consequence of Equation 4.23 (Theorem 4.14).
(b) Let $m_2, \ldots, m_n \leftrightarrow H$. To prove Equation 4.25b, one only needs to prove that $P(m_1 \wedge H\,|\,d_i) \geq P(m_1\,|\,d_i)\,P(H\,|\,d_i)$ where the equality holds only if m_1 and H do not share common disorders other than d_i.
Case 1: d_i is not in m_1 or H.
Without loss of generality, let d_i not be in m_1. Then, m_1 and d_i are independent of each other by Lemma 4.11 and thus $P(m_1\,|\,d_i) = P(m_1)$. It then follows from Theorem 4.14 that

$$P(m_1 \wedge H \wedge d_i) \geq P(m_1) \, P(H \wedge d_i) = P(m_1 \,|\, d_i) \, P(H \wedge d_i)$$

where equality holds only if m_1 and H do not share any common disorder.
Case 2: d_i appears in both m_1 and H.
Let $m_1 \leftrightarrow h \vee m_1 : d_i$. Note that $m_1 : d_i$ cannot be in H because H involves
manifestations different than m_j; thus, both h and H are context sets of
$m_1 : d_i$. Then, by Equation 4.1a and Lemma 4.12

$$
\begin{aligned}
\alpha &= P(m_1 \wedge H \wedge d_i) \\
&= P((h \vee m_1 : d_i) \wedge H \wedge d_i) \\
&= P(h \wedge H \wedge d_i) + P(m_1 : d_i \wedge H) - P(m_1 : d_i \wedge h \wedge H) \\
&= P(h \wedge H \wedge d_i) + c_{i1} \, P(H \wedge d_i) - c_{i1} \, P(h \wedge H \wedge d_i) \\
&= (1 - c_{i1}) \, P(h \wedge H \wedge d_i) + c_{i1} \, P(H \wedge d_i).
\end{aligned}
$$

Since d_i and h are independent by Lemma 4.11, then

$$
\begin{aligned}
\beta &= P(m_1 \,|\, d_i) \, P(H \wedge d_i) \\
&= [P(h \,|\, d_i) + P(m_1 : d_i \,|\, d_i) - P(m_1 : d_i \wedge h \,|\, d_i)] \, P(H \wedge d_i) \\
&= [P(h) + c_{i1} - c_{i1} \, P(h)] \, P(H \wedge d_i) \\
&= (1 - c_{i1}) P(h) \, P(H \wedge d_i) + c_{i1} \, P(H \wedge d_i).
\end{aligned}
$$

Then, by Theorem 4.14,

$$\alpha - \beta = (1 - c_{i1}) \, [P(h \wedge H \wedge d_i) - P(h) \, P(H \wedge d_i)] \geq 0$$

where the equality holds only if h and $H \wedge d_i$ do not share any common
disorder. Noticing that d_i is not in h and $m_1 \leftrightarrow h \vee m_1 : d_i$, this is equivalent
to saying that $\alpha = \beta$ only if m_1 and H do not have any common disorder
other than d_i.   □

proof of Theorem 4.20.
From probability theory, proving the lemma is equivalent to proving

$$\alpha = P(d_1 \wedge d_2 \wedge m_1) \, P(m_1) \leq \beta = P(d_1 \wedge m_1) \, P(d_2 \wedge m_1)$$

where the equality holds only if either $c_{11} = 0$ or $c_{21} = 0$.
Let $\gamma = 1 - \prod\limits_{\substack{d_i \in causes(m_1) \\ i \neq 1,2}} (1 - c_{ij} \, p_i)$. Then, by Equations 4.24, we have

$$
\begin{aligned}
P(m_1) &= 1 - (1 - c_{11} \, p_1) \, (1 - c_{21} \, p_2) \, \gamma, \\
P(d_1 \wedge m_1) &= [1 - (1 - c_{11}) \, (1 - c_{21} \, p_2) \, \gamma] \, p_1, \\
P(d_2 \wedge m_1) &= [1 - (1 - c_{11} \, p_1) \, (1 - c_{21}) \, \gamma] \, p_2, \\
P(d_1 \wedge d_2 \wedge m_1) &= [1 - (1 - c_{11}) \, (1 - c_{21}) \, \gamma] \, p_1 \, p_2.
\end{aligned}
$$

By a straightforward but lengthy calculation, we have

$$\beta - \alpha = \gamma \, p_1 \, p_2 \left[(1 - c_{11}) \, (1 - c_{21}) + (1 - c_{11} \, p_1) \, (1 - c_{21} \, p_2) \right.$$
$$\left. - (1 - c_{11}) \, (1 - c_{21} \, p_2) - (1 - c_{11} \, p_1) \, (1 - c_{21}) \right]$$
$$= \gamma \, p_1 \, p_2 c_{11} \, c_{21} \, (1 - p_1) \, (1 - p_2) \geq 0.$$

The only situation where the above equation equals zero is either c_{11} or c_{21} being zero.   □

proof of Theorem 4.21.
(a) Since m_1 and m_2 do not share any common disorders and d_1 is not a cause of m_2, m_2 is independent of m_1 and d_1 by Theorem 4.14. Then

$$P(d_1 \,|\, m_1 \wedge m_2) = \frac{P(m_1 \wedge m_2 \wedge d_1)}{P(m_1 \wedge m_2)} = \frac{P(m_1 \wedge d_1) \, P(m_2)}{P(m_1) \, P(m_2)} = P(d_1 \,|\, m_1).$$

To prove (b) and (c), let $h = \displaystyle\bigvee_{\substack{d_i \in causes(m_1) \\ d_i \neq d_1}} m_1 : d_i$. Then $m_1 = h \vee m_1 : d_1$ and h is

independent of d_1, and both h and m_2 are context sets of $m_1 : d_1$. Then by Theorem 4.14,

$$P(m_1) = P(h) + c_{11} \, p_1 - c_{11} \, p_1 \, P(h),$$
$$P(m_1 \wedge d_1) = p_1 \left[P(h) + c_{11} - c_{11} \, P(h) \right]$$
$$= P(m_1) - P(h) \, (1 - p_1),$$
$$P(m_1 \wedge m_2) = P(h \wedge m_2) + c_{11} \, P(m_2 \wedge d_1) - c_{11} \, P(h \wedge m_2 \wedge d_1),$$
$$P(m_1 \wedge m_2 \wedge d_1) = P(h \wedge m_2 \wedge d_1) + c_{11} \, P(m_2 \wedge d_1) - c_{11} P(h \wedge m_2 \wedge d_1)$$
$$= P(m_1 \wedge m_2) - [P(h \wedge m_2) - P(h \wedge m_2 \wedge d_1)].$$

For brevity, let

$$\alpha = P(m_1 \wedge m_2 \wedge d_1) \, P(m_1) \text{ and}$$
$$\beta = P(m_1 \wedge d_1) \, P(m_1 \wedge m_2).$$

Then the comparison of $P(d_1 \,|\, m_1 \wedge m_2)$ and $P(d_1 \,|\, m_1)$ is equivalent to that of α and β. By the above derivation, we have

$$\alpha - \beta = P(m_1 \wedge m_2) \, P(h) \, (1 - p_1) - [P(h \wedge m_2) - P(h \wedge m_2 \wedge d_1)] \, P(m_1).$$

(b) Since d_1 is not a cause of m_2, it is independent of m_2. Then $P(h \wedge m_2 \wedge d_1) = P(h \wedge m_2) \, p_1$, then

$$\alpha - \beta = [P(m_1 \wedge m_2) \, P(h) - P(m_1) \, P(h \wedge m_2)] \, (1 - p_1).$$

Substituting $P(m_1)$ and $P(m_1 \wedge m_2)$ by equations derived earlier,

$$\alpha - \beta = c_{11} \, p_1 \, (1 - p_1) [P(m_2) \, P(h) - P(h \wedge m_2)] < 0$$

since h and m_2 share some common disorders and thus by Theorem 4.14 $P(m_2) \, P(h) - P(h \wedge m_2) < 0$.
(c) Since h and m_2 do not share common disorders, they are therefore independent of each other. However, m_1 and m_2 share a common disorder

d_1. Then by Theorem 4.14,

$$\alpha - \beta = P(m_1 \wedge m_2)\, P(h)\, (1 - p_1) - [P(m_2) - P(m_2 \wedge d_1)]\, P(h)\, P(m_1)$$
$$> P(m_1)\, P(m_2)\, P(h)\, (1 - p_1) - [P(m_2) - P(m_2 \wedge d_1)]\, P(h)\, P(m_1)$$
$$= P(m_1)\, P(h)\, [P(m_2 \wedge d_1) - P(m_2)\, p_1] > 0$$

since d_1 is a cause of m_2 and thus by Theorem 4.16 $P(m_2 \wedge d_1) > P(m_2)\, p_1$.
(d) Proof is by the example in the text immediately after the Theorem.   □

proof of Theorem 4.22.
By Assumption 2.1′, $d_i \wedge d_j = false$ for $i \neq j$. By Assumption 3, $m_j \leftrightarrow \bigvee_{d_k \in causes(m_j)} m_j : d_k$. It then follows that

$$m_j \wedge d_i \leftrightarrow (\bigvee_{d_k \in causes(m_j)} m_j : d_k) \wedge d_i \leftrightarrow m_j : d_i.$$

Therefore, we have $P(m_j \wedge d_i) = P(m_j : d_i)$. Dividing both sides by $P(d_i) = p_i$, the theorem follows immediately.   □

proof of Theorem 4.23.
By the same argument as in the proof of Theorem 3.22,

$$m_1 \wedge \cdots \wedge m_n \wedge d_i \leftrightarrow m_1 : d_i \wedge \cdots \wedge m_n : d_i.$$

Since all causation events involve different manifestations, they are contexts of each other. Then, by successively applying Equation 4.3b (Assumption 2.2), it follows that

$$P(m_1 \wedge \cdots \wedge m_n \wedge \,|d_i) = P(m_1 : d_i \wedge \cdots \wedge m_n : d_i \,|d_i)$$
$$= \prod_{j=1}^{n} P(m_j : d_i \,|d_i)$$
$$= \prod_{j=1}^{n} P(m_j \,|d_i),$$

where the last equality is by Theorem 3.22.   □

5
Diagnostic Strategies in the Probabilistic Causal Model

> "But if probability is a measure of the importance of our state of ignorance, it must change its value whenever we add new knowledge. And so it does."
>
> Thornton C. Fry,
> *Probability and Its Engineering Uses*

In the probabilistic causal model described in the last chapter, symbolic causal knowledge and numeric probabilistic knowledge are integrated in a coherent and formal fashion. The relative likelihood $L(D_I, M^+)$ was developed to evaluate the plausibility of hypothesis D_I given M^+, and was shown to be appropriate for identifying the Bayesian optimal diagnostic hypothesis. Recall that earlier, in Chapter 3, we defined the solution for a diagnostic problem to be the set of all irredundant covers of a given M^+. One difficulty concerning this definition is how to further disambiguate these alternatives (in some problems the number of irredundant covers of the given M^+ may be fairly large). The relative likelihood measure may be used to overcome this difficulty if we redefine the problem solution as the hypothesis with the highest relative likelihood value, i.e., the most probable one.

The next question then arises: how can one effectively construct or search for the most probable hypothesis from the vast hypothesis space during problem-solving? Clearly, generating all possible hypotheses $D_I \subseteq D$ and then ranking them by their relative likelihood is computationally untractable for most real-world applications because there are 2^D potential hypotheses.[*]

This issue can be addressed in a number of ways. One could start by ranking all hypotheses $D_I \in 2^D$ of size 1, proceeding to those of size two, then to those of size three, and so forth to a point where one can be sure that the most probable hypothesis has been generated. This kind of breadth first enumeration strategy would usually involve significant unnecessary work by generating large numbers of unlikely candidates. Alternatively, one could generate plausible hypotheses using some *ad hoc*

---

* The term "potential hypothesis" or "hypothesis" is used in this chapter to refer to any set of disorders $D_I \subseteq D$. Therefore, there are a total of $|2^D|$ potential hypotheses for a given problem.

heuristics and then rank them by the relative likelihood measure. However, such an approach has only been partially successful to date in situations involving multiple simultaneous disorders, sometimes lacks a theoretical or domain–independent basis, and can be shown to fail in certain situations [Catanzarite79, Josephson87, Miller82, Pauker76, Pople82]. Another possible approach, based on parsimonious covering theory, is to generate and rank only "parsimonious covers" using various symbolic notions of parsimony. Unfortunately, this latter approach would also generally involve significant unnecessary work in some situations since the algorithms, e.g., *BIPARTITE* in Chapter 3, use only symbolic causal associations and parsimony criteria to generate hypotheses. They have no way of knowing whether or not a parsimonious cover is a probable hypothesis. In addition, as revealed in Section 4.3.1, once probabilistic knowledge is introduced into a causal model, exceptional situations exist where existing symbolic criteria of parsimony could fail to identify the most probable hypothesis.

The goal of this chapter is thus to set forth a strategy for *selectively* generating diagnostic hypotheses that both greatly limits the number of hypotheses considered and, at the same time, is still guaranteed to identify the most probable hypothesis (or hypotheses if a tie exists for the relatively most probable hypothesis). This strategy integrates the use of both symbolic causal associations and probability theory: the symbolic causal associations between manifestations and disorders and the covering principle are used for disorder evocation and hypothesis formulation, while probabilistic knowledge is used to focus search attention and finally to select the most probable hypotheses.

In Section 5.1, a best–first heuristic search algorithm is presented which takes a "closed" diagnostic problem $P = <D,M,C, M^+>$ and returns the most probable hypothesis (or hypotheses if a tie exists) of M^+ as the problem solution. The term "closed" refers to situations where the presence/absence of each manifestation in M is known *a priori*. In Section 5.2, this "closed world" algorithm is then extended to solve "open" problems where the presence/absence of manifestations are gradually made known during the problem–solving process. In particular, and in contrast to closed problems where every manifestation is known either to be present or be absent, when the open problem–solving process stops, manifestations whose presence/absence are not known are considered *unknown*, and are not assumed to be absent (i.e., this is an "open-world" problem). Section 5.3 discusses the issue of the "quality" of problem solutions resulting from these algorithms, develops a measure for solution quality, and presents algorithms for problem–solving based on this measure. Finally, Section 5.4 gives a comparison between the probabilistic causal model and two other models which are also centered on formalizing the causal relations in probability theoretic terms.

5.1. Closed Problem–Solving

The process of identifying the most probable hypothesis for a closed problem presented here is a best–first process of selectively generating plausible hypotheses. The process starts with the null hypothesis $\varnothing$, a hypothesis that no disorder is present. Then at any point during problem–solving an existing hypothesis is selected and expanded to generate a set of new hypotheses, each of which is a proper superset of the chosen hypothesis that includes exactly one additional disorder.[*] In other words, expansion is a process of generating supersets of a selected hypothesis. As this search process goes on, more and more hypotheses are generated (made explicit) and evaluated. The process stops when the most probable hypothesis is generated and identified. Hence, the real issues are how to select an existing hypothesis to expand so that as few hypotheses as possible are generated during the search process, and how to determine that the most probable hypothesis(es) has been generated and identified and thus that the process can be terminated.

5.1.1. Bounding a Hypothesis

In the search process outlined above, among all of the hypotheses in 2^D, some of them are generated or made explicit while others are not. Now the question is, which of the existing hypotheses should be selected next for expansion? In other words, we need some criterion on how likely it is that a hypothesis expansion will lead to the most probable cover(s), i.e., some measure of its merit with respect to search. As discussed earlier, any generated D_I not only explicitly represents a hypothesis, but also implicitly represent other hypotheses which are its proper supersets and thus can be generated from it through a sequence of expansions. Let $\hat{D}_I \supseteq D_I$ be the most probable hypothesis among all $D_J \supseteq D_I$, i.e., $L(\hat{D}_I, M^+) = \max\{L(D_J, M^+) \,|\, D_J \supseteq D_I\}$. Then $L(\hat{D}_I, M^+)$ can be used as a measure of D_I's merit: an existing hypothesis D_I is more promising if the best (most probable) hypothesis that can be generated from it has a higher relative likelihood. Unfortunately, the value $L(\hat{D}_I, M^+)$ cannot easily be calculated from D_I. However, if a lower and upper bound on this likelihood, to be called the *bounds on* D_I for short, can be determined, this information can then be used for selecting the most promising existing hypothesis for expansion. For instance, consider two existing hypotheses D_I and D_J which are bounded by $[a, b]$ and $[c, d]$, respectively. That is, $a \leq \max\{L(D_K, M^+) \,|\, D_K \supseteq D_I\} \leq b$ and $c \leq \max\{L(D_L, M^+) \,|\, D_L \supseteq D_J\} \leq d$. If $b > d$, then it is more likely that the most probable hypothesis among supersets of D_I is better than that of supersets of D_J. Therefore, expanding D_I is a more

---

(*) The term *supersets* as used here includes D_I itself. When all supersets of D_I and not itself is intended, the term *proper supersets* is used.

promising step than expanding D_J. If, further, $a > d$, i.e., the lower bound on D_I is greater than the upper bound on D_J, then it is certain that expanding D_J will never yield a hypothesis better than the best one among supersets of D_I. Thus, D_J together with all its supersets can be discarded from any further consideration. As seen here, these bounds may greatly help to narrow the focus during the search for a most probable hypothesis. In the rest of this section we identify such bounds and analyze their properties. In the next section we discuss their use during the search process.

The lower and upper bounds on hypothesis D_I are closely related to the relative likelihood measure $L(D_I, M^+)$ defined in Chapter 4. For the reader's convenience, the equations related to this measure (Equations 4.18a,b,c,d) are cited and renumbered below:

$$L(D_I, M^+) = L_1(D_I, M^+) \, L_2(D_I, M^+) \, L_3(D_I, M^+) \tag{5.1a}$$

where

$$L_1(D_I, M^+) = \prod_{m_j \in M^+} P(m_j|D_I) = \prod_{m_j \in M^+} \left[1 - \prod_{d_i \in D_I} (1 - c_{ij}) \right] \tag{5.1b}$$

$$L_2(D_I, M^+) = \prod_{m_l \in M - M^+} P(\overline{m_l}|D_I) = \prod_{d_i \in D_I} \prod_{m_l \in effects(d_i) - M_+} (1 - c_{il}), \tag{5.1c}$$

$$L_3(D_I, M^+) = \prod_{d_i \in D_I} \frac{p_i}{(1 - p_i)}. \tag{5.1d}$$

Note here that, by Equation 5.1c, for a closed problem, all manifestations not in M^+ are assumed to be absent. Also note that both L_2 and L_3 are products over d_i in D_I, so they can be combined into a single product over D_I. For brevity, let

$$\alpha_i = L_2(\{d_i\}, M^+) \, L_3(\{d_i\}, M^+) = \left[\prod_{m_l \in effects(d_i) - M^+} (1 - c_{il}) \right] \frac{p_i}{1 - p_i}$$

for all $d_i \in D_I$. Then $L_2(D_I, M^+) \, L_3(D_I, M^+) = \prod_{d_i \in D_I} \alpha_i$, and thus Equation 5.1a can be rewritten as

$$L(D_I, M^+) = L_1(D_I, M^+) \prod_{d_i \in D_I} \alpha_i. \tag{5.2}$$

Equation 5.2 is a convenient form of Equation 5.1 for the forthcoming derivation. Note that for many if not most real-world diagnostic problems, $\alpha_i < 1$ because the prior probabilities of disorders are usually very small and each product $\prod_{m_l \in effects(d_i) - M^+} (1 - c_{il})$ is less than 1. Also remember that if D_I is not a cover of M^+, then $L(D_I, M^+) = 0$ because $L_2(D_I, M^+) = 0$ and thus it cannot be in the solution.

Now the lower and upper bounds on hypothesis D_I are derived. First, consider the lower bound on D_I. Let $D_J \supseteq D_I$ be the most probable hypothesis among all supersets of D_I, i.e., $L(D_J, M^+) \geq L(D_K, M^+)$ for all $D_K \supseteq D_I$. Then, we have $L(D_J, M^+) \geq L(D_I, M^+)$. Thus, $L(D_I, M^+)$ can be chosen as the lower bound for $L(D_J, M^+)$ regardless whether or not we know the exact identity of D_J.

Now consider the upper bound on D_I, i.e., the upper bound of $L(D_J, M^+)$, denoted as $UB(D_I, M^+)$. Since D_J is the most probable hypothesis among all supersets of D_I, the upper bound of $L(D_J, M^+)$ is the upper bound of $L(D_K, M^+)$ for all $D_K \supseteq D_I$. Since $L_1(D_K, M^+) \leq 1$ for all such D_K, then by Equation 5.2, for any $D_K \supseteq D_I$

$$L(D_K, M^+) \leq \prod_{d_j \in D_K} \alpha_j = \prod_{d_i \in D_I} \alpha_i \prod_{d_k \in D_K - D_I} \alpha_k \leq \prod_{d_i \in D_I} \alpha_i \prod_{\substack{d_k \in D - D_I \\ \alpha_k > 1}} \alpha_k.$$

Thus we define

$$UB(D_I, M^+) = \prod_{d_i \in D_I} \alpha_i \prod_{\substack{d_k \in D - D_I \\ \alpha_k > 1}} \alpha_k. \tag{5.3a}$$

In cases where $\alpha_k \leq 1$ for all $d_k \in D$ (which is common for many diagnostic applications), the second factor becomes one and can be dropped from the equation. In these situations, we have

$$UB(D_I, M^+) = \prod_{d_i \in D_I} \alpha_i. \tag{5.3b}$$

One important property of function $UB(D_I, M^+)$ is that it is monotonically non–increasing when D_I is enlarged by including more disorders. This is given in the following lemma.

lemma 5.1: For any $D_K \supset D_I$, $UB(D_K, M^+) \leq UB(D_I, M^+)$. Moreover, if $\alpha_i < 1$ for all $d_i \in D$, then $UB(D_K, M^+) < UB(D_I, M^+)$.

For brevity, in the text that follows the two quantities $L(D_I, M^+)$ and $UB(D_I, M^+)$ associated with hypothesis D_I are sometimes referred to as the *L value* and *UB value* of D_I, respectively. From the above derivation, they are indeed the lower and upper bounds on D_I as intended. This is formally stated in the following lemma.

lemma 5.2: Let $D_J \supseteq D_I$ be the most probable hypothesis among all supersets of D_I. Then

$$L(D_I, M^+) \leq L(D_J, M^+) \leq UB(D_I, M^+).$$

Figure 5.1 below gives an example of a very simple diagnostic problem. This problem has six disorders d_1 through d_6 and five manifestations m_1 through m_5 (real–world problems are generally much larger). The prior probabilities p_i are shown below each $d_i \in D$ and causal strengths c_{ij} are shown adjacent to each causal link $<d_i, m_j> \in C$. $M^+ = \{m_1, m_3, m_4\}$ is the set of all present manifestations. This example problem will be used through the rest of this chapter for illustrative purposes along with the development of problem–solving algorithms.

example: Using the probabilities in Figure 5.1, for $M^+ = \{m_1, m_3, m_4\}$, we have

$$\alpha_1 = 0.00404, \quad \alpha_2 = 0.088889, \quad \alpha_3 = 0.175,$$
$$\alpha_4 = 0.015, \quad \alpha_5 = 0.010526, \quad \alpha_6 = 0.004082.$$

The relative likelihood of hypothesis $\{d_2, d_3\}$ is computed as

$$L(\{d_2, d_3\}, M^+) = L_1(\{d_2, d_3\}, M^+) \, \alpha_2 \, \alpha_3$$
$$= (1 - (1 - 0.9)(1 - 0)) \, (1 - (1 - 0)(1 - 0.5))$$
$$(1 - (1 - 0.3)(1 - 0.8)) \cdot 0.088889 \cdot 0.175$$
$$= 0.00602.$$

The relative likelihood of $\{d_1, d_4\}$ (which is not a cover of M^+) is zero because

$$L_1(\{d_1, d_4\}, M^+)$$
$$= (1 - (1 - 0.2)(1 - 0)) \, (1 - (1 - 0.8)(1 - 0.2)) \, (1 - (1 - 0)(1 - 0))$$
$$= 0.$$

The upper bounds of relative likelihood of all supersets of these two hypotheses are

$$UB(\{d_2, d_3\}, M^+) = \alpha_2 \, \alpha_3 = 0.088889 \cdot 0.175 = 0.01556,$$

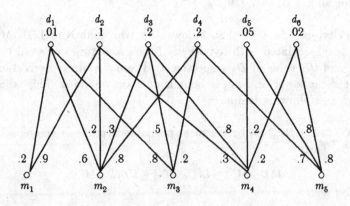

Figure 5.1. A abstract diagnostic problem in the probabilistic causal model.

$$UB(\{d_1, d_4\}, M^+) = \alpha_1 \, \alpha_4 = 0.00404 \cdot 0.015 = 0.0000606.$$

Since $UB(\{d_1, d_4\}, M^+) < L(\{d_2, d_3\}, M^+)$, hypothesis $\{d_1, d_4\}$ and all of its supersets can be discarded as far as a search for a most probable hypothesis is concerned because none of these sets of disorders will be more probable than hypothesis $\{d_2, d_3\}$. □

5.1.2. An Algorithm for Closed Problems

A best–first heuristic search process for the most probable hypothesis is now formulated, culminating in algorithm *SEARCH* which will be presented shortly. Before going into the details of this algorithm and establishing its correctness, we first describe two routines it uses, namely *Expand* and *Update*, and discuss the underlying ideas in an informal fashion. While reading this subsection, the reader is suggested to look ahead to Figure 5.2, where a portion of the search process for solving the problem illustrated in Figure 5.1 is given. Rows 2 and 3 of Table 5.1 provide the L and UB values of relevant hypotheses.

The function *Expand* below expands a selected hypothesis D_I during the search process. When D_I is not a cover of M^+, the expansion is based on an arbitrarily selected manifestation $m_j \in M^+$ not covered by D_I. Function *Expand* returns a set of new hypotheses where each possible cause d_k of m_j has been added into D_I to form a new hypothesis (note that a new hypothesis $D_I \cup \{d_k\}$ thus covers more of M^+ than D_I does). On the other hand, if D_I is a cover of M^+, then it is expanded in such a way that each disorder not in D_I is added into D_I to form a new hypothesis. The reason for separating the two cases is to reduce the total number of non–cover hypotheses generated ($causes(m_j)$ is usually a small subset of $D - D_I$). For example, although the diagnostic problem given in Figure 5.1 has a total of 22 non–cover hypotheses, it will be seen in a later example that we will only generate five of them (including the initial hypothesis $\emptyset$) before the most probable hypothesis is identified.

```
1. function Expand(D_I)
2.      variable d_k disorder, m_j manifestation;
3.      begin
4.          if D_I is not a cover of M^+
5.          then return { D_I ∪ { d_k } | d_k ∈ causes(m_j)
                        for an arbitrary m_j ∈ M^+ − effects(D_I)}
6.          else return { D_I ∪ { d_k } | d_k ∈ D − D_I}
7.      end.
```

example: As Figure 5.2 shows, the initial hypothesis $\emptyset$ is a non–cover since $M^+ \neq \emptyset$. Manifestation m_3 is arbitrarily selected from M^+ for expanding $\emptyset$. Since by Figure 5.1 manifestation m_3 has three causes, d_1, d_3, and d_4, three new hypotheses are generated. On the other hand, the expansion of cover $\{d_2, d_3\}$ (at the bottom of Figure 5.2) generates four new hypotheses because there are 4 disorders not in this hypothesis (i.e., d_1, d_4, d_5, and d_6).   □

During problem–solving, algorithm *SEARCH* maintains two sets: *Frontier* and *Candidates*. *Frontier* is the set containing all hypotheses which have been generated but not expanded yet (may contain covers as well as non-covers of M^+). *Frontier* contains only the initial hypothesis $\emptyset$ at the beginning of problem–solving, i.e., it is initialized to be $\{\emptyset\}$. *Candidates* is the set of all hypotheses which are both *covers* of M^+ and have been *expanded* already. *Candidates* is initialized to be empty. It will be seen later that the most probable hypothesis, i.e., the desired solution, is chosen from hypotheses in the set *Candidates*. Thus, at any moment during the search process, any cover D_I of M^+ that already has been generated by previous expansions must either be in *Frontier* or *Candidates*.

When the function *Expand* is called to expand some hypothesis D_I in *Frontier*, sets *Frontier* and *Candidates* are then changed accordingly. The procedure *Update* uses function *Expand* to expand a selected hypothesis D_I chosen from *Frontier*, and updates *Frontier* and *Candidates* as follows.

```
1. procedure Update(D_I)
2.      variable S set of hypotheses;
3.      begin
4.          S := Expand(D_I);
5.          Frontier := Frontier − {D_I};
6.          if D_I is a cover of M^+ then Candidates := Candidates ∪ {D_I};
7.          for each D_J ∈ S and D_J ∉ Frontier ∪ Candidates do
8.              Frontier := Frontier ∪ {D_J};
9.          endfor
10.     end.
```

Since D_I is expanded at line 4, it is removed from *Frontier* at line 5. If D_I is a cover of M^+, it is added into *Candidates* at line 6. For each newly generated hypothesis $D_J \in Expand(D_I)$, if it is neither in *Frontier* nor *Candidates*, then it is added into *Frontier* at line 8. Thus, after *Update*(D_I) is called, *Frontier* continues to contain all hypotheses generated but not expanded, while *Candidates* continues to be the set of all covers already expanded.

We now turn to algorithm *SEARCH* itself, shown below. Starting with *Frontier* $= \{\emptyset\}$ and *Candidates* $= \emptyset$, the algorithm always selects hypothesis $D_I \in$ *Frontier* with the largest *UB* value (line 7) to expand next (line 8). A new expansion generally reduces the largest *UB* value in the current *Frontier* since *UB* is monotonically non–increasing during the expansion process (see Lemma 5.1). Thus, expanding D_I generally narrows the focus of the search.

```
1. procedure SEARCH(D,M,C, M⁺)
2.      variable D_I hypothesis, Frontier Candidates set of hypotheses,
        upper real;
3.      begin
4.          Frontier := { ∅ };
5.          Candidates := ∅ ;
6.          while Frontier ≠ ∅ do        {* search part of the space 2^D *}
7.              select D_I from Frontier with the largest UB value;
8.              Update(D_I);                {* hypothesis generation *}
9.              if Frontier = ∅ then upper := 0
10.                 else upper := max{ UB(D_K, M⁺) | D_K ∈ Frontier};
11.             S := { D_J ∈ Candidates | L(D_J, M⁺) > upper and
                           L(D_J, M⁺) ≥ L(D_K, M⁺) for all D_K ∈ Candidates};
12.             if S ≠ ∅
13.                 then return S          {* a solution is found and returned *}
14.         endwhile
15.     end.
```

After each hypothesis expansion, some covers of M^+ have been generated, and these are stored either in *Frontier* or in *Candidates*. However, some other covers have not been generated yet. A very important property of this search process, which will be formally stated in Lemma 5.5, is that for any such ungenerated cover D_J, there is a D_I in *Frontier* such that $D_J \supset D_I$, so D_J could still be generated through one or more expansions starting with D_I. In this sense, the set of all hypotheses in *Frontier* implicitly represents all ungenerated covers of M^+. Then, from the definition of upper–bound UB and Lemma 5.2, the largest UB value among all hypotheses in *Frontier* (line 10) is an upper bound on the relative likelihoods of all covers not in *Candidates* (either explicitly in *Frontier* or supersets of those in *Frontier*). If this upper bound is less than the L value of any hypothesis in *Candidates*, then $S \neq \emptyset$ (line 12), and the search process stops because it is now certain that some hypothesis in *Candidates* is more probable than each and every hypothesis represented by *Frontier*. At this point the hypothesis in *Candidates* with the largest L value is identified to be the overall most probable one, and returned as the problem solution (line 13).

In some rare situations, after algorithm *SEARCH* has been executed for a period of time, the following scenario may occur: *Frontier* contains only one hypothesis D_I, all $D_J \in Expand(D_I)$ are covers of M^+ and have already been expanded (and thus they are all in *Candidates*), and $UB(D_I, M^+)$ is greater than the L values of all covers in *Candidates*. In this situation, the solution set S formed at line 11 is empty, so the process must continue. After D_I is selected for expansion at line 7, since all of its immediate descendents are already in *Candidates*, procedure *Update* will simply remove D_I from *Frontier* (line 5 of *Update*) without adding any new hypothesis into that set (line 7 of *Update*). Therefore, *Frontier* becomes $\emptyset$ after the execution of *Update*(D_I) (line 8). This is detected by the condition of the **if** statement at line 9, and *upper* is subsequently assigned 0. As shown by Lemma 5.4, all covers of M^+ are now in *Candidates*. Thus, *upper* = 0 will guarantee the correct construction of S at line 11 and then terminate the procedure.

A simple example should clarify the problem–solving strategy adopted by algorithm *SEARCH*. This example applies *SEARCH* to the small problem in Figure 5.1. Figure 5.2 illustrates how a portion of hypothesis space is gradually made explicit, and Table 5.1 gives L and *UB* values of hypotheses generated in the process.

example: In Figure 5.2, after expanding hypotheses $\emptyset$ with respect to m_3, $\{d_3\}$ has the largest *UB* value among all three hypotheses in *Frontier* (Table 5.1), so it is selected for expansion with respect to m_1 which is the only present manifestation not covered by $\{d_3\}$. Since $\{d_3\}$ is not a cover of M^+, it is removed from *Frontier* but not added to *Candidates*. Now *Frontier* has grown to contain 4 hypotheses according to function *Expand*: $\{d_1\}$, $\{d_1,d_3\}$, $\{d_2,d_3\}$, $\{d_4\}$. Among them, $\{d_2,d_3\}$ has the largest *UB* value and is a cover of M^+. It is then expanded and moved from *Frontier* to *Candidates*, and its four descendants are added to *Frontier*. Next, $\{d_4\}$ is selected and expanded against m_1, resulting in *Frontier* = $\{\{d_1\}$, $\{d_1,d_3\}$,

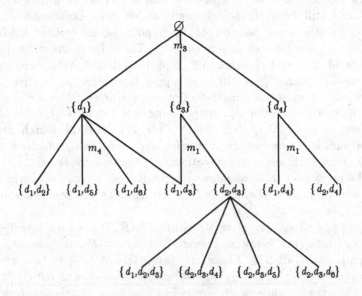

Figure 5.2. A portion of space 2^D generated by algorithm *SEARCH*. The sequence of hypotheses expanded: $\emptyset$, $\{d_3\}$, $\{d_2,d_3\}$, $\{d_4\}$, $\{d_1\}$, $\cdots$

Table 5.1. Important values associated with each generated hypothesis

D_I	$\varnothing$	$\{d_1\}$	$\{d_3\}$	$\{d_4\}$	$\{d_1,d_3\}$	$\{d_2,d_3\}$
$UB(D_I, M^+)$	1	.00404	.175	.015	.0007071	.0155556
$L(D_I, M^+)$	0	0	0	0	.0001018	.00602
$le(D_I, M^+)$	.32299	.0012835	.0220405	.0045515	.0000858	.0005294

D_I	$\{d_1,d_2,d_3\}$	$\{d_2,d_3,d_4\}$	$\{d_2,d_3,d_5\}$	$\{d_2,d_3,d_6\}$	$\{d_1,d_4\}$
$UB(D_I, M^+)$	.0000629	.0002333	.0001637	.0000635	.0000606
$L(D_I, M^+)$	0	0	0	0	.0001018
$le(D_I, M^+)$	.0000019	.0000044	.0000038	.0000019	.0000181

D_I	$\{d_2,d_4\}$	$\{d_1,d_2\}$	$\{d_1,d_5\}$	$\{d_1,d_6\}$
$UB(D_I, M^+)$	.0013333	.0003591	.0000425	.0000165
$L(D_I, M^+)$	.000072	.0000793	.0000014	.0000005
$le(D_I, M^+)$	.0002627	.0000755	.0000129	.0000052

$\{d_1,d_2,d_3\}$, $\{d_2,d_3,d_4\}$, $\{d_2,d_3,d_5\}$, $\{d_2,d_3,d_6\}$, $\{d_1,d_4\}$, $\{d_2,d_4\}\}$, and $Candidates = \{\{d_2,d_3\}\}$. Note again that since $\{d_4\}$ is not a cover of M^+, it is not added into $Candidates$. Now, $L(\{d_2,d_3\}, M^+) = 0.00602$ is found to be greater than the UB values of all hypotheses in $Frontier$ (see Table 5.1), and thus $\{d_2,d_3\}$ is identified to be the most probable hypothesis for the given M^+ so algorithm $SEARCH$ stops.

For the small knowledge base used in the above example (Figure 5.1), there are a total of $2^6 = 64$ potential hypotheses, among which 42 are covers and 22 are non–covers. When the most probable hypothesis is identified as illustrated above, 12 sets of disorders are generated among which 5 are non–covers and 7 are covers.   □

Next we discuss some important issues concerning the efficiency of algorithm $SEARCH$. During the search process, every newly generated hypothesis is added into $Frontier$ unless it has already been generated before (see procedure $Update$), and every expanded hypothesis is added into $Candidates$ if it is a cover of M^+. This guarantees that no cover of M^+ will be thrown away during the search process, as shown by Lemmas 5.4 and 5.5, and thus can subsequently be identified should the need arise. The main reason to do this is to establish a general problem–solving framework so that problem–solving algorithms in subsequent sections (Sections 5.2 and 5.3) can easily be developed. Such generality, however, may cause severe efficiency problems, especially when the hypothesis space of the diagnostic problem at hand is large (large number of possible disorders). *Candidates* and especially *Frontier* will grow very rapidly so that their sizes may become practically unmanageable.

If the task of problem–solving is simply to find the most probable cover(s) with the highest likelihood (L value), then efficiency can be greatly improved by slightly modifying the above algorithms. For example, we can allow *Candidates* to contain only the expanded hypothesis(es) with the highest L value known so far. Thus, the size of *Candidates* will be reduced to one or a few hypotheses, and operations involving *Candidates* will become much faster. More importantly, the size of *Frontier* can also be controlled. This can be done as follows. First, conduct a preliminary depth–first or other heuristic (not necessarily admissible) search to identify a cover D_I for the given M^+, and then initialize *Candidates* to be $\{D_I\}$, instead of $\varnothing$, before the search starts. The search process itself goes on in the same way as before except that any newly generated hypothesis D_J resulting from calling *Expand* will not be added into *Frontier* unless $UB(D_J)$ is equal to or greater than the L value of covers in the current *Candidates*. All other newly generated hypotheses will simply be discarded because they and all hypotheses that can be generated from them (i.e., their supersets) are guaranteed to have smaller L values than the ones in the current *Candidates*. This hypothesis pruning technique is very common in AI branch–and–bound search. Moreover, since the initial cover in *Candidates* excludes every newly generated hypothesis with smaller L value from entering *Frontier* at a very early stage of the search, the space actually being searched is much more significantly narrowed. This is because a hypothesis generated at an earlier stage (thus containing fewer disorders) is usually associated with a larger number of supersets.

The modifications to algorithms *SEARCH* and *Update* outlined above could bring very significant savings in computation if the problem size is large. For example, in an experimental run of algorithm *SEARCH* over a problem with 48 disorders and four present manifestations, the *Frontier* set grew to exceed 20,000 hypotheses before a cover was found. However, when *Candidates* was initialized to be $\{D_I\}$, where D_I was a cover found by a depth–first search, and the pruning technique was adopted in *Update*, the maximum size of *Frontier* was drastically reduced to about a hundred hypotheses!

5.1.3. Correctness of Algorithm *SEARCH*

Before the formal statement of the correctness of algorithm *SEARCH* is given, some useful lemmas are established. Lemma 5.3 first gives an important property of function *Expand*.

lemma 5.3: Let $D_J \supset D_I$ be a cover of M^+ in a diagnostic problem. Then there is a $D_K \in Expand(D_I)$ such that $D_J \supseteq D_K$.

An immediate consequence of Lemma 5.3 is that any proper superset of D_I which covers M^+ can be generated by successive expansions starting with D_I. Therefore, *any* cover of M^+ can be generated by a series of successive expansions starting with hypothesis $\emptyset$, the only hypothesis contained in *Frontier* when algorithm *SEARCH* begins problem–solving. Next, we prove that procedure *Update* correctly updates *Frontier* and *Candidates*.

lemma 5.4 [Correctness of *Update*]: If at line 8 of algorithm *SEARCH* the following statements
(1) *Frontier* is the set of all hypotheses which have been generated but not yet expanded;
(2) *Candidates* is the set of all covers which have been expanded
are true before the execution of *Update*(D_I) where $D_I \in$ *Frontier*, then they are also true after the execution of *Update*(D_I). In other words, *Update*(D_I) preserves the truth of the above statements.

Having established that procedure *Update* correctly updates *Frontier* and *Candidates*, we now prove an important property concerning unknown hypotheses during the execution of algorithm *SEARCH*.

lemma 5.5: At the beginning of each pass through the **while**–loop (line 6) in algorithm *SEARCH*, for any *cover* D_R of M^+ which has not been generated by previous hypothesis expansions (i.e., for any cover $D_R \notin$ (*Frontier* $\cup$ *Candidates*)), there exists some $D_S \in$ *Frontier* such that $D_R \supset D_S$.

By Lemma 5.5, as mentioned earlier, all covers of M^+ which are not in *Candidates* are explicitly or implicitly represented by *Frontier* either as its members or as proper supersets of its members. Combining this with Lemma 5.2, the following result immediately holds.

corollary 5.6: Following each execution of *Update* at line 8 of algorithm *SEARCH*, if $L(D_I, M^+) \geq \max\{ UB(D_K, M^+) | D_K \in$ *Frontier*$\}$ for a given cover D_I of M^+, then $L(D_I, M^+) \geq L(D_J, M^+)$ for any D_J which is either in *Frontier* or has not been generated yet.

If a D_I with $L(D_I, M^+) \geq \max\{ UB(D_K, M^+) | D_K \in$ *Frontier*$\}$, as in Corollary 5.6, happens to be the most probable one (largest L value) in *Candidates*, then it is the most probable hypothesis of all and is a member of the solution set for the problem. This is why *SEARCH* stops when all of such D_I are found (lines 1 and 12). Corollary 5.6 thus leads to the proof of the correctness of algorithm *SEARCH*.

theorem 5.7 [Correctness of *SEARCH*]: For any diagnostic problem $P = <D,M,C, M^+>$, *SEARCH*(D,M,C, M^+) will terminate and return a solution of problem P.

As illustrated by earlier examples and as shown by the above lemmas and theorems, $SEARCH$ will find the most probable hypothesis(es) as the solution for the given problem and then stop. However, if instead of stopping at this point we remove the identified most probable hypothesis from $Candidates$, the search process can be resumed to identify the second most probable hypothesis in the same way as before. Thus, the same search process could be used as a supplier of probable hypotheses: upon request, it can successively provide the first, second, third, etc. most likely hypotheses. This feature of the best–first search process may have certain uses in real–world diagnostic applications. One such use will be addressed in Section 5.3.

5.2. Open Problem–Solving

Most diagnostic problems in the real–world are not closed, i.e., the presence/absence of all manifestations is not known *a priori*. Instead, as discussed in Chapter 1, some of these manifestations are "discovered" to be present or absent during the diagnostic process through the test part (questioning–answering) of the hypothesize–and–test cycle [Pople82] [Josephson82,84] [Elstein78] [Kassirer78] [Rubin75]. In this section algorithm $SEARCH$ is extended to capture this well–recognized sequential nature of the diagnostic process. Like sequential problem–solving methods presented in Chapter 3, external function calls for more information about the unknown manifestations (functions like *Moremanifs* and *Nextman* of algorithm *BIPARTITE* in Chapter 3) must be provided.

5.2.1. Formulation

In closed problem–solving as presented in the preceding section, a manifestation is either present (in M^+) or absent (not in M^+). However, in most real world applications, when the diagnostic process is completed some manifestations are known to be present, some others are known to be absent, and the presence/absence of still others is unknown (e.g., their presence was not checked because they are not relevant to the hypothesized diagnoses, or testing for them was too costly or risky relative to their diagnostic merit). Therefore, M, the set of all manifestations, is actually partitioned into three disjoint subsets in open problems: present ones, absent ones, and unknown ones. Consequently, all absent manifestations should be explicitly represented in the problem specification, not just assumed to be $M - M^+$. Also note that this partition is not fixed; instead, it changes during the problem–solving process. Initially, all manifestations are unknown. Then the set of known present manifestations and the set of known absent manifestations are gradually enlarged upon receiving answers about the presence/absence of selected manifestations.

Recall that in Chapter 4, we took M^+ to represent the joint event that all manifestations m_j in M^+ are present and all other manifestations m_l (i.e., those in $M - M^+$) are absent. That is, $M^+ \leftrightarrow \underset{m_j \in M^+}{\wedge} m_j \quad \underset{m_l \in M - M^+}{\wedge} \overline{m_l}$.

Now, to capture the sequential and open nature of problem–solving, we interpret our notation somewhat differently as follows. Let M^+ denote the set of all present manifestations $\{m_1, m_2, \ldots, m_k\}$ known so far, and M^- denote the set of all absent manifestations $\{m_{k+1}, m_{k+2}, \ldots, m_n\}$ known so far. Then $M^+ \cap M^- = \varnothing$, and $M^i = M - (M^+ \cup M^-)$ denotes the set of manifestations whose presence or absence is unknown. In other words, M^+ represents the event that all manifestations in M^+ are present but says nothing about other manifestations $(M^+ \leftrightarrow \underset{m_j \in M^+}{\wedge} m_j)$, and M^- represents the event that all manifestations in M^- are absent but says nothing about other manifestations $(M^- \leftrightarrow \underset{m_l \in M^-}{\wedge} \overline{m_l})$. The set notation $D_I \subseteq D$ still represents the event that all disorders in D_I are present and all other disorders are absent $(D_I \leftrightarrow \underset{d_i \in D_I}{\wedge} d_i \underset{d_k \in D - D_I}{\wedge} \overline{d_k})$.

Fortunately, this extended problem formulation does not cause any difficulty, because the appropriate probabilistic formulas needed for open problem–solving were already derived in Chapter 4. Algorithm *SEARCH* for closed problem–solving is primarily based on Equations 5.1a to d. These formulas were actually consequents of a more general equation, namely Equation 4.16, which is reproduced and renumbered below.

$$P(m_1 \wedge m_2 \wedge \cdots \wedge m_k \wedge \overline{m_{k+1}} \wedge \cdots \wedge \overline{m_n} \mid D_I)$$

$$= \prod_{j=1}^{k} P(m_j \mid D_I) \prod_{l=k+1}^{n} P(\overline{m_l} \mid D_I)$$

$$= \prod_{j=1}^{k} \left(1 - \prod_{i=1}^{r} (1 - c_{ij})\right) \prod_{l=k+1}^{n} \prod_{i=1}^{r} (1 - c_{il}) \tag{5.4}$$

where $m_1, m_2, \ldots, m_k, m_{k+1}, \ldots, m_n$ are n distinct manifestations in M, and $D_I = \{d_1, d_2, \ldots, d_r\} \subseteq D$.

Recalling Lemma 4.8 of Chapter 4, for an absent manifestation $\overline{m_j}$, $P(\overline{m_j} \mid D_I) = 1$ if $m_j \notin effects(D_I)$. Thus by Equation 5.4,

$$P(M^+ \wedge M^- \mid D_I)$$

$$= \prod_{m_j \in M^+} \left(1 - \prod_{d_i \in D_I} (1 - c_{ij})\right) \prod_{d_i \in D_I} \prod_{m_l \in M^- \cap effects(d_i)} (1 - c_{il}). \tag{5.5}$$

The relative likelihood of $D_I \subseteq D$ given M^+ and M^- can conveniently be defined by the following equations:

$$L(D_I, M^+, M^-) = L_1(D_I, M^+, M^-) L_2(D_I, M^+, M^-) L_3(D_I, M^+, M^-) \quad (5.6a)$$

where

$$L_1(D_I, M^+, M^-) = \prod_{m_j \in M^+} \left(1 - \prod_{d_i \in D_I} (1 - c_{ij}) \right), \quad (5.6b)$$

$$L_2(D_I, M^+, M^-) = \prod_{d_i \in D_I} \prod_{m_l \in M^- \cap effects(d_i)} (1 - c_{il}), \quad (5.6c)$$

$$L_3(D_I, M^+, M^-) = \prod_{d_i \in D_I} \frac{p_i}{1 - p_i}. \quad (5.6d)$$

Similar to Equation 5.3, for any given hypothesis D_I, the upper bound UB on L values of all of D_I's supersets D_J can be defined as

$$UB(D_I, M^+, M^-) = \prod_{d_i \in D_I} \alpha_i \prod_{\substack{d_k \in D - D_I \\ \alpha_k > 1}} \alpha_k \quad (5.7)$$

where

$$\alpha_i = L_2(\{d_i\}, M^+, M^-) L_3(\{d_i\}, M^+, M^-)$$

$$= \left[\prod_{m_l \in M^- \cap effects(d_i)} (1 - c_{il}) \right] \frac{p_i}{1 - p_i}.$$

Note that the only difference between Equations 5.6 and 5.1, and between Equations 5.7 and 5.3 is that all absent manifestations $\overline{m_l}$ are explicitly given in M^-, and are not assumed to be in $M - M^+$.

The solution to an open problem is then defined to be the set of disorders $D_I \subseteq D$ which has the highest relative likelihood by Equations 5.6 when no further information about any remaining unknown manifestations is available.

5.2.2. Algorithm and Correctness

Based on the above extended problem formulation, a problem–solving algorithm for open problems is given below which is similar to its closed counterpart. The correctness of the algorithm is only informally justified without a detailed proof.

Algorithms *Expand* and *Update* used in *SEARCH* stay the same except they now work on the current M^+ and M^-, and the calculations of L and UB values are based on Equations 5.6 and 5.7. Some modifications must be made to algorithm *SEARCH* so that information about additional manifestations being either present or absent can be handled. As new entities are added to M^+ and M^- during the diagnostic process, say by receiving answers to questions like "Is manifestation m_j present?", the bounds (L and UB values) of all hypotheses in *Frontier* and in *Candidates* must be modified based on newly established m_j or $\overline{m_j}$ (see Equations 5.6 and 5.7). Moreover, if m_j is now given to be present, some hypotheses in *Candidates* may not cover the new manifestation m_j, and thus they should be removed from *Candidates* (remember that any hypothesis in *Candidates* must be a cover of the current M^+). Algorithm *Modify*, given below, does the appropriate revision. It enlarges M^+ or M^-, depending on whether m_j or $\overline{m_j}$ is established, respectively, and modifies *Candidates* accordingly. Note that the change of M^+ and M^- by *Modify* requires that L and UB values of hypotheses in *Frontier* and *Candidates* be revised, although it is not explicitly specified in the procedure.

1. **procedure** *Modify*(x)
2.   **variable** m_j **manifestation**;
3.   **begin**
4.   **if** $x = \overline{m_j}$ **then** $M^- := M^- \cup \{m_j\}$ {* m_j now known to be absent *}
5.   **else begin**   {* m_j now known to be present *}
6. $M^+ := M^+ \cup \{m_j\}$;
7.   **for** $D_I \in$ *Candidates* **and** $m_j \notin effects(D_I)$
                    do *Candidates* := *Candidates* $- \{D_I\}$ **endfor**
8.   **endif**
9.   **end.**

A new search algorithm for open problem–solving, *SEARCH-OPEN*, can now be presented. This algorithm calls external functions *Moreanswers* and *Newanswer* to obtain information about the presence/absence of an additional manifestation, and incorporates the revision of *Candidates* (and implicitly L and UB values of all hypotheses in *Frontier* and *Candidates*) by procedure *Modify* into the heuristic search process described in algorithm *SEARCH* in the last section.

1. **procedure** *SEARCH-OPEN*(D,M,C)
2.   **variable** D_I **hypothesis**, *Frontier Candidates* **set of hypotheses**,
            M^+ M^- **sets of manifestations**, *upper* **real**;
3.   **begin**
4.   *Frontier* := $\{\emptyset\}$;
5.   *Candidates* := $\emptyset$;
6. $M^+ := \emptyset$;
7. $M^- := \emptyset$;
8.   **while** *Frontier* $\neq \emptyset$ **do**   {* search part of the space 2^D *}
9.   **while** *Moreanswers* **do**   {* receiving new clues *}
10.   *Modify*(*Newanswer*)
11.   **endwhile**;
12.   select $D_I \in$ *Frontier* with the largest UB value;
13.   *Update*(D_I);   {* hypothesis generation *}
14.   **if** *Frontier* = $\emptyset$ **then** *upper* := 0
15.   **else** *upper* := max$\{UB(D_K, M^+, M^-) | D_K \in$ *Frontier*$\}$;

16. $S := \{ D_J \in Candidates \mid L(D_J, M^+, M^-) > upper$ and
             $L(D_J, M^+, M^-) \geq L(D_K, M^+, M^-)$ for all $D_K \in Candidates \}$;
17.   **if** $S \neq \emptyset$ **and not** *Moreanswers*
18.   **then return** S {* a solution is found and returned *}
19.   **endwhile**
20.   **end**.

Similar to functions *Moremanifs* and *Nextman* in algorithm *BIPARTITE*, procedure *SEARCH-OPEN* also employs two external functions, namely *Moreanswers* and *Newanswer*, to interact with the user. These functions are application–specific, and thus are not specified here. The boolean function *Moreanswers* is true if some unknown manifestation m_j (in $M' = M - (M^+ \cup M^-)$) can be confirmed to be present/absent. Then the function *Newanswer* returns either m_j or $\overline{m_j}$ as is appropriate. In general, information about new manifestations might be obtained at various times during problem–solving, depending on the details of the implementation of the "question generation" process. For instance, inquiry about new manifestations might be made after each hypothesis expansion, or after a most probable hypothesis for the current M^+ is identified, or at some appropriate time based on the analysis of hypotheses in *Candidates* and *Frontier*, etc. In the algorithm *SEARCH-OPEN*, we arbitrarily choose to do this at the beginning of its execution and after each hypothesis expansion. The procedure *Modify* at line 9 will revise M^+ or M^-, and *Candidates* as well.

The outer **while** loop (lines 8 to 19) of *SEARCH-OPEN* will not stop until S becomes non–empty (i.e., the most probable cover(s) of the current M^+ has been found) and "*Moreanswers* = false" (i.e., no further information about M' is available). Since the presence of further manifestations can neither be confirmed nor denied, hypotheses in S are the most probable covers of the final M^+ and are returned as the problem solution.

Both M^+ and M^- are initialized to $\emptyset$ (lines 6 and 7), indicating the beginning of the hypothesize–and–test process. The inner **while** loop (lines 9 to 11) allows answers of one or more manifestations to be obtained. The revision of M^+, M^- and *Candidates* at line 10 of *SEARCH-OPEN* guarantees that, as with *SEARCH* for closed problems, all covers of the current M^+ are either in *Frontier* $\cup$ *Candidates*, or are proper supersets of some members of *Frontier*.

theorem 5.8 [Correctness of *Modify*]: During the execution of *SEARCH-OPEN*, if the statement "all covers of the current M^+ are either in *Frontier* $\cup$ *Candidates* or are proper supersets of some members of *Frontier*" is true before the execution of *Modify* at line 10, it will still be true after its execution.

By Theorem 5.8, as with the closed problem–solving algorithm, all covers of the current M^+ are represented either explicitly or implicitly by *Frontier* and *Candidates* during the evolution of M^+ and M^-. Analogous to the proofs of Lemmas 5.3 through 5.7, the correctness of *SEARCH-OPEN* can be established in the context of evolving M^+ and M^-. The major advantage of *SEARCH-OPEN* over its closed counterpart *SEARCH* is that its sequential nature more closely mimics the repetitive "hypothesize–and–test" process of human diagnosis. However, *SEARCH-OPEN* pays an additional cost in that the L and UB values for existing hypotheses must be recomputed whenever M^+ or M^- is enlarged. This cost may be fairly high when the problem becomes large because the size of *Frontier* is generally of exponential order of the size of M^+.

In summary, based on the formal probabilistic causal model presented in Chapter 4, problem–solving algorithms for closed and open problems have now been given. These best–first search algorithms integrate the use of symbolic and probabilistic knowledge so that problem–solving is more efficient and accurate.

5.3. The Quality of Problem Solutions

In the probabilistic causal model, in order to handle some of the computational difficulties involved, we disregard constants $P(M^+)$ and $\prod_{d_i \in D}(1 - p_i)$ in Bayes' theorem and use the relative likelihood (L value) of a hypothesis as the measure of its plausibility (see Section 4.2.3 and Equations 4.16 and 17 of Chapter 4). Problem–solving strategies based on relative likelihood, as shown in preceding sections, are appropriate if the goal of problem–solving is to identify only the *single most probable* hypothesis(es) with the highest L value. In many real–world diagnostic applications, however, identifying the single most probable hypothesis (or hypotheses if a tie exists) does not really solve the problem. For example, if D_{max} is identified to be the most probable hypothesis of a given case, and it has relative likelihood measure $L(D_I, M^+) = 0.006$, then how comfortable or confident is one in concluding that D_{max} alone is a reasonable solution of the given problem? If the relative likelihood of all other hypotheses is very much smaller than 0.006, then this conclusion is probably acceptable. If, however, there are some other hypotheses with relative likelihood smaller but comparable to 0.006, then D_{max} alone may not be acceptable as a problem solution (its posterior probability may be quite small even though its relative likelihood is the largest). In the latter situation, a human diagnostician might include more than one hypothesis in his conclusion as alternative possibilities, or might pursue the diagnostic process further by asking appropriate questions to disambiguate among the more probable hypotheses.

The relative likelihood of the most probable hypothesis alone does not directly tell us whether we should accept the single most probable hypothesis as the problem solution, or whether we should include more hypotheses, and if so, how many more should be included. That is, it provides us no sense of the "quality" of a problem solution. The main reason for this difficulty is that by using the relative likelihood measure, we lose the measure of the absolute strength or "belief" in a hypothesis for a given case. However, if instead the posterior probability is used, say $P(D_{\max}|M^+) = 0.7$, then we can conclude that $D_{\max}$ is the real cause of M^+ with 0.7 probability. In other words, the quantities $P(M^+)$ and $\prod_{d_i \in D}(1 - p_i)$,

which makes the difference between the posterior probability and our relative likelihood measure, are not merely normalization factors of syntactical use. It carries some information important for assessing the absolute belief of diagnostic hypotheses. Thus, by replacing posterior probability with relative likelihood to measure hypothesis plausibility, we get rid of the problem of the expensive computation of $P(M^+)$, but face a new problem of assessing and controlling the "quality" of a diagnostic problem's solution.

In this section, a diagnostic problem–solving strategy is developed which still avoids the direct computation of $P(D_I|M^+)$, yet also controls the quality of the problem solution. A quantity between 0 and 1, called a *comfort measure* (abbreviated CM), is used to measure the quality of the problem solution. A plausible *solution* is defined to be a *minimum* number of hypotheses such that the sum of their posterior probabilities is guaranteed to *exceed* the given CM value, even if the exact values of these posterior probabilities are not known. The problem–solving strategy derived here is a direct extension of algorithm $SEARCH$ for closed problems (see Section 5.1). The heuristic best–first algorithm $SEARCH$ is able to identify *the* single most likely hypothesis (or hypotheses if a tie exists) in a provably–correct manner. In contrast, the methods presented in this section are oriented towards finding a set of most probable hypotheses (usually with different posterior probabilities) satisfying the given comfort measure.

To do this, techniques are developed to calculate lower and upper bounds of the posterior probabilities $P(D_I|M^+)$ of existing hypotheses D_I as their estimates. These bounds are refined closer to the real $P(D_I|M^+)$ whenever new hypotheses are generated during the search process. These bounds are completely different from the L and UB values of Section 5.1 (see Section 5.1.1). To avoid confusion, the lower and upper bounds of $P(D_I|M^+)$ used here will be called $inf(D_I)$ and $sup(D_I)$, respectively. In other words, we are looking for ways to determine $inf(D_I)$ and $sup(D_I)$ such that $inf(D_I) \leq P(D_I|M^+) \leq sup(D_I)$ for any given D_I, and we want these bounds as tight (i.e, as close to $P(D_I|M^+)$) as possible. As mentioned earlier, the search process in algorithm $SEARCH$ can be extended to successively generate the most likely hypothesis(es), the second most likely, the third most likely, etc., by continuing the process of hypothesis expansion and evaluation. It is the integration of best–first search and the techniques for bounding posterior probabilities that enables us to find a solution satisfying the given *CM* criterion. The example problem given in Figure 5.1 will again be used in this section for illustrative purposes.

5.3.1. Comfort Measure and Estimating Posterior Probabilities

Let a "comfort measure" *CM* be given with $0 < CM \leq 1$, representing how certain we wish to be that a collection of diagnostic hypotheses $\{D_1, D_2, \ldots, D_K\}$ includes the actual set of causative disorders D^+ that are present. For example, $CM = 0.95$ means that we want D^+ to be included in $\{D_1, \ldots, D_k\}$ with a probability of 0.95. Given *CM*, the solution of a diagnostic problem can be defined as follows.

definition 5.1: For a diagnostic problem $P = <D,M,C, M^+>$ and a comfort measure $0 < CM \leq 1$, $Sol(P) = \{D_1, \ldots, D_K\} \subseteq 2^D$ is said to be a *solution* if

(1) $P(D_1 \vee \cdots \vee D_K | M^+) = \sum_{I=1}^{K} P(D_I | M^+) \geq CM$, and

(2) $|Sol(P)|$ is minimum.

The existence of a solution for any diagnostic problem as defined here immediately follows from the facts that D_I in the hypothesis space 2^D form a mutually exclusive and exhaustive set, so $\sum_{D_I \in 2^D} P(D_I | M^+) = 1$, and $0 < CM \leq 1$. Hypothesis D_1 through D_K in the solution are considered to be plausible alternatives for the correct answer, though with possibly different posterior probabilities. Since, as mentioned earlier, hypotheses not covering M^+ have zero relative likelihoods and posterior probabilities, all hypotheses in a solution must be covers of M^+. To satisfy condition 2, i.e., that the size of $Sol(P)$ be as small as possible, we can select the K most probable hypotheses satisfying condition 1. However, even selecting hypotheses in such a way, the solution of a problem may not be unique if more than one hypothesis has the same relative likelihood value. For example, let $Sol(P) = \{D_1, \ldots, D_K\}$ be a solution of a problem, and let D_K have the least posterior probability among all hypotheses in $Sol(P)$. If, however, another hypothesis $D_R \notin Sol(P)$ has the same posterior probability as D_K, then the set $\{D_1, \ldots, D_{K-1}, D_R\}$ is also a solution. In general two or more distinct hypotheses are unlikely to have exactly the same likelihood value, and even if so, the alternative solutions only differ on hypotheses with the lowest likelihood, i.e., on the least significant hypotheses. Therefore, the problem–solving strategy presented here is only concerned with finding *a* solution for a given problem.

Deriving the problem solution according to Definition 5.1 above would appear to require calculation of posterior probabilities, thus leading to prohibitive computations as explained earlier. That this is not the case will be demonstrated with the problem–solving algorithm *SEARCH-CM* presented in the next subsection which, instead of using posterior probabilities, uses their lower and upper bounds (inf and sup values) to determine a solution. Algorithm *SEARCH-CM* is the same as *SEARCH* except that it constructs the solution according to Definition 5.1. Thus, at any moment during the problem–solving process, among all hypotheses in 2^D, some of them will have been generated or made explicit, and others not. Among the explicit hypotheses, some will be covers of M^+ and others will be non-covers (with zero L value). In the context of such a problem–solving strategy, it is now shown that it is possible to estimate effectively the lower and upper bounds of posterior probabilities of individual hypotheses without actually calculating the posterior probabilities involved. This is done by using L values and UB values (see Section 5.1.1 for respective equations) of just those hypotheses already made explicit at any given moment during the problem–solving.

Since all D_I in 2^D are mutually exclusive and exhaustive, $P(M^+)= \sum_{D_J \in 2^D} P(M^+|D_J) P(D_J)$. Then, from Equation 5.1 and by Bayes' theorem, we can represent the posterior probability of D_I given M^+ in terms of relative likelihoods:

$$P(D_I|M^+) = \frac{P(M^+|D_I) P(D_I)}{\sum\limits_{D_J \in 2^D} P(M^+|D_J) P(D_J)} = \frac{L(D_I, M^+) \prod\limits_{d_k \in D} (1 - p_k)}{\sum\limits_{D_J \in 2^D} L(D_J, M^+) \prod\limits_{d_k \in D} (1 - p_k)}$$

$$= \frac{L(D_I, M^+)}{\sum\limits_{D_J \in 2^D} L(D_J, M^+)} = \frac{L(D_I, M^+)}{\sum\limits_{\substack{D_J \in 2^D \\ D_I \text{ covers } M^+}} L(D_J, M^+)} \qquad (5.8)$$

The last equality comes from the fact that $L(D_J, M^+) = 0$ if D_J does not cover M^+, as explained earlier.

Equation 5.8 cannot be used directly in a large problem (one with a large disorder set D) because it requires the generation of all members of 2^D (or at least all covers of M^+) and calculation of their relative likelihood values. However, it can be used to derive lower and upper bounds for $P(D_I|M^+)$ when only some hypotheses have been generated or made explicit.

At any moment during problem–solving, let $L_{known} = \sum L(D_I, M^+)$ for all covers D_I which have been generated so far. Assume somehow we have derived a value $L_{est} \geq \sum L(D_J, M^+)$ for all covers D_J which have not been generated yet. Then we have,

$$L_{known} \leq \sum_{\substack{D_J \in 2^D \\ D_I \text{ covers } M^+}} L(D_J, M^+) \leq L_{known} + L_{est}$$

and thus, from Equation 5.8, we have a lower–bound $inf(D_I)$ and an upper–bound $sup(D_I)$ on $P(D_I|M^+)$ given by

$$inf(D_I) = \frac{L(D_I, M^+)}{L_{known} + L_{est}} \leq P(D_I|M^+) \leq \frac{L(D_I, M^+)}{L_{known}} = sup(D_I). \quad (5.9)$$

It is these bounds, not the true posterior probabilities of hypotheses, that are used during problem–solving to determine if a solution according to Definition 5.1 (i.e., satisfying the given comfort measure) can be formed. Note that by Equation 5.9, if $P(D_I|M^+) \geq P(D_J|M^+)$ then $sup(D_I) \geq sup(D_J)$ and $inf(D_I) \geq inf(D_J)$ for any D_I and D_J because $L(D_I, M^+) \geq L(D_J, M^+)$ while L_{known} and L_{est} are constants at any given time.

The upper–bound $sup(D_I)$ of $P(D_I|M^+)$ is easy to derive because L_{known} can be obtained by accumulating L values of each newly generated cover during the search process. Thus the real problem here is how to define and obtain L_{est}, the estimated upper–bound of the sum of L values of all unknown covers, without actually generating these covers and calculating their L values.

To derive L_{est}, we first develop an upper–bound on the *sum* of L values of all *proper* supersets of an individual D_I, i.e., an upper–bound on $\sum_{D_J \supset D_I} L(D_J, M^+)$. It will be seen later that L_{est} can be defined in terms of these upper–bounds for some already generated hypotheses D_I. Since by Lemma 5.2, $L(D_J, M^+) \leq UB(D_I, M^+)$ for all $D_J \supset D_I$, and since D_I has $2^{|D-D_I|} - 1$ proper supersets,[(*)] one could simply use

$$UB(D_I, M^+) (2^{|D-D_I|} - 1)$$

as an upper bound for $\sum_{D_J \supset D_I} L(D_J, M^+)$. Although easy to compute, this sum is too loose a bound and will lead to much unnecessary computation. A much tighter bound can be derived in which the product of $|D - D_I|$ 2's in the above is replaced by a product of $|D - D_I|$ numbers of slightly larger than 1. By the definition of UB (Equations 5.3), we have the following lemma concerning the relationship of UB values between a hypothesis D_I and its proper superset D_J.

(*) There are a total of $|D - D_I|$ disorders not in D_I. For each $D_J \in 2^{D-D_I}$, except $\varnothing$, $D_I \cup D_J \supset D_I$ and they are the only proper supersets of D_I. Therefore, D_I has a total of $2^{|D-D_I|} - 1$ proper supersets.

lemma 5.9: For any $D_J \supset D_I$,

$$UB(D_J, M^+) \leq UB(D_I, M^+) \prod_{d_k \in D_J - D_I} \alpha_k$$

where the equality holds if $\alpha_k \leq 1$ for all $d_k \in D_J$.

The quantity $\alpha_k = L_2(\{d_k\}, M^+) L_3(\{d_k\}, M^+)$ used here was defined in Section 5.1.1.

Using Lemmas 5.9 and 5.2, the upper bound of the sum of L values of all proper supersets of D_I can be obtained by summing the above equation over all such supersets. This leads to one of the most important results in this section, stated in the next theorem.

theorem 5.10: Let D_I be a cover of M^+. Then

$$\sum_{D_J \supset D_I} L(D_J, M^+) \leq UB(D_I, M^+) \Big[\prod_{d_j \in D - D_I} (1 + \alpha_j) - 1 \Big]. \tag{5.10}$$

For notational convenience, let $l_{est}(D_I, M^+)$ denote the upper bound of the sum of L values of all $D_J \supset D_I$. Then we have

$$l_{est}(D_I, M^+) = UB(D_I, M^+) \Big[\prod_{d_j \in D - D_I} (1 + \alpha_j) - 1 \Big]. \tag{5.11}$$

Note that, as discussed earlier, now this estimate of the upper bound is the multiplication of $UB(D_I, M^+)$ and a product of $|D - D_I|$ numbers each of which is only slightly larger than one because α_j are usually much smaller than one.

example: Again, consider the example problem given in Figure 5.1. Let $D_I = \{d_2, d_3\}$. Then by Equations 5.3b, 5.10 and 5.11,

$$l_{est}(\{d_2, d_3\}, M^+) = \alpha_2 \alpha_3 [(1 + \alpha_1)(1 + \alpha_4)(1 + \alpha_5)(1 + \alpha_6) - 1]$$

$$= 0.0155556 \cdot 0.0340318 = 0.000529$$

$$\geq \sum_{D_J \supset \{d_2, d_3\}} L(D_J, M^+)$$

even though the exact value of $\sum_{D_J \supset \{d_2, d_3\}} L(D_J, M^+)$ is not known.   □

For any given hypothesis D_I, we can now readily compute its relative likelihood $L(D_I, M^+)$ by Equations 5.1 or 5.2; the upper-bound of the relative likelihoods of all its *individual* supersets $UB(D_I, M^+)$ by Equation 5.3; and the upper-bound of the *sum* of the relative likelihoods of all its proper supersets $l_{est}(D_I, M^+)$ by Equation 5.11. These three values associated with each hypothesis play important roles in the problem-solving process presented in the next subsection.

5.3.2. Problem–Solving Strategy

Algorithm *SEARCH-CM* for solving diagnostic problems formulated according to Definition 5.1 is now presented together with an illustrative example. The correctness of the algorithm is then established and its efficiency is discussed.

Similar to algorithm *SEARCH*, algorithm *SEARCH-CM* generates new hypotheses by expanding an existing hypothesis using function *Expand*. It also maintains two sets, *Frontier* and *Candidates*, as before. At any moment during the search process, any cover D_I of M^+ that already has been generated by previous expansions must either be in *Frontier* or *Candidates*. Therefore, we have

$$L_{known} = \sum_{\substack{D_I \in Frontier \cup Candidates \\ D_I \ covers \ M^+}} L(D_I, M^+). \tag{5.12}$$

It was shown earlier (Lemma 5.5) that at any moment during the search process, any cover of M^+ which has not been generated is a proper superset of some hypothesis $D_J \in Frontier$. Since $l_{est}(D_I, M^+)$ is an upper–bound of the sum of L values of all proper supersets of D_I (by Theorem 5.10), we define

$$L_{est} = \sum_{D_I \in Frontier} l_{est}(D_I, M^+)$$

$$= \sum_{D_I \in Frontier} UB(D_I, M^+) \left[\prod_{d_j \in D - D_I} (1 + \alpha_j) - 1 \right]. \tag{5.13}$$

It is clear that $L_{est} \geq \sum L(D_J, M^+)$ for all D_J which have not been generated. Thus, at any moment during the search process we can compute L_{known} and L_{est} by Equations 5.12 and 5.13, respectively, from the current *Frontier* and *Candidates*, and in turn compute *inf* and *sup* of any hypothesis by Equation 5.9. Since *Frontier* and *Candidates* are initialized to $\{\emptyset\}$ and $\emptyset$, respectively, for a given problem we have $L_{known} = L(\emptyset, M^+)$ and $L_{est} = l_{est}(\emptyset, M^+)$ initially, derived from Equations 5.12 and 5.13. (In the case where $M^+ \neq \emptyset$ then $\emptyset$ does not cover M^+, and therefore $L_{known} = L(\emptyset, M^+) = 0$ initially.)

When the function *Expand* is called to expand some hypothesis D_I in *Frontier*, not only sets *Frontier* and *Candidates* need to be changed, but also L_{known} and L_{est}. So the procedure *Update* is extended to *Update-CM* to update L_{known} and L_{est} as well.

```
1. procedure Update-CM(D_I)
2.      variable S set of hypotheses;
3.      begin
4.          S := Expand(D_I);
5.          Frontier := Frontier − {D_I};
6.          L_est := L_est − l_est(D_I, M^+);
```

7.   **if** D_I is a cover of M^+ **then** $Candidates := Candidates \cup \{D_I\}$;
8.   **for** each $D_J \in S$ **and** $D_J \notin Frontier \cup Candidates$ **do**
9. $Frontier := Frontier \cup \{D_J\}$;
10. $L_{est} := L_{est} + l_{est}(D_J, M^+)$;
11.   **if** D_J covers M^+ **then** $L_{known} := L_{known} + L(D_J, M^+)$
12.   **endfor**
13.   **end**.

Sets *Frontier* and *Candidates* are treated the same as in *Update*, so after *Expand*(D_I), *Frontier* continues to contain all hypotheses generated but not expanded, and *Candidates* continues to be the set of all covers already expanded. Correspondingly, since D_I is removed from *Frontier*, $l_{est}(D_I, M^+)$ is subtracted from L_{est} at line 6. For each D_J added into *Frontier*, $l_{est}(D_J, M^+)$ is added to L_{est} at line 10, so that L_{est} is updated to be

$$\sum_{D_J \in Frontier} l_{est}(D_J, M^+)$$

for the updated new *Frontier*. At line 11, for each D_J added into *Frontier*, if D_J is also a cover of M^+ then $L(D_J, M^+)$ is added to L_{known} (such D_J's are new covers of M^+ generated by the current expansion of D_I). Thus, L_{known} is updated to be

$$\sum_{\substack{D_I \in Frontier \cup Candidates \\ D_I \, covers \, M^+}} L(D_I, M^+)$$

for the updated *Frontier* and *Candidates*.

After each expansion and update, algorithm *SEARCH-CM* calls a function *Testsol* to test if the solution for the given problem can be formed by selecting hypotheses from *Candidates*. Among all hypotheses $D_I \in Candidates$, a set of those with their L values greater than or equal to the largest UB value of all hypotheses in *Frontier* is selected and passed to *Testsol* (as shown earlier by Corollary 5.6, these hypotheses D_I are more probable than those in *Frontier* and those which have not been generated yet, and thus they are the most probable covers of all). Algorithm *Testsol* then successively selects hypotheses in descending order of their L values. If K hypotheses $D_1, D_2, \ldots, D_K$ are selected in this way such that

$$\sum_{I=1}^{K} inf(D_I) \geq CM > \sum_{I=1}^{K-1} sup(D_I), \tag{5.14}$$

then the set of these K hypotheses is returned as a solution of the given problem (recall that all hypotheses in *Candidates* are covers). Note that in Equation 5.14, instead of the posterior probabilities of hypotheses, the lower and upper bounds are used to determine if a solution can be formed according to Definition 5.1. The appropriateness of this test criterion can be informally justified as follows. Recall that $inf(D_I) \leq P(D_I, M^+) \leq sup(D_I)$

(Equation 5.9), so Equation 5.14 implies that

$$\sum_{I=1}^{K} P(D_I|M^+) \geq CM > \sum_{I=1}^{K-1} P(D_I|M^+).$$

Since these K hypotheses are most probable ones, and K of them together satisfy the CM but $K - 1$ of them do not, they compose a smallest set of hypotheses satisfying the given CM, thus meeting the two conditions set in Definition 5.1. The formal proof of this criterion (Lemma 5.11) and an illustrative example is given later. If no such set of hypotheses can be found (either because not enough most probable hypotheses can be identified and selected from *Candidates*, or because the *inf* and *sup* values are not refined enough), then the procedure returns an empty set of hypotheses indicating the need for further expansions. Function *Testsol* is given below.

1. **function** *Testsol*(S)
2.   **variable** *Sol* **set of hypotheses**;
3.   **begin**
4. $Sol := \emptyset$;
5.   **while** $S \neq \emptyset$ **and** $\sum_{D_J \in Sol} sup(D_J) < CM$ **do**
6.   select D_I from S with the largest $L(D_I, M^+)$;
7. $S := S - \{D_I\}$;
8. $Sol := Sol \cup \{D_I\}$;
9.   **if** $\sum_{D_J \in Sol} inf(D_J) \geq CM$ **then return** (Sol)
10.   **endwhile**;
11.   **return** ($\emptyset$)
12.   **end**.

When *Testsol* is called in *SEARCH-CM* (to be given shortly), the parameter S it takes is the set of all covers in the current *Candidates* with their L values greater than the largest UB value among all members of the current *Frontier* (see lines 12 and 13 of *SEARCH-CM*). In other words, as discussed earlier, S is the set of hypotheses which have been identified to be more probable than all other hypotheses. Variable *Sol* is used to store the partially formed solution, and is initially empty. During each pass of the **while**–loop (lines 5 to 10), the hypothesis D_I with the largest L value is selected and moved from S (line 7) to *Sol* (line 8). The test condition of line 9 is the same as the first inequality of Equation 5.14. At the beginning of the **while**–loop (line 5), if $S = \emptyset$, then there are no more hypotheses left for further selection; if $CM \leq \sum_{D_J \in Sol} sup(D_J)$, then the second inequality of

Equation 5.14 will be violated. In either case, no solution satisfying Equation 5.14 can be found, the loop terminates and returns $\emptyset$. If both conditions at line 5 are met, and the condition at line 9 is also met after one more hypothesis is selected and moved from S into Sol, then both inequalities of Equation 5.14 are satisfied, and Sol is thus a solution according to Definition 5.1 and can be returned to $SEARCH\text{-}CM$ at line 9.

We now turn to algorithm $SEARCH\text{-}CM$. Whenever function $Testsol$ fails to form a solution from hypotheses in set S (selected from $Candidates$), algorithm $SEARCH\text{-}CM$ always selects hypothesis $D_I \in Frontier$ with the largest UB value to expand next. A new expansion generally reduces the largest UB value of the current $Frontier$, and thus leads to more hypotheses in $Candidates$ which may be selected to form a solution (i.e., leads to an enlarged S passing to $Testsol$). Also, by generating more hypotheses, L_{known} and L_{est} are refined, leading to the refinement of inf and sup values of individual hypotheses (narrowing the bounds on their posterior probabilities). Thus, each expansion leads the search closer to a solution. Algorithm $SEARCH\text{-}CM$ is given below.

1. **procedure** $SEARCH\text{-}CM(D,M,C, M^+,CM)$
2.   **variable** D_J **hypothesis**, $Frontier$ $Candidates$ S $Solution$ **set of hypotheses**, L_{known} L_{est} upper **real**;
3.   **begin**
4. $Frontier := \{\varnothing\}$;
5. $Candidates := \varnothing$;
6. $L_{known} := L(\varnothing, M^+)$;
7. $L_{est} := l_{est}(\varnothing, M^+)$;
8.   **while** $Frontier \neq \varnothing$ **do**   {* search in the space 2^D *}
9.   select D_I from $Frontier$ with the largest UB value;
10. $Update\text{-}CM(D_I)$;   {* hypothesis generation *}
11.   **if** $Frontier = \varnothing$ **then** $upper := 0$
12.   **else** $upper := \max\{UB(D_K, M^+) | D_K \in Frontier\}$;
13. $S := \{D_J \in Candidates | L(D_J, M^+) > upper\}$;
14. $Solution := Testsol(S)$;   {* test for solution *}
15.   **if** $Solution \neq \varnothing$
16.   **then return** $(Solution)$ {* a solution is found returned *}
17.   **endwhile**
18.   **end**.

There are two major differences between algorithms $SEARCH$ and $SEARCH\text{-}CM$. The first difference concerns L_{known} and L_{est} used to calculate lower and upper bounds inf and sup of hypotheses. These two values are initialized at lines 6 and 7 in $SEARCH\text{-}CM$, and updated after each hypothesis expansion by procedure $Update\text{-}CM$. The second difference concerns the problem solution. In algorithm $SEARCH$, the solution is the single most probable hypothesis (or multiple hypotheses in the unusual situation where they have the same highest L value). This hypothesis is the one in $Candidates$ whose L value is the largest and exceeds $upper$, the largest UB value among all hypotheses in $Frontier$ (see lines 10 and 11 in

SEARCH). On the other hand, the solution in *SEARCH-CM* is a set of K hypotheses whose L values are the highest, the second highest, the third highest, and so forth, such that the sum of their posterior probabilities exceeds the given CM value. Therefore, *SEARCH-CM* first selects all hypotheses from *Candidates* whose L values are larger than *upper* (thus they are the first, the second, etc. most probable ones) at line 13, and then tries to form a solution from them by calling *Testsol* at line 14. If *Testsol* returns a non–empty set of hypotheses, this set is then returned by *SEARCH-CM* as a solution for the given problem (line 15). Otherwise, the **while**-loop continues to select new nodes from *Frontier* for expansion. A simple example should clarify the problem–solving strategy adopted by algorithm *SEARCH-CM*.

example: In Figure 5.2 of Section 5.1, a hypothesis subspace generated by algorithm *SEARCH* to find a most probable hypothesis for the small problem given in Figure 5.1 was shown. Table 5.1 gives $L(D_I)$, $UB(D_I)$, and $l_{est}(D_I, M^+)$ for some generated hypotheses D_I. Let the comfort measure CM be given to be 0.95. The first few steps of expansions are the same as was done by *SEARCH*. As illustrated in Section 5.1, after expanding hypotheses $\varnothing$, $\{d_3\}$, $\{d_2,d_3\}$, and $\{d_4\}$ in that order, we have *Frontier* $= \{\{d_1\}, \{d_1,d_3\}, \{d_1,d_2,d_3\}, \{d_2,d_3,d_4\}, \{d_2,d_3,d_5\}, \{d_2,d_3,d_6\}, \{d_1,d_4\}, \{d_2,d_4\}\}$, and *Candidates* $= \{\{d_2,d_3\}\}$. Then, $\{d_2,d_3\}$ is identified to be the most probable hypothesis for the given M^+ with $L(\{d_2,d_3\}, M^+) = 0.00602$. If identifying the single most probable diagnostic hypothesis was the goal of problem–solving, the algorithm could terminate, as was done by *SEARCH*. However, since the goal is to identify a smallest set of hypotheses whose posterior probabilities sum to more than CM, further work is necessary.

Considering all hypotheses in the current *Frontier*, $\{d_1\}$ and $\{d_1,d_4\}$ are not covers; their relative likelihood is zero. Then from Equation 5.12 and 5.13 and Table 5.2,

$$L_{known} = 0.0001018 + 0.0000448 + 0.0001084 + 0.0000654$$

$$+ 0.0000254 + 0.000072 + 0.00602$$

$$= 0.0064378;$$

$$L_{est} = 0.0012835 + 0.0000858 + 0.0000019 + 0.0000044$$

$$+ 0.0000038 + 0.0000019 + 0.0000181 + 0.0002627$$

$$= 0.0016621.$$

Therefore, for the most probable cover $\{d_2,d_3\}$, we have from Equation 5.9

$$inf(\{d_2,d_3\}) = 0.00602 / (0.0064378 + 0.0016621) = 0.743,$$

$$sup(\{d_2,d_3\}) = 0.00602 / 0.0064378 = 0.935,$$

that is, $0.734 \leq P(\{d_2,d_3\} \mid M^+) \leq 0.935$. Since $sup(\{d_2,d_3\}) < CM = 0.95$, the single most probable hypothesis is not sufficient as a problem solution according to Definition 5.1, so problem–solving continues.

To identify the second most probable cover of M^+ in this example, additional expansions are performed until more hypotheses are expanded and added into *Candidates*, and the hypothesis in *Candidates* with the second largest L value exceeds the largest UB value among all members of *Frontier*. After successively expanding six hypotheses $\{d_1\}$, $\{d_2,d_4\}$, $\{d_1,d_3\}$, $\{d_1,d_2\}$, $\{d_2,d_3,d_4\}$, and $\{d_2,d_3,d_5\}$, the hypothesis $\{d_2,d_3,d_4\}$ in *Candidates* is found to be the second most likely cover, with relative likelihood 0.0001084. (Note that at this time we have identified that $\{d_1,d_3\}$, $\{d_1,d_2\}$ $\{d_2,d_4\}$, and $\{d_2,d_4,d_5\}$ also have their L values greater than the largest UB value of hypotheses in the current *Frontier*, and that they are thus the third through sixth most probable covers of M^+.) At this moment, L_{known} is calculated to be 0.0065296 and L_{est} to be 0.000048.

As occurs after each expansion, the algorithm now tries to form a solution using function *Testsol*. If a solution cannot be formed, further expansions may be needed to either identify more hypotheses, or to achieve a better approximation of *inf* and *sup* values of hypotheses by reducing L_{est} and increasing L_{known}. Among the six most probable covers of M^+ identified so far, the sum of *inf* values of the first four of them is given by

$$Sum_1 = inf(\{d_2,d_3\}) + inf(\{d_2,d_3,d_4\}) + inf(\{d_1,d_3\}) + inf(\{d_1,d_2\})$$
$$= 0.91523 + 0.01648 + 0.01548 + 0.01206 = 0.959,$$

and the sum of *sup* values of the first three most probable ones is given by

$$Sum_2 = sup(\{d_2,d_3\}) + sup(\{d_2,d_3,d_4\}) + sup(\{d_1,d_3\})$$
$$= 0.92196 + 0.01660 + 0.01559 = 0.954.$$

As calculated above, both Sum_1 and Sum_2 are greater than the given CM value. $Sum_1 > CM$ implies that the sum of posterior probabilities of the first four most probable hypotheses exceeds the given CM, and thus they are sufficient to form a solution (see condition 1 of Definition 5.1). However, $Sum_2 > CM$ implies, or at least does not preclude, the possibility that the sum of posterior probabilities of the first three most probable hypotheses might still exceed CM. In other words, the first four most probable hypotheses might not satisfy the minimum cardinality condition set for a solution (condition 2 of Definition 5.1). The reason for such uncertainty is that the current *inf* and *sup* values form bounds which are too coarse concerning the involved posterior probabilities. Further expansions are needed to narrow these bounds. After three more expansions (expanding hypotheses $\{d_2,d_3,d_6\}$, $\{d_1,d_2,d_3\}$, and $\{d_1,d_4\}$), L_{known} is increased to 0.0065298, and L_{est} reduced to 0.0000264. Now,

$$inf(\{d_2,d_3\}) + inf(\{d_2,d_3,d_4\}) + inf(\{d_1,d_3\})$$
$$= 0.91821 + 0.01653 + 0.01553 = 0.9503,$$

$$sup(\{\,d_2,d_3\,\}) + sup(\{\,d_2,d_3,d_4\,\})$$

$$= 0.92193 + 0.0166 = 0.9385.$$

Since $0.9385 < CM < 0.9503$, we now can conclude that $\{\{\,d_2,d_3\,\},\ \{\,d_2,d_3,d_4\,\},\ \{\,d_1,d_3\,\}\}$ is a solution of the given problem as specified in Definition 5.1. $\square$

For the small knowledge base used in the above example, there are a total of $2^6 = 64$ hypotheses. When a solution is obtained by algorithm *SEARCH-CM* as illustrated above, 31 hypotheses are generated. The apparent inefficiency (about half of all possible hypotheses are generated) is presumably due to the fact that the problem size is unrealistically small, the prior probabilities of some disorders are unusually high (0.2 for p_3 and p_4), and that more than half of all manifestations (3 out of 5) are taken to be present, something which was done to facilitate the numerical illustration given above. In most real–world applications where, in general, only a small fraction of all possible manifestations are present, only a small fraction of all possible hypotheses would be generated before a solution is reached.

5.3.3. Correctness of Algorithms

In this subsection, the correctness of *Update-CM*, *Testsol*, and *SEARCH-CM* are established.

theorem 5.11 [Correctness of *Update-CM*]: If at line 10 of algorithm *SEARCH-CM* the following statements

(1) *Frontier* contains all hypotheses which have been generated but not yet expanded;

(2) *Candidates* is the set of all covers which have been expanded;

(3) $L_{known} = \displaystyle\sum_{\substack{D_I \in Frontier\,\cup\,Candidates \\ D_I covers\ M^+}} L(D_I, M^+)$; and

(4) $L_{est} = \displaystyle\sum_{D_J \in Frontier} l_{est}(D_J, M^+)$

are all true before the execution of *Update-CM(D_I)* where $D_I \in Frontier$, then they are all also true after the execution of *Update-CM(D_I)*.

Since procedure *Update-CM* correctly updates *Frontier*, *Candidates*, L_{known}, and L_{est}, Lemma 5.5 and Corollary 5.6 for *SEARCH* also hold for *SEARCH-CM*. Thus, any cover D_I of M^+ is either in *Candidates* (has been expanded) or in *Frontier* (has been generated but not expanded) or has not been generated. Then, by Corollary 5.6, covers in *Candidates* with their L values greater than or equal to the largest UB value of all members of *Frontier* are not less probable than any other covers. Thus, these covers in *Candidates* compose a set of the most probable hypotheses. Among them, the one with the largest L value is the most probable hypothesis, the one with the second largest L value is the second most probable hypothesis, etc. It is for this reason that algorithm $SEARCH$-CM constructs the set S as it does at line 13 and passes it to function $Testsol$ to see if a solution can be formed from hypotheses in S.

To establish the correctness of function $Testsol$, it is necessary to show first that Equation 5.14 is appropriate as a test condition for a solution.

lemma 5.12: Let $D_1, D_2, \ldots, D_K$ be K most probable hypotheses of M^+ for a problem $P = <D,M,C,M^+>$ ordered in descending order of their L values (i.e., D_1 is the most probable one, and D_K is the least probable one among the K hypotheses). Let CM be the given comfort measure. Then $S = \{D_1, D_2, \ldots, D_K\}$ is a solution for problem P if the inequality given in Equation 5.14 is met, i.e., if

$$\sum_{I=1}^{K} inf(D_I) \geq CM > \sum_{I=1}^{K-1} sup(D_I). \qquad (5.14)$$

theorem 5.13 [Correctness of $Testsol$]: Let $S = \{D_1, \ldots, D_N\}$ be a set of N most probable hypotheses of a given problem $P = <D,M,C,M^+>$, and let D_1 through D_N be ordered in descending order of their L values. If the most probable K ($K \leq N$) of them, $D_1, \ldots, D_K$, satisfy the inequalities of Equation 5.14, then $Testsol(S) = \{D_1, \ldots, D_K\}$ is a solution of P according to Definition 5.1. Otherwise, $Testsol(S) = \emptyset$, indicating failure to identify a solution.

Finally, the correctness of algorithm $SEARCH$-CM is established.

theorem 5.14 [Correctness of $SEARCH$-CM]: For any diagnostic problem $P = <D,M,C,M^+>$, $SEARCH$-$CM(D,M,C,M^+,CM)$ will terminate and return a solution of problem P.

5.3.4. Efficiency Considerations

In presenting algorithm $SEARCH$-CM, a number of efficiency issues have been ignored to keep the presentation as straightforward as possible. We now turn to these issues which would especially be of concern to someone interested in implementing the algorithms as computer programs.

Algorithm $SEARCH$-CM, like all best–first heuristic search procedures, should in general be relatively efficient. However, some specific statements in $SEARCH$-CM and in the sub–routines it calls may be implemented more efficiently than as shown. For example, if a record is kept of $UB(D_I, M^+)$ and $\prod_{d_k \in D - D_I} (1 + \alpha_k)$ for each known hypothesis D_I, then for any hypothesis $D_J = D_I \cup \{d_i\}$ which is generated by $Expand(D_I)$, we have $UB(D_J, M^+) = UB(D_I, M^+) \alpha_i$ if $\alpha_i < 1$ or $UB(D_J, M^+) = UB(D_I, M^+)$ otherwise (see Equations 5.3), and $\prod_{d_k \in D - D_J} (1 + \alpha_k) = [\prod_{d_k \in D - D_I} (1 + \alpha_k)] / (1 + \alpha_i)$.

In this incremental form the calculations for $l_{est}(D_I, M^+)$ and L_{est} in procedure *Update* are quite tractable. As another example, in lines 5 and 9 of function *Testsol*, the summations of *inf* and *sup* of selected hypotheses can be cumulated in each iteration of the **while**-loop, not recalculated over and over again. Lines 9, 12 and 13 of algorithm *SEARCH-CM* can also be implemented more efficiently if *Frontier* and *Candidates* are implemented by ordered lists (in the descending order of *UB* and *L* values, respectively) rather than sets.

So far, we have always considered the hypothesis space to be the space of all subsets of D, i.e., 2^D, which is usually very large when the total number of possible disorders is large. However, as discussed in Chapter 3, in many real–world problems one is only interested in disorders that are capable of causing some of the given present manifestations, i.e., all disorders *relevant* to the given M^+. In such a situation the scope of problem–solving can be restricted to *causes*(M^+) which is usually a very small subset of D. Then the whole search space for both algorithms *SEARCH* and *SEARCH-CM* is substantially reduced (from 2^D to $2^{causes(M^+)}$).

Another efficiency issue is more subtle, and requires careful consideration. Requiring a minimum size set of hypotheses for a solution (condition 2 of Definition 5.1) might sometimes lead to excessive effort on the part of algorithm *SEARCH-CM*. Consider the following situation. Let $D_1, \ldots, D_K$ be K most probable hypotheses for a given M^+ where $\sum_{I=1}^{K} P(D_I|M^+) = CM + \delta$ for positive δ very close to zero, and $\sum_{I=1}^{K-1} P(D_I|M^+) < CM$. Thus, $\{D_1, \ldots, D_K\}$ is a solution of the problem by Definition 5.1. Applying algorithm *SEARCH-CM*, since $inf(D_I) \le P(D_I|M^+)$, we would have $\sum_{I=1}^{K} inf(D_I) < CM$ until $\sum_{I=1}^{K} P(D_I|M^+) - \sum_{I=1}^{K} inf(D_I) < \delta$, which, since $\delta \approx 0$, implies that L_{est} is close to zero and L_{known} is close to the sum of L values of all covers of M^+ (i.e., until almost all covers are generated and expanded) which is computationally formidable. One way for an implementor to cope with this potential problem is to loosen the definition of a problem solution slightly to allow it, in some cases, to contain one more than the minimum number of hypotheses. Thus, the problem solution might be formally redefined as follows.

definition 5.2: A set $S = \{D_1, \ldots, D_K\}$ is said to be an *almost minimum solution* of problem $P = <D, M, C, M^+>$ if

(1) $P(D_1 \vee \cdots \vee D_K|M^+) = \sum_{I=1}^{K} P(D_I|M^+) \ge CM$, and

(2) among all $T \subset 2^D$ satisfying $\sum_{D_I \in T} P(D_I|M^+) \ge CM$, $|S| - |T| \le 1$.

If one is willing to accept almost minimum solutions, the test condition for identifying a problem solution can then be relaxed as given by the following theorem.

theorem 5.15: Let $D_1, \ldots, D_K$ be K most probable covers for a problem $P = <D,M,C,M^+>$, ordered in descending order of $L(D_I, M^+)$. Let CM be the given comfort measure. Then $S = \{D_1, \ldots, D_K\}$ is an almost minimum solution for problem P if

$$\sum_{I=1}^{K} inf(D_I) \geq CM > \sum_{I=1}^{K-1} inf(D_I) \quad \text{and} \tag{5.15a}$$

$$\sum_{I=1}^{K} inf(D_I) > \sum_{I=1}^{K-1} sup(D_I). \tag{5.15b}$$

Equations 5.15a and 5.15b are more relaxed than Equation 5.14 because they are implied by 5.14 but not vice versa. Most importantly, some computation may be saved in worst case scenarios as was discussed earlier. This is illustrated by the example below.

example: Reconsider the example illustrated in Section 5.3.2, where the last three hypothesis expansions (expanding $\{d_2,d_3,d_6\}$, $\{d_1,d_2,d_8\}$, and $\{d_1,d_4\}$) were necessary to satisfy Equation 5.14. These expansions would not have been necessary if an almost minimum solution were acceptable. Before these four expansions, as shown in Section 5.3.2, we have

$$inf(\{d_2,d_3\}) + inf(\{d_2,d_3,d_4\}) + inf(\{d_1,d_3\}) + inf(\{d_1,d_2\}) = 0.959$$
$$inf(\{d_2,d_3\}) + inf(\{d_2,d_3,d_4\}) + inf(\{d_1,d_3\})$$
$$= 0.91523 + 0.01648 + 0.01548 = 0.947,$$

and

$$sup(\{d_2,d_3\}) + sup(\{d_2,d_3,d_4\}) + sup(\{d_1,d_3\}) = 0.954.$$

Thus, the conditions set by Equations 5.15a and 5.15b are met by these *four* most probable hypotheses and they are returned as an almost minimum solution of the problem. As shown in Section 5.3.2, the first three of these four hypotheses are enough to form a solution (with minimum size), but by allowing one extra hypothesis, namely $\{d_1,d_2\}$, to be included, fewer hypotheses are generated and expanded during problem-solving.   □

In summary, the comfort measure CM provides a criterion for controlling the "quality" of a problem solution, and by computing and refining $inf(D_I)$ and $sup(D_I)$ values for each known hypothesis, not only the relative likelihood, but also the range of the posterior probabilities of hypotheses D_I can be obtained and made progressively more precise during problem-solving.

This allows identification of a solution such that the probability for the correct diagnosis to be among the hypotheses in the solution is at least as high as the given CM value. Moreover, the size of the resultant solution set provides a meaningful measure of the specificity of the solution. Smaller size solutions indicate that a higher degree of specificity is achieved, while larger size solutions indicate that the solution is relatively nonspecific (too many alternatives are offered). Such nonspecificity is largely due to the fact that the given M^+ is not "specific" or "focused". By a specific or focused M^+ we mean one which closely matches the pattern of manifestations expected by some hypothesis D_I, and thus gives strong support to that hypothesis. A nonspecific M^+, on the other hand, does not closely match a pattern of manifestations produced by any possible D_I, and thus tends to render weak support to a lot of hypotheses. Therefore a large solution size may be used as an indicator that further inquiry for more manifestations (making M^+ more specific) or consultation with a human expert might be needed.[*]

There are other possible criteria that might be adopted for "quality control" of a problem solution. For example, a solution of a problem could be defined as a set of n most–probable hypotheses for a desired number n. There are several problems with this "n–most–likely" criterion. First, it is difficult to specify the desired number n from a users' viewpoint, at least in as natural and meaningful a fashion as the comfort measure we proposed. Second, a fixed n may be too large for some cases, thus causing unnecessary search, yet too small for other cases, thus making the search end too early. In other words, determining a reasonable value for n *a priori* would require the user of a problem–solving system to know in advance how many hypotheses are reasonable *for a specific* M^+. Also, by using an n–most–likely criterion, the specificity of M^+ inherent in problems is not revealed by the solution of a problem–solving system. As another alternative, a solution could be defined as a set of most–probable hypotheses such that the ratio of hypotheses in the solution is within a given range. This seems more meaningful than the fixed number hypothesis criterion and can be considered as an approximation of the comfort measure. However, neither of these alternative approaches identifies the risk that the actually occurring hypothesis is missing from the solution unless some kind of bounds on posterior probabilities of existing hypotheses can be developed. This then raises the question of how tight these bounds should be. It is based on these considerations that a comfort measure is proposed here as a coherent means to control the quality of the problem–solving and to drive a search process to its completion.

(*) In the NESTOR system, Cooper has developed similar techniques for estimating lower and upper bounds for posterior probabilities and suggested the use of these bounds to evaluate the quality of problem solutions [Cooper84]. This will be discussed in detail in Section 5.4 where NESTOR is compared with the probabilistic causal model.

5.4. Comparison to Related Work

Recently, some others have used ideas similar to ours in different formulations and have developed various strategies to find the most probable hypothesis based on underlying causal networks. In this section, we briefly review two approaches taken by others, NESTOR [Cooper84] and Belief Networks [Pearl86a,b, 88], and compare them with the probabilistic causal model developed here. Although both of these models are based on more general causal networks involving intermediate states and causal chaining, their key ideas can be revealed in the two–layer (bipartite) network setting. In the following discussion, the comparison is thus made for the more restricted bipartite networks.

5.4.1. Cooper's NESTOR

In NESTOR, if A is a direct cause of B, then by the conditional probability $P(B|A)$ is meant $P(A\ causes\ B|A)$. This conditional probability $P(B|A)$ is the same as our causal strength from A to B. To the authors' knowledge, NESTOR is the only other system which explicitly considers the realization of a cause–effect relation as a probabilistic event. NESTOR also requires that knowledge of prior probabilities of disorders (either for individual disorders or for sets of multiple disorders) and causal strengths for all direct causal links be available.

In NESTOR, a hypothesis can consist of multiple disorders. For a given set of findings F (known present and absent manifestations) and a hypothesis H_I (presence/absence of disorders in bipartite networks), similar to our approach NESTOR uses not the posterior probability $P(H_I|F)$, but a relative measure $P(F|H_I)\,P(H_I) = P(F \wedge H_I)$ as the score for H_I. Thus, the tremendous effort that would be required to compute $P(F)$ is saved. A method was developed in NESTOR to evaluate this relative likelihood measure for a given H_I and F from the causal strengths and prior probabilities of disorders. A best–first search algorithm very similar to our search algorithm was also developed for finding the most probable hypothesis (one with the largest relative likelihood).

Having noted the similarity of these two independently developed models in basic underlying ideas for problem formulation and problem–solving, we can now consider some significant differences between them. Unlike our probabilistic causal model which is based on formalization of key notions and on mathematical proofs, NESTOR is less formal and is oriented more towards being a working medical diagnostic system. In NESTOR, intervals, not point probabilities, are used for both the probabilities required as part of the knowledge base (prior probabilities of disorders and causal strengths for direct causal links) and for the probabilities derived during a computation. Also, each entity (disorder, manifestation or intermediate entities) may be in one of multiple states (e.g., high, middle, low), instead of only being either present or absent. Computations heavily depend on heuristics which allow domain–specific knowledge to play appropriate roles. This gives NESTOR the advantage in flexibility in accommodating domain–specific knowledge and tolerance for the limitations of the knowledge that is available. NESTOR's main disadvantage is its lack of formalization. Some important notions are not clearly defined, and some derivations are not based on formal proofs but on informal qualitative analysis. For example, the exact probabilistic meaning of $P(F|H_I)$ for a group of findings F and a group of disorders H_I is not explicitly defined, and why the computation of $P(F|H_I)$ is represented by causal strengths associating individual entities in that particular way is not clearly demonstrated. These things were formally established in our model through the concept of "joint–causation event" (Section 4.2.2).

Nonetheless, it is interesting to note that a number of important *results* we derived from the basic assumptions of our model were independently *assumed* by Cooper in terms of heuristics of computation in NESTOR. This is satisfying in that it suggests that the intuitions underlying NESTOR's heuristics are consistent with the results derived in the probabilistic causal model. As an example, consider the computation of $P(F|H_I)$. To make the comparison of how the two models approach computation of $P(F|H_I)$ clear, in what follows we consider that each entity can only be either present or absent, that every probability is a point value, and that the causal networks are acyclic and bipartite.

A set of heuristics is used by NESTOR in order to utilize domain–specific knowledge of the causal relations between entities. When no such knowledge is available, some of these rules are reduced to the same results we derived from our model. For example, the combined causal effect on a manifestation m_j from a set of present disorders observes the Bernoulli law (combination of convergent links in NESTOR terminology). This is illustrated in Figure 5.3a where the individual causal strengths from d_1 and d_2 to m_j are a and b, respectively. The combined effect of d_1 and d_2 on m_j is treated like a single link of strength $c = a + b - a\,b$ in NESTOR. This is equal to the measure $1 - (1 - a)(1 - b)$ formalized in our model as a joint–causation event in Chapter 4. The same equation is formally proved in Lemmas 4.16 and 4.18 for different settings. On the other hand, if a disorder d_i is a direct cause of several present manifestations, then NESTOR assumes the causal effects on each of these manifestations are independent of each other (combination of divergent links in NESTOR terminology). This is illustrated in Figure 5.3b where d_i may cause m_1 and m_2 with the strengths a and b, respectively. Then the combined strength that d_i causes both m_1 and m_2 is $c = a\,b$. This is proved by Theorem 4.4 in our model in Chapter 4. To compute the final result of $P(F|H_I)$ for a given hypothesis H_I, NESTOR first combines all convergent links, resulting in a network with only divergent or separate links. NESTOR then multiples the strengths of these remaining links. It is easy to show that this gives the same results as our formula for L_1 and L_2 in computing relative likelihoods (see Equations 4.16 and 4.18).

The issue of "quality control" for diagnostic problem solving using relative likelihoods is also a concern of NESTOR. NESTOR not only uses an algorithm which is capable of successively generating the n most probable hypotheses for a given number n, but this algorithm also reflects the importance of estimating the posterior probability, not just the relative merit, of a hypothesis in order to gain confidence in that hypothesis. Similar to what we did in Section 5.3, such estimates are provided by a pair of upper and lower bounds for the posterior probability of a given hypothesis. To calculate these bounds, the sum of likelihood values of all existing hypotheses and an upper bound on the sum of likelihood values of all unknown hypotheses are used. After normalization and simplification, the NESTOR formula for the first sum is exactly our L_{known}, but the second sum is weaker than our L_{est}. NESTOR essentially uses the prior probability $P(D_J)$ as the upper bound of the relative likelihood for unknown hypothesis D_J and $1 - \sum_{D_I \text{ is known}} P(D_I)$ as the upper bound of the sum of likelihoods of all unknown hypotheses. After normalization this amounts to

$$L_{est}^* = \frac{1}{P(\varnothing)} - \sum_{D_I \text{ is known}} L_3(D_I, M^+) \text{ where } L_3(D_I, M^+) = \prod_{d_i \in D_I} \frac{p_i}{1 - p_i}. \text{ Here and}$$

in the following, we use L_{est}^* to refer to the approach used in NESTOR.

The comfort measure developed in Section 5.3 has some advantages over NESTOR's approach. First, the comfort measure is a more natural and meaningful measure for solution quality control than the n–most–likely criterion, as discussed earlier in Section 5.3. Second, using L_{est}^* to provide a bound on posterior probability often leads to generation of the majority of potential hypotheses, something which is practically intractable in larger

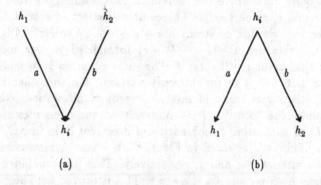

(a)   (b)

Figure 5.3. Combined causal strength from multiple causal links.
(a) Combined strength from convergent links: $c = a + b - a b$.
(b) Combined strength from divergent links: $c = a b$.

real–world problems. For example, using L_{est}^* on the example given in Section 5.3, 60 of the 64 possible hypotheses would be generated before the given CM is satisfied, while using our formula, only 31 of them are generated. The reason for this performance difference is that we used $UB(D_J, M^+) = L_2(D_J, M^+) L_3(D_J, M^+)$ as the upper bound for unknown hypothesis D_J, a measure which is much smaller than $L_3(D_J, M^+)$ used in L_{est}^* because $L_2(D_J, M^+)$ is usually much smaller than 1.[*] To further investigate this matter, two experiments were conducted. Experiment 1 tested all possible M^+ sets for the diagnostic problem given in Fig. 5.1 (a total of 31 different M^+ sets are possible, excluding $M^+ = \varnothing$). Experiment 2 used 30 randomly generated M^+ sets, 10 each where $|M^+| = 3, 4, 5$, respectively, on a randomly created diagnostic problem with $|D| = 10$ and $|M| = 10$ and $p_i < 0.1$ for all $d_i \in D$. The efficiency of problem solving was measured using the average of the ratio of the total number of hypotheses generated over the size of the hypothesis space for all different M^+. For hypothesis space size, we used $2^{causes(M^+)}$ instead of 2^D. The results of these experiments are given in Table 5.2.

Three points can be made in considering the results of these experiments. First, in both experiments, the equation developed in Section 5.3 has a significantly better efficiency (lower average ratio 0.608 and 0.288) than the model using L_{est}^* (higher average ratio 0.909 and 0.884). Second, experiment 2 is closer to real–world problems than experiment 1 in terms of problem size, prior probability range, and percentage of all manifestations known to be present. As anticipated (see discussion at end of Section 5.3.2), our method shows significant efficiency improvement in experiment 2 over experiment 1, but the results from the model using L_{est}^* were only slightly better. Third, the degree of variation of the ratios for all cases, measured by coefficients of variation (standard deviation divided by the

Table 5.2. Fraction of Hypothesis Space Explored by L_{est} and L_{est}^*.

model	Experiment 1			Experiment 2		
	mean	standard deviation	coefficient of variation	mean	standard deviation	coefficient of variation
Peng & Reggia	0.608	0.175	0.288	0.288	0.117	0.406
Cooper	0.909	0.097	0.107	0.884	0.126	0.143

(*) NESTOR was intended to apply on general causal networks which allow intermediate entities and causal chaining, and thus are more complicated than the two layer networks we have considered so far. Since it is difficult to calculate L_2 values for hypotheses in this more general setting, prior probabilities were used as upper bounds for posterior probabilities for hypotheses.

mean), were also different for both models. The fairly high degree of variation of our model (0.283 and 0.406) indicates that the efficiency varies a lot for different inputs (different M^+). We conjecture that more "specific" or "focused" M^+ sets tend to generate fewer hypotheses before a solution is reached than less specific M^+ sets. This should make our model even more efficient in real–world applications than in randomly generated examples as studied here because, for many real–world problems, the given findings are usually quite specific (since they are caused by a set of disorders which are actually occurring). However, the degree of variation using L^*_{est} is considerably lower (0.107 and 0.143) which implies that the specificity of M^+ can only make a very small difference from the average behavior. Combining the above arguments, it is fair to predict that our model is practically more tractable than the earlier approach developed by Cooper, at least for two layer bipartite networks.

In summary, both our probabilistic causal model and NESTOR focus on cause–effect associations between individual entities by establishing the realization of such relationships as a category of probabilistic events. They both assume causation independence (explicitly stated in our model as an assumption and implicitly embedded in heuristic rules in NESTOR) for diagnostic problem–solving. This idea distinguishes these two models from other systems for diagnostic problem–solving. From this common basis, the definition of a problem solution, the evaluation of hypotheses based on relative likelihoods, and the problem–solving strategies bear strong similarity between these two models.

5.4.2. Pearl's Belief Networks

In the past several years another formulation for solving diagnostic problems based on causal networks has also been derived from formal probability theory [Pearl86a,b, 88]. Since this model focuses on the update of "beliefs" of entities (defined as posterior probabilities of entities, given input data) upon receiving new evidence, such networks are called *belief networks*. As with our causal network, when applied to diagnostic problems a belief network is a directed acyclic graph where nodes represent diagnostic entities and links represent causal relationship between individual entities (links are directed from causes to effects). Based on the causal relationship formulated by such a network structure, probability theory, or more specifically Bayes' Theorem, is applied to solve various diagnostic problems. For brevity, in what follows we concentrate on analyzing the probability assumptions made in the belief network model and only briefly discuss the strategies proposed for problem–solving.

Unlike our probabilistic causal model and NESTOR, the belief network model uses traditional conditional probabilities to capture causal relations. The real advance of the belief network model over traditional Bayesian systems lies in the independence assumption. Instead of simply assuming that effects are conditionally independent given individual causes, as has been done for some previous Bayesian classification systems (see [Charniak83, Ben–Bassat80]), more complicated interactions between entities in the general network structure are taken into consideration in making the independence assumption. After careful analysis of the causal relations in real–world situations, important interdependencies in the causal world were noted which motivated the following assumptions underlying a belief network [*] [Pearl86b].

Consider a triple of nodes h_1, h_2 and h_3, where h_1 is connected to h_2 via h_3. As illustrated in Figure 5.4, the two links connecting pairs { h_1, h_3 } and { h_2, h_3 } can join at the midpoint, h_3, in one of the three possible ways: (1) *tail–to–tail* (Figure 5.4a), (2) *head–to–tail* (Figure 5.4b), and (3) *head–to–head* (Figure 5.4c). Now consider cases (1) and (3) (case (2) does not exist in bipartite networks), and assume that h_1, h_2 and h_3 are the only nodes involved. Intuitively one can argue that in case (1), h_1 and h_2 are conditionally independent given h_3 (i.e., $P(h_1 \wedge h_2 | h_3) = P(h_1 | h_3) P(h_2 | h_3)$); and that in case (3), h_1 and h_2 are marginally independent (e.g., $P(h_2 | h_1) = P(h_2)$) but may become dependent, given h_3.

These very reasonable observations are *consequents* of assumptions in our probabilistic causal model. Actually, conditional independence of tail–

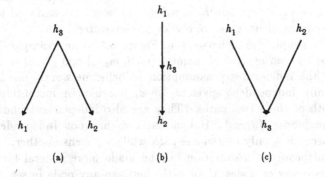

Figure 5.4. Causal links join at a midpoint.
(a) Tail–to–tail connection where h_3 is a direct cause of both h_1 and h_2.
(b) Head–to–tail connection where h_3 is an effect of h_1 and a cause of h_2.
(c) Head–to–head connection where h_3 is an effect of both h_1 and h_2.

---

[*] In a belief network model, a node can be in one of several possible states, not just present or absent. To demonstrate the basic ideas, in these discussions we only consider binary state nodes.

to–tail connections, as in case (1) above, is a special case of Theorem 4.19 (Manifestation Interdependence). This theorem says that two entities can interact through their common causes (ancestors) but the instantiation [*] of such an ancestor (i.e., it is designated as being either present or absent) may *cut off* this interaction if it is their only common cause. Interdependency of head–to–head connections in case (3) is a special case of Theorem 4.20 which says that the instantiation of a common effect (descendent) of two disorders may *open* a channel for these two disorders to interact. This illustrates that, similar to our model, common causes and common effects play different roles in the interdependency between two entities.

Belief networks generalize the above intuitions into an independence assumption. The generalization goes as follows for a bipartite network. First, consider a path between two nodes h_1 and h_2. If there is a tail–to–tail connection node X in that path, then from case (1), an instantiation of X will *block* the interaction between h_1 and h_2 through that path. If X is a head–to–head connection node, then from the intuition of case (3), such an interaction will be blocked by not instantiating X. Next, consider all paths between h_1 and h_2. Let S be a set of instantiated nodes. Nodes h_1 and h_2 are said to be *separated* by S if for each path between these two nodes, either a tail–to–tail connection node in that path is in S or a head–to–head connection node is not in S. In other words, S separates h_1 and h_2 by blocking all paths between them, and thus cuts off all channels for interaction. Therefore, two nodes h_1 and h_2 in a belief network are assumed to be conditionally independent, given S, if they are separated by S.

Take the simple causal network in Figure 5.5 as an example. There are two paths between m_1 and d_3, namely (m_1, d_1, m_3, d_3) and $(m_1, d_1, m_2, d_2, m_4, d_3)$. Then, by the independence assumption in belief networks, m_1 and d_3 are conditionally independent given d_1 or $\overline{d_1}$ because an instantiation of d_1 blocks both of these two paths. They are also independent under the set $\{d_1, d_2\}$, or under $\{d_1, m_3\}$. But m_1 and d_3 are not independent under $\{d_2, m_3\}$ because d_2 only blocks one path while m_3 opens another.

This independence assumption can be made more general for independence of two sets of nodes: if all paths between any node in set A and any node in set B are separated by S, then A and B are conditionally independent, given S.

Although the independence assumption in belief networks appears different than the results derived in the probabilistic causal model, it can be shown that they achieve the same result with respect to entity interdependency. In other words, nodes h_1 and h_2 are separated by set S and thus conditionally independent in a belief network iff they are conditionally

---

(*) Instantiating a variable means to assign it one of its possible values or states. Here, since we only consider entities with two possible values, instantiating a node means to assign it to be either present or absent. Similarly, to instantiate a set of nodes is to designate each node in that set as being either present or absent.

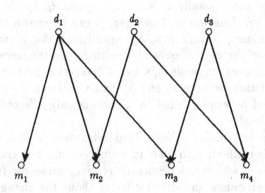

Figure 5.5. A multi-connected causal network where there
are two paths between nodes m_1 and d_3.

independent, given S, in the probabilistic causal model. In what follows we
informally explain how several key features of the probabilistic causal
model can be considered to be the same as consequents of the independence
assumption in belief networks.

Consider two disorders d_1 and d_2 in the probabilistic causal model.
Because they do not have any further causes, all paths between them must
contain some head–to–head connection nodes. If none of these nodes is
instantiated, then no path is open between them. Then by the independence assumption in belief networks, these two disorders are marginally
independent. In other words, our disorder independence assumption can be
viewed as a consequent of the independence assumption in belief networks.
Also, since a hypothesis D_I in the probabilistic causal model represents an
instantiation of all disorders (recall that D_I represents that all d_i in D_I are
present and all other disorders are absent in the probabilistic causal
model), D_I instantiates tail–to–tail connection nodes in all paths between
two manifestations m_1 and m_2, and thus m_1 and m_2 are conditionally
independent given D_I. This, as given in Theorem 4.10, is a crucial step in
deriving the relative likelihood formula, and thus this formula could also
be derived from the independence assumption in belief networks.

Now we turn our attention to problem–solving strategies in belief networks based on the above independence assumptions. The basic approach
centers on a special kind of network, *singly–connected–graphs*, which can
be extended for more general networks. A singly connected graph is a network where there is at most one path between any pair of nodes. Different
parts of a singly connected graph can easily be separated by instantiating
a tail–to–tail node (disorder) or not instantiating a head–to–head node
(manifestation). The influence between these parts is thus blocked by such
an instantiation. For example, instantiation of a disorder node d_i effectively partitions a bipartite, singly–connected network into several parts,

each of which associates with a manifestation causally connected to d_i. These parts are conditionally independent, given d_i, by the independence assumption in belief networks. Moreover, it can be shown that because of singly–connectedness, a link $< h_i, h_j >$ partitions the network into two regions. Input in the region associated with h_i can influence node h_j only through its influence on node h_i's belief (posterior probability) and the local causal relation between h_i and h_j, and vice versa. In other words, in singly–connected networks, belief in a node is only affected by its neighbors, i.e., it is local.

These properties enable a distributed relaxation method for problem-solving. In this method, each node in a singly–connected graph is an autonomous processor which independently receives messages from all of its neighbors (direct causes and direct effects) about the change of beliefs at those nodes, updates its own belief based on these messages, and then sends messages about its new belief to all its neighbors. The process of updating a node's belief is called *fusion* because all messages received are fused together; the process of sending messages is called *propagation*. This fusion and propagation process continues until the whole network (or the part of it which can be reached from the input nodes) has been updated and the network reaches an equilibrium where each node has its belief revised to reflect the presence of new data. This process can be shown to take only time proportional to the diameter of the network [Pearl86b].

Besides the belief revision process outlined above, finding the most probable multiple–node hypothesis (best explanation) is also an important diagnostic task which is one of the goals for our model as well as for NESTOR. For this task, the distributed method for belief revision can be extended to find the best or most probable instantiation of all nodes which are not instantiated by input data. This is called *belief commitment*. Belief commitment is basically the same as belief revision except that the rules for fusion and propagation are modified. The goal now is to let a node be committed to the best (most probable) instantiation, and not to obtain beliefs of different possible states of that node for the given input data. Its correctness was proved and this process also requires only time proportional to the network diameter [Pearl86a]. When all uninstantiated nodes are disorders (such as with two layer bipartite networks in our model), then the most probable instantiation of disorders in a belief network is the same as our problem solution and that of NESTOR.

Unfortunately, this distributed problem–solving method in belief networks cannot be directly applied to more general multi–connected networks, which are what occur in many real–world diagnostic problems. In such networks the messages may circulate indefinitely around loops so the process may never converge to an equilibrium state. (See Figure 5.5 for an example of a multi–connected network.) To avoid this difficulty, a set of cycle–cut nodes can be found from a given multi–connected network. By instantiating all nodes in that set, the given network becomes a singly–

connected one. The final solution (whether revision or commitment of beliefs) can then be obtained based on all such possible instantiations [Pearl 86a]. Finding a minimum cycle–cut set from a given graph is NP hard, and the number of possible instantiations is exponential to the size of the cycle–cut set. Therefore, in general, solving a diagnostic problem using this method would in the worst case need time exponential to the network size. This problem of computational complexity is common to all three models. An approach based on the probabilistic causal model is presented in Chapter 7 to cope with this problem.

Although the probabilistic causal model, NESTOR, and belief networks have different formulations and styles, what is common to all three models is that they go beyond the explicit statistical associations between disorders and manifestations underlying traditional Bayesian classification and concentrate on understanding the characteristics of cause–effect relations crucial to diagnostic inference. The strong similarities in the fundamentals among these three independently developed models suggests that a deeper and closer–to–reality understanding of causal relations has been reached. The new view of the probabilistic nature of causality captured in these models may provide new techniques for knowledge engineering in diagnosis and other areas involving causal inferences.

5.5. Mathematical Appendix

proof of lemma 5.1.

Let $d_k \in D - D_I$. If $\alpha_k > 1$ then, from Equation 5.3a, α_k is a factor of $UB(D_I, M^+)$, therefore,

$$UB(D_I \cup \{d_k\}, M^+) = UB(D_I, M^+).$$

If $\alpha_k \leq 1$, then

$$UB(D_I \cup \{d_k\}, M^+) = UB(D_I, M^+) \, \alpha_k \leq UB(D_I, M^+)$$

where equality holds only if $\alpha_k = 1$. Combining the above two cases, the lemma follows immediately. $\square$

proof of Lemma 5.2.

The first part of the lemma is obvious. To prove the second part, note that by Lemma 5.1, $L(D_J, M^+) \leq UB(D_J, M^+) \leq UB(D_I, M^+)$. $\square$

proof of Lemma 5.3.

By the definition of function *Expand*, the lemma is proven in two cases.

Case 1: D_I is not a cover of M^+. Then, $M^+ - effects(D_I) \neq \emptyset$ (see the definition of cover in Section 3.1.2). Let an arbitrary manifestation $m_j \in M^+ - effects(D_I)$ be chosen to expand D_I. Then any $D_J \supset D_I$ covering M^+ must cover m_j, i.e., $(D_J - D_I) \cap causes(m_j) \neq \emptyset$. Therefore,

$D_J \supseteq D_I \cup \{d_k\} \supset D_I$ for some $d_k \in causes(m_j)$.

Case 2: D_I is a cover of M^+. Then any $D_J \supset D_I$ is also a cover and $(D_J - D_I) \subseteq (D - D_I) \neq \emptyset$. Therefore, $D_J \supseteq D_I \cup \{d_k\}$ for some $d_k \in D - D_I$. $\square$

proof of Lemma 5.4:

(1) Since D_I is expanded (line 4 of *Update*), its deletion from *Frontier* (line 5) does not invalidate statement (1) concerning *Frontier*. For each D_J generated by expanding D_I, if it has not been expanded before, then it is not in *Candidates*, thus, adding such a D_J to *Frontier* (line 9) does not invalidate statement (1). Neither does omitting D_J from *Frontier* if D_J is already in *Candidates*, since in this case it was previously expanded. Since these are the only places related to *Frontier*, the statement (1) concerning *Frontier* remains true after *Update*(D_I).

(2) Obvious by line 6, the only alteration to *Candidates* in *Update*. $\square$

proof of Lemma 5.5.

The proof is by induction on the number of hypothesis expansions (number of passes of the **while**–loop) performed.

Base case: At the beginning of the first pass of the **while**–loop, no expansions have been performed. Then *Frontier* $^{~} = \{\emptyset\}$. The lemma holds trivially since $D_R \supseteq \emptyset$ for all covers D_R of M^+.

Induction step: Assume the lemma holds for *Frontier*$^{(n)}$ which contains all hypotheses generated but not yet expanded when some $n \geq 0$ hypothesis expansions have been performed. Now show that if any $D_I \in Frontier^{(n)}$ is selected for expansion during the $(n+1)^{th}$ pass, the lemma holds for the resulting *Frontier*$^{(n+1)}$. Let D_R be a cover of M^+ which has not been generated after D_I is expanded. Then by the inductive hypothesis, $D_R \supset D_J$ for some $D_J \in Frontier^{(n)}$. If there is such a D_J in *Frontier* which is not equal to D_I, then $D_J \in Frontier^{(n+1)}$ because only D_I is removed from *Frontier*$^{(n)}$ by procedure *Update* (line 5).

Now consider the situation where D_I is the only one among members in *Frontier* to be a proper subset of D_R. Then by Lemma 5.3 and the fact that D_R is not generated by expanding D_I, $D_R \supset D_S$ for some $D_S \in Expand(D_I)$. It remains to be shown that such a D_S cannot have been expanded before, so $D_S \notin Candidates^{(n)}$, and thus by lines 7 and 8 of *Update*, $D_S \in Frontier^{(n+1)}$. Assume the contrary, that D_S had been expanded before during the kth pass of the **while**–loop where $k \leq n$. Then by Lemma 5.3, there exists some $D_{T_k} \in Expand(D_S)$ such that $D_R \supset D_{T_k} \supset D_S$. Repeating the above argument if D_{T_k} has also been expanded before, etc., since there are only n hypothesis expansions before D_I is expanded, there must exist some D_{T_n} such that $D_R \supset D_{T_n} \supset D_S$, which has been generated but not expanded after the first n expansions, thus belonging to *Frontier*$^{(n)}$. Since D_{T_n} is a descendant of D_I, $D_{T_n} \neq D_I$. This contradicts the assumption that D_I is the only proper subset of D_R among all members of *Frontier*$^{(n)}$. $\square$

proof of Corollary 5.6.

By Lemma 5.5, for any such D_J, there exists some D_L in the current *Frontier* such that $D_J \supset D_L$. Then by Equation 5.3a and Lemma 5.1, we have

$$L(D_J, M^+) \leq UB(D_J, M^+) \leq UB(D_L, M^+)$$
$$\leq \max\{UB(D_K, M^+) | D_K \in Frontier\} \leq L(D_L, M^+). \qquad \Box$$

proof of Theorem 5.7.

Note that by initializations of lines 4 and 5, the statements in Theorem 5.3 about *Frontier* and *Candidates* are true before the **while**–loop of procedure *SEARCH* (lines 6 to 14) started. Then by Theorem 5.3, they will always be true after each call of *Update* in line 8. Thus, any cover of M^+ is either in *Frontier* $\cup$ *Candidates* or has not been generated. Then, by Corollary 5.6, all hypotheses $D_J \in S$ (S is formed at line 11) are the most probable hypotheses.

Since for any problem there exists a solution, it only needs to be shown that such S can be obtained in a a finite amount of time of the execution of algorithm *SEARCH*. Assume the contrary that such an S can never be found within a finite amount of time. Then $S = \emptyset$ at line 12 is always true, and the **while**–loop continues forever. On the other hand, since the hypothesis space 2^D is finite, and no hypothesis which has been generated can be generated again by any of its supersets (descendants), each time after the execution of $Update(D_I)$ at line 8, the current *Frontier* is different from all previous ones. Then after a finite amount of time, the current *Frontier* becomes $\emptyset$, and the current *Candidates* becomes the set of all covers of M^+ (Theorem 5.3). At this time *upper* $= \max\{UB(D_K, M^+) | D_K \in \emptyset\} = 0$ (line 9). Thus $S = \{D_J \in Candidates | L(D_J, M^+) \geq L(D_K, M^+)$ for all $D_K \in Candidates\} \neq \emptyset$ must be a solution. $\qquad \Box$

proof of Theorem 5.8.

Since x is about a previously unknown manifestation, it is not in M^+ or M^-.

Case 1: $x = \overline{m_j}$. Since M^+ is not changed in this case, the theorem holds trivially.

Case 2: $x = m_j$. Then by line 6, the set of present manifestations $M_{new}+ = M^+ \cup \{m_j\}$ where M^+ is the set of present manifestations before the execution of *Modify*. Now consider any cover D_I of M_{new}^+. They also cover M^+, thus are either in *Frontier* $\cup$ *Candidates* or are proper supersets of some member of *Frontier* before the execution of line 7. On the other hand, line 7 deletes from *Candidates* those D_J which are covers of M^+ but not M_{new}^+. Thus, D_I is not affected and the theorem holds. $\qquad \Box$

proof of Lemma 5.9.

From Equation 5.1a

$$UB(D_J, M^+) = \prod_{d_j \in D_J} \alpha_j \prod_{\substack{d_k \in D - D_J \\ \alpha_k > 1}} \alpha_k = \prod_{d_i \in D_I} \alpha_i \prod_{d_j \in D_J - D_I} \alpha_j \prod_{\substack{d_k \in D - D_J \\ \alpha_k > 1}} \alpha_k$$

$$\leq \prod_{d_i \in D_I} \alpha_i \prod_{d_j \in D_J - D_I} \alpha_j \prod_{\substack{d_k \in D - D_I \\ \alpha_k > 1}} \alpha_k = UB(D_I, M^+) \prod_{d_j \in D_J - D_I} \alpha_j$$

where the inequality comes from the facts that $D - D_I \supset D - D_J$ and $\alpha_k > 1$ for $d_k \in D_J - D_I$ in the last product. $\qquad \square$

proof of Theorem 5.10.
Consider any $D_J \supset D_I$. If $|D_J| = |D_I| + 1$, then $D_J = D_I \cup \{d_j\}$ for some $\{d_j\} \subset D - D_I$. From Lemma 5.9 and the definition of UB, $L(D_J, M^+) \leq UB(D_J, M^+) \leq UB(D_I, M^+)\, \alpha_j$. Therefore, for all such D_J

$$\sum_{\substack{D_J \supset D_I \\ |D_J| = |D_I| + 1}} L(D_I, M^+) \leq \sum_{\{d_j\} \subseteq D - D_I} UB(D_I, M^+)\, \alpha_j$$

$$= UB(D_I, M^+) \left[\sum_{\{d_j\} \subseteq D - D_I} \alpha_j \right].$$

Similarly, if $|D_J| = |D_I| + 2$, then $L(D_J, M^+) \leq UB(D_J, M^+) \leq UB(D_I, M^+)\, \alpha_j \alpha_k$ for some $\{d_j, d_k\} \subset D - D_I$. Therefore, for all such D_J

$$\sum_{\substack{D_J \supset D_I \\ |D_J| = |D_I| + 2}} L(D_J, M^+) \leq \sum_{\{d_j d_k\} \subseteq D - D_I} UB(D_I, M^+)\, \alpha_j \alpha_k$$

$$= UB(D_I, M^+) \left[\sum_{\{d_j d_k\} \subseteq D - D_I} \alpha_j \alpha_k \right].$$

Then for all proper supersets of D_I, we have

$$\sum_{D_J \supset D_I} L(D_J, M^+)$$

$$\leq UB(D_I, M^+) \left[\sum_{\{d_j\} \subseteq D - D_I} \alpha_j + \sum_{\{d_j d_k\} \subseteq D - D_I} \alpha_j \alpha_k + \cdots + \prod_{d_j \in D - D_I} \alpha_j \right]$$

$$= UB(D_I, M^+) \left[\prod_{d_j \in D - D_I} (1 + \alpha_j) - 1 \right]. \qquad \square$$

proof of Theorem 5.11.
(1) and (2) are the same as in Theorem 5.3 (the correctness of *Update-CM*).
(3) Let $X = \{D_K \in Frontier \cup Candidates \,|\, D_K$ covers $M^+\}$. To show that *Update-CM* preserves statement (3) is equivalent to showing that the changes of L_{known} exactly correspond to the changes of X. The only places *Frontier* or *Candidates* can be modified in *Update* are lines 5, 7, and 9. However, lines 5 and 7, which only involve D_I, do not change X because if D_I is not a cover of M^+, then $D_I \notin X$ before and after the execution of *Update*(D_I), while if D_I covers M^+, while if D_I covers M^+, lines 5 and 7

merely move D_I from *Frontier* to *Candidates*. Thus we only need to consider the changes of X brought by line 9. For all D_J added into *Frontier* at line 9, only those which are also covers will be added into X. Precisely for these D_J, their L values are added to L_{known} (line 11), thus statement (3) is preserved.

(4). By reasoning similar to that for (3) where lines 6 and 10 for changing L_{est} correspond to changes to *Frontier* at lines 5 and 9. □

proof of Lemma 5.12.

By Equation 5.9, since $P(D_I|M^+) \geq inf(D_I)$, $\sum_{I=1}^{K} P(D_I|M^+) \geq \sum_{I=1}^{K} inf(D_I) \geq CM$, so condition 1 given in Definition 5.1 is met.

Suppose that another set of hypotheses T also satisfies condition 1 of the problem solution and $|T| = |S| - n$ where $n > 0$. Since D_1 through D_K are a set of K most probable hypotheses and if $P(D_I|M^+) \geq P(D_J|M^+)$ then $sup(D_I) \geq sup(D_J)$, then by Equation 5.14,

$$\sum_{D_J \in T} sup(D_J) \leq \sum_{I=1}^{K-n} sup(D_I) \leq \sum_{I=1}^{K-1} sup(D_I) < CM.$$

On the other hand, since T satisfied condition 1,

$$\sum_{D_J \in T} sup(D_J) \geq \sum_{D_J \in T} P(D_J|M^+) \geq CM.$$

This is a contradiction. Therefore, S has the smallest possible size among all sets of hypotheses satisfying condition 1, and thus it satisfies condition 2 of Definition 5.1. □

proof of Theorem 5.13.

If the K most probable hypotheses in S satisfy Equation 5.14, it is obvious that the test at line 9 will be satisfied during the Kth pass of the **while**-loop ($S \neq \emptyset$ and $\sum_{D_J \in Sol} sup(D_J) < CM$ are always true before the Kth pass of the loop). Then by Lemma 5.12, the set of hypotheses *Sol* returned at line 9 is a solution of the given problem. Conversely, if there do not exist such K hypotheses, among the N hypotheses given in S satisfying Equation 5.14, then either $\sum_{J=1}^{N} inf(D_J) < CM$ or $\sum_{J=1}^{K} sup(D_J) \geq CM > \sum_{J=1}^{K} inf(D_J)$ for some $K \leq N$. The test at line 9 will always fail. In the first case, $S = \emptyset$ at line 5 after N iterations. In the second case, $\sum_{D_J \in Sol} sup(D_J) \geq CM$ after K iterations. In either case, the **while**-loop terminates and returns $\emptyset$. □

proof of Theorem 5.14.

Note that $L_{known} = L(\emptyset, M^+) = 0$ if $\emptyset$ does not cover M^+ (when $M^+ \neq \emptyset$), therefore, regardless of whether $\emptyset$ covers M^+ or not, by initializations of lines 4 to 7, the statements in Theorem 5.11 about *Frontier*, *Candidates*, L_{known}, and L_{est} are true before the **while**-loop of procedure *SEARCH-CM* (lines 8 to 17) started. Then by Theorem 5.11, they will always be true after each call of *Update-CM* in line 10. Thus, any cover of M^+ is either in *Frontier* $\cup$ *Candidates* or has not been generated. Then, by Corollary 5.6, all hypotheses $D_J \in S$ (S is formed at line 13) are more probable than any other hypothesis. If the most probable K of them satisfy Equation 5.14, then by Theorem 5.13, *Solution* = *Testsol*(S) (line 14) is a solution of the given problem. Since for any problem there exists a solution, it only needs to be shown that such S can be obtained in a finite amount of time of the execution of algorithm *SEARCH-CM*. Assume the contrary, that such an S can never be found. Then *Solution* $= \varnothing$ at line 15 is always true (Theorem 5.13), and the **while**-loop continues forever. On the other hand, since the hypothesis space 2^D is finite, and no hypothesis which has been generated can be generated again by any of its supersets (descendants), each time after the execution of *Update-CM*(D_I) at line 10, the current *Frontier* is different from all previous ones. Then after a finite amount of time, the current *Frontier* becomes $\varnothing$, and the current *Candidates* becomes the set of all covers of M^+ (by Theorem 5.11). At this time *upper* $= 0$ at line 11, thus $S = $ *Candidates*. Then the K most probable hypotheses $D_1, D_2, \ldots, D_K$ in S for some $K \leq 2^{|D|}$ must be a solution of the given problem. To show that they satisfy Equation 5.14, notice that now

$$L_{known} = \sum_{D_I \in Candidates} L(D_I, M^+) = \sum_{D_I \in 2^D} L(D_I, M^+)$$

and

$$L_{est} = \sum_{D_I \in \varnothing} l_{est}(D_I, M^+) = 0.$$

Therefore, by Equations 5.8 and 5.9, $inf(D_I) = sup(D_I) = P(D_I | M^+)$ for all $D_I \in 2^D$. $\square$

proof of Theorem 5.15.

By Equation 5.9, since $P(D_I | M^+) \geq inf(D_I)$, $\sum_{I=1}^{K} P(D_I | M^+) \geq \sum_{I=1}^{K} inf(D_I) \geq$ *CM*. Condition 1 given in Definition 5.2 is then met if Equation 5.15a is met. To establish condition 2 of Definition 5.2 from Equations 5.15a and b, suppose that another set of hypotheses T also satisfies condition 1 of Definition 5.2, and $|S| - |T| = n$ where $n > 1$. Since D_1 through D_{K-n} are $K - n$ most probable hypotheses and $|T| = K - n$, then $\sum_{I=1}^{K-n} P(D_I | M^+) \geq$ $\sum_{D_J \in T} P(D_J | M^+)$, and in turn $\sum_{I=1}^{K-n} sup(D_I) \geq \sum_{D_J \in T} sup(D_J)$. Since T satisfies condition 1 of Definition 5.2, we then have

$$\sum_{I=1}^{K-2} sup(D_I) \geq \sum_{I=1}^{K-n} sup(D_I) \geq \sum_{D_J \in T} sup(D_J) \geq \sum_{D_J \in T} P(D_J|M^+) \geq CM.$$

On the other hand, since $inf(D_K) \leq inf(D_{K-1}) \leq sup(D_{K-1})$, we have from Equation 5.15b that $(\sum_{I=1}^{K-1} sup(D_I)) - sup(D_{K-1}) < (\sum_{I=1}^{K} inf(D_I)) - inf(D_K)$, i.e., $\sum_{I=1}^{K-2} sup(D_I) < \sum_{I=1}^{K-1} inf(D_I)$. Then by Equation 5.15a, $\sum_{I=1}^{K-2} sup(D_I) < CM$. This contradicts the previous derivation that $\sum_{I=1}^{K-2} sup(D_I) \geq CM$. Therefore, condition 2 is met if both Equations 5.15a and 5.15b are met.   □

6
Causal Chaining

> "Where there is a causal sequence or chain of several events, A causing B, B causing C, C causing D, and D causing E, we can regard E as the effect of any or all of the preceding events."
> I. Copi, *Introduction to Logic*

In Chapters 3 – 5, we focused on the simplest type of diagnostic problems where the underlying causal networks consist of only two layers (sets M and D) and developed problem-solving algorithms for these problems. It was assumed there that disorders are directly causally-associated with measurable manifestations. In contrast, in many real-world diagnostic problems indirect causal associations between disorders and manifestations occur through *causal chaining* of intermediate states: "d causes s" and "s causes m" may be two existing causal associations which, during problem-solving, may be chained together to form "d causes m". For example, in diagnosing a plumbing system, the manifestation $m =$ "no water pressure at faucet 6" might be caused by abnormal state $s =$ "pipe 17 is blocked", and this in turn might be caused by the disorder $d =$ "frozen water in pipe 17". In medicine, manifestation $m =$ "left hemiparesis" (weakness on the left side) might be caused by $s =$ "right cerebral hemisphere damage", which in turn might be caused by disorder $d =$ "right intracerebral hematoma" (bleeding into the cerebrum or brain). In these cases and others, the causal chaining

$$d \rightarrow s \rightarrow m$$

is one of many involved in diagnostic inference.

Causal chaining in abductive inference models should reflect the transitive nature of causation, and may involve several rather than just two steps, as is the case in the above examples. This is analogous to chaining in rule-based deductive systems, but chaining is used here for causally-motivated abduction rather than rule-based deduction (theorems). We will use the term "pathological state" or "syndrome" for intermediate states or concepts such as "block in pipe 17" or "right cerebral hemisphere damage". Pathological states represent diagnostic categories that are generally not directly observable and thus are not manifestations, but they are not ultimate causative entities either and thus are not disorders.

In this chapter we develop diagnostic methods to handle causal chaining for problems involving different types of underlying causal networks where partial solutions may be known *a priori*. We will deal with networks containing only symbolic causal knowledge. (Extensions of the probabilistic causal model to networks involving causal chaining are under way at the time this book is going to press.) The methods developed in this chapter are direct extensions of the problem–solving methods developed in the previous chapters. We begin by extending the problem formulation of Chapter 3 to include pathological states.

6.1. Problem Formulation and Taxonomy of Causal Networks

6.1.1. Diagnostic Problems with Causal Chaining

The diagnostic problems of interest here include entities called *pathological states*. These entities are not diagnoses but syndromes which must be accounted for, yet at the same time they are abstractions that are not directly measurable. To represent these intermediate entities, or objects, the formulation of a diagnostic problem given in Chapter 3 (Section 3.1.1) is extended.

definition 6.1: A *diagnostic problem* P is a 5–tuple $< H,D,M,C,H^+ >$ where:
$H = \{ h_1, \ldots, h_n \}$ is a finite, non–empty set of *hypothesis elements* or entities;

$D \subseteq H$ is a non–empty distinguished set called *disorders*,

$M \subseteq H$ is a non–empty distinguished set called *manifestations*,

$C \subseteq H \times H$ is a relation called *causation* such that
   (1) for all $h_i \in H$, $< h_i,h_i > \notin C^+$ where C^+ is the transitive closure of C;
   (2) $domain(C) = H - M$, $range(C) = H - D$; and

$H^+ \subseteq H$ is a distinguished set of entities said to be present.

Here H represents all entities or diagnostic concepts of interest: manifestations, disorders, and pathological states (syndromes) (see Figure 6.1 below). D, a special subset of H, represents the causative disorders that may appear in final diagnoses (i.e., those entities which can spontaneously occur). M, a special subset of H, represents all manifestations, i.e., measurable abnormalities whose presence/absence can be determined by physical measurement. These two sets are the same as in two layered formulation in Chapter 3. Other entities of H (i.e., those in $H - (D \cup M)$) represent all intermediate pathological states. The causation relation C represents the direct causal associations among the entities in H. An association $< h_i,h_j > \in C$ means h_i may directly cause h_j. Note that, as before, this association does *not* mean that h_i necessarily causes h_j, but only that it *might*. This reflects the real world situation in many cases. C^+, the transitive closure of C, represents all direct and indirect causal associations among all entities in H that can be obtained through transitivity of the causal relation. Thus, the first condition in the definition of relation C specifies that the causal network is a finite acyclic graph (nothing can cause itself, directly or indirectly, i.e., no cycle exists in the network). The second condition specifies that in such a causal network every $d_i \in D$ has at least one outgoing link but no incoming link, every $m_j \in M$ has at least one incoming link but no outgoing link, and every intermediate entity in $H - (D \cup M)$ has both kinds of links. It should be clear from this that D and M are disjoint.

H, D, M, and C together specify the general problem environment wherein diagnostic inference is conducted. They correspond to the knowledge base in a knowledge–based system. H^+, a special subset of H, represents the features which are taken to be present in a specific given problem (unlike the general knowledge in H, D, M and C, H^+ is knowledge about a specific case). It corresponds to the input to a knowledge–based system. Note that, unlike M^+ in previous chapters, H^+ is not restricted to a subset of M but may contain pathological states or disorders as well (i.e., H^+ may contain a *volunteered partial solution*). As before, we will use $<H,D,M,C,?>$ to denote an underlying causal network when emphasis is on the general knowledge rather than a specific case.

Figure 6.1 below gives a graphic representation of an example of a diagnostic causal network $<H,D,M,C,?>$ where the relation C is shown as links between nodes representing diagnostic entities. All entities belong to H, with d_1, d_2, d_3 being disorders in D, m_1 through m_6 being manifestations in M, and h_4 through h_8 being intermediate entities or syndromes in $S = H - (D \cup M)$.

We call the causal networks defined in this way *hyper–bipartite networks*. While these networks involve fairly general causal chaining, they do not involve causal associations between disorders in D, or between manifestations in M. Among hyper–bipartite problems, it is useful to further distinguish two special cases: *layered* problems where causal networks are partitioned by relation C into disjoint layers of entities, and *bipartite* problems where there are only two layers of entities, namely, a set of disorders and a set of manifestations.

definition 6.2: A diagnostic problem $P = <H,D,M,C,H^+>$ is called

(1) a *layered problem* if H can be partitioned into non–empty disjoint sets $M = H^0$, H^1, ..., $H^L = D$, and $C = C_1 \cup C_2 \cup \cdots \cup C_L$ where $C_l \subseteq H^l \times H^{l-1}$ for $l = 1$ to L;

(2) a *bipartite problem* if $H = D \cup M$.

Figure 6.2 illustrates the networks for layered and bipartite problems. In a layered problem, relations $C_l \subseteq H^l \times H^{l-1}$ have $domain(C_l) = H^l$ and

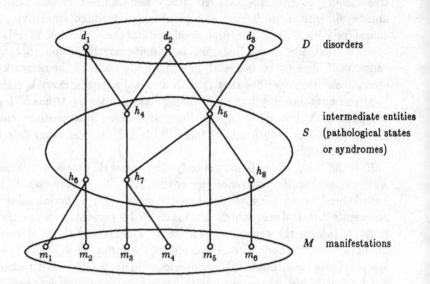

Figure 6.1. A causal network $< H,D,M,C,? >$ of a simple diagnostic problem where causal chains exist.

$range(C_l) = H^{l-1}$ for $l = 1$ to L. In a bipartite problem relation $C \subseteq D \times M$
has $domain(C) = D$ and $range(C) = M$. Thus, the two layer diagnostic prob-
lems we dealt with in Chapter 3 are special cases of the hyper–bipartite
problems considered here, namely, bipartite problems (problems without
intermediate states) where H^+ is restricted to being a subset of M. In the
next section, we will extend the problem–solving methods developed for
bipartite problems in Chapter 3 to solve layered problems and then general
hyper–bipartite problems.

Similar to Chapter 3, for a hyper–bipartite diagnostic problem P, we
define the following sets or functions based on the relation C, its transitive
closure C^+, and its reflexive and transitive closure C^*.

definition 6.3: For $h_i \in H$ in a diagnostic problem $P = < H,D,M,C,H^+ >$,
$effects(h_i) = \{ h_j \mid < h_i,h_j > \in C \}$, the set of entities directly caused by h_i;
$causes(h_i) = \{ h_j \mid < h_j,h_i > \in C \}$, the set of entities which can directly cause
h_i;
$effects^+(h_i) = \{ h_j \mid < h_i,h_j > \in C^+ \}$, the set of all entities that may be
directly or indirectly caused by h_i;
$causes^+(h_i) = \{ h_j \mid < h_j,h_i > \in C^+ \}$, the set of entities that can directly or
indirectly cause h_i; and
$effects^*(h_i) = \{ h_i \} \cup effects^+(h_i) = \{ h_j \mid < h_i,h_j > \in C^* \}$;
$causes^*(h_i) = \{ h_i \} \cup causes^+(h_i) = \{ h_j \mid < h_j,h_i > \in C^* \}$.

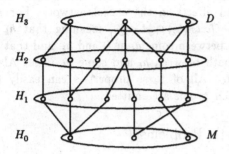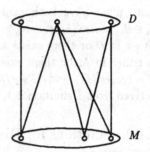

Figure 6.2. Some special types of diagnostic problems.
(a) A layered problem.
(b) A bipartite problem.

Generalizing the above concepts from elements of H to subsets of H, we define

definition 6.4: For any $H_I \subseteq H$ in a diagnostic problem
$P = <H,D,M,C,H^+>$,

$$effects(H_I) = \bigcup_{h_i \in H_I} effects(h_i),$$

$$effects^+(H_I) = \bigcup_{h_i \in H_I} effects^+(h_i),$$

$$effects^*(H_I) = \bigcup_{h_i \in H_I} effects^*(h_i);$$

$$causes(H_I) = \bigcup_{h_i \in H_I} causes(h_i),$$

$$causes^+(H_I) = \bigcup_{h_i \in H_I} causes^+(h_i),$$

$$causes^*(H_I) = \bigcup_{h_i \in H_I} causes^*(h_i);$$

example: in Figure 6.1 we have

$effects(h_5) = \{h_7, h_8, m_5\}$,
$causes(h_5) = \{d_2, d_3\}$,
$effects^+(h_5) = \{h_7, h_8, m_3, m_4, m_5, m_6\}$,
$causes^*(h_5) = \{h_5, d_2, d_3\}$,
$effects(\{d_1, d_3\}) = \{h_4, h_5, h_6\}$,
$causes^+(\{m_1, m_5\}) = \{h_6, h_5, d_1, d_2, d_3\}$. ☐

Certain properties of hyper–bipartite problems can be described using these concepts. For all $d_i \in D$, $causes(d_i) = \emptyset$, meaning that disorders have no further causes. For all $m_j \in M$, $effects(m_j) = \emptyset$, meaning that manifestations cannot cause anything. For all $h_k \in H - M$, $effects(h_k) \neq \varnothing$; and for all $h_k \in H - D$, $causes(h_k) \neq \varnothing$, meaning that any intermediate state must have both causes and effects in the causal network. For all $h_k \in H$, $causes^*(h_k) \cap D \neq \varnothing$ and $effects^*(h_k) \cap M \neq \varnothing$, meaning that h_k is either in D or there exists a path between some d_i in D and h_k, and that h_k is either in M or there exists a path between h_k and some m_j in M. Also, $H = causes^*(M)$ and $H = effects^*(D)$. All of these properties can easily be derived from Definition 6.1, so their proofs are omitted.

6.1.2.   Solutions for Diagnostic Problems

Now we generalize the concepts of explanation and problem solution from bipartite causal networks to hyper–bipartite ones.

definition 6.5: $H_I \subseteq H$ is said to be a *cover* of $H_J \subseteq H$ if $H_J \subseteq effects^*(H_I)$. A cover of H_J is said to be *irredundant* if none of its proper subsets is also a cover of H_J.

definition 6.6: E is an *explanation* of H^+ for a diagnostic problem $P = <H,D,M,C,H^+>$ iff
(1) E is an irredundant cover of H^+, and
(2) $E \subseteq D$.

Note that now the concept of covering is generalized from a relationship between $D_I \subseteq D$ and $M_J \subseteq M$ to any two subsets H_I and H_J of H. In particular, H_I and H_J are not required to be disjoint, and H_I can be considered to be a cover of itself. However, an explanation is restricted to being a subset of D for otherwise (if it contains some non–ultimate entities) the diagnostic process is considered incomplete. Similar to Chapter 3, we can define the problem solution as follows.

definition 6.7: The *solution* of a diagnostic problem $P = <H,D,M,C,H^+>$, designated as $Sol(P)$, is the set of all explanations of H^+.

For example, in Figure 6.1, $\{d_1,d_2\}$ and $\{d_1,d_3\}$ are the only explanations for $H^+ = \{m_1,m_5\}$, and therefore they compose the solution for a problem based on this H^+.

We proceed to characterize further properties of covers and explanations in the following lemmas. These properties are very similar to those of bipartite problems discussed in Chapter 3.

lemma 6.1: If H_K is a cover of H_J in a diagnostic problem, then there exists a $H_I \subseteq H_K$ which is an irredundant cover of H_J.

theorem 6.2 (Explanation Existence Theorem): There exists at least one explanation for H^+ for any diagnostic problem $P = <H,D,M,C,H^+>$.

lemma 6.3: If H_I is an irredundant cover of H_J, then for any $h_i \in H_I$, there exists some $h_j \in H_J$ which is uniquely covered by h_i, i.e., $h_j \in effects^*(h_i)$ but $h_j \notin effects^*(H_I - \{h_i\})$.

lemma 6.4: If H_I is an irredundant cover of H_J, then $|H_I| \leq |H_J|$. More specifically, if E is an explanation of H^+ for a diagnostic problem, then $|E| \leq |H^+|$.

Corollary 6.5: $E = \emptyset$ is the only explanation for $H^+ = \emptyset$.

6.2. Solving Layered and Hyper–Bipartite Problems

We now turn to solving layered and hyper–bipartite diagnostic problems where causal chaining plays an important role. Two algorithms, *LAYERED* and *HYPER-BIPARTITE*, are developed to solve these two types of more complicated problems. Since both algorithms employ the basic ideas of algorithm *BIPARTITE* during problem–solving and represent tentative hypotheses in generator–set form, it is recommend that the reader review algorithm *BIPARTITE* and the algebra for generator–sets presented in Chapter 3. Techniques for handling volunteered information will also be developed at the end of this chapter in a general form. Before then, we assume that $H^+ = M^+ \subseteq M$, i.e., it only contains present manifestations.

6.2.1. Transitivities of Sets of Irredundant Covers

Recall that the underlying causal networks of layered problems are partitioned into disjoint layers, and causal associations exist only between entities in adjacent layers (Figure 6.2). For clarity, we will use superscripts to denote layer numbers, e.g., G_i^J is a generator at layer J, Q^I is a generator-set at layer I, etc. Before presenting algorithm *LAYERED*, it is necessary to have a deeper understanding of how diagnostic elements (individually as well as in groups) are chained together in the framework of irredundant covering.

In first–order predicate calculus, if $A \to B$ and $B \to C$ are two axioms in a model,[*] it can be inferred that $A \to C$. In a rule based expert system, if $A \to B$ and $B \to C$ are two rules in the knowledge base, then $A \to C$ can be used as a compound rule. In the extended causal network model, as we mentioned earlier, similar chaining exists. Because cause–effect relations

---

[*] The arrows here represent logical implications.

are generally transitive, if h_i can cause h_j and h_j can cause h_k, then h_i can be viewed as implicitly or indirectly causing h_k. The notion of causal chaining can also be represented using the functions *causes* and *effects* defined in Section 6.1. If $h_i \in causes^*(h_j)$ and $h_j \in causes^*(h_k)$, then $h_i \in causes^*(h_k)$. Also, if $h_k \in effects^*(h_j)$, $h_j \in effects^*(h_i)$, then $h_k \in effects^*(h_i)$. That is, causal chaining can also be viewed as "effect chaining".

One could thus convert a causal network of a complicated problem, such as a layered or hyper–bipartite network, into a bipartite network by replacing H by $D \cup M$ and C by $C' = C^* \cap (D \times M)$. Relation C' here can be viewed as representing compiled associations between disorders and manifestations. Consequently, solving these more complicated problems could be achieved by applying algorithm *BIPARTITE* to the converted bipartite networks. This approach, however, abandons many of the potential benefits of using more general causal structures in the inference process, e.g., natural knowledge representation, efficient knowledge acquisition and maintenance, generating questions based on tentative hypotheses consisting of intermediate pathological states, etc. Rather than collapsing layered/hyper–bipartite networks into bipartite networks, approaches which directly use these more general networks need to be developed.

In parsimonious covering theory, the basic units used during problem–solving are not only individual hypothesis elements but also individual covers and groups of covers, as was demonstrated in problem–solving of bipartite problems in Chapter 3. In order to develop effective problem–solving techniques for layered/hyper–bipartite problems, it is therefore also necessary to inquire about the causal transitivities of various kinds of covers, i.e., how these covers can be chained together during the inference process. It is clear that the notion of cover is transitive. If X is a cover of Y and Y is a cover of Z, then X is also a cover of Z because $Z \subseteq effects^*(Y) \subseteq effects^*(X)$. However, a counter–example based on Figure 6.3 shows that transitivity does not hold for *individual* irredundant covers, i.e., if X is an irredundant cover of Y and Y is an irredundant cover of Z, then X is not necessarily an irredundant cover of Z. In Figure 6.3, let $Z = \{h_1, h_2, h_3, h_4\}$ at layer K. Z has three irredundant covers at layer J: $\{h_5, h_7\}$, $\{h_6, h_7\}$, and $\{h_6, h_8\}$. Let $Y = \{h_5, h_7\}$ and $X = \{h_9, h_{10}\}$. Then X is an irredundant cover of Y at layer I but not of Z because $\{h_{10}\}$ alone is also a cover of Z. However, as we will show in Theorem 6.7, causal transitivity does hold for *sets* of irredundant covers, a fact whose importance and usefulness will be seen later in the development of problem–solving techniques.

Recall that covers can be represented by the compact form of generators and generator–sets (see Section 3.3). If $[G_l]$ is a set of covers of M^+ in a problem, then any $Y \in [G_l]$ is a cover of M^+ and thus can account for the presence of all $m_j \in M^+$. If X is a cover of Y, then X is also a cover of M^+ and therefore can account for the presence of all $m_j \in M^+$. It is for this reason that we have the following definition.

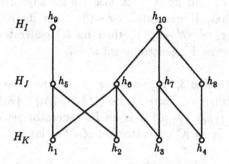

Figure 6.3. An example of a layered problem where irredundant covers are not transitive.

definition 6.8: In a diagnostic problem $P = <H,D,M,C,H^+>$, $X \subseteq H$ is said to be a cover of generator G_I if it covers some $Y \in [G_I]$; the cover is irredundant if none of its proper subsets is also a cover of G_I. Similarly, X is said to be a cover of generator–set G if it covers some $Y \in [G]$; the cover is irredundant if none of its proper subsets is also a cover of G.

Note that if $G_I = \varnothing$, then $\varnothing$ is its only cover because $[G_I] = [\varnothing] = \{\varnothing\}$ and $\varnothing$ is the only irredundant cover of $\varnothing$ (by Corollary 6.5). From the definition, X is a cover of generator–set G iff it covers some $G_I \in G$. If $G = \{\varnothing\}$, then $[G] = \{\varnothing\}$. Therefore, $\varnothing$ is the only cover of G. If $G = \varnothing$ then $[G] = \varnothing$. Therefore $G = \varnothing$ has no cover at all.

example: In Figure 6.3, let $G^J = \{(\{h_5\}\ \{h_7\})\ (\{h_6\}\ \{h_7,h_8\})\}$ be a generator–set at layer J, representing all irredundant covers at layer J of $Z = \{h_1,h_2,h_3,h_4\}$ at layer K. Then $\{h_{10}\}$ is an irredundant cover of G^J while $\{h_9,h_{10}\}$ is not.   ☐

Having defined covers and irredundant covers of a generator/generator–set, it is natural to use a generator–set at one layer to represent the set of irredundant covers of a given generator/generator–set at a lower layer in a layered problem. This generalization is given in the next definition.

definition 6.9: In a layered diagnostic problem, generator–set G^{I_k} at layer I is said to be an *irredundant cover generator–set* (*IC generator–set*) of generator G^J_k at layer $J < I$ if $[G^{I_k}] = \{X \subseteq H^I | X$ is an irredundant cover of $G^J_k\}$; generator–set G^I at layer I is said to be an *irredundant cover generator–set* (*IC generator–set*) of generator–set G^J at layer $J < I$ if $[G^I] = \{X \subseteq H^I | X$ is an irredundant cover of $G^J\}$.

By definition, if G^I is an IC generator–set of G^J, then for all $X \in \lfloor G^I \rfloor$, X covers some $Y \in \lfloor G^J \rfloor$ and no $X' \subset X$ also covers any member in the class $\lfloor G^J \rfloor$. Also note that, if generator $G_k^J = \varnothing$, then its IC generator–set is $\{\varnothing\}$; if generator–set $G^J = \{\varnothing\}$, then its IC generator–set is $\{\varnothing\}$; if $G^J = \varnothing$, then it has no IC generator–set at all.

example: In Figure 6.3, representing Z in the previous example in generator–set form, we have $G^K = \{(\{h_1\} \ \{h_2\} \ \{h_3\} \ \{h_4\})\}$. Then $G^J = \{(\{h_5\} \ \{h_7\}) \ (\{h_6\} \ \{h_7,h_8\})\}$ is an IC generator–set of G^K at layer J, and $G^I = \{(\{h_{10}\})\}$ is an IC generator–set of G^J at layer I.   □

An immediate advantage of this generalization is that a generator–set G^0 can be used to represent the present manifestations in more general situations. Recall that $M^+ \subseteq M$ represents all manifestations $m_j \in M^+$ that are present. Sometimes the presence of manifestations is not that clear: some uncertainty may exist about which manifestations are present. For instance, suppose manifestations m_1 and m_2 are definitely present, but at the same time one is unsure of whether the third present manifestation is m_3 or m_4. Then the present manifestations can easily be represented as a generator $(\{m_1\}\{m_2\}\{m_3,m_4\})$ or as a generator–set $\{(\{m_1\}\{m_2\}\{m_3,m_4\})\}$, incorporating the uncertainty about m_3 and m_4. The earlier notation M^+ can be considered as a special case of this extended notation where generator–set $G^0 = \{(\{m_j\} \mid m_j \in M^+)\}$.

Intuitively, it seems plausible that, unlike individual irredundant covers, IC generator–sets are transitive, and this result is now established through Lemma 6.6 and Theorem 6.7.

lemma 6.6: Let $X \subseteq H^{I+1}$ be an irredundant cover of $Z \subseteq H^{I-1}$ in a layered problem. Then there exists some $Y \subseteq H^I$ such that X is an irredundant cover of Y and Y is an irredundant cover of Z.

theorem 6.7 [Transitivity of IC Generator–Sets]: In a layered diagnostic problem, let G^{I+1} be an IC generator–set of G^I, and G^I be an IC generator–set of G^{I-1}. Then G^{I+1} is an IC generator–set of G^{I-1}.

The transitivity of IC generator–sets, as stated in Theorem 6.7, provides a way of chaining irredundant covers during diagnostic inference in a layered problem. The implication is that if $M^+ \subseteq H^0 = M$ is given as present, then *BIPARTITE* could first be applied to obtain G^1 such that $\lfloor G^1 \rfloor$ is the set of all irredundant covers of M^+ at layer 1. An extended version of *BIPARTITE* could then use G^1 to obtain IC generator–set G^2 of G^1 at layer 2, and so forth to obtain G^3, G^4,..., such that each one is an IC generator–set of its predecessor at one layer lower. If $H^L = D$ is the top layer, then G^L at layer L will thus eventually be obtained. By the transitivity of IC generator–sets, G^L implicitly represents the set of all irredundant covers of M^+ at D, and thus gives the solution of the layered problem.[*]

6.2.2. Algorithm *LAYERED* and Its Correctness

Algorithm *LAYERED* utilizes the transitivity property of IC generator–sets to solve a layered problem by solving a sequence of bipartite problems. An extended version of algorithm *BIPARTITE*, named *ICGS* (for irredundant covering of generator–sets), is called repeatedly to compute the IC generator–set at one layer of a generator–set one layer lower, starting at H^1 and working upwards until layer $H^L = D$ is reached. In some real–world situations, new questions for further hypothesis disambiguation may be best generated based on some tentative hypotheses at intermediate and higher layers. Therefore, whenever the IC generator–set at layer I is computed, algorithm *LAYERED* asks for new manifestations. If such manifestations exist, all of its causes at layer I are evoked and used to update the IC generator–set at that layer in the same way as was done in algorithm *BIPARTITE*. This approach thus permits (but does not require) the focused seeking of further clarification at many points during problem–solving.

To develop algorithm *LAYERED*, we first establish algorithm *ICGS* by showing how to transform the problem of computing an IC generator–set $G^{(I+1)}{}_k$ of a generator G^I_k into a bipartite diagnostic problem. The idea is as follows. For each g_j in generator G^I_k, a distinguished "pseudo–manifestation" or "pseudo–element" m_{b_j} is created. All such pseudo–manifestations m_{b_j} can be viewed as forming a "manifestation set" M_b, and the set of $h_i \in causes(g_i)$ for all $g_i \in G^I_k$ can be viewed as forming a "disorder set" D_b. The causal associations between elements in D_b and elements in M_b are set up as follows: for any $m_{b_j} \in M_b$, $causes(m_{b_j}) = causes(g_j)$. Thus, D_b, M_b and their causal associations compose a bipartite problem. Formally, this transformation is given in the following lemma where P is a given layered problem and P_b is the bipartite problem corresponding to layers I and $I+1$ in P.

lemma 6.8: Let $G^I_k = (g_1, g_2, ..., g_n)$ be a generator at layer $H^I \neq D$ in a layered problem $P = <H, D, M, C, M^+>$. Let $P_b = <D_b \cup M_b, D_b, M_b, C_b, M_b^+>$ where
$$D_b = \bigcup_{j=1}^{n} causes(g_j),$$
$M_b = \{m_{b_1}, m_{b_2}, \ldots, m_{b_n}\}$, where each m_{b_j} is the pseudo–element correspond-

---

(*) Counterexamples can easily be formed to show that transitivity does not hold for either individual or sets of minimum covers. That is, unlike irredundant covers, finding all minimum covers of M^+ at one layer does not necessarily lead to minimum covers at a higher layer. This is another reason that we prefer irredundancy to minimality as a parsimony criterion in parsimonious covering theory.

ing to $g_j \in G_k^I$,

$C_b = \{<h_i, m_{b_j}> \mid h_i \in D_b,\ m_{b_j} \in M_b,$ and there exists some $h_j \in g_j$ where $<h_i, h_j> \in C$ in $P\}$,

$M_b^+ = M_b$.

Then,

(a) P_b is a bipartite diagnostic problem; and

(b) $G^{(I+1)_k}$ is a IC generator–set of G_k^I in problem P iff $[G^{(I+1)_k}]$ is the solution of P_b.

Lemma 6.8 is crucial to problem–solving of layered problems because it formally equates the process that finds an IC generator–set of a given generator in a layered problem to the process that finds the solution of a bipartite problem. This is achieved by treating each g_j in the given generator as a pseudo–element m_{b_j} having the same set of causes as g_j. The following lemma extends the result to IC generator–sets of a generator–set.

lemma 6.9: Let $G^I = (G_1^I, G_2^I, \ldots, G_N^I)$ be a generator–set at layer I in a layered problem P, and let $G^{(I+1)_k}$ be an IC generator–set of $G_k^I \in G^I$. If G^{I+1} is an IC generator–set of G^I, then $[G^{I+1}] = \{X \mid X \in [G^{(I+1)_k}]$ and there does not exist $X' \in [G^{(I+1)_{k'}}]$ where $X' \subset X,\ k, k' = 1, 2, \ldots, N\}$.

This lemma indicates that $[G^{I+1}] \subseteq [\bigcup_{G_k^I \in G^I} G^{(I+1)_k}]$ where G^{I+1} is an IC generator–set of G^I at one layer higher and $G^{(I+1)_k}$ is an IC generator–set of an individual $G_k^I \in G^I$. It also indicates that if $X \in [G^{(I+1)_k}]$ is a redundant cover of G^I, then there must exist some $X' \in [G^{(I+1)_{k'}}]$ (where $k' \neq k$) which is a proper subset of X and irredundantly covers G^I. Therefore, in general G^{I+1} cannot be constructed by simply taking the union of the individual $G^{(I+1)_k}$. An additional check may be performed to remove possible redundancies among them. This can be done by the residual operation defined in Chapter 3 (Section 3.3).

example: In Figure 6.3, let generator–set $G^K = \{(\{h_1\}\ \{h_2\}\ \{h_3\}\ \{h_4\})\}$. Then the IC generator–set for G^K at layer J is $G^J = \{(\{h_6\}\ \{h_7, h_8\})\ (\{h_5\}\ \{h_7\})\}$. The IC generator–set of $(\{h_6\}\ \{h_7, h_8\})$ at layer I is $G^{I_1} = \{(\{h_{10}\})\}$ while the IC generator–set of $(\{h_5\}\ \{h_7\})$ at layer I is $G^{I_2} = \{(\{h_9\}\ \{h_{10}\})\}$. It is clear that $G^I \neq G^{I_1} \cup G^{I_2}$ because $\{h_{10}\} \in [G^{I_1}]$ is a proper subset of $\{h_9, h_{10}\} \in [G^{I_2}]$. Using the residual operation to remove this redundancy, we obtain

$$G^I = res(G^{I_1}, G^{I_2}) \cup res(G^{I_2}, G^{I_1}) = G^{I_1} \cup \emptyset = \{(\{h_{10}\})\}.\qquad \square$$

The algorithm $ICGS$ given below takes as input a generator–set G^I at layer I and returns its IC generator–set G^{I+1} at layer $I+1$. By Lemmas 6.8 and 6.9, this algorithm is a generalization of algorithm $BIPARTITE$ for bipartite problem–solving.

```
1. function ICGS(G)      {* G is G^I *}
2.        variables g_j element–set, G_k generator, Q Q_k generator–set;
3.        begin
4.            Q := ∅;            {* initialization, Q becomes G^{I+1} *}
5.            for G_k ∈ G do     {* while some generator in G not processed *}
6.                Q_k := {∅};
7.                for g_j ∈ G_k do  {* compute IC generator–set of G_k as Q_k *}
8.                    Q_K := revise(Q_k, causes(g_j))
9.                endfor;
10.               Q := res(Q, Q_k);      {* remove possible redundancy from Q *}
11.               Q := Q ∪ res(Q_k, Q)  {* remove possible redundancy from Q_k *}
                                        {* and construct new Q *}
12.           endfor;
13.           return Q              {* Q is the IC generator–set of G *}
15.       end.
```

In function $ICGS$, the **for** loop (lines 7 to 9), an extended version of algorithm $BIPARTITE$, computes the IC generator–set of a chosen generator $G_k \in G$. A few modifications are made here relative to $BIPARTITE$. First, in line 8, function "$revise$" is applied to $causes(g_j)$, not $causes(m_1)$, because the g_j's are treated as pseudo–elements.[*] Second, no external functions $Moremanifs$ or $Nextman$ are needed since G is given as input. Instead, a **for** statement is used to select each $g_j \in G_k$ sequentially (line 7). The rest of the operations are the same as in $BIPARTITE$. When the **for** loop ends (line 9), Q_k is the IC generator–set one layer higher for generator G_k. To obtain the IC generator–set for the whole generator–set G, each time the IC generator–set Q_k for some $G_k \in G$ is computed, it is checked against the current Q for any duplicates or redundancy, where Q is the IC generator–set of all previously selected G_k's. If such duplicates or redundancy exist in either Q_k or Q, they are removed by the two residual operations in lines 10 and 11. The union operation in line 11 is then used to construct the IC generator–set Q of all G_k's in G selected up to this moment. When the outer loop (lines from 5 to 12) ends, Q is returned as the IC generator–set one layer higher of the given generator–set G.

The following theorem establishes the correctness of the function $ICGS$.

theorem 6.10: If G^I is a generator–set at layer $H^I \neq D$ in a layered diagnostic problem, then $G^{I+1} = ICGS(G^I)$ is an IC generator–set of G^I at layer

---

(*) Function $revise$ is described in Section 3.4.1.

H^{I+1}.

Problem–solving for layered diagnostic problems can iteratively apply *ICGS* to find IC generator–sets at layer 2, 3, . . . , up to layer L $(H^L = D)$, starting with G^1 where $[G^1]$ is the set of all irredundant covers of M^+ at layer H^1. In addition to this, as mentioned earlier, it may be convenient to try to discover new manifestations incrementally whenever an IC generator–set is computed by *ICGS* at any layer. Combining these two considerations together, algorithm *LAYERED* which solves layered diagnostic problems involving causal chaining is given below. For convenience of presentation, a notation for the function *causes* is adopted here which concerns finding causes of an entity at a higher layer:

$$\text{for } I > 1, \; causes^I(h_i) = causes(causes^{I-1}(h_i)) \text{for any } h_i \in H.$$

That is, $causes^I(h_i)$ is the set of all causes of h_i at layer I higher in the network.

```
1.  function LAYERED(H,D,M,C)
2.      variables j k integer, G generator–set;
3.      begin
4.          k := 1;              {* initialization of layer index k *}
5.          G := {∅};           {* initialization of the solution generator–set *}
6.      repeat
7.          if G ≠ {∅} then G := ICGS(G);
                            {* compute IC generator–set of G one layer higher *}
8.          while Moremanifs do
9.              G := revise(G, causes^k(Nextman))
                            {* incorporate causes of new manifestation into G *}
10.         endwhile;
11.         k := k + 1     {* increment layer index *}
12.     until G is at D;
13.     return G           {* generator–set for Sol(P) *}
14.     end.
```

In this algorithm, computation is carried out primarily by line 7 and by the **while** loop (lines 8 to 10). By calling function *ICGS*, line 7 gives the IC generator–set of generator–set G at one layer higher. The **while** loop calls function "*revise*" to incorporate the causes of any newly discovered manifestation into the current generator–set G. Variable k indicates the layer number at which the current IC generator–set is being computed, so $causes^k(Nextman)$ gives the causes of the new manifestation at layer k, the current layer. The termination condition for the **repeat** loop "G is at D" is an abbreviation for the requirement that the set of all hypothesis elements in G is a subset of D, i.e., $\bigcup_{\substack{g_i \in G_I \\ G_I \in G}} g_i \subseteq D$. In other words, the algorithm terminates when an IC generator–set at layer D is computed and no more manifestations can be obtained. The correctness of this algorithm is established by the next theorem.

theorem 6.11 (Correctness of *LAYERED*): Let $P = <H,D,M,C,M^+>$ be a layered diagnostic problem. Then $Sol(P) = [LAYERED(H,D,M,C)]$.

6.2.3. Pseudo–Layers in Hyper–Bipartite Problems

Hyper–bipartite diagnostic problems are the most general problems formulated in this chapter. In general H, the set of all elements, is not partitioned into disjoint layers in a hyper–bipartite problem. If, however, a systematic transformation could be found to view or treat a hyper–bipartite problem as if it were a layered one while preserving the problem solution, then it could be solved by algorithm *LAYERED*. Actually, there are a number of such transformations. In the following, a simple one is presented and its corresponding problem–solving algorithm is seen to require only a minor change to *LAYERED*.

The basic idea of this transformation can best be explained by first trying to generate pseudo–layers from the given hyper–bipartite problem as follows: $H^0 = M$, $H^1 = causes(H^0)$, $H^2 = causes(H^1)$, etc. Thus, for the hyper–bipartite problem given in Figure 6.4a, the first two pseudo–layers would be $H^0 = \{m_1,m_2,m_3,m_4,m_5\}$ and $H^1 = \{h_5,h_1,h_3,h_2,h_4,h_8\}$.

Two problems arise, however, when one tries to generate H^2 by simply equating it to $causes(H^1)$. First, h_5 and h_8 of H^1 are in D and their causes sets are empty. Second, $h_3 \in causes(h_1)$ is already in H^1, and so is $h_4 \in causes(h_2)$. In other words, layers thus generated may not be disjoint. To overcome the first problem, an extended *causes* function, called *extcauses* is defined for all $h_i \in H$ and $H_I \subseteq H$:

$$extcauses(h_i) = \begin{cases} \{h_i\} & \text{if } h_i \in D, \\ causes(h_i) & \text{otherwise;} \end{cases} \text{ and}$$

$$extcauses(H_I) = \bigcup_{h_i \in H_I} extcauses(h_i).$$

Also, for notational convenience, we define:

$$extcauses^0(h_i) = \{h_i\}, \quad extcauses^{l+1}(h_i) = extcauses(extcauses^l(h_i));$$
$$extcauses^0(H_I) = H_I, \quad extcauses^{l+1}(H_I) = extcauses(extcauses^l(H_I)).$$

Since the causal networks formulated in this model are finite acyclic graphs, it is clear from the definition of function *extcauses* that for each $m_j \in M$, $extcauses^{N_j}(m_j) = causes^*(m_j) \cap D$, and $extcauses^N(M) = D$ for some finite numbers N_j and N. Thus, function *extcauses* not only makes sense when applied to elements of D, but also guarantees that after a finite number of applications to M, the set D of the given network can be

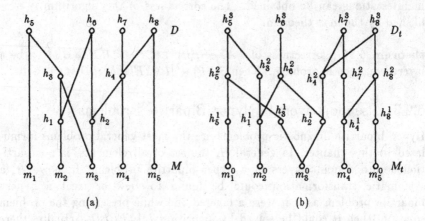

Figure 6.4.   An example of transforming a hyper–bipartite
problem into a layered problem using the function *trans*
described in the text. $P_t = trans(P)$ is composed of
pseudo–layers derived from P while preserving the problem solution.
(a) A hyper–bipartite problem $P = <H,D,M,C,?>$.
(b) A layered problem $P_t = trans(P)$ transformed from P.

obtained.

example: In Figure 6.4a, applying function "extcauses" on M of problem
$\dot{P}$ three times, the following sets can be generated:

$extcauses^0(M) = \{ m_1, m_2, m_3, m_4, m_5 \} = M,$

$extcauses(M) = \{ h_5, h_1, h_3, h_2, h_4, h_8 \},$

$extcauses^2(M) = \{ h_5, h_3, h_6, h_4, h_7, h_8 \},$

$extcauses^3(M) = \{ h_5, h_6, h_7, h_8 \} = D.$ □

Sets $extcauses^I(M)$ cannot be directly used as layers to construct a layered
problem because they may not be disjoint, as is clearly shown in the above
example. To handle this problem, a superscript notation for renaming (or
labeling) is adopted: every element in $extcauses^I(M)$ is marked with superscript I. Thus, for $I \neq J$, h_k^I and h_k^J are considered to be two different elements in the transformed layered problem. Combining function $extcauses$
and this superscript notation, pair–wise disjoint sets of hypothesis elements
can be generated from a given hyper–bipartite problem. These sets will be
called *pseudo–layers* derived from the given hyper–bipartite problem P. As
will be seen later, they form the layers of the layered problem P_t derived
from P.

example: In Figure 6.4b, the four pseudo–layers derived from the problem P (Figure 6.4a) are as follows:

$$H^0 = \{\, m_1^0, m_2^0, m_3^0, m_4^0, m_5^0 \,\}, \qquad H^1 = \{\, h_5^1, h_1^1, h_3^1, h_2^1, h_4^1, h_8^1 \,\},$$
$$H^2 = \{\, h_5^2, h_3^2, h_6^2, h_4^2, h_7^2, h_8^2 \,\}, \qquad H^3 = \{\, h_5^3, h_6^3, h_7^3, h_8^3 \,\}.$$

If superscripts are ignored, then H^0 in P_t is the same as M in P while H^3 in P_t is the same as D in P. $\qquad\qquad\qquad\qquad\qquad\qquad\qquad\qquad\square$

Pseudo–layer generation during this transformation should stop when the pseudo–layer corresponding to D of the given problem is generated; any further pseudo–layers will be the same as D. In the above example, no pseudo–layers should be generated after layer $H^3 = D$ is generated. H_t, the set of all hypothesis elements of transformed problem P_t, is thus composed of pseudo–layers H^0 through H^3 derived from P.

To transform a hyper–bipartite problem to a layered one while preserving the solution, not only must H be transformed to a set of disjoint layers, but C must also be preserved appropriately. Based on the pseudo–layer generation process discussed above, the transformation of relation C to C_t is informally described as follows. First, if $< h_i, h_j > \in C$ in P, then $< h_i^{K+1}, h_j^K > \in C_t$ in P_t for some K. However, for some $h_i \in D$ in P, it is possible that both h_i^K and h_i^{K+1} may exist in P_t. For example, consider $h_5 \in D$ of the hyper–bipartite problem in Figure 6.4a, for which h_5^1, h_5^2, and h_5^3 are all in the transformed problem. In situations like this, it is also necessary to consider h_i^{K+1} to be a pseudo–cause of h_i^K. Combining the above two situations together, $< h_i^{K+1}, h_j^K > \in C_t$ in P_t iff $h_i \in extcauses(h_j)$ in P, thus preserving the causal associations given in C of P. Based on the pseudo–layer generation and causal association transformation processes described above, the function *trans*, which transforms a given hyper–bipartite problem into a layered problem while preserving the solution, is formally defined.

definition 6.10: Let $P = < H, D, M, C, M^+ >$ be a hyper–bipartite problem. Then function *trans* is defined as $trans(P) = < H_t, D_t, M_t, C_t, M_t^+ >$ where $H_t = H^0 \cup H^1 \cup \ldots \cup H^N$ where

$H^0 = M_t = \{\, h_i^0 \,|\, h_i \in M \,\}$,

$H^I = \{\, h_i^I \,|\, h_i \in extcauses(h_j) \text{ where } h_j^{I-1} \in H^{I-1} \,\}$ for $I > 0$, and

$D_t = H^N$ is the first layer thus generated such that for every $h_i^N \in H^N$, $h_i \in D$;

$C_t = C_1 \cup C_2 \cup \cdots \cup C_N$ where

$C_I = \{\, < h_i^I, h_j^{I-1} > \,|\, h_i \in extcauses(h_j) \,\}$ for $1 \leq I \leq N$;

$M_t^+ = \{\, h_i^0 \,|\, h_i \in M^+ \,\}$.

lemma 6.12: If $P = < H, D, M, C, M^+ >$ is a hyper–bipartite diagnostic problem, then $P_t = < H_t, D_t, M_t, C_t, M_t^+ > = trans(P)$ is a layered problem.

Figure 6.4b gives the layered problem P_t derived from the hyper–bipartite problem P of Figure 6.4a by function *trans*. Here, each layer of P_t is a pseudo–layer of P (H^0 through H^3 as given earlier), and causal associations are represented by links between elements in adjacent layers. Next, we establish that the transformation function *trans* preserves the problem solution, i.e., if the superscripts are ignored, then $Sol(P)$ equals $Sol(P_t)$.

lemma 6.13: Let $P = <H,D,M,C,M^+>$ be a hyper–bipartite diagnostic problem. Let $P_t = <H_t,D_t,M_t,C_t,M_t^+> = trans(P)$ where H_t consists of layers $H^0 = M_t$, H^1, . . . , $H^N = D_t$. Then $E_t = \{h_1^N, h_2^N, \ldots, h_k^N\} \in Sol(P_t)$ iff $E = \{h_1, h_2, \ldots, h_k\} \in Sol(P)$.

6.2.4. Algorithm *HYPER–BIPARTITE* and Its Correctness

The previous subsection demonstrated that hyper–bipartite problems could be transformed into layered problems, and by implication could be solved by using algorithm *LAYERED*. It is, however, unwise to really transform a hyper–bipartite problem network to a layered one. Such a transformation would lose the natural causal relations supported by the hyper–bipartite model in many domains, and this in turn could cause difficulties in knowledge base updating and answer justification. The reason for defining such a transformation function is to lay the groundwork for formally establishing the correctness of the problem–solving algorithm developed below. Fortunately, the actual transformation used during hyper–bipartite problem–solving does not need to be as complete as the function *trans*, and the transformation does not really change the knowledge base. First, those hypothesis elements in a network which are not relevant to the given manifestations of a specific problem (i.e., those which are not in $causes^*(M^+)$) can be ignored since they will not be evoked during the inference process at all. Second, as shown in algorithm *LAYERED* for layered problem–solving, the causal network is only referenced during the hypothesis evocation phase through the function *causes*, while the hypothesis formation phase (function *revise*) only involves algebraic manipulations of existing hypotheses and newly evoked elements. In other words, function *revise* only operates on elements and covers at one pseudo–layer. Therefore, actually renaming the duplicate entities h_i becomes unnecessary (duplicate elements only occur in different pseudo–layers). The algorithm *HYPER–BIPARTITE* for hyper–bipartite problem–solving, given next, is identical to algorithm *LAYERED* except that all calls to function *causes* are replaced by calls to function *extcauses*. Likewise, the function *ICGS'* which replaces function *ICGS* at line 7 in algorithm *HYPER–BIPARTITE*, is identical to function *ICGS* except that the call to $causes(g_j)$ in *ICGS* is replaced by $extcauses(g_j)$. Thus, pseudo–layers are not really constructed, but the algorithm now behaves as if they exist.

```
1. function HYPER-BIPARTITE(H,D,M,C)
2.      variables j k integer, G generator-set;
3.      begin
4.          k := 1;                    {* initialization of layer index k *}
5.          G := {∅};                 {* initialization of eventual solution G *}
6.          repeat
7.              if G ≠ {∅} then G := ICGS'(G);
                        {* compute IC generator-set of G at pseudo-layer k *}
8.              while Moremanifs do
                        {* update G by new manifestations at pseudo-layer k *}
9.                  G := revise(G, extcauses^k(Nextman) )
10.             endwhile;
11.             k := k + 1             {* move one pseudo-layer higher *}
12.         until G is at D;
13.         return G
14.     end.
```

theorem 6.14 [Correctness of *HYPER-BIPARTITE*]: If $P = \langle H,D,M,C,M^+ \rangle$ is a hyper-bipartite problem then $Sol(P) = [HYPER\text{-}BIPARTITE(H,D,M,C)]$.

6.3. Volunteered Partial Solutions

As described earlier, in some real world diagnostic problems not only measurable findings (manifestations) are given, but confirmed disorders or pathological states can be given as well. For example, a physician might tell a consultant: "This 56 year old diabetic woman complains of chest pain · · · " indicating the known presence of a disorder (diabetes). A diagnostic algorithm should be able to assimilate and use this kind of information effectively in arriving at a correct diagnosis. To include these situations in the extended model, H^+, the set of features given as present for a particular case, is not restricted to be a set of manifestations as we have done so far. Instead, H^+ can contain some disorders and pathological states as well. First, we discuss the simplest case (i.e., bipartite problems).

Consider extending the concept of a bipartite problem to $P = \langle H,D,M,C,H^+ \rangle$ where H^+ may not be a subset of M. Let $M^+ \subseteq M$ be the set of all manifestations known to be present, and $D^+ \subseteq D$ be the set of confirmed or volunteered disorders. Then $H^+ = M^+ \cup D^+$. Since D^+ is confirmed to be present, intuitively, any diagnostic explanation or plausible hypothesis must contain D^+ as a subset. This is why we call D^+ a *volunteered partial solution*. The next theorem shows that the covering requirement of explanations defined in parsimonious covering theory (definitions 3.5 and 6.5) already captures this intuition.

theorem 6.15: Let E be an explanation of $H^+ = M^+ \cup D^+$ for an extended bipartite problem $P = <H,D,M,C,H^+>$ where $M^+ \subseteq M$ and $D^+ \subseteq D$. Then, $D^+ \subseteq E$.

For a given set of present manifestations in a problem, the problem solution may be quite different depending on whether or not there exists volunteered information.

example: Take problem P_1 of Chapter 3 (Figure 3.4) and let $H^+ = \{m_1, m_4, m_5, d_7\}$. The solution to this problem is

$$S_1 = \{\{d_1, d_7\}, \{d_2, d_7\}, \{d_3, d_7, d_8\}, \{d_4, d_7, d_8\}\}.$$

This is different from the solution for the case of $H^+ = \{m_1, m_4, m_5\}$ which, as computed in Chapter 3, is

$$S_2 = \{\{d_1, d_7\}, \{d_1, d_8\}, \{d_1, d_9\}, \{d_2, d_7\}, \{d_2, d_8\}, \{d_2, d_9\}, \{d_3, d_8\}, \{d_4, d_8\}\}.$$

As given in Chapter 3 (see Figure 3.6), $S_2 = [G]$, where $G = \{(\{d_3, d_4\}\ \{d_8\}) (\{d_1, d_2\}\ \{d_7, d_8, d_9\})\}$ is a generator–set. When a new manifestation m_j is given, $revise(G, causes(m_j))$ can be used to update the existing hypotheses since every $h_j \in causes(m_j)$ may cover m_j. In the case where a confirmed disorder is given, such as d_7 in this example, one may naturally think of using $revise(G, \{d_7\})$ to update the existing hypotheses since d_7 is the only element which may cover itself. In fact, starting with $H^+ = \{m_1, m_4, m_5\}$, let $G^{vol} = revise(G, \{d_7\})$. From the definitions of functions *division*, *residual*, *augmented residual*, and *revise* given in Chapter 3, we have $G^{vol} = F \cup res(Q, F)$ where

$$F = div(G, \{d_7\}) = \{(\{d_1, d_2\}\ \{d_7\})\},$$

$$Q = augres(G, \{d_7\}) = \{(\{d_3, d_4\}\ \{d_8\}\ \{d_7\})\},$$

so,

$$res(Q, F) = \{(\{d_3, d_4\}\ \{d_8\}\ \{d_7\})\}.$$

Thus,

$$G^{vol} = \{(\{d_1, d_2\}\ \{d_7\}) (\{d_3, d_4\}\ \{d_8\}\ \{d_7\})\}.$$

It is clear that $[G^{vol}] = S_1$.   □

This example reveals that updating the existing hypotheses when a newly confirmed disorder is given can be done in a similar way as is done for a newly given present manifestation. The difference is that one uses $revise(G, \{d_i\})$ instead of $revise(G, causes(m_j))$. Note that by the definition of function *extcauses* in the last subsection, $revise(G, \{d_i\})$ and $revise(G, causes(m_j))$ are both just special cases of $revise(G, extcauses(x))$ where x can be either a newly discovered manifestation m_j (then $extcauses(x) = causes(m_j))$, or a newly confirmed disorder d_i (then

$extcauses(x) = \{d_i\}$).   Therefore, algorithm *BIPARTITE* for bipartite problem–solving can readily be adopted to handle confirmed or volunteered disorders. The only necessary change is to replace the function *causes* by the function *extcauses* in the algorithm.

This basic idea can also be adopted in problem–solving for layered and hyper–bipartite problems with volunteered partial solutions. However, some new considerations may arise. First, intermediate pathological states not in M nor D can also be given as confirmed. Second, like manifestations, these confirmed or volunteered syndromes can be given at any stage of the diagnostic process. For example, in a layered diagnostic problem–solving process, a confirmed syndrome h_i at layer H^K may be available either before or after the intermediate hypothesis G^K at layer H^K is formed. To cope with these situations, a measure of the height of a node h_i relative to M in a hyper–bipartite problem network is helpful (such heights would be the layer numbers if the problem is a layered one). If a given new fact is a confirmation of a manifestation or an intermediate state with height lower than the height of the current layer (pseudo–layer), it will be treated in a way similar to new manifestations in algorithms *LAYERED* or *HYPER–BIPARTITE*, i.e., first find all of its causes at the current layer using the *extcauses* function, and then incorporate these causes into the current generator–set. If disorders or intermediate states with height higher than the current layer are given voluntarily during the problem–solving, then a wait list can be used to hold temporarily all of these elements until the appropriate time. An algorithm for solving hyper–bipartite problems involving volunteered partial solutions can be found in [Peng85]. The basic idea of the algorithm is illustrated through the following example.

example: Consider the hyper–bipartite problem given in Figure 6.4a. Let the height of an element $h_i \in H$ be defined as the minimum path length from h_i to any $m_j \in M$. Figure 6.4b gives the pseudo–layers and extended causal associations between elements in adjacent pseudo–layers. The lowest pseudo–layer in which an element h_i appears is the height of that element. Suppose that three elements, m_2, m_3 and h_7 are known to be present (h_7 is volunteered information). Since the height of h_7 is two, it will not be processed, but held temporarily in a waiting list. Incorporating m_2 and m_3 into the initial generator–set G (see line 9 of algorithm *HYPER–BIPARTITE*), we have the generator–set at pseudo–layer 0 as

$$G^0 = \{(\{ m_2\}\{ m_3\})\}.$$

Applying $ICGS'$ over G^0, we have a generator–set at pseudo–layer 1 as

$$G^1 = \{(\{ h_1\}\{ h_3, h_2\})\}.$$

Suppose that it is now revealed that h_2 is also present. Since h_2 is of height 1, it is immediately incorporated into G^1 by *revise*, leading to a revised generator–set at the current layer (layer 1)

$$\hat{G}^1 = revise(G^1, \{h_2\}) = \{(\{h_1\}\{h_2\})\}.$$

Applying $ICGS'$ again, this time over $\hat{G}^1$, we have a generator–set at pseudo–layer 2 as

$$G^2 = \{(\{h_6\})(\{h_3\}\{h_4\})\}.$$

Since h_7 in the waiting list has height two, it is now incorporated into G^2, leading to the revised generator–set

$$\hat{G}^2 = \{(\{h_6\}\{h_7\})(\{h_3\}\{h_4\}\{h_7\})\}.$$

Now, suppose that one more manifestation m_4 is also given to be present. Applying the extended causes function $extcauses$, all causes of m_4 of height two are found (the process is currently at pseudo–layer 2): $extcauses^2(m_4) = \{h_7, h_8\}$. Inspection of $\hat{G}^2$ shows that every hypothesis it generates contains one of these two causes of m_4, namely h_7, so incorporating $\{h_7, h_8\}$ into $\hat{G}^2$ does not cause any change to the current generator–set. One more application of $ICGS'$ over the current generator–set $\hat{G}^2$ gives a generator–set at pseudo–layer 3

$$G^3 = \{(\{h_6\}\{h_7\})(\{h_5\}\{h_7\})\}.$$

Because now all elements in G^3 are members in D, we have $Sol(P) = [G^3]$. It can be verified that the two hypotheses $\{h_6, h_7\}$ and $\{h_5, h_7\}$ generated by G^3 are the only subset of D which irredundantly cover all given present elements $\{m_2, m_3, m_4, h_2, h_7\}$. □

6.4. Mathematical Appendix

proof: of Lemma 6.1.
Analogous to Lemma 3.3, but using Definition 6.5. □

proof of Theorem 6.2.
Since $H^+ \subseteq H = effects^*(D)$, D is a cover of H^+. The theorem then follows from the definition of explanation and Lemma 6.1. □

proof of Lemma 6.3.
Analogous to Lemma 3.5. □

proof of Lemma 6.4.
Analogous to Lemma 3.6. □

proof of Corollary 6.5.
$H^+ = \emptyset = effects^*(\emptyset)$, therefore, $\emptyset$ covers $H^+ = \emptyset$ and has no proper subset. Thus $\emptyset$ is an explanation of $H^+ = \emptyset$. Also, since $\emptyset$ is a proper subset of any non–empty set of entities, it follows that $E = \emptyset$ is the only explanation of H^+. □

proof of Lemma 6.6.

Since all layers are disjoint, $Z \subseteq effects^*(X)$ iff $Z \subseteq effects^+(X) = effects^*(effects(X))$ where $effects(X) \subseteq H^I$, i.e., Z is covered by $effects(X)$ which is in turn covered by X. Then by Lemma 6.1, there exists some $Y \subseteq effects(X)$ where Y is an irredundant cover of Z. Suppose that there exists some $X' \subset X$ which also covers Y; then X' also covers Z, contradicting the fact that X is an irredundant cover of Z. Therefore, X is an irredundant cover of Y. $\qquad\square$

proof of Theorem 6.7.

First show that every $X \in [G^{I+1}]$ is an irredundant cover of G^{I-1}. From the definition of IC generator–set, X is an irredundant cover of some $Y \in [G^I]$ and Y is an irredundant cover of some $Z \in [G^{I-1}]$. Therefore, by the transitivity of covers, X is a cover of Z, thus X covers G^{I-1}. Suppose that there exists some $X' \subset X$ which is an irredundant cover of G^{I-1} (irredundantly covers some $Z' \in [G^{I-1}]$). Then by Lemma 6.6, there exists some $Y' \subseteq H^I$ such that X' irredundantly covers Y' and Y' irredundantly covers Z'. Thus $Y' \in [G^I]$ and X' is a cover of G^I. This contradicts that X is an irredundant cover of G^I.

Conversely, let $X \subseteq H^{I+1}$ be an irredundant cover of G^{I-1}. Then X is an irredundant cover of some $Z \in [G^{I-1}]$. By Lemma 6.6, there exists some $Y \subseteq H^I$ such that X irredundantly covers Y and Y irredundantly covers Z, i.e., $Y \in [G^I]$ and $X \in [G^{I+1}]$. $\qquad\square$

proof of Lemma 6.8.

(a). Since $g_j \neq \varnothing$ and $causes(g_j) \neq \varnothing$ for all $g_j \in G_k^I$, then from the definition of C_b and the one-to-one correspondence between $m_{b_j} \in M_b$ and $g_j \in G_k^I$, $range(C_b) = M_b$ and $domain(C_b) = D_b$. Thus, P_b is a bipartite problem.

(b). From the definition of C_b and D_b, we have $h_i \in causes(m_{b_j})$ in P_b iff $h_i \in causes(g_j)$ in P. Then, in P, $E \subseteq H^{I+1}$ covers G_k^I iff E covers some $X \in G_k^I$ iff for all $g_j \in G_k^I$: $E \cap causes(g_j) \neq \varnothing$; in P_b, E covers M_b^+ iff for all $m_{b_j} \in M_b^+$: $E \cap causes(m_{b_j}) \neq \varnothing$. Therefore, $E \subseteq H^{I+1}$ is a cover of G_k^I in P iff E is a cover of M_b^+ in P_b. Then it immediately follows that $E \subseteq H^{I+1}$ is an irredundant cover of G_k^I in P iff E is an irredundant cover of M_b^+ in P_b. $\qquad\square$

proof of Lemma 6.9.

For any $X \in [G^{I+1}]$, X covers some $G_k^I \in G^I$. If there exists some $X' \in [G^{(I+1)_k}']$ and $X' \subset X$, then X' also covers G^I, which contradicts that X is an irredundant cover of G^I.

Conversely, for any $X \in [G^{(I+1)_k}]$ where there does not exists $X' \in [G^{(I+1)_k}']$ such that $X' \subset X$, then, X covers G^I. Suppose that X is not an irredundant cover of G^I, then there exists $X_1 \subset X$ which irredundantly covers G^I, and therefore irredundantly covers some $G_{k'}^J \in G^J$. This is a contradiction. Thus, $X \in [G^{I+1}]$. $\qquad\square$

proof of Theorem 6.10.

By induction on $|G^I|$.

Base case: $|G^I| = 0$, i.e., $G^I = \varnothing$. Then $[G^I] = \varnothing$ contains no members. Therefore, G^I has no cover at layer $I+1$, i.e., $G^{I+1} = \varnothing$. On the other hand, $G^I = \varnothing$ makes the loop of lines 5 to 12 not be executed and *ICGS* terminates and returns $Q = \varnothing$ (obtained at line 4 as initialization).

Induction step: Assume the lemma holds for $0 \le |G^I| < N$ for some N. Now consider $|G^I| = N$, i.e., $G^I = (G_1^I, G_2^I, \ldots, G_N^I)$. Then by the inductive hypothesis, Q is the IC generator–set of $G^I - (G_N^I)$ after $N - 1$ times of executions of the outer loop (lines 5 to 12). Since there is one more generator, namely G_N^I, left in G^I, the outer loop will be executed one more time where the execution of line 6 and the inner loop (lines 7 to 9) with $G_k = G_N^I$ computes Q_k as an IC generator–set of G_N^I (by Lemma 6.8 and Theorem 3.19). Two residual operations in line 10 and line 11 remove all duplicate and redundant covers of G^I from $[Q_k]$ and $[Q]$, respectively (Lemma 3.14.c). Then, by Lemma 6.9, their union in line 11 yields Q being the IC generator–set of G^I, the execution of function *ICGS* terminates and returns Q.   □

proof of Theorem 6.11.

By induction on L, the number of layers in the causal network of a layered problem. (Recall that by the definition of layered problems, $M = H^0$ and $H^L = D$.)

Base case: $L = 1$, i.e., P is a bipartite problem. Since $G = (\varnothing)$, line 7 will not be executed in the first pass. The **while** loop (lines 8 to 10) is the same as *BIPARTITE* since $k = 1$ by initialization at line 4. Then $[G]$ is the set of all irredundant covers of M^+ in layer $H^1 = D$ after line 10. The **repeat** loop (lines 6 to 12) will then stop since G is at D, and the execution of the function *LAYERED* terminates and returns G with $[G] = Sol(P)$ by Theorem 3.19.

Induction step: Assume the theorem holds for $1 \le L < N$ for some N. Now consider a problem P with $L = N$. By the inductive hypothesis, after $N - 1$ times executions of the outer loop (lines 6 to 12), G is computed such that $[G]$ is the set of all irredundant covers of M_1^+ at layer H^{L-1}, where $M_1^+ \subseteq M^+$ is the set of all present manifestations received so far. Since G is not in D, this loop has to be executed once again. After the execution of line 7, by Lemma 6.10, the new G at layer $H^L = D$ is the IC generator–set of previous G at layer H^{N-1}. Because of the transitivity of IC generator–sets, more precisely by Theorems 6.7, $[G]$ is the set of all irredundant covers of M_1^+ at the top layer. If $M_1^+ = M^+$, i.e., there are no more manifestations (*Moremanifs* = False), then the **while** loop (lines 8 to 10) will be skipped, and the **until** condition is satisfied. Thus the function terminates and returns G with $[G] = Sol(P)$. If $M_1^+ \subset M^+$, i.e., there are more manifestations (*Moremanifs* = True), the **while** loop will be executed to update G so that any $E \in [G]$ covers these new manifestations as well. This loop is the same as *BIPARTITE* except now $causes^N(Nextman)$, instead $causes(Nextman)$, is used as the second argument in function revise. Thus, causes of *Nextman* at layer N are incorporated into G. Analogous to the proof of Theorem 3.19, when the **while** loop stops, G is updated so that $[G]$ is the set of all irredundant covers of M^+ at layer $H^L = D$. The function then terminates and returns G with $[G] = Sol(P)$. □

proof of Lemma 6.12.

By the definition, $m_j^0 \in M_t = H^0$ in P_t iff $m_j \in M$ in P. Thus $M_t \neq \emptyset$ and $effects(m_j^0) = \emptyset$ for all $m_j^0 \in M_t$. It is obvious that $h_i^I \in H_t^I$ iff $h_i \in extcauses^I(M)$ for all $I > 0$. Since there exists a finite number N such that $extcauses^N(M) = D$, then $d_i^N \in D_t = H^N$ in P_t iff $d_i \in D$ in P. Thus $D_t \neq \emptyset$. Superscripts attached in every entity in H_t make H^I and H^J disjoint for $I \neq J$. Then, the only thing that needs to be shown is that $domain(C_I) = H^I$ and $range(C_I) = H^{I-1}$ for every C_I, $1 \leq I \leq N$.

By the definition of C_t, it is obvious that $C_I \subseteq H^I \times H^{I-1}$. Then, from the definition of H^I in P_t, for any $h_i^I \in H^I$, there is some $h_j^{I-1} \in H^{I-1}$ such that there are h_i and h_j in P where $h_i \in extcauses(h_j)$. Thus, $< h_i^I, h_j^{I-1} > \in C_I$. Since it holds for all $h_i^I \in H^I$, it follows that $domain(C_I) = H^I$. For any $h_j^{I-1} \in H^{I-1}$ in P_t, $extcauses(h_j) \neq \emptyset$ in P by definition of $extcauses$. Therefore, there exists some $h_i \in extcauses(h_j)$ and thus there exists $h_i^I \in H^I$. By the definition of C_t, for such h_i^I and h_j^{I-1}, $< h_i^I, h_j^{I-1} > \in C_I$. Since it holds for all $h_j^{I-1} \in H^{I-1}$, it follows that $range(C_I) = H^{I-1}$. □

proof of Lemma 6.13.

By Definition 6.10, for every $m_j^0 \in M_t^+ \subseteq M_t$ in P_t iff its counterpart $m_j \in M^+ \subseteq M$ in P.

Moreover, since for any $m_j \in M$, $causes^*(m_j) \cap D = extcauses^N(m_j)$, therefore, for any $m_j \in M$ and $d_i \in D$, $< d_i, m_j > \in C^*$ iff $d_i \in extcauses^N(m_j)$ in P. On the other hand, by Definition 6.10, $< d_i^N, m_j^0 > \in C_t^*$ in P_t iff $d_i \in extcauses^N(m_j)$ in P. Based on the above equivalence, it follows that $E_t = (d_1^N, d_2^N, \ldots, d_k^N)$ is a cover of M_t^+ iff $E = (d_1, d_2, \ldots, d_k)$ is a cover of M^+. The irredundancy then follows immediately from Lemma 6.3. □

proof of Theorem 6.14.

Let $M^+ = \{m_1, m_2, \ldots, m_s\}$ in P. And Let $P_t = < H_t, D_t, M_t, C_t, M_t^+ > = trans(P)$ where $D_t = H^N$ and $M_t^+ = \{m_1^0, m_2^0, \ldots, m_s^0\}$. By Lemma 6.13,

(1) $E = (h_1, h_2, \ldots, h_r) \in Sol(P)$ iff $E_t = (h_1^N, h_2^N, \ldots, h_r^N) \in Sol(P_t)$.

Since P_t is a layered problem, then

(2) $E_t \in Sol(P_t)$ iff $E_t \in [LAYERED(H_t, D_t, M_t, C_t)$.

By definition 6.10 of function *trans*, $h_i^1 \in causes(m_j^0)$ in P_t iff $h_i \in extcauses(m_j)$ in P; and $h_i^{l+1} \in causes(h_j^l)$ in P_t iff $h_i \in extcauses(h_j)$ in P. Since all other operations are the same in algorithms *LAYERED* and *HYPER-BIPARTITE*, it follows that when *HYPER-BIPARTITE* works on pseudo-layers $1, 2, \ldots, k$ and stops after $k = K \leq N$ iterations of the

repeat loop where K is the smallest number such that $extcauses^K(M^+) \subseteq D$ in P, then,

(3) $X_t = (h_1^K, h_2^K, \ldots, h_s^K) \in [G^K]$ in P_t iff $E \in$ $[HYPER\text{-}BIPARTITE(H,D,M,C)] = [G]$ in P, where $[G^K]$ is the set of all irredundant covers of M_t^+ at layer H^K in P_t.

Since G is at D, then G^K is at D_t. Therefore, IC generator–sets of G^K at layers $H^{K+1}, H^{K+2}, \ldots, H^N$ in P_t, namely, $G^{K+1}, G^{K+2}, \ldots, G^N$ are the same as G^K except for the different superscripts attached on their entities. Thus

(4) $E_t \in [LAYERED(H_t,D_t,M_t,C_t)]$ iff $X_t = (h_1^K, h_2^K, \ldots, h_s^K) \in [G^K]$.

Combining (1), (2), (4), and (3), it follows that $E \in Sol(P)$ in P iff $E \in [HYPER\text{-}BIPARTITE(H,D,M,C)]$.   □

proof of Theorem 6.15.

Since E is an explanation of H^+, E covers H^+. Therefore, for any $h_i \in H^+$, particularly for any $d_i \in D'$, there exists a $d_j \in E$ such that $d_i \in effects^*(d_j)$. Since $< d_j, d_i > \notin C$, $d_i \in effects^*(d_j)$ implies that $d_i = d_j$. Since it is true for all $d_i \in D'$, it follows that $D' \subseteq E$.   □

7
Parallel Processing for Diagnostic Problem–Solving

> "Information is represented in long–term memory
> as a network of associations among concepts.
> Information is retrieved by spreading activation
> from concepts in working memory through the
> network structure."
> John R. Anderson

In the probabilistic causal model described in this book, as well as in some
others, probabilistic inference is combined with AI symbol processing
methods for diagnostic problem–solving. In these models disorders and
manifestations (and perhaps intermediate states) are connected by causal
links associated with probabilities representing the strength of causal association. A hypothesis, consisting of zero or more disorders, with the *highest*
posterior probability under the given set of manifestations (findings) is
typically taken as the optimal problem solution. Conventional sequential
search approaches in AI for solving diagnostic problems formulated in this
fashion, such as the ones presented in Chapter 5 of this book and the
search algorithm in NESTOR [Cooper84], suffer from combinatorial explosion when the number of possible disorders is large. This is because they
potentially must compare the posterior probabilities of all or a notable
portion of possible combinations of disorders. Pearl's belief network model
adopts a parallel revision method to find global optimal solutions for the
special case of singly–connected causal networks within polynomial time of
the network diameter [Pearl87]. However, as discussed in Section 5.4, for a
non–singly–connected causal network, which is the case for most diagnostic
problems, Pearl's approach requires separate computation for each instantiation of the set of "cycle–cut" nodes, and thus still leads to combinatorial difficulty when this set of cycle–cut nodes is large. All of these problems raise the issue of whether the probabilistic causal model described in
this book might be formulated as a highly parallel computation, i.e., as a
"connectionist model", so that combinatorial explosion can be avoided.

Connectionist modeling based on a "neural style" of computing has been
shown to offer an alternative approach for solving some other difficult
problems with reduced time complexity, such as the "traveling salesman
problem" or optimization of VLSI layout [Hopfield85, Kirkpatrick83].

Utilizing rich interactions of large number of processing nodes acting in parallel, a connectionist network can derive a best or near best solution for such problems within a reduced time. This suggests that such techniques may also be applicable to approximate diagnostic problem–solving as formulated in this book.

There are many different ways to cast diagnostic problem–solving as a connectionist model. In this chapter, a specific model will be developed for solving two–layer (bipartite) diagnostic problems. In this model a diagnostic problem is viewed as a non–linear optimization problem. To solve this problem, global optimization criteria derived from the probabilistic causal model are decomposed into local optimization criteria which are used by nodes in a connectionist model to update their activation levels. Through parallel node interactions, nodes representing disorders compete with each other to account for each "individual" present manifestation, yet complement each other to account for all present manifestations. When equilibrium is reached, the network settles into a locally optimal state in which some fully activated disorder nodes (winners) together compose the diagnosis for the given case, while all other disorder nodes are fully deactivated. Various experiments, both based on randomly generated bipartite problems as well as a medical example, have been conducted. The results of these experiments show that the connectionist approach may yield very high accuracy for solving diagnostic problems in a much reduced time. Before going into details of the model, a brief introduction to the basics of connectionist parallel processing is given.

7.1. Connectionist Models and Diagnosis

7.1.1. Basics of Connectionist Models

A connectionist model is a network of simultaneously active processing elements (nodes and connections) whose local interactions over time lead to global system behavior. It is convenient to view any connectionist model as having a network and an activation rule. The *network* consists of a set of *nodes* (units) connected together via directed *links*. Nodes directly connected to one another are said to be *neighbors* of each other. Each node n_i in the network has a numeric activation level $a_i(t)$ associated with it at time t, and the overall pattern of activation, vector $\vec{A}(t) = (a_1(t), a_2(t), \cdots, a_n(t))$, represents the current *state* of the network at time t. A node's activation level, or output derived from it, is communicated from a node to its neighbors at each moment in time. The total input activation $in_j(t)$ that node n_j receives from its neighbors in this fashion at any moment is used to update its own level of activation. Numeric connection strengths called *weights* are often associated with the links in the network and are used during computations that update node activations. A weight on the link *from* node n_i *to* node n_j is often designated w_{ji}. If activation of node n_i

tends to increase the activation of neighboring node n_j, then the connection from n_i to n_j is an *excitatory link*, and this is usually designated by $w_{ji} > 0$ on that link. Conversely, if activation of node n_i tends to decrease activation in n_j, then the connection is said to be an *inhibitory link*, and this is designated by $w_{ji} < 0$. The matrix of weights **W** is generally thought of as long-term memory, and may be a function of time, although we will consider **W** to be fixed here (i.e., no learning occurs).

The *activation rule* of a connectionist model is a local procedure that each node follows in updating its activation level in the context of input from neighboring nodes. Often, all nodes simultaneously update their activation levels as a function of their input and current activation, i.e., the ith node computes its activation level at time $t + 1$ as $a_i(t + 1) = f_i(in_i(t), a_i(t))$. The key points here are that massive, explicit parallelism is involved as activation spreads throughout a network, and that all information processing occurs through *local* interactions between neighboring nodes.

What the nodes, links, activation levels, etc. in a connectionist model represent varies from model to model (see [Reggia & Sutton, 1988] for a review). Here, we are specifically concerned with connectionist models that represent long-term associative memory. Information in human long-term memory is often viewed by cognitive psychologists as a network of associations between concepts [Anderson, 1983]. Starting during the mid-1960's, a class of network models similar to connectionist models was initially studied in cognitive psychology. These associative networks have nodes which each represent a conceptual unit (e.g., the concept "dog", the phoneme "f" in a speech system, a line segment in an image) and links which each represent a relationship or association between conceptual units. This representation of one concept per node and one association per link is the basis for designating them as having a *local representation* of information. Networks of this type include both semantic networks as well as other associative networks modeling "lower level" non-semantic information.

The activation rule that implements information retrieval in these associative networks, often referred to as *spreading activation*, typically produces an *intersection search*. For example, if two nodes in a network are activated by an external influence, some form of activation (numeric or symbolic) will propagate out from both nodes in an unguided, breadth-first fashion until a point of intersection occurs between the two expanding regions of activation. This point, or the paths from the source nodes to it, would indicate a possible relationship between the concepts represented by the original source nodes. Sometimes it is desired that a single node among a set of initially possible "intersected" nodes be activated in such a fashion, and this is often referred to as a *winner-takes-all* phenomenon. In connectionist models, a winner-takes-all output is usually produced by "competing" nodes having mutually inhibitory connections.

There are several examples today where self–processing associative networks, implemented as models of cognitive mechanisms, have qualitatively or quantitatively simulated various measurable human behavioral phenomena. For example, an associative network model of letter perception was able to account for why people perceive letters better in the context of their occurrence in a written word, and even made testable predictions about letter perception that were subsequently verified [McClelland81; Rumelhart82]. As another example, an associative network mapping printed words into their spoken form was able to simulate how long it took to pronounce aloud a word as a function of its spelling [Reggia88].

Connectionist models based on associative networks are best distinguished from neural models (brain models). Their networks represent concepts and associations, entities in the cognitive domain rather than biophysical structures. Further, while many of these models use a neuron–like activation rule borrowed from the neural modeling literature, many do not. For example, propagation of symbolic labels is sometimes used to implement spreading activation. Even where numerical activation rules are used, non–neuron–like paradigms such as *competitive activation rules* can prove useful [Reggia89]. With this latter approach, nodes actively compete in a non–neuron–like fashion for sources of activation that appear in a network. The point is that self–processing associative networks can be viable models of mental functional processes and/or useful computational methods independent of how they may be viewed as arising from a neurobiological substrate.

Connectionist models in general are fundamentally different from more traditional information processing models (like the algorithms presented in earlier chapters of this book) in at least two ways. First, they are *self–processing*. More traditional information processing models typically consist of a passive data structure (associative network, set of production rules, etc.) which is manipulated by an active external process/procedure (abductive inference mechanism, rule interpreter, etc.). In contrast, the nodes and links in a connectionist model are *active* processing agents; there is typically no external active agent that operates on them. Second, connectionist models exhibit global behavior derived from *concurrent local interactions* of their numerous components. The external process that manipulates the underlying data structures in more conventional models in AI and cognitive science typically has global access to the entire network/rule set, and processing is strongly and explicitly sequentialized (e.g., conflict resolution in rule–based systems). An important implication of these distinctions is that anything associated with a connectionist model that is characterized as "intelligent behavior" is a *global* property that somehow emerges from the concurrent local interactions between neighboring nodes. This notion of intelligence as an *emergent property* is a fundamental principle underlying connectionist models.

7.1.2. Connectionist Modeling of Diagnostic Problem–Solving

Connectionist modeling techniques are often considered to be useful for "low level" information processing (e.g., signal processing) tasks but of limited value for supporting the "high level" problem–solving methods used in contemporary AI systems. Thus, at first glance it might appear that there is little hope for using connectionist models for diagnostic problem–solving. However, recent advances have been made both in applying connectionist methods to a number of AI tasks [Hinton81, Touretzky85,86, Ballard86] as well as to solving global optimization problems [Kirkpatrick83, Hopfield85]. This raises the issue of whether one might formulate a diagnostic problem as a connectionist model, and if so, how to go about it. While a variety of approaches might be taken (e.g., [Goel88, Mulsant88, Hripcsak89]), we will develop a connectionist model here that uses a local representation and whose activation rule is derived directly from the probabilistic causal model described in Chapter 4 of this book.

To focus information processing and prevent spreading activation from saturating a network with activation, connectionist models often employ inhibitory links (links with negative weights) between incompatible or competing nodes [Grossberg80, McClelland81, Rumelhart82, Feldman82]. In contrast, the approach we take here uses a *competitive activation mechanism* to control spreading activation [Reggia85b,87]. A distinct characteristic of competition–based connectionist models is that there is no need for inhibitory links between conceptually incompatible or competing nodes. The mutual–inhibition between these nodes is realized not through explicit inhibitory links but through competition: neighboring nodes of a source node *actively* compete for the output of that source node, and the ability of a neighboring node to compete for activation increases as its own activation level increases or as its rival's activation level decreases [Reggia85b, 87].

As noted above, when equilibrium is reached in many connectionist model applications a single "winner" node that is fully activated is desired, while "losing" nodes should be fully inactive. Such a desired state is referred to as a *single-winner-takes-all* or *choice* phenomenon [Feldman82, Carpenter87]). A competitive activation mechanism has at least two advantages in the context of an associative network with a local representation where single–winner–takes–all behavior is desired. First, most connections/links in semantic/associative networks correspond to empirical associations with at least theoretically measurable frequencies of occurrence (e.g., how frequently a disorder causes a manifestation). In contrast to this well–defined correspondence between connectionist model components (excitatory connections) and the entities being modeled (measurable associations), there is no generally recognized analogous real–world correspondence to inhibitory connections (e.g., how strongly a disorder inhibits another disorder). In this sense, models without inhibitory links are somewhat closer to current psychological perspectives and AI models than those with inhibitory links. Second, by eliminating inhibitory links, not only is the enormous storage for these links saved, but also the fanout of each node may be drastically reduced, thus leading to less computation at each node. The experience of our group in implementing connectionist/neural network models on a parallel machine suggests that reduced fanout is an important factor in producing speed–up on parallel architectures, especially with large networks [Tagamets87].

In diagnostic problem–solving situations, where a hypothesis or solution usually consists of more than one disorder, implementing competitive dynamics via a competitive activation mechanism would appear to be even more desirable. This is because, in general, a *multiple–winners–take–all* phenomenon rather than a single–winner–takes–all phenomenon is desired. In other words, it may be desirable that several disorder nodes be fully activated simultaneously. If a set of competing nodes with direct, mutually–inhibitory links tries to sustain multiple winners simultaneously, these winners tend to extinguish each others' activation. Further, in some situations, two nodes may be considered to be in competition, while in other situations the same two nodes may not be competitors and may actually "cooperate" to formulate a solution to a problem. This is illustrated by the simple diagnostic problem shown in Figure 7.1. When manifestation m_2 alone is present, disorders d_1 and d_2 would "compete" with each other to explain or account for the presence of m_2. However, if instead manifestations m_1 and m_3 are present, both d_1 and d_2 should "cooperate" with each other and both would be necessary in the solution hypothesis to account for or cover the two present manifestations. Moreover, it is not difficult to imagine situations where the same disorders are competing with each other with respect to some present manifestations while at the same time cooperating with each other with respect to other present manifestations. In other words, the inter–relationship between disorders during diagnostic inference is not simply a static mutually–excitatory or mutually–inhibitory relationship, but a more complex dynamic function of the network and the problem input (the latter being the set of manifestations given to be present). Thus it is at least very difficult, if not impossible, to model these dynamic inter–disorder relationships through simple inhibitory links with static weights.

The underlying conjecture motivating the work discussed in this chapter is that the dynamically changing functional relationships between disorders and appropriate "multiple–winners–take–all" behavior may be realized through the use of a competitive activation mechanism [Peng89b]. This seems plausible because, as noted earlier, by competitive mechanism one can dispense with the inhibitory links usually utilized to support winner selection. The goal is thus to construct a specific competition–based connectionist model to carry out diagnostic problem–solving with high accuracy, i.e., to yield the most probable hypothesis in most cases. The

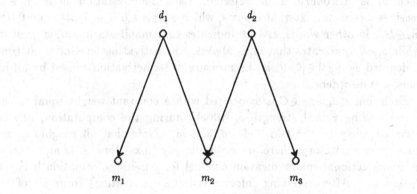

Figure 7.1. A very simple diagnostic problem consisting of
two disorders $\{d_1, d_2\}$ and three manifestations $\{m_1, m_2 m_3\}$.

emphasis here is thus on the computational and problem–solving aspects of connectionist modeling rather than its cognitive or neurobiological aspects. To the extent that our conjecture is correct, this approach can be used as a computationally efficient problem–solver for diagnostic problems.

7.2. A Specific Connectionist Model Architecture

In this section, we introduce a specific connectionist model using a competition–based activation rule to find the most probable hypothesis as formulated in the probabilistic causal model of Chapter 4. A "local" or "unit–value" representation is used: nodes, representing concepts, are connected by links whose weights represent association strengths between nodes. These links are also viewed as channels for sending information between nodes. At each moment of time, each node receives information about the activation levels of its immediate neighboring nodes (nodes connected to it via direct links), and then uses this information to calculate its own activation level. Through this process of spreading activation, the network settles down to equilibrium representing a solution to a problem.

A two–layer probabilistic causal network, as defined in Chapter 4, can be used directly as a connectionist model network: D and M are two sets of nodes, and C is the set of links connecting nodes between these two layers. There are no inhibitory or other intra–set links between any pair of disorder nodes or between any pair of manifestation nodes. In this formulation, each node is associated with a dynamically changing activation level. For a disorder node $d_i \in D$, its activation level at time t during the computation, denoted $d_i(t) \in [0, 1]$, serves as a measure of confirmation. Initially, $d_i(0) = p_i$. When $d_i(t) \approx 1.0$ at time t, the disorder d_i is confirmed to be occurring and thus becomes an element of the solution; when $d_i(t) \approx 0.0$ then d_i is disconfirmed or rejected. Each manifestation node $m_j \in M$ receives a constant external input s_j which equals 1.0 if $m_j \in M^+$, and 0.0 if $m_j \in M^-$. In other words, $s_j = 1.0$ indicates that manifestation m_j is present, while $s_j = 0.0$ indicates that m_j is absent. The activation level of m_j at time t, denoted as $m_j(t) \in [0, 1]$, is the measure of its activation caused by all its causative disorders.

Each link $< d_i, m_j > \in C$ is associated with a constant weight equal to the corresponding causal strength c_{ij} which, during the computation, can be accessed solely by the two nodes d_i and m_j. Note that all weights c_{ij} are positive or excitatory: there are no inhibitory links. Link $< d_i, m_j >$ serves as a bidirectional communication channel for passing information between d_i and m_j. After receiving information (i.e., activation) from all of its immediate neighboring nodes, a node updates its activation level a small amount (the specific activation rule used is given below) and then sends its current activation level to all of its immediate neighbors. Moreover, for each $m_j \in M^+$, its neighboring nodes (nodes in $causes(m_j)$) are competing with each other for m_j's activation because they are competing to cover m_j. This relaxation–plus–competition process continues until equilibrium is reached at time t_e. If the model converges on a set of "winners", i.e., for each d_i, $d_i(t_e)$ approximates either 1 or 0, then the set of disorders $D_S = \{ d_i \, | \, d_i(t_e) \approx 1 \}$ is taken to be the connectionist model's problem solution, i.e., the connectionist model derives D_S as its candidate for the most probable cover D_{max} of the given features M^+. The crucial point here is that a set of disorders D_S is to be derived through the concurrent *local* interactions occurring in the connectionist model where D_S represents a hypothesis about the identity of the "globally" optimal set of disorders D_{max} as determined by the relative likelihood measure $L(D_I, M^+)$ in the probabilistic causal model. Since each node's processing is driven solely by local information, it is not guaranteed *a priori* that the resultant locally–optimal solution will correspond to a globally–optimal solution.

Now the question remains as to what the local activation rules should be for disorder and manifestation nodes such that the model will have the desired behavior, i.e., it will reach equilibrium, converge on a set of multiple "winners" D_S, and D_S will be consistent with D_{max}, the most probable hypothesis. This question is answered in the next section.

7.3. Equations for Updating Node Activations

In this subsection, an approach to deriving local activation rules for use in connectionist models is developed. For the reader's convenience, the relative likelihood measure derived in Chapter 4 (Equation 4.7) is cited and renumbered below: for any $D_I \subset D$ and the given sets of present manifestations M^+,

$$L(D_I, M^+) = \prod_{m_j \in M^+} [1 - \prod_{d_i \in D_I} (1 - c_{ij})] \prod_{m_l \in M^-} \prod_{d_i \in D_I} (1 - c_{il}) \prod_{d_i \in D_I} \frac{p_i}{1 - p_i} \quad (7.1)$$

where, as we discussed earlier, $M^- = M - M^+$ is assumed to represent the set of all absent manifestations for a closed problem.

Viewing a diagnostic problem as a non–linear optimization problem, we will decompose the globally optimal criterion (a continuous form of Equation 7.1) into a local optimal criterion for each disorder node, and then use these local criteria to derive activation rules for individual nodes. Thus, the global optimization problem of finding a set of disorders (D_S) which maximizes $L(D_S, M^+)$ is decomposed into a set of concurrent local problems for all individual disorder nodes.

7.3.1. Optimization Problem

Let $|D| = n$, i.e., let there be n possible disorders. Then in the connectionist model outlined in the last section, any hypothesis $D_I \subseteq D$ can be considered as one of the 2^n corners of the n–dimensional hypercube $[0, 1]^n$, and thus can be represented as an n–dimensional vector $\vec{X} = (x_1, x_2, \ldots, x_n)$ where $x_i = 1$ if $d_i \in D_I$ and $x_i = 0$ otherwise. Thus, a diagnostic problem can be viewed as a discrete optimization problem: finding one of the corners of hypercube $[0, 1]^n$ which maximizes Equation 7.1. Instead of jumping from corner to corner in searching for a solution, if we allow $\vec{X}$ to go through the interior of the hypercube and still guarantee that the computation settles down into one of the corners, we can reformulate the problem as a continuous optimization problem. This can be done by generalizing the optimization function Equation 7.1 from a discrete domain $\{0, 1\}^n$ to the continuous domain $[0, 1]^n$. Define $Q(\vec{X})$ to be

$$Q(\vec{X}) = \prod_{m_j \in M^+} [1 - \prod_{i=1}^{n}(1 - c_{ij} x_i)] \prod_{m_l \in M^-} \prod_{i=1}^{n}(1 - c_{il} x_i) \prod_{i=1}^{n} \frac{1 - x_i (1 - p_i)}{1 - p_i x_i} \quad (7.2)$$

where $\vec{X}$ is a vector in $[0, 1]^n$. Noticing that $c_{ij} = 0$ if $<d_i, m_j> \notin C$, then for any $\vec{X}$ in $\{0, 1\}^n$ (i.e., for any corner of the hypercube), Equation 7.2 becomes Equation 7.1.

Based on the above generalization of Equation 7.1, the problem of finding D_{max} with the greatest value of Equation 7.1 for the given M^+ is thus transformed into a continuous non–linear optimization problem. The non–linear equation $Q(\vec{X})$ is the *objective function* against which the maximum value is desired; and $x_i \in \{0, 1\}$, $i = 1, 2, \ldots, n$ are *constraints* [Collatz75]. In other words, among all vectors $\vec{X}$ in $[0, 1]^n$ whose elements are either one or zero (i.e., those which satisfy the constraints) we want to find the one which will maximize $Q(\vec{X})$, the objective function.

The way that our connectionist model approaches this optimization problem is to continuously update $d_i(t)$ and $m_j(t)$ based on "local" information using equations derived from $Q(\vec{X})$. At time t, the activation levels

$d_i(t)$ of all disorder nodes d_i compose a vector $\vec{D}(t) = (d_1(t), d_2(t), \ldots, d_n(t))$ where $d_i(t) \in [0, 1]$. Thus $\vec{D}(t)$ is a vector in $[0, 1]^n$. Applying the objective function Equation 7.2 to $\vec{D}(t)$, we have

$$Q(\vec{D}(t))$$

$$= \prod_{m_j \in M^+} [1 - \prod_{i=1}^{n}(1 - c_{ij} d_i(t))] \prod_{m_l \in M^-} \prod_{i=1}^{n}(1 - c_{il} d_i(t)) \prod_{i=1}^{n} \frac{1 - d_i(t)(1 - p_i)}{1 - p_i d_i(t)} \quad (7.3)$$

Initially, $\vec{D}(0) = (d_1(0), d_2(0), \ldots, d_n(0)) = (p_1, p_2, \ldots, p_n)$ is the vector of prior probabilities p_i of all $d_i \in D$. Ideally, when equilibrium is achieved at time t_e, the model will converge on a set of multiple winners, i.e., $\vec{D}(t_e) = (d_1(t_e), d_2(t_e), \ldots, d_n(t_e))$, where $d_i(t_e)$ approaches either 0 or 1. $\vec{D}(t_e)$ represents a hypothesis D_S where $d_i \in D_S$ iff $d_i(t_e) \approx 1$. At this time, as noted earlier, $Q(\vec{D}(t_e)) = L(D_S, M^+)$. Therefore, D_S will maximize Equation 7.1 iff $\vec{D}(t_e)$ will maximize Equation 7.3. How $d_i(t)$ should be updated based on local information to maximize Equation 7.3 is derived shortly, but we first consider the updating of $m_j(t)$.

7.3.2. Updating $m_j(t)$

The value $m_j(t)$ is the current activation of node m_j caused by or induced from current activations of all of its causative disorders. Motivated by Equations 7.1 and 7.3, we define a local activation rule for each $m_j \in M$ to be

$$m_j(t) = 1 - \prod_{i=1}^{n}(1 - c_{ij} d_i(t)) = 1 - \prod_{d_i \in causes(m_j)}(1 - c_{ij} d_i(t)) \quad (7.4)$$

where the second equality is from the fact that $c_{ij} = 0$ if $<d_i, m_j> \notin C$. This activation rule is a local computation since it only depends on current activation levels of m_j's causative disorders (those in $causes(m_j)$) which are directly connected to m_j in the causal network. Initially, $m_j(0) = 1 - \prod_{i=1}^{n}(1 - c_{ij} p_i) = P(m_j)$ (see Equation 4.24a in Chapter 4). At equilibrium time t_e, one would anticipate

$$m_j(t_e) = 1 - \prod_{i=1}^{n}(1 - c_{ij} d_i(t_e)) = 1 - \prod_{d_i \in D_S}(1 - c_{ij}) = P(m_j | D_S)$$

if a multiple–winners–take–all result occurs. This is also consistent with the underlying probabilistic causal model (Equation 4.13a in Chapter 4).

7.3.3. Updating $d_i(t)$

A local activation rule for updating $d_i(t)$ is now derived in two steps. First, the global optimization function $Q(\vec{D}(t))$ is decomposed into partially localized optimization functions $q_i(d_i(t))$ for each disorder node d_i; then, q_i is used to derive a local activation rule for $d_i(t)$ which only depends on information from its immediate neighbors (i.e., information only from $m_j \in effects(d_i)$). Let $M_i^+ = M^+ \cap effects(d_i)$ and $M_i^- = M^- \cap effects(d_i)$. These are the present manifestations which disorder d_i could cause and the manifestations expected by d_i but actually absent, respectively (i.e., M_i^+ and M_i^- partition $effects(d_i)$). Then from the global optimization function Equation 7.3, we define

$$q_i(d_i(t)) = \prod_{m_j \in M_i^+} [1 - \prod_{k=1}^n (1 - c_{kj} d_k(t))]$$

$$\prod_{m_l \in M_i^-} \prod_{k=1}^n (1 - c_{kl} d_k(t)) \prod_{k=1}^n \frac{1 - d_k(t)(1 - p_k)}{1 - p_k d_k(t)} \tag{7.5}$$

where $d_i(t)$ is the only argument for function q_i, while all $d_k(t)$, $k \neq i$, are considered to be its parameters. Note that the first two products in Equation 7.5 are taken over M_i^+ and M_i^-, which are local to d_i, not over M^+ and M^- as in Equation 7.3. In this sense, Equation 7.5 is a partially localized version of Equation 7.3 ("partially" because the parameters $d_k(t)$ for $k \neq i$ are still present).

Viewing $q_i(d_i(t))$ as an objective function and $d_i(t)$ as being constrained to $\{0, 1\}$, we decompose the global optimization problem of $\vec{D}(t)$ into local optimization problems of its elements $d_i(t)$: derive whichever of $d_i(t) = 1$ or $d_i(t) = 0$ that will maximize q_i, i.e., whichever of $q_i(1)$ or $q_i(0)$ is greater, if all other $d_k(t)$ are fixed. If $q_i(1) > q_i(0)$, $d_i(t)$ should increase in order to obtain local optimization. Likewise, if $q_i(1) < q_i(0)$, $d_i(t)$ should decrease. Thus we define the ratio $r_i(t) = \dfrac{q_i(1)}{q_i(0)}$ which will be used to govern the updating of $d_i(t)$ in the connectionist model. It can be proven (see Appendix) that the ratio

$$r_i(t) = \prod_{m_j \in M_i^+} [1 + c_{ij} \frac{1 - m_j(t)}{m_j(t) - c_{ij} d_i(t)}] \prod_{m_l \in M_i^-} (1 - c_{il}) \frac{p_i}{1 - p_i}. \tag{7.6a}$$

Note that $r_i(t)$ is completely determined by information local to node d_i; all $d_k(t)$, c_{kj}, and c_{kl} for $k \neq i$ are no longer present. The quantity $r_i(t)$ is used to indicate whether $d_i(t)$ should increase ($r_i(t) > 1$) or decrease ($r_i(t) < 1$) and by how much. In this sense $r_i(t)$ represents the combined "input activation" to the ith disorder from its manifestations, and the factors of the two products in Equation 7.6a can be viewed as individual inputs from specific manifestations.

Decisions based on local information have been used in many sequential approximation algorithms for various combinatorial problems. The difference here is that the local decision in our connectionist model only causes a *slight change* of the state at a time, and more importantly, such changes, through successive parallel node interactions, are reversible or non-monotonic in the sense that a previously increased activation at one node can be decreased later due to the influence of activations of its neighboring nodes (this will be further demonstrated through examples later). This might be viewed as analogous to backtracking in sequential algorithms except that it is a local, concurrent phenomenon here.

Different input values and activation rules for disorders and manifestations in this model reflect the different roles they play in diagnostic problem–solving. Moreover, analogous to Equation 7.1, the three parts in the product of Equation 7.6a represent the influence on disorder $d_i(t)$ from d_i's present manifestations, expected but absent manifestations, and prior probability, respectively. The relationship between $r_i(t)$ and related node activations and link weights are easily seen to agree with intuition. For example, factors associated with $m_j \in M_i^+$ are greater than 1.0, representing positive support for d_i from its present manifestations; while factors associated with $m_l \in M_i^-$ are less than one, representing evidence against d_i from its expected but absent manifestations. Similarly, a greater c_{ij} will increase $r_i(t)$ more while a greater c_{il} will have an opposite effect. The interesting relation that an increase of $m_j(t)$ will tend to reduce $r_i(t)$ is also justifiable because the higher $m_j(t)$ is, the more full m_j is covered by its disorders and thus it requires less additional coverage from d_i.

Note that the last two parts in Equation 7.6a are constants for an individual disorder node for a given M^+, so this equation can be rewritten as

$$r_i(t) = K_i \prod_{m_j \in M_i^+} [1 + c_{ij} \frac{1 - m_j(t)}{m_j(t) - c_{ij} d_i(t)}] \tag{7.6b}$$

where $K_i = \prod_{m_l \in M_i^-} (1 - c_{il}) \frac{p_i}{1 - p_i}$ is a constant that can be computed and stored at each disorder node before the iterative process starts. Therefore, at any time t, computation for the current $r_i(t)$ only requires the current $m_j(t)$ of all $m_j \in M_i^+$. Whether a manifestation m_j is in M^-, and thus is involved in computing K_i once (before the iterative process starts) or it is in M^+, and thus is involved in iteratively computing $r_i(t)$ thereafter, can be determined by m_j's input value s_j. Thus, s_j can be considered as a gate to communication channels of m_j. At the beginning of a simulation, all m_j send their s_j values to their respective disorders. For each disorder node d_i, those $s_j = 0$ it receives indicate manifestations in M^- and are first used to compute K_i once, and then to "close" the corresponding links during the subsequent iterations.

Another point is that division by $m_j(t) - c_{ij} d_i(t) = 0$ in Equation 7.6b might arise for a manifestation $m_j \in M_i^+$. By Equation 7.4, this could occur only in two situations: d_i is the only causative disorder of m_j having a non-zero activation, or all disorders capable of causing m_j have zero activations. The first situation implies that all disorders in $causes(m_j)$ except d_i are rejected, leaving d_i as the only possible winner to account for the presence of m_j; thus d_i's activation should increase toward 1.0 to be eventually accepted. Thus, using a very large $r_i(t)$ value as an approximation in this situation is appropriate. The second situation is impossible if activations of disorders change smoothly. This is because when activations of all disorders in $causes(m_j)$ are close to zero, m_j becomes very close to zero and the term $(1 - m_j(t)) / (m_j(t) - c_{ij} d_i(t))$ in Equation 7.6b therefore becomes very large. This would make $r_i(t)$ greater than 1 for some of these disorders d_i and increase their activations, and in turn increase $m_j(t)$. Therefore, to prevent this "dividing by zero" exception in Equation 7.6b, testing for $m_j(t) = c_{ij} d_i(t)$ was done before the division in the simulations that follows. If equality holds, then a very large constant (say, 99999.0) is used to approximate "infinity" as the quotient. This will make $r_i(t)$ greater than 1.0 and cause the increase of $d_i(t)$ as desired. The only exception which can make this technique fail to work properly is the rare symmetric situation where several common causes of a manifestation always have the same (or very close) activation because they have the same prior probability and symmetric causal associations. How to handle this situation will be discussed later.

As discussed earlier, $r_i(t) = q_i(1) / q_i(0)$ indicates the desired direction of change of $d_i(t)$ in order to achieve local optimization, i.e., $d_i(t)$ should increase when $r_i(t) > 1$ and decrease when $r_i(t) < 1$. Therefore, $r_i(t) - 1$, when bounded by -1 and 1, is taken to be the change rate of $d_i(t)$. The reason to bound the change rate is to ensure that for each iteration, $d_i(t)$ only changes a small amount. Put more precisely, define the *ramp function* $f(x)$ to be

$$f(x) = \begin{cases} 1 & \text{if } x > 1 \\ -1 & \text{if } x < -1 \\ x & \text{otherwise.} \end{cases} \tag{7.7}$$

This leads to the following differential equation expressing the local activation rule for $d_i(t)$:

$$\dot{d}_i(t) = f(r_i(t) - 1) (1 - d_i(t)) \tag{7.8a}$$

where $\dot{d}_i(t)$ is the derivative or rate of change of $d_i(t)$. Changing this into an iterative approximate form, we have

$$d_i(t + \Delta) = d_i(t) + f(r_i(t) - 1) (1 - d_i(t)) \Delta \tag{7.8b}$$

where Δ is a small number (discussed below). The factor $(1 - d_i(t))$ ensures that $d_i(t + \Delta)$ will never exceed 1. To ensure $d_i(t + \Delta) \geq 0$, we set it to 0.0 if $d_i(t + \Delta)$ is less than 0.0 from Equation 7.8b. Thus, the dynamics of Equation 7.8a are approximated in the simulations that follow by:

$$d_i(t + \Delta) = \max\{0.0, \ d_i(t) + f(r_i(t) - 1) (1 - d_i(t)) \Delta \}. \tag{7.8c}$$

Thus, as desired, $d_i(t)$ is guaranteed to be in $[0, 1]$ at any time t.

To see how competition plays a role in this computation, note that by Equation 7.4 we can rewrite Equation 7.6b of $r_i(t)$ as

$$r_i(t) = K_i \prod_{m_j \in M_i^+} \left[1 + c_{ij} \frac{(1 - c_{ij}\, d_i(t)) \prod_{\substack{d_k \in causes(m_j) \\ d_k \neq d_i}} (1 - c_{kj}\, d_k(t))}{1 - (1 - c_{ij}\, d_i(t)) \prod_{\substack{d_k \in causes(m_j) \\ d_k \neq d_i}} (1 - c_{kj}\, d_k(t)) - c_{ij}\, d_i(t)} \right]$$

$$= K_i \prod_{m_j \in M_i^+} \left[1 + \frac{c_{ij}}{\dfrac{1}{\prod_{\substack{d_k \in causes(m_j) \\ d_k \neq d_i}} (1 - c_{kj}\, d_k(t))} - 1} \right]. \tag{7.6c}$$

This equation shows that for any disorder d_i, $r_i(t)$ will tend to decrease if activation $d_k(t)$ of some other $d_k \in causes(M_i^+)$ increases, and $r_i(t)$ will tend to increase if $d_k(t)$ decreases. In this sense, d_i competes with all other $d_k \in causes(M_i^+)$, and whether $d_i(t)$ should increase or decrease depends on this competition as well as the constant K_i. However, this competition is not a rigid inhibition, as with some other connectionist models using inhibitory links. In this model, as indicated by Equation 7.6c, a fully activated disorder d_k may not necessarily prevent its competitor d_i from also being activated by support from some other manifestations that d_i does not share with d_k, provided such manifestations exist. Some simple example simulations are given in the next section to illustrate the competitive dynamics involving disorders more clearly (see Table 7.1).

7.4. Experiments and Analysis

After deriving activation rules for manifestation and disorder nodes (Equations 7.4 and 7.8c), a number of experiments were conducted in which the parallel computation of the connectionist model was simulated by a computer program on a sequential machine. The purpose of these experiments was to test whether the model would converge on a set of multiple winners at equilibrium time t_e (defined as $d_i(t_e)$ approximating to 1 or 0 for all d_i), and whether the resultant hypothesis D_S would compare favorably with the most probable hypothesis $D_{\max}$. This section describes these experiments and analyzes the experimental results.

7.4.1. Basic Experimental Methods and Results

The parallel computation of the connectionist model was simulated by a sequence of iterations, each of which consists of two steps. At step 1, all disorder nodes d_i send their activation $d_i(t)$ to their immediate neighbors (their respective manifestation nodes). Each manifestation node $m_j \in M^+$ then updates its current activation $m_j(t)$ by Equation 7.4 using $d_i(t)$ only from its causative disorder nodes. At step 2, all manifestation nodes $m_j \in M^+$ send their activation values $m_j(t)$ to their immediate neighbors (their respective disorder nodes). Each disorder node d_i then updates its current activation by Equation 7.8c. This iterative process stops when the network reaches equilibrium state at time t_e. (A network reaches equilibrium at time t if $|d_i(t) - d_i(t - \Delta)| < 0.0001$ for every disorder node d_i in the network during a simulation.) Then all disorder nodes d_i with $d_i(t_e) > 0.95$ are accepted and compose the solution set D_S, while all disorder nodes d_k with $d_k(t_e) < 0.05$ are rejected. If there is any disorder with its activation level stabilized between 0.05 and 0.95, it is reported as a case of not converging on a set of multiple winners.

One factor of importance to the experiments is the size of Δ, the incremental interval for updating node activation. Too small a value of Δ, say 0.01, results in a very slow rate of convergence, typically taking 800 to 1,000 iterations for a case to settle down to a solution. Too large a value, say 0.1, could lead to incorrect solutions in some cases. Based on empirical observations, Δ was determined as follows. Initially, Δ was set to 0.005. After each iteration, Δ was incremented by 0.005 if it was less than 0.2. Then Δ stayed at 0.2 until equilibrium was reached. The small values of Δ early in the simulation make the approximation Equation 7.8c closer to the differential Equation 7.8a, thus tending to minimize error due to coarse discretization of t in the simulation. After about 40 iterations, $d_i(t)$ values are close to their final values in most situations, so the larger Δ (0.2) then helps fast convergence at the end of a simulation.

To provide the reader with a concrete example of what these simulations were like, Table 7.1 below shows representative example of simulations for different M^+ sets using the simple causal network given in Figure 7.2. For the three different M^+ sets shown at the top of Table 7.1, three different D_S sets, $\{d_2\}$, $\{d_1,d_2\}$, and $\{d_1,d_3\}$, were generated as diagnostic results by the connectionist model. Note that in each of these examples the connectionist simulation converges with a single- or multiple–winners–take–all solution, and each D_S turns out to be the same as the respective most probable hypothesis D_{max}. When $M^+ = \{m_2\}$, the single present manifestation m_2 makes d_1 and d_2 competitors since one of them is sufficient to account for the presence of m_2. Eventually, one of them, d_2, wins, and activations at all other disorder nodes die out. When $M^+ = \{m_1,m_2,m_3\}$, none of the disorders alone is capable of covering or accounting for the given M^+, but $\{d_1,d_2\}$ or $\{d_1,d_3\}$ could, so in this case d_2 and d_3 can be viewed as competitors. Which of these two disorders is better was determined competitively. In this particular case, d_2 won and d_3 lost. Also note that d_1 and d_2 are competitors with respect to m_2. However, one of them being fully activated does not prevent another from also being fully activated by support from other present manifestations.

The competitive dynamics is even more interesting when $M^+ = \{m_1,m_2,m_3,m_4\}$. Comparing activations of individual disorders early

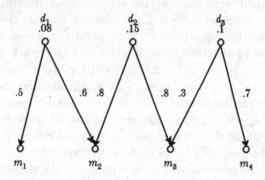

Figure 7.2. A simple causal network with prior probabilities
attached to each disorder and causal strengths attached
to each causal link.

Table 7.1. Disorder activation levels for different M^+ sets.

number of itera- tions	$M^+=\{m_2\}$			$M^+=\{m_1,m_2,m_3\}$			$M^+=\{m_1,m_2,m_3,m_4\}$		
	d_1	d_2	d_3	d_1	d_2	d_3	d_1	d_2	d_3
0	0.08	0.15	0.1	0.08	0.15	0.1	0.08	0.15	0.1
1	0.076	0.148	0.096	0.085	0.154	0.096	0.085	0.154	0.105
2	0.069	0.145	0.087	0.094	0.163	0.089	0.094	0.163	0.113
5	0.027	0.139	0.034	0.147	0.212	0.04	0.147	0.212	0.166
10	0.0	0.293	0.0	0.305	0.358	0.0	0.305	0.356	0.32
20	0.0	0.685	0.0	0.69	0.714	0.0	0.69	0.698	0.697
30	0.0	0.92	0.0	0.921	0.927	0.0	0.92	0.746	0.923
40	0.0	0.989	0.0	0.989	0.99	0.0	0.989	0.659	0.989
50	0.0	1.0	0.0	1.0	1.0	0.0	1.0	0.479	1.0
60							1.0	0.192	1.0
65							1.0	0.0	1.0

in the simulation, d_2 seems to be in the best position (it has a larger prior
probability, *and* it gets more support from M^+ initially through two
stronger links). If some sequential approximation approach is taken, d_2
may thus be selected as part of the solution (final diagnosis) because it is
the best among all three disorders based on local information. On the
other hand, since d_1 is the only disorder which can account for m_1, and d_3
the only disorder which can account for m_4, both of them should also be
included in the solution, thus resulting in a diagnosis having three disorders which, as it turns out, is neither parsimonious nor the most probable.

If inhibitory links were used between competitors, then it is likely that d_1 and d_3 would be suppressed by the high activation of d_2, resulting in a non–cover solution of d_2 alone, or there would be a failure to achieve clear–cut winners–take–all behavior because d_1 and d_3 would directly inhibit each other. Here, however, because the early superiority of d_2 is not final, the activations of d_1 and d_3 gradually increase subsequently due to the support they receive from m_1 and m_4, respectively (the higher $d_2(t)$ initially does not prevent the increase of $d_1(t)$ and $d_3(t)$ because there are no inhibitory links between them). Thus, d_1 and d_3 become more and more competitive relative to d_2 and eventually take all support from m_2 and m_3 away from d_2, so $d_2(t)$ drops to zero eventually. This simple example shows how the parallel interactions through the competitive model of Equations 7.4 and 7.8 can work properly in different situations.

A thorough set of experiments was done for three significantly larger examples of diagnostic problems which we will call example–1, example–2, and example–3. Each of these examples has a causal network of 10 disorder nodes and 10 manifestation nodes. Example–1 and example–2 were randomly generated, i.e., for each d_i, what its prior probability p_i is, how many manifestations are causally associated with it, which are they, and what their respective causal strengths are, were all generated randomly and independently. The only restriction was that all p_i's in example–1 be less than 0.10, while in example–2 the p_i's were restricted to be less than 0.20. Finally, example–3 is the same as example–2 except that all prior probabilities in example–3 are assigned to be twice those in example–2. The reason for restricting p_i's to small numbers is that in most real–world diagnostic problems prior probabilities of disorders are very small. The details of these three example networks are given in an Appendix in Section 7.8.

For each of these example networks, all possible 1024 cases, each corresponding to a distinct $M^+ \subseteq M$ (i.e., $\varnothing$, $\{m_1\}$, $\{m_2\}$, $\{m_1, m_2\}$ $\cdots$), were tested. For each M^+, the sequential search algorithm $SEARCH$ presented in Chapter 5 was used to find target hypothesis D_{max}, the globally most probable hypothesis for the given M^+. D_{max} was then compared with D_S, the hypothesis obtained by the program simulating the connectionist model. The cases in which $D_S = D_{max}$ were recorded.

In these experiments all 3072 cases converged (no oscillations occurred), and each case resulted in a set of winning disorders being fully activated while all other disorders were fully deactivated (no disorder had an activation level between 0.5 and 0.95 at equilibrium). In other words, multiple–winners–take–all behavior was realized in all of these experimental cases. Most of these cases (more than 95%) converged after 80 to 100 iterations. A few took several hundreds of iterations or more to converge. The simulation results for these experiments are given in the second row of Table 7.2. This table shows that the solutions D_S from the connectionist model exactly agreed with the most probable hypothesis D_{max} (i.e., $D_S = D_{max}$) in about 70 – 80% cases for the three example networks (73.2% correct for all 3072 cases). This demonstrates that global optimization can be achieved in the majority of cases via local optimization in the connectionist model. For those mis–matched cases where $D_S \neq D_{max}$, further study revealed that most of them are the second or third best hypotheses in terms of their posterior probabilities. For example, among the 215 mis–matched cases in example–1, 134 and 53 of them are the second and the third best hypotheses, respectively. Thus, only 28 (less than 3%) of all 1024 cases resulted in hypotheses worse than the third best one, so 97% achieve globally or near–globally optimal solutions. Similar results were also obtained for example–2 and example–3 (percentages of cases where D_S is worse than the third best hypothesis are 8% and 8.6%, respectively).

7.4.2. Resettling Process

For cases where $D_S \neq D_{max}$, the inconsistency is due to the mis–behavior of some disorder nodes whose local optimization does not lead to a globally optimal solution. That is, either some node d_i is fully activated based on local information and competition but does not belong to D_{max} (it should have been rejected), or d_i is fully deactivated but it does belong to D_{max} (it should have been accepted). The hypothesis D_S generated by the parallel computation gives us a mechanism for seeking a remedy to such inconsistencies. Even though D_S does not indicate which disorder nodes might have gone wrong when D_S was computed, we know that if any node $d_i \in D_S$ went wrong, its $d_i(t_e)$ should be zero, not one; and if $d_i \notin D_S$ went wrong, its $d_i(t_e)$ should be one, not zero. This information, which is not available before D_S is generated, can be used as the basis for a "resettling process," repeating simulations that involve partially instantiating the causal network. The full resettling process is performed after D_S is generated when the first parallel computation reaches equilibrium and goes as follows (n is the total number of disorders):

Table 7.2. Experimental results using activation rule Equation 7.8b.

	example–1	example–2	example–3	total
total number of cases	1024	1024	1024	3072
number of correct cases after the first parallel computation	809 (79.0%)	692 (67.6%)	748 (73.0%)	2249 (73.2%)
number of correct cases after a partial resettling process	980 (95.7%)	951 (92.9%)	967 (94.4%)	2898 (94.3%)
number of correct cases after a full resettling process	1022 (99.8%)	1018 (99.4%)	1018 (99.4%)	3058 (99.5%)

After the network stabilizes with D_S, n more parallel computations are performed, each of which is done on the given original network with one disorder node d_i's activation being instantiated: $d_i(0)$ is set and clamped to 0 if it is in D_S, or to 1 if it is not in D_S. The n hypotheses $D_S^{(1)}$, $D_S^{(2)}$, ..., $D_S^{(n)}$ resulting from these n partially–instantiated networks are then compared with D_S, and the one among the $n + 1$ hypotheses maximizing Equation 7.1 or 7.3 is taken as the solution for the given case.

This full resettling process can be viewed as a way of escaping from the local optimum reached in the first run of the computation. Now, n more local optima are generated and they are guaranteed to be different from D_S because of the way the partial–instantiation is implemented (although there may be duplicates among these n new hypotheses). Therefore, this process is expected to greatly improve accuracy assuming D_S from the first computation at least approximates D_{max}. Experimental results (see the fourth row of Table 7.2) show that after the full resettling process, the total number of cases where the connectionist model resulted in the most probable hypothesis was markedly increased (99.5% of all 3072 cases were correct). Furthermore, in all of the cases where $D_S \neq D_{max}$ after resettling, the solutions obtained from the connectionist model were the second most probable hypotheses.

Unfortunately, the price we pay for such a high accuracy via a full resettling process is that instead of one parallel computation, now $n + 1$ computations would be required, where n is the total number of disorders. A trade–off between accuracy and cost can be achieved by only resettling with $d_i(0)$ to zero for each $d_i \in D_S$ in turn so that only $|D_S|$ more computations need be performed. Usually $|D_S|$ is drastically smaller than $|D| = n$, especially in large real–world problems, so this would cost much less than resettling with every d_i in D. In the three example networks, as shown in the third row of Table 7.2, this partial resettling process resulted in $D_S = D_{max}$ in over 94% of all cases in these three example networks.

7.4.3. Convergence with Multiple–Winners–Take–All

We now discuss the issue of convergence, i.e., whether this model will always reach equilibrium, and when equilibrium is reached, whether it is guaranteed that every disorder node will approximate zero/one activation. Although we do not have analytical results and existing analysis of competition–based models are not directly applicable [Seidman87], all 3072 cases of the three examples converged on multiple winners. To further investigate this problem, the same 3072 cases were tested again with randomly assigned initial activations for all disorder nodes. Now, instead of setting the initial activation $d_i(0)$ to p_i, the prior probability for each disorder d_i, $d_i(0)$ is set to a very small positive random number (0.00001 to 0.0001). All cases again converged on multiple winners, and almost the same degree of accuracy was achieved. The experimental results are given in Table 7.3. This not only shows that the model is somewhat insensitive to the initial activations of disorder nodes, but also suggests a way to overcome potential situations where some disorders stabilized on activation values somewhere in between 0.05 and 0.95. Since such a situation represents a delicate and uncommon symmetry of a network involving $r_i(t) = 1$ in the simulation, changes to the initial $d_i(0)$ for all d_i by random assignment may well bring the system out from the symmetry.

7.4.4. Altered Activation Rule Using A Sigmoid Function

It is also interesting to ask how sensitive the results obtained above are to the specific form of the activation updating rule Equation 7.8a for $d_i(t)$. To examine this issue, we repeated some of the experimental simulations after altering the local activation rule for disorders. Consider Equation 7.7, the ramp function f used to bound the activation change rate of $d_i(t)$, which looks somewhat like a sigmoid function. One of the nice properties of the sigmoid function is that it asymptotically reaches its minimal and maximal values when its argument approaches negative and positive infinity, respectively. In the next set of experiments, a different activation rule for $d_i(t)$ based on a sigmoid function was applied to the same three examples as before. The activation rule is defined as follows:

$$d_i(t + 1) = \frac{1}{1 + e^{-(r_i(t) - 1)/T(t)}} \tag{7.9}$$

where t is the number of iterations, and $T(t)$ is a parameter sometimes called *temperature* in *simulated annealing* systems [Kirkpatrick83, Ackley85]. In the experiments that follow, similar to simulated annealing used in thermodynamic networks, the computation is allowed to start with a high T value that was gradually reduced by a factor δ, i.e., $T(t + 1) = T(t)\,\delta$. Although the connectionist modeling method discussed here is not

Table 7.3. Experimental results with small random initial activations for disorder nodes.

	example–1	example–2	example–3	total
total number of cases	1024	1024	1024	3072
number of correct cases after the first parallel computation	788 (77.0%)	693 (67.7%)	727 (71.0%)	2208 (71.9%)
number of correct cases after a partial resettling process	980 (95.7%)	942 (92.0%)	959 (93.7%)	2881 (93.8%)
number of correct cases after a full resettling process	1018 (99.4%)	1016 (99.2%)	1014 (99.0%)	3048 (99.2%)

simulated annealing, we refer to δ as the "annealing constant" and the updating rule for $T(t)$ as the "annealing schedule" by analogy.

This new activation rule (Equation 7.9) and the one used in previous experiments (Equation 7.8) are both based on $r_i(t)$, and both will cause $d_i(t+1)$ to increase (decrease) when $r_i(t)$ is greater (less) than 1. The two differences are that in Equation 7.9 a sigmoid function replaces the ramp function f of Equation 7.7, and the activation $d_i(t+1)$ is directly computed from the current $r_i(t)$ rather than via its derivative as in Equation 7.8a. The activation $d_i(t)$ on each iteration is determined by $r_i(t)$ and $T(t)$. The smaller $T(t)$ is, the steeper the curve of the sigmoid function will be. When $T(t)$ approaches 0.0, the magnitude of $r_i(t) - 1$ becomes relatively insignificant, so $d_i(t+1)$ should always approach either 1.0 or 0.0, depending on the sign of $r_i(t) - 1$. In the experiments, we set the initial value of $T(0) = 2.0$, and $\delta = 0.8$.

As might be expected, this new activation rule takes less time for the system to converge than before. Except for a few cases, convergence was reached within 20 iterations which is much faster than the 80 – 100 iterations typically needed when Equation 7.8c was used as the activation rule. Some exceptional cases did not converge with the initial setting $T(0) = 2.0$ and $\delta = 0.8$ but resulted in oscillating behavior. To make them converge, we adjusted the annealing schedule by setting the initial temperature $T(0)$ to a value much higher than 2.0, sometimes as high as 100 (this, of course, results in a longer time for those cases to reach equilibrium). All of them now converged. Surprisingly to us, not only did this new rule work as well as the original one, but in fact it resulted in much higher accuracy: in 87.2% of all 3072 cases $D_S = D_{max}$ without any resettling. This figure rose to 99.4% correct with only *partial* resettling, as reported in Table 7.4. Accuracy in both situations is significantly higher than the corresponding 73.2% and 94.3% achieved using Equation 7.8c.

Table 7.4. Experimental results using activation rule Equation 7.9.

	example–1	example–2	example–3	total
total number of cases	1024	1024	1024	3072
number of correct cases after the first parallel computation	927 (90.5%)	859 (83.9%)	894 (87.3%)	2680 (87.2%)
number of correct cases after a partial resettling process	1015 (99.1%)	1019 (98.5%)	1020 (99.6%)	3054 (99.4%)
number of correct cases after a full resettling process	1021 (99.7%)	1024 (100%)	1023 (99.9%)	3068 (99.9%)

7.5. A Medical Application Example

In this section, the connectionist formulation developed in this chapter is applied to a medical diagnostic problem to show its applicability to larger, more realistic networks [Wald89]. The causal network under consideration is for neuropsychiatric diagnosis. The disorder set D of the network consists of 26 disorders from psychiatry and neurology which affect mental status (examples of such disorders are alcohol intoxication, Alzheimers disease, anorexia nervosa, etc.). A list of 56 symptoms and signs (e.g., acute–anxiety, affect–depressed, insomnia, etc.) was assembled for each disorder. Manifestations other than symptoms and signs, such as laboratory results, were omitted. All manifestations used in this model were assumed to be acute or subacute and to occur in a right–handed patient.

There are 384 causal links in the network, each of which connects a disorder to a manifestation. Connection weights (causal strengths) and subjective disorder prior probabilities were estimated and agreed upon by two physicians, one in psychiatry and one in neurology. As an example of the probability estimates used in the network, the connection weight between the disorder node "major depression" and the manifestation node "decreased appetite" is 0.7. Table 7.5 gives an example list of all manifestation nodes connecting to the disorder node "anorexia nervosa". Table 7.6 provides an example list of all disorder nodes connecting to the manifestation node "gait ataxia". The prior probabilities (initial activation values) of disorder nodes range between 0.001 and 0.09 and reflect relative frequency of the disorders. For example, "catatonic schizophrenia", a rare disorder, is given an initial activation of 0.001, while "major depression", a relatively common disorder, is given an initial activation of 0.09. The network's 384 links are distributed among the 26 disorders with an average of 15 links per disorder; the range is from 6 to 33. The 56 manifestations have an average of about 7 connections each; the range is from 1 to 17.

On first thought, this network may not seem impressive, but it should be understood that the potential "hypothesis space" involved with such a network is enormous compared to the examples in the preceding section. A

Table 7.5. Manifestations of anorexia nervosa and their associated causal strengths.

weight–loss	1.00
body–image–disturbance	0.90
vomiting–or–nausea	0.70
amenorrhea	0.70
complaint–of–appetite–decreased	0.50
psychomotor–agitation	0.50
insomnia	0.50

Table 7.6. Disorders causing gait ataxia and their associated causal strengths.

Wernickes–encephalopathy	0.95
delirium–tremens	0.90
alcohol–intoxication	0.85
brainstem–infact	0.70
brainstem–hematoma	0.70
brainstem–tumor	0.70
infectious–delirium	0.70
Wilsons–disease	0.50
B–12–deficiency	0.40
dominant–hemisphere–tumor	0.30
encephalitis	0.25

network with 10 disorders represents $2^{10} = 1,024$ possible diagnostic hypotheses; in contrast, a network with 26 disorders represents $2^{26} = 67,108,864$ possible hypotheses. In addition, this network is based on a "real" diagnostic application. The network structure (causal associations) and connection weights were provided by physicians and were not randomly generated. As a result, the connectionist model used in this experiment is not only larger, but also more realistically structured, permitting us to begin assessing the feasibility of applying this approach to real–world diagnostic problems.

Five groups of test cases are used to test the connectionist model. Manifestations are chosen randomly from the total set of 56 possible manifestations based on a uniform distribution. Each group of test cases consists of ten different sets of manifestations (M^+). Each case in the first test group has $|M^+| = 1$, i.e., contains one present manifestation; each case in the second group has $|M^+| = 3$; and each of the cases in the other three groups has $|M^+|$ equal to 5, 7, or 9 [*]

For each test case, the three globally optimal solutions (those with highest likelihood L) were identified by the sequential algorithm *SEARCH* of Chapter 5. Then, they were run using the connectionist model described in the previous section. In this experiment, Equation 7.9, the sigmoid function, was used for updating activations of disorder nodes. Each case was run for 80 iterations. A resettling process was not performed.

Some preliminary runs of the simulation showed that oscillations

---

(*) In any randomly generated test case where amenorrhea is present and weight–loss is not, the case was discarded and a new one generated. This is because amenorrhea is only caused by anorexia nervosa in the causal network used in the experiment, while anorexia nervosa has a causal strength of 1.0 on the link between it and weight–loss. Thus, a case with amenorrhea but not weight–loss is inconsistent with the causal network. This conflict occurs because the causal network used in the experiment is restricted to neuropsychiatric disorders; it does not include other non–neuropsychiatric causes of amenorrhea.

occurred much more frequently than in the random network examples described earlier, and a lot of these cases could not be corrected by using a high initial temperature. Further analysis of the behavior of the model revealed that the network will always go through a "critical period", starting at a "critical temperature". During this period, the activations of all disorder nodes are decreasing to a very low level before some of them (those in the solution) jump to 1.0 [Wald89]. If, at this time, two competing disorders of the same manifestation have activations very close to each other, and if the temperature difference between time intervals is too coarse, then both of them will jump to a high activation level together at the same time, and then drop to a very low activation level at the next time instant, thus resulting in oscillations (and they will quickly pull other disorder nodes into the oscillations). Analysis shows that as long as $T(0)$ is higher than the critical temperature, which is usually less than 1.0, increasing $T(0)$ will not bring the network out of the oscillation. However, if δ is sufficiently small so that the small difference between activations of the two rival nodes can be differentiated, the oscillations can be avoided. The interested reader is referred to [Wald89] for the details of the analysis and a way to effectively decide the critical point and thus suitable $T(0)$ and δ values for a given network. The results described below are for $T(0) = 1.0$ and $\delta = 0.95$.

Simulation results in this case showed that all cases converged to stable answers. Among the all 50 cases, 37 (74%) of them produced the most probable cover of the given M^+ (the globally optimal answers). Another 8 simulations gave the second or third most probable covers, so 45 (90%) of all cases gave one of the three globally most optimal answers. Considering the relatively large knowledge base (28 disorders and 56 manifestations) and the fact that resettling was not used, those are reasonably good results. The detailed accounts of the experiment can be found in [Wald89].

One thing concerning this experiment that differs from real–world diagnosis is that the input (i.e., M^+) for each case was randomly generated, not obtained from real clinical records. In general, manifestations of a real patient are not randomly spread. Instead, they are more closely related to the disorders that really occur. Whether this fact would improve the performance of the connectionist model in real–world applications remains to be seen.

7.6. Summary

In summary, a specific competition–based connectionist model can be constructed to solve diagnostic problems formulated as causal networks. The diagnostic problem–solving can be regarded as a non–linear optimization problem, and the equations governing node activation updating in the connectionist model are thus derived by decomposing the global optimization criterion to criteria local to individual nodes. This model was run over all 1024 possible different cases for each of three randomly generated example networks. The experiments showed that diagnostic problems can be solved by this connectionist model within acceptable accuracy (73.2% of globally optimal answers if Equation 7.8c is used, and 87.2% if Equation 7.9 is used) when only a single parallel computation to equilibrium is performed, and can be done with a very high accuracy when a partial resettling process is also performed (greater than 99% with Equation 7.9). The model was also tested on a larger and more realistic causal network, consisting of 28 disorders and 56 manifestations, and remarkably good performance was observed (74% of globally optimal answers, and 90% of one of the three globally optimal answers without using resettling).

These experiments show that the competitive connectionist models offer a good alternative to sequential approaches using traditional AI techniques. They may avoid the combinatorial difficulties faced by existing sequential approaches, yet perform the problem–solving with quite high accuracy, i.e., provide globally optimal or near globally optimal solutions in most cases. The experiments we have conducted were all on two–layer causal networks. It remains to extend this connectionist model to more general networks such as hyper–bipartite networks defined in Chapter 6, where nodes representing intermediate concepts such as syndromes are also connected by causal links. Exploring this approach further and applying it to other non–linear optimization problems as well as real–world diagnostic applications should shed further light on its strengths and weaknesses.

7.7. Mathematical Appendix

Proof of Equation 7.6: By the definition of $r_i(t)$ and $q_i(d_i(t))$,

$$r_i(t) = \frac{q_i(1)}{q_i(0)}$$

$$= \frac{\displaystyle\prod_{m_j \in M_i^+} \left[1 - \prod_{\substack{k=1 \\ k \neq i}}^{n}(1 - c_{kj}\, d_k(t))\, (1 - c_{ij})\right]}{\displaystyle\prod_{m_j \in M_i^+} \left[1 - \prod_{\substack{k=1 \\ k \neq i}}^{n}(1 - c_{kj}\, d_k(t))\right]}$$

$$\frac{\displaystyle\prod_{m_l \in M_i^-} \prod_{\substack{k=1 \\ k \neq i}}^{n}(1 - c_{kl}\, d_k(t))\, (1 - c_{il}) \displaystyle\prod_{\substack{k=1 \\ k \neq i}}^{n} \frac{1 - d_k(t)\,(1 - p_k)}{1 - p_k\, d_k(t)} \;\; \frac{p_i}{1 - p_i}}{\displaystyle\prod_{m_l \in M_i^-} \prod_{\substack{k=1 \\ k \neq i}}^{n}(1 - c_{kl}\, d_k(t)) \displaystyle\prod_{\substack{k=1 \\ k \neq i}}^{n} \frac{1 - d_k(t)\,(1 - p_k)}{1 - p_k\, d_k(t)} \;\; \frac{1}{1}}$$

$$= \prod_{m_j \in M_i^+} \frac{1 - \prod_{\substack{k=1 \\ k \neq i}}^{n} (1 - c_{kj}\, d_k(t))\, (1 - c_{ij})}{1 - \prod_{\substack{k=1 \\ k \neq i}}^{n} (1 - c_{kj}\, d_k(t))} \prod_{m_l \in M_i^-} (1 - c_{il})\, \frac{p_i}{1 - p_i}. \qquad (I)$$

To simplify Equation I, consider a factor of the first product. By Equation 7.4,

$$m_j(t) = 1 - \left[\prod_{\substack{k=1 \\ k \neq i}}^{n} (1 - c_{kj}\, d_k(t)) \right] (1 - c_{ij}\, d_i(t)). \qquad (II)$$

From Equation II, we have

$$1 - \prod_{\substack{k=1 \\ k \neq i}}^{n} (1 - c_{kj}\, d_k(t)) = 1 - \frac{1 - m_j(t)}{1 - c_{ij}\, d_i(t)} = \frac{m_j(t) - c_{ij}\, d_i(t)}{1 - c_{ij}\, d_i(t)}, \quad \text{and} \qquad (III)$$

$$1 - \left[\prod_{\substack{k=1 \\ k \neq i}}^{n} (1 - c_{kj}\, d_k(t)) \right] (1 - c_{ij}) = 1 - \frac{1 - m_j(t)}{1 - c_{ij}\, d_i(t)} (1 - c_{ij})$$

$$= \frac{m_j(t) - c_{ij}\, d_i(t) + c_{ij}(1 - m_j(t))}{1 - c_{ij}\, d_i(t)} \qquad (IV)$$

Dividing Equation IV by Equation III, we have

$$\frac{1 - \prod_{\substack{k=1 \\ k \neq i}}^{n} (1 - c_{kj}\, d_k(t))\, (1 - c_{ij})}{1 - \prod_{\substack{k=1 \\ k \neq i}}^{n} (1 - c_{kj}\, d_k(t))}$$

$$= \frac{m_j(t) - c_{ij}\, d_i(t) + c_{ij}(1 - m_j(t))}{1 - c_{ij}\, d_i(t)} \; \frac{1 - c_{ij}\, d_i(t)}{m_j(t) - c_{ij}\, d_i(t)}$$

$$= \frac{m_j(t) - c_{ij}\, d_i(t) + c_{ij}(1 - m_j(t))}{m_j(t) - c_{ij}\, d_i(t)}$$

$$= 1 + c_{ij} \frac{1 - m_j(t)}{m_j(t) - c_{ij}\, d_i(t)}. \qquad (V)$$

Substituting Equation V to Equation I, $r_i(t)$ is simplified as

$$r_i(t) = \prod_{m_j \in M_i^+} \left[1 + c_{ij} \frac{1 - m_j(t)}{m_j(t) - c_{ij}\, d_i(t)} \right] \prod_{m_l \in M_i^-} (1 - c_{il})\, \frac{p_i}{1 - p_i} \qquad (7.6a)$$

$\square$

7.8. Appendix of Experimental Networks

The following table contains prior probabilities for disorders and causal strengths for causal associations for the three example networks used in experiments. See Section 7.4.1 for the description of these networks.

example–1		example–2		example–3	
$p_1 = 0.026$	$p_2 = 0.014$	$p_1 = 0.17$	$p_2 = 0.07$	$p_1 = 0.34$	$p_2 = 0.14$
$p_3 = 0.054$	$p_4 = 0.06$	$p_3 = 0.03$	$p_4 = 0.12$	$p_3 = 0.06$	$p_4 = 0.24$
$p_5 = 0.003$	$p_6 = 0.023$	$p_5 = 0.135$	$p_6 = 0.18$	$p_5 = 0.27$	$p_6 = 0.36$
$p_7 = 0.048$	$p_8 = 0.079$	$p_7 = 0.075$	$p_8 = 0.03$	$p_7 = 0.30$	$p_8 = 0.06$
$p_9 = 0.098$	$p_{10} = 0.027$	$p_9 = 0.14$	$p_{10} = 0.05$	$p_9 = 0.28$	$p_{10} = 0.10$
$c_{12} = 0.31$	$c_{14} = 0.85$	$c_{12} = 0.06$	$c_{14} = 0.68$	$c_{12} = 0.06$	$c_{14} = 0.68$
$c_{17} = 0.30$	$c_{27} = 0.50$	$c_{16} = 0.10$	$c_{17} = 0.51$	$c_{16} = 0.10$	$c_{17} = 0.51$
$c_{32} = 0.29$	$c_{34} = 0.64$	$c_{21} = 0.53$	$c_{23} = 0.81$	$c_{21} = 0.53$	$c_{23} = 0.81$
$c_{35} = 0.15$	$c_{36} = 0.11$	$c_{24} = 0.09$	$c_{25} = 0.85$	$c_{24} = 0.09$	$c_{25} = 0.85$
$c_{38} = 0.72$	$c_{39} = 0.62$	$c_{28} = 0.13$	$c_{29} = 0.34$	$c_{28} = 0.13$	$c_{29} = 0.34$
$c_{43} = 0.88$	$c_{48} = 0.27$	$c_{2,10} = 0.85$	$c_{32} = 0.54$	$c_{2,10} = 0.85$	$c_{32} = 0.54$
$c_{51} = 0.72$	$c_{52} = 0.92$	$c_{35} = 0.45$	$c_{36} = 0.90$	$c_{35} = 0.45$	$c_{36} = 0.90$
$c_{54} = 0.07$	$c_{55} = 0.47$	$c_{37} = 0.59$	$c_{3,10} = 0.29$	$c_{37} = 0.59$	$c_{3,10} = 0.29$
$c_{59} = 0.73$	$c_{5,10} = 0.96$	$c_{42} = 0.74$	$c_{45} = 0.52$	$c_{42} = 0.74$	$c_{45} = 0.52$
$c_{66} = 0.32$	$c_{67} = 0.26$	$c_{47} = 0.65$	$c_{49} = 0.32$	$c_{47} = 0.65$	$c_{49} = 0.32$
$c_{71} = 0.05$	$c_{72} = 0.80$	$c_{53} = 0.72$	$c_{58} = 0.49$	$c_{53} = 0.72$	$c_{58} = 0.49$
$c_{75} = 0.73$	$c_{78} = 0.58$	$c_{63} = 0.09$	$c_{65} = 0.66$	$c_{63} = 0.09$	$c_{65} = 0.66$
$c_{82} = 0.04$	$c_{84} = 0.26$	$c_{6,10} = 0.44$	$c_{73} = 0.22$	$c_{6,10} = 0.44$	$c_{73} = 0.22$
$c_{86} = 0.23$	$c_{87} = 0.69$	$c_{74} = 0.46$	$c_{75} = 0.21$	$c_{74} = 0.46$	$c_{75} = 0.21$
$c_{8,10} = 0.51$	$c_{92} = 0.12$	$c_{76} = 0.76$	$c_{7,10} = 0.43$	$c_{76} = 0.76$	$c_{7,10} = 0.43$
$c_{97} = 0.95$	$c_{9,10} = 0.67$	$c_{81} = 0.29$	$c_{82} = 0.34$	$c_{81} = 0.29$	$c_{82} = 0.34$
$c_{10,4} = 0.43$	$c_{10,5} = 0.18$	$c_{88} = 0.25$	$c_{91} = 0.39$	$c_{88} = 0.25$	$c_{91} = 0.39$
$c_{10,6} = 0.11$		$c_{94} = 0.20$	$c_{95} = 0.90$	$c_{94} = 0.20$	$c_{95} = 0.90$
		$c_{96} = 0.48$	$c_{97} = 0.38$	$c_{96} = 0.48$	$c_{97} = 0.38$
		$c_{10,2} = 0.74$	$c_{10,8} = 0.27$	$c_{10,2} = 0.74$	$c_{10,8} = 0.27$

8
Conclusion

> Alice: "Would you tell me, please, which way I
> ought to go from here?"
> Cheshire Cat: "That depends a good deal on
> where you want to get to."
> Lewis Carroll

In this book we have presented parsimonious covering theory as a formal model for diagnostic problem–solving. The basic model (Chapter 3) of this theory and its various extensions (Chapters 4 to 7) capture important abductive features of the diagnostic inference process in a mathematically rigorous fashion. To conclude this book, we first summarize what was accomplished in developing this theory in Section 8.1. Viewing diagnostic problem–solving as a special type of general abductive inference, parsimonious covering theory can be considered as a first step toward formalization of abduction, and thus may find applications for some non–diagnostic problems. The potential generality of this theory is discussed in Section 8.2, along with some of its non–diagnostic applications. Finally, in Section 8.3, we outline some limitations and potential extensions to the current form of this formal model.

8.1. A Summary of Parsimonious Covering Theory

In essence, parsimonious covering theory is a formal model of diagnostic inference which centers on pairwise cause–effect relationships between individual elements and tries to find the best or most plausible explanations (sets of disorders) for a set of given manifestations (findings). The formulation of diagnostic problems in this theory provides a more natural knowledge representation than the traditional rule–based paradigm in knowledge engineering systems. This not only makes it easier to acquire knowledge from domain experts and organize it in the knowledge base, but also makes some important relevant concepts much more clear. For example, the best explanation, a vague notion representing the goal of general abduction, is realized or formalized in this framework by two principles based on causal relations in a diagnostic world: *the covering principle* which states that a disorder can account, explain or cover manifestations caused by that disorder; and *the parsimony principle* which states that the "simplest" or most parsimonious cover is the most plausible (see Section 3.1).

Based on this basic framework, an algorithm *BIPARTITE* for problem-solving in bipartite (two layer) causal networks was developed initially and proven to find all irredundant covers for a given set of manifestations (Section 3.4). Whenever a new manifestation is given, this algorithm incorporates the causes of the new finding into the existing hypotheses to form the set of all irredundant covers for all currently known manifestations. This repetitive process mimics the hypothesize–and–test reasoning common to many abductive tasks and produces explanations that are intuitively plausible. This problem–solving strategy also provides some limited ability to justify the solution obtained and can easily be modified to accommodate volunteered partial solutions (Section 6.3).

Although very simple, the basic formulation of parsimonious covering theory summarized above captures some key ideas of abduction in general and diagnostic inference in particular. Further, it provides the framework for a variety of theoretical extensions that gradually extend the power of the theory. The first extension was to formally integrate probability theory, the best established theory of uncertainty, into the framework of parsimonious covering theory to capture the uncertain nature of cause–effect relationships (Chapter 4). The resulting probabilistic causal model uses an approach quite different from traditional Bayesian classification. In previous Bayesian approaches, only the occurrence and non–occurrence of entities like manifestations and disorders were considered, and the causal relations between these entities are implicitly embedded in conditional probabilities between them. Concentrating on causal relations, the probabilistic causal model postulates that, besides disorders and manifestations, there is another kind of event, namely causation events, that reflects the occurrence of the causal effects. This is a fundamentally new approach to multimember classification in diagnostic problem–solving. Based on a set of probabilistic assumptions, which are reasonable in many applications and are consistent with the assumptions underlying parsimonious covering theory, a formal probability calculus was derived from probability theory and causal networks for bipartite diagnostic problems.

The resultant probabilistic causal model avoids the difficulties confronted by traditional Bayesian approaches when applied in multiple–disorder hypothesis situations: either a set of unrealistic assumptions must be made or a huge number of probabilities must be available. Based on a relative likelihood measure of diagnostic hypotheses derived from the probabilistic causal model, a provably correct best–first search algorithm, *SEARCH*, can be used to find the best (most probable) hypothesis(es) for the given set of manifestations. A measure of quality control for problem-solving in this model called a "comfort measure" was proposed to compensate for the lack of absolute belief while using relative likelihoods to measure hypothesis merit.

Moreover, the probabilistic causal model observes the covering principle in the sense that if a hypothesis is not a cover of the given set of manifestations, then its relative likelihood equals zero. It also provides the theoretical foundation for objectively justifying various subjective parsimony criteria, such as relevancy, irredundancy, and minimum cardinality. This model possesses a number of interesting properties which are in agreement with intuition (e.g., manifestations with common disorders are positively correlated, disorders are negatively correlated given their common manifestations, non-monotonic evidence accumulation, etc.; see Section 4.3). All of these properties further strengthen the plausibility of this model.

Intermediate states or entities, which connect measurable manifestations and ultimate disorders (abnormalities) through causal chaining, are also very important in diagnostic inference and can be found in many real-world diagnostic applications. For this reason, parsimonious covering theory was generalized from two layer bipartite networks to much more general causal networks in a straight-forward manner (Chapter 6). By adding intermediate states (syndromes) in various ways, causal chaining is realized. The generalized causal network is thus capable of representing more precisely knowledge of a much broader range of diagnostic problems. This also contributes to computational efficiency, naturalness of representation, and problem-solving flexibility.

Finding the most probable or plausible hypothesis can be a very time consuming computational task, in some cases involving search of a sizable portion of the whole search space, which is exponential to the number of possible disorders. This issue might be addressed by incorporating application-specific knowledge and other heuristics into the algorithms developed in this book to restrict the actual space searched. However, we elected to consider instead a competitive connectionist approach for solving this difficulty (Chapter 7). A two layer causal network can be considered as a connectionist network where disorders and manifestations are nodes interacting via connecting causal links. Disorders independently compete with each other to cover present manifestations (inputs) through local and highly parallel computations. When the present manifestations are indicated, the network settles into an equilibrium state representing a plausible hypothesis (always a locally optimal solution, often a globally optimal one). A resettling process can then be performed to further increase the accuracy. This approach provides a general and very satisfactory method to approximate problem solutions while using highly parallel computations, at least for the cases used in our experiments.

In summary, as a theoretical model, parsimonious covering theory and its extensions formalize many fundamentally important features of diagnostic inference in a general and rigorous fashion and provide computationally feasible problem-solving algorithms for various diagnostic tasks. While the theory faces a number of limitations (see Section 8.3 below), it forms a substantial theoretical foundation for constructing knowledge-based diagnostic systems capable of handling a broad range of problems.

8.2. Generality of the Theory: Non–Diagnostic Applications

Besides diagnosis, there are many other problems which can be categorized as abductive, or have abductive aspects to their problem–solving. We suspect that parsimonious covering theory, a theory of one kind of abduction, may find more widespread application, perhaps with some modifications, in such non–diagnostic problems. In Chapter 1 we mentioned several of these areas. Here, we give a more detailed discussion of the potential applications in two areas, namely, word–sense disambiguation in natural language processing and theory formation in learning.

Natural Language Processing

Very recently, a growing number of AI researchers have been working with the assumption that abductive inference underlies natural language processing [Charniak85, Dasigi89]. For example, like diagnostic problem–solving, natural language processing involves context–sensitive disambiguation of word senses and inferences about plausible explanations (e.g., garden path sentences, ellipses, and anaphora resolution) at a low level. Similar examples exist for high level natural language processing such as inferring the plans of the participants in a dialog so as to interpret the dialog coherently [Litman87], or inferring the plans of the protagonists in a story [Charniak86].

More specifically, an analogy between diagnostic problem–solving as formulated in parsimonious covering theory and word sense interpretation in natural language processing can be identified, as listed in Table 8.1. In terms of the knowledge used, both tasks involve the use of *associative knowledge*, i.e., associations between conceptual entities. Like disorders and manifestations associated by causal relations in diagnostic problems, natural language processing also involves associations between linguistic entities (e.g., word senses or meanings) and their manifestations (i.e., words). Presumably any type of associative relation could be involved: temporal, causal, spatial, similarity and so forth. Also the structure of such associative knowledge in both tasks is *ambiguous*, i.e., for any given concept there are typically multiple associations of the same kind with other related concepts that can be viewed as alternatives. For example, similar to a manifestation having multiple possible causative disorders, a word (e.g., *fly*) may also have multiple possible senses or meanings (e.g., small insect, baseball hit high in the air, to perform a task rapidly, etc.). The similarity also exists in problem–solving. Like an explanation, the "meaning" of a sequence of words as a multiple–component hypothesis must be *constructed* from individual elementary semantic concepts such as word senses. Disambiguation of a cue W (word) in alternative hypotheses is context–sensitive, i.e., it depends upon other cues that form the context of cue W and thus a parsimony principle may play a role in this disambiguation. Probabilistic knowledge about the uncertainty of associations and about the average frequency of occurrence of entities may also play some role in the disambiguation (e.g., the word "ball" is more likely associated with the "toy" sense than with the "dance" sense).

There are some substantial differences, of course, between diagnostic inference and natural language processing. For example, the order of manifestations in diagnostic problem–solving is usually irrelevant or insignificant to a plausible solution, but the order of words in a sentence is usually an important piece of information used in word sense disambiguation. Also, in diagnosis, if several hypotheses cannot be further discriminated, they may all be accepted as a tentative problem solution. But in natural language processing a single coherent explanation is generally desired. Despite these differences, the strong similarities between these two categories of problems suggest the possibility of applying parsimonious covering theory to solve certain natural language processing problems.

At least one such exploratory application exists [Dasigi89]. This is an experimental prototype which automatically generates natural language interfaces for medical diagnostic expert systems. The prototype is domain–independent in the same sense that a generic expert system shell is domain–independent. Given a knowledge base for a specific medical application, a vocabulary extractor extracts and indexes the linguistic information which it contains. In addition, an indexed domain–independent knowledge base that contains linguistic knowledge common to many

Table 8.1. The analogy with word sense disambiguation

Parsimonious Covering Theory	Word Sense Disambiguation and Interpretation
manifestation m_j	word
intermediate pathophysiological states	word senses and partial interpretations
disorder d_i	assertion/proposition
causal relation	associations (e.g., between words and senses)
$causes(m_j)$	set of higher level concepts associated with concept m_j (e.g., set of all senses of a word)
$effects(d_i)$	concept in terms of which concept d_i can manifest itself (e.g., synonyms of a concept)
observed manifestations	input text
diagnostic explanation (i.e., a set of disorders)	interpretation (e.g., a set of assertions)

domains is used. A natural language interface is generated for the specific application domain defined by the knowledge base using this knowledge plus a parsimonious covering inference mechanism.

Several modifications to the original parsimonious covering theory of diagnostic inference were introduced to handle the aspects of natural language processing that differ from diagnosis. By choosing representations in terms of descriptions for words that take the order of the words into account, the lack of sensitivity of parsimonious covering theory to word order is significantly reduced. Unlike the unstructured entities in parsimonious covering theory, the complex structure of words is taken into account in the hypothesis construction process. The syntactic (e.g., noun/adjective, subject/object) and semantic (word senses) aspects of covering are integrated in a mutually cooperative manner. In this system, a hypothesis is required, on the one hand, to cover words parsimoniously according to their semantic categories so that the syntactic descriptions in the linguistic knowledge base are satisfied, and on the other hand, concurrently to cover the words semantically with one or more domain-specific entities. For the syntactic aspect of parsimonious covering, irredundancy was chosen as a criterion for parsimony so that no potentially useful cover is thrown away. Because entities are structured with semantic associations among them, a new criterion of parsimony, called *cohesiveness*, was used for the semantic aspect of covering. The term "cohesiveness" used here refers to how well a cover fits into its surrounding context and can be viewed as a generalization of the minimum cardinality criterion. Reconciliation between the syntactic and semantic aspects of covering is achieved by satisfying the heuristic that parsimonious domain–specific entities covering a group of words (a semantic cover) belong to the set of semantic categories under which the words are grouped (a syntactic cover). Thus, these two aspects of covering proceed hand in hand, syntactic covering aiding semantic covering by grouping words together corresponding to their various salient semantic categories, while the semantic aspect of covering helps throw away all non–promising (non–unified) groupings so as to focus the syntactic aspect of covering.

The prototype implementation suggests that it may be possible to combine effectively concurrent syntactic and semantic covering of natural language processing in the framework of parsimonious covering theory. It still remains to be seen if, ultimately, parsimonious covering can be extended to model abductive inference occurring in natural language processing in its full generality, namely, where the intentions and plans of the discourse participants and subjects are complex and play a significant role in understanding the discourse.

Learning and Discovery

In recent years, researchers modeling learning and discovery, especially in developing computational models of theory formation, have shown increasing interest in abduction [Thagard89, O'Rorke88,89]. When a new observation contradicts the prediction of an existing theory, a new theory (possibly a revision of the old one) is called on so that the new theory can explain or account for the new observation as well. Like in diagnostic problems, here the purpose of a new theory is to form a plausible explanation for all observations, and the relationships connecting the theory (or its components) to observations are mainly causal associations. Based on this abductive nature, some computational models of theory formation have been developed which are capable of recapturing some revolutionary events in the history of science where new theories emerged from crises of the old theories, e.g., Lavoisier's oxygen theory over Stahl's phlogiston theory for combustion and calcination and Darwin's theory of evolution by natural selection over creationism, and some others [Thagard89, O'Rorke88,89]. In contrast to parsimonious covering theory, these abductive models of scientific theory formation involve a broader, less restricted framework for their application but their rules and principles governing computation are heuristic in nature. However, some key concepts and principles such as explanations, plausibility of explanations, hypothesis generation and revision, priority of data, etc. which are formally defined in parsimonious covering theory are also used in these models. Table 8.2 below gives a rough analogy between concepts in parsimonious covering theory for diagnosis and those in theory formation models. It is interesting to observe that there is a great deal of overlap in the underlying principles of these independently–developed theory formation models and those of parsimonious covering theory.

As an application–independent theoretical model, parsimonious covering theory provides a useful perspective for evaluating the heuristic rules of these models, analyzing their applicability, and critiquing their limitations. To see how this can be done, consider the "Theory of Explanatory

Table 8.2. The analogy with models for theory formation

Parsimonious Covering Theory	Models for Theory Formation
present manifestation m_j	fact to be explained
disorder d_i	theory component/proposition
$causes(m_j)$	components of rival theories that can individually explain a given fact
$effects(d_i)$	facts which can be explained by a component
hypothesize–and–test	theory evolution and emergence of new theory
diagnostic explanation	theory/explanatory hypothesis

Coherence" (TEC) [Thagard89]. In TEC, each of the rival theories is represented by a set of hypothesis components. A hypothesis component (or a group of them) is associated with all observed facts or evidence for which it can explain or causally account. The plausibility of hypothesis components, and in turn a scientific theory, is based on the notion of *coherence*. Coherence is a combination of considerations of symmetry, explanatory ability, analogy and other criteria, although explanation is the most important one. Moreover, the measure for explanatory ability of a hypothesized scientific theory is essentially "simplicity", i.e., a simpler scientific theory is better than a more complex alternative. Thus, in this respect, the underlying intuitions are the same for both parsimonious covering theory and TEC. They differ in the detailed definition of the notion of simplicity.

Based on qualitative arguments, a set of seven principles was identified by Thagard to determine the plausibility or coherence of hypothesis (scientific theory) components. It is interesting to analyze some of these principles using the results about hypothesis plausibility derived from parsimonious covering theory. According to one principle in TEC, if a group of hypothesis components can together explain a piece of evidence, then the degree of coherence of each of these components is inversely proportional to the number of components in that group. Thus, for two groups of rival hypothesis components (from two different theories) capable of explaining the same evidence, the one with fewer hypotheses, all else being roughly the same, will be preferred, because its members have a higher degree of coherence. This is very similar to one of the plausibility criteria, namely *minimum cardinality*: explanatory hypotheses with a fewer number of hypothesized components are preferable. This criterion was adopted in an early version of parsimonious covering theory and was discussed in Chapters 2 and 3. In applying it to specific diagnostic problems, it became evident that minimum cardinality is an inadequate measure of hypothesis plausibility. As we pointed out before, for example, in medical diagnosis two common diseases are often more plausible than a single rare disease in explaining a given set of symptoms [Reggia85a], and in electronic diagnosis analogous examples exist [Reiter87]. For this reason, parsimonious covering theory as well as other models of diagnostic inference have adopted a more relaxed criterion of plausibility: *irredundancy*. Although it does not always favor the smallest set of propositions, irredundancy is a preferable criterion because it handles cases like the medical and electronics examples above while still constraining the number of hypothesis components. Probabilistic analysis in Section 4.3.1 gave an objective evaluation of these subjective parsimony criteria based on posterior probability, indicating that except in rare cases, the most probable hypothesis is irredundant. On the other hand, minimum cardinality is only appropriate when all hypothesis components have very small and about equal prior probabilities and their causal association strengths to the evidence are fairly large.

Whether and to what extent this result holds for theory formation needs to be further investigated.

Another TEC principle states that if many relevant observations are unexplained, then the coherence of a hypothesis component is reduced. To a certain extent this implies that plausibility of a hypothesis component increases when new evidence supporting it is given. However, as shown by Theorem 4.21 in Section 4.3.3, new evidence may sometimes cause a decrease in the likelihood of a hypothesis component that causes it, if that evidence supports a rival causative hypothesis more strongly at the same time.

The main reason for the above discussed discrepancies between TEC and parsimonious covering theory seems to be that the former is based on the presumption that, in theory formation and some other nondiagnostic domains, the probabilities do not exist. Therefore, the computation must solely rely on symbolic associations. However, one should note that strict probabilities do not really exist in diagnostic applications either. Nevertheless, people do have different beliefs on different hypothesis components and on how strongly they are associated with evidence. That is, some measure, be it subjective or objective, numeric or nonnumeric, of "prior plausibility" or "intrinsic merit" and "conditional plausibility" of causation do exist and are essential not only in diagnosis, but also in other domains such as theory formation. The results with parsimonious covering theory suggest that it may be useful to develop a plausibility measure to accommodate such information more accurately than simply counting hypothesis components or the pieces of evidence explained by a proposed theory.

8.3. Future Research Directions

As a first step towards an abstract model of diagnostic inference, parsimonious covering theory and its extensions presented in this book concentrate on formalizing some essential aspects of that inference process. In doing so, the theory unavoidably simplifies real–world problems a great deal. A number of issues of both practical and theoretical importance have been left out of the current theory. Some of these issues (such as handling non–manifestation problem features, generating questions, justifying hypotheses, etc.) may be handled heuristically based on application–specific knowledge when one tries to develop a practical diagnostic system based on parsimonious covering theory [Reggia83a,85d]. This leads to the question: How can one incorporate these domain–specific heuristics into parsimonious covering theory in a coherent manner so that the power and generality of the theory can be increased? These and other issues may eventually be treated formally within the theoretical framework of parsimonious covering theory and they present a rich area for future research. We briefly discuss some of them now.

As we mentioned in Chapter 2, sometimes some non–causative facts may affect the likelihood of hypotheses. For instance, in medicine, "setting factors" such as a patient's age, sex, previous disease history, etc. may affect the plausibility of a diagnostic hypothesis because these factors specify the particular environment, context or setting within which the diagnostic problem occurs. In a different environment, i.e., in a different subspace in probability theoretic terms, the prior probabilities of individual disorders as well as the causal strengths between disorders and manifestations may be different. Also, risk factors, the severity of a disorder, and the cost of testing for new evidence and potential benefits or lack of such benefits from possible treatment may affect the diagnostic process. These non–causal factors are not yet included in parsimonious covering theory.

For problem–solving, parsimonious covering theory only formalizes half of the "hypothesize–and–test" cycle of the diagnostic inference process, namely the "hypothesize" part which deals with hypothesis formation and updating based on the arrival of new evidence. The "test" part of the cycle has largely been left out of the theory and submerged in external functions for question generation such as *Moremanifs* and *Nextman*. New evidence gathered from answering generated questions may be used to verify, discriminate and modify existing hypotheses. More informative questions may help guide the direction and narrow the focus of attention of the search process much better than less informative ones. Thus, the ability to generate good questions based on the available information and on the current hypotheses may be crucial for the efficiency and effectiveness of problem–solving. Question generation and setting factors were handled by heuristics in KMS.HT, a domain–independent diagnostic problem–solving shell based on parsimonious covering theory [Reggia81,83a]. It would be of interest to see how to treat them, or at least some of their aspects, formally in the framework of parsimonious covering theory.

In some real world applications, temporal and spatial factors of causal relations should also be taken into consideration, and this is not done in the current version of parsimonious covering theory. For example, in medicine, the temporal order in which symptoms appear and evolve can sometimes provide useful information for diagnosis. Neurological localization, a process which determines the site or sites of nervous system damage based on observations of a patient, is an example in which spatial/anatomical relationships are used as a crucial part of the knowledge base for diagnosis [Goldberg78, Reggia78]. How to incorporate temporal and spatial factors into parsimonious covering theory is thus another direction for further research. Exploratory studies of this latter issue are underway.

In parsimonious covering theory, disorders are not directly related to each other via direct associations, and neither are manifestations. In other words, there is no internal structure in the sets D and M. A causal network relating disorders and manifestations (possibly through intermediate states) can be geometrically viewed as planar or flat. In the real world, however, relations do exist among disorders as well as among manifestations. For example, among other things, disorders can be organized into a taxonomy containing disorder classes at different levels of abstraction. In medicine, diseases can be categorized into classes such as heart problems, liver problems, kidney problems, etc., based on organ involvement; or infection, cancer, abnormal immunity, etc., based on etiological consideration. Based on similarity, each of these classes represents a group of disorders and can itself be further divided into subclasses. This is also the case for manifestations. Fevers can be organized into a class entity "fever", and "heart rhythm irregularity" can be used to represent a large number of different kinds of abnormal heart rhythms. A taxonomy can be represented as an *is-a hierarchy*, i.e., a subclass B of A is a descendent of A in the hierarchy ("*B isa A*") because B is a type of A. For example, classifying based on organ involvement, the disease "viral hepatitis" is a type of "inflammatory hepatocellular disease" which, in turn, is a type of "hepatocellular disease" which, in turn, is a type of "hepatobiliary disease". On the other hand, the same disease can be classified based on etiology as a type of "viral infection" which, in turn, is a type of "infection". Disorder set D and manifestation set M can thus be organized into tangled is–a hierarchies in general, and the current parsimonious covering theory does not accommodate this structure.

This additional structural knowledge is very important for diagnostic inference. A widely accepted view of human diagnostic problem–solving behavior is that problem–solving is carried out at multiple levels of abstraction [Elstein78, Kassirer78, Reggia87a, Pople82,85]. For example, given the manifestation "fever", an experienced physician may quickly form a few plausible high–level diagnostic hypotheses such as "infection", "cancer", and "inflammation" by using the high–level causal associations between them. Each of these "high–level" disorder classes can be refined to many specific disorders within the classes. Such causal relationships between high level entities can be considered as abstractions of the relationships of their specific individual members. Thus, the taxonomy or classification of individual entities and the causal relationship between entities at different levels would add one more dimension to the flat causal network formulated in parsimonious covering theory, as illustrated by Figure 8.1.

Using high level causal associations is an efficient diagnostic strategy: it serves to focus problem–solving attention by avoiding the consideration of unnecessarily detailed disorders initially, and enables one to conduct inference with incomplete information concerning manifestations (it may be the case that not the specific manifestations but only some broader classes such "fever" are given in the initial phase of the diagnosis). Incorporating multiple levels of abstraction involving causal relations into parsimonious covering and extending the problem–solving methods to accommodate this

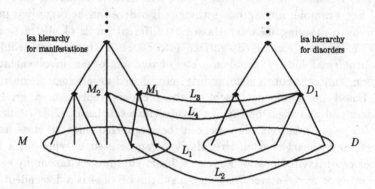

Figure 8.1. An illustration of high level causal associations. L_1 and L_2 are causal links between terminal disorders and manifestations, similar to those currently formulated in parsimonious covering theory. In contrast, L_3 and L_4 are high level links between class nodes, representing a summary or abstraction of causal relationships between terminal descendants of respective class nodes. These two high level links have different semantics because all descendants of M_1, but only some descendants of M_2, can be caused by descendants of D_1.

information would greatly enhance the theory's representation and inference ability. Some work along these lines already has been done. It has systematically categorized the semantics of high–level causal associations and developed methods for exception–handling and refinement/synthesis of causal links during problem–solving [Chu90].

Finally, we have concentrated on the representation and use of causal associations for diagnostic inference in developing parsimonious covering theory. This knowledge of causal associations as used in the theory is generally obtained from human diagnosticians' experience and thus it is sometimes referred to as *experiential knowledge*. This experiential knowledge can answer the question of whether or not two diagnostic entities are causally associated but not the question of *why* they are (or are not) causally associated. Knowledge of the underlying mechanisms responsible for experiential diagnostic causal associations is often referred to as *mechanistic knowledge*. Relying on experiential knowledge alone has its disadvantages. In some problem domains, "rules of thumb" and past statistical experiential knowledge may be inadequate for successful diagnostic problem–solving. Also, even if the experiential approach works for typical cases, there may be unusual scenarios which defy a diagnostician's expectations. The consequences of such anomalies, particularly in domains such as medical diagnosis or nuclear reactor monitoring, can be serious.

It is therefore desirable or necessary in some diagnostic situations to utilize not only experiential knowledge but also mechanistic knowledge about the *structure* and *function* of the interacting parts of the system being diagnosed. For example, information such as "The retina transduces visual information into electrical activity that travels down the optic nerve" or "The battery provides the energy needed to start the engine" describe normal functions. Modeling information like this concerning the underlying mechanism of a system can provide a deeper understanding of why things are causally associated at the surface or experiential level, and thus potentially may enable an automated diagnostic system to deal with problem situations beyond those which have been anticipated by the knowledge base author. In addition, if mechanism modeling is used in conjunction with experiential causal knowledge in a knowledge base, the integrity of the knowledge base can be examined by looking for and eliminating any inconsistencies between the two representations whenever new information is added. The need to eliminate inconsistencies in knowledge bases is becoming increasingly important as their areas of application become more and more complex and their sizes become larger and larger.

Integrating mechanistic knowledge with experiential knowledge in parsimonious covering theory is a very important direction for future research. Several issues must be addressed in this context. For example, a suitable approach to knowledge representation, in the context of diagnostic problem–solving, should be developed for mechanism modeling to adequately describe how the system components are structured and are functioning through interactions. Also, the relationships between a mechanism model and surface experiential knowledge must be established so that abnormal states in a system and their underlying causes can be related to each other. This would enable one to determine the consistency of a knowledge base by comparing the diagnostic associations extracted from the mechanism model with those stated explicitly from experience. Such interrelationships should also facilitate the coherent use of both experiential and mechanistic knowledge during diagnostic inference.

8.4. A Final Note

Any theory is only a hypothetical model of the real world. Although it captures key features in a rigorous manner, parsimonious covering theory as presented in this book is only a hypothetical model of the abductive inference process that humans conduct to solve diagnostic problems. Development of a sound and fully general theory, i.e., a good model of the real world, will itself be a process involving hypothesize–and–test cycles. Now that a hypothesis has been made in the form of parsimonious covering theory, the next step is to test it, i.e., to build systems and compare their behavior with systems based on other theories as well as human performance. Such experiments will ultimately test the plausibility and applicability of this theory, and reveal its real limitations. It is hoped that the parsimonious covering theory and its probabilistic extensions as presented in this book may become one more step along the path to a greater goal — establishing a general formal logic for abduction.

Bibliography

[Ackley85] Ackley, D., Hinton, G., and Sejnowski, T., "A Learning Algorithm for Boltzmann Machines", *Cognitive Science*, **9**, 1985, 147–169.

[Adams76] Adams, J., "A Probabilistic Model of Medical Reasoning and the MYCIN Model", *Mathematical Bioscience*, **32**, 1976, 177–186.

[Addis85] Addis, T. *Designing Knowledge-Based Systems*, Prentice Hall, NJ. 1985.

[Ahuja86] Ahuja, S. and Reggia, J. "Classification of Phonological Errors – An Abductive Reasoning Approach", *Proc. First Intl. Conf. on AI and Its Impact on Medicine and Biology*, Montpelier, France, 28–54.

[Ballard86] Ballard, D., "Parallel Logical Inference and Energy Minimization", *Proc. of National Conference on Artificial Intelligence*, AAAI, 1986, 203–208.

[Basili85] Basili, V., and Ramsey, C., "ARROWSMITH – P: A Prototype Expert System for Software Engineering Management", in Karna, K., (ed.), *Proc. Expert Systems in Government Symposium*, McLean, VA, 1985, 252–264.

[Ben-Bassat80] Ben-Bassat, M. et al, "Pattern-Based Interactive Diagnosis of Multiple Disorders: The MEDAS System", *IEEE Transaction on Pattern Analysis and Machine Intelligence*, **2** (2), March 1980, 148–160.

[Bennett81] Bennett, J. and Hollander, C., "DART: An Expert System for Computer Fault Diagnosis", *Proc. of International Joint Conference on Artificial Intelligence*, IJCAI, 1981, 843–845.

[Bernstein78] Bernstein, L., Siegel, E. and Ford, W., "The Hepatitis Knowledge Base Prototype", *Proc. 2nd Annu. Symp. Comp. Appl. Med. Care*, Nov. 1978, 366–367.

[Buchanan70] Buchanan, B., Sutherland, E., and Feigenbaum, E., "Rediscovering Some Problems of Artificial Intelligence in the Context of Organic Chemistry", *Machine Intelligence*, **5**, Meltzer and Michie (eds.), Edinburgh University Press, 1970.

[Carpenter87] Carpenter, G. and Grossberg, S., "A Massively Parallel Architecture for a Self-Organizing Neural Pattern Recognition Machine", *Computer Vision, Graphics and Image Processing*, **37**, 1987, 54–115.

[Catanzarite79] Catanzarite, V. and Greenburg, A., "Neurologist – A Computer Program for Diagnosis in Neurology", *Proc. 3rd Symp. Comp. Appl. Med. Care*, IEEE 1979, 64–72.

[Chandrasekaran79] Chandrasekaran, B., et al, "An Approach to Medical Diagnosis Based on Conceptual Structure", *Proc. of International Joint Conference on Artificial Intelligence, IJCAI,* 1979, 134–142.

[Charniak83] Charniak, E., "The Bayesian Basis of Common Sense Medical Diagnosis", *Proc. of National Conference on Artificial Intelligence, AAAI,* 1983, 70–73.

[Charniak85] Charniak, E. and McDermott, D., *Introduction to Artificial Intelligence,* Addison–Wesley, Reading, MA., 1985, chapters 8, 10.

[Chu90] Chu, B. and Reggia, J., "Modeling Diagnosis at Multiple Levels of Abstraction", submitted.

[Collatz75] Collatz, L. and Wetterling, W., *Optimization Problems,* Springer–Verlag, 1975.

[Coombs84] Coombs, M. (Ed.) *Developments in Expert Systems,* Academic Press, 1984.

[Coombs87] Coombs, M. and Hartley R., "The MGR Algorithm and Its Application to the Generation of Explanations for Novel Events", Tech. Report MCCS–87–97, Computer Research Laboratory, New Mexico University, 1987.

[Cooper84] Cooper, G., *NESTOR: A Computer-Based Medical Diagnostic Aid That Integrates Causal and Probabilistic Knowledge,* STAN–CS–84–1031 (Ph. D. Dissertation), Dept. of Computer Science, Stanford University, Nov. 1984.

[Dasigi89] Dasigi, V., and Reggia, J., "Parsimonious Covering as a Method for Natural Language Interfaces to Expert Systems", *Artificial Intelligence in Medicine,* **1**, 1989, 49–60.

[Davies72] Davies, P., "Symptom Diagnosis Using Bahadur's Distribution", *Bio-Med. Comp.,* **3**, 1972, 69–89.

[Davis76] Davis, R., "Application of Metalevel Knowledge to the Construction, Maintenance and Use of Large Knowledge Base", MEMO AIM–283, Stanford AI Laboratory, Stanford, CA, 1976.

[Davis77] Davis, R., Buchanan, B., and Shortliffe, E, "Production Rules as a Representation for a Knowledge–based Consultation Program", *Artificial Intelligence,* **8**, 1, 1977, 15–45.

[deDombal75] deDombal, F., "Computer Assisted Diagnosis of Abdominal Pain", in Rose and Mitchell (eds.), *Advances in Medical Computing,* Churchill–Livingston, 1975, 10–19.

[deKleer87] de Kleer, J. and Williams, B. "Diagnosing Multiple Faults", *Artif. Intell.* **32**, 1987, 97–130.

[Dempster68] Dempster, A., "A Generalization of Bayesian Inference", *Journal of Roy. Statis. Soc.,* **B30**, 1968, 205–247.

[Duda73] Duda, R., and Hart, P., *Pattern Classification and Scene Analysis,* Wiley–Interscience, 1973.

[Duda76] Duda, R., et al, "Subjective Bayesian Methods for Rule–Based Inference Systems", *Proc. AFIPS,* 1976, 1075–1082.

[Duda78] Duda, R., et al, "Development of the PROSPECTOR Consultation System for Mineral Exploration", Final Report, SRI Project 5821 and 6415, SRI International Inc., Menlo Park, CA., 1978.

[Elstein78] Elstein, A., Shulman, L., and Sprafka, S., *Medical Problem Solving - An Analysis of Clinical Reasoning*, Harvard University Press, 1978.

[Erman80] Erman L., and Lesser, V., "The HEARSAY-II Speech Understanding System: A Tutorial", in Lea (Ed.), *Trends* 1980, 361–381.

[Fahlman75] Fahlman, S., "Symbol-Mapping and Frames", *SIGART Newsletter*, **53**, 1975, 7–8.

[Fahlman79] Fahlman, S., *NETL - A System for Representing and Using Real-World Knowledge*, MIT Press, Cambridge, MA. 1979.

[Feldman82] Feldman, J., and Ballard, D., "Connectionist Models and Their Properties", *Cognitive Science*, **6**, 1982, 205–254.

[Findler79] Findler N. (Ed.), *Associative Networks: The Representation and Use of Knowledge by Computers*, New York, Academic Press, 1979.

[Flehinger75] Flehinger, B., and Engle, R., "HEME: A Self-Improving Computer Program for Diagnosis-Oriented Analysis of Hematologic Diseases", *IBM J. Res. Develop.*, Nov. 1975, 557–564.

[Friedman77] Friedman, R., and Gustafson, D., "Computers in Clinical Medicine - A Critical Review", *Comp. and Biomed. Res.*, **10**, 1977, 199–204.

[Fryback78] Fryback, D., "Bayes' Theorem and Conditional Nonindependence of Data in Medical Diagnosis", *Comp. and Biomed. Res.*, **11**, 1978, 423–434.

[Goel88] Goel, A., Ramanujam, J., and Sadayappan, P., "Towards a 'Neural' Architecture for Abductive Reasoning", *Proc. IEEE Intl. Conf. on Neural Networks*, Vol. I, 1988, 681–688.

[Goldberg78] Goldberg, R., and Kastner, J., "An Explicit Description of Anatomical Knowledge as an Aid to Diagnosis: A Spatial Network Model", CBM-TM-78, Dept. of Computer Science, Rutgers University, 1978.

[Gordon85] Gordon, J., and Shortliffe, E., "A Method for Managing Evidential Reasoning in a Hierarchical Hypothesis Space", *Artificial Intelligence*, **26**, 1985, 323–357.

[Gorry68] Gorry, G., and Barnett, G., "Experience with a Model of Sequential Diagnosis", *Comp. and Biomed. Res.*, **1**, 1968, 490–507.

[Grossberg80] Grossberg, S., "How Does a Brain Build a Cognitive Code", *Psychological Review*, **87**, 1980, 1–51.

[Gupta85] Gupta, M., Kandel, A., Bandler, W., and Kiszka, J., (eds.) *Approximate Reasoning in Expert Systems*, North-Holland (Amsterdam), 1985.

[Gustafson77] Gustafson, D. et al, "A Probabilistic System for Identifying Suicide Attemptors", *Comp. and Biomed. Res.*, **10**, 1977, 83–89.

[Hinton81] Hinton, G., "Implementing Semantic Networks in Parallel Hardware", in G. Hinton and J. Anderson (eds.) *Parallel Models of Associative Memory*, Erlbaum, 1981, 161–187.

[Hopfield84] Hopfield, J., "Neurons with Graded Response Have Collective Computational Properties Like Those of Two–State Neurons", *Proc. Natl. Acad. Sci. USA*, **81**, 1984, 3088–3092.

[Hopfield85] Hopfield, J., and Tank, D., "Neural Computation of Decisions in Optimization Problems", *Biological Cybernetics*, **52**, 1985, 141–152.

[Hripcsak89] Hripcsak, G., "Toward Data Analysis Using Connectionist Models", *Proc. Symp. Comp. Appl. Med. Care, IEEE*, 1989, in press.

[Jelliffe72] Jelliffe, R., Buell, J., and Kalaba, R., "Reduction of Digitalis Toxicity by Computer–Assisted Glycoside Dosage Regimens", *Ann. Intl. Med.*, **77**, 1972, 891–906.

[Johnson81] Johnson, et al "Expertise and Error in Diagnostic Reasoning", *Cognitive Science*, **5**, 1981, 235–283.

[Josephson82] Josephson, J., "Explanation and Induction", Ph. D. Thesis, Dept. of Philosophy, Ohio State University, 1982.

[Josephson84] Josephson, J., Chandrasekaran, B., and Smith, J., "Assembling the Best Explanation", *IEEE Workshop on Principles of Knowledge–Based Systems*, Denver, CO. Dec., 1984.

[Josephson87a] Josephson, J., Chandrasekaran, B., Smith, J., and Tanner, M., "A Mechanism for Forming Composite Explanatory Hypotheses", *IEEE Trans. System, Man, and Cybernetics*, **17** (3), 1987, 445–454.

[Josephson87b] Josephson, J., "A Framework for Situation Assessment", *Proceedings of the Knowledge–Based Systems Workshop*, 1987, 76–85.

[Kahn] Kahn, G., Nowlan, S. and McDermott, J. "Strategies for Knowledge Acquisition", *IEEE Trans. on Pattern Analysis and Machine Intelligence*, **7**, 1985, 511–522.

[Karp72] Karp, R., "Reducibility Among Combinatorial Problems", *Complexity of Computer Computations*, Miller, R., and Thatcher, J. (eds.), Plenum Press, New York, 1972, 85–103.

[Kassirer78] Kassirer, J., and Gorry, G., "Clinical Problem Solving: A Behavioral Analysis", *Ann. Intl. Med*, **89**, 1978, 245–255.

[Kautz86] Kautz, H. and Allen, J., "Generalized Plan Recognition", *Proc. of National Conference on Artificial Intelligence, AAAI*, 1986, 32–37.

[Kirkpatrick83] Kirkpatrick, S., Gelatt, C., and Vecchi, M., "Optimization by Simulated Annealing", *Science*, **220**, 1983, 671–680.

[Knapp77] Knapp, R. et al, "A Computer–Generated Diagnostic Decision Guide – A Comparison of Statistical Diagnosis and Clinical Diagnosis", *Comp. Biol. Med.*, **7**, 1977, 223–230.

[Leaper72] Leaper, D., Horrocks, J., Staniland, J., and deDombal, F., "Computer–Assisted Diagnosis of Abdominal Pain Using Estimates Provided by Clinicians", *Brit. Med. J.*, **4**, 1972, 359–354.

[Ledley59] Ledley, R., Lusted, L., "Reasoning Foundation of Medical

Diagnosis: Symbolic Logic, Probability, and Value Theory Aid Our Understanding of How Physicians Reason", *Science*, **130**, 9, 1959, 9–21.

[Lindsay80] Lindsay, R., et al, *DENDRAL*, McGraw-Hill, New York, 1980.

[Litman87] Litman, D. and Allen, J., "A Plan Recognition Model for Subdialogues in Conversation", *Cognitive Science*, **11**, 1987, 163–200.

[Mattys79] Mattys, H., et al, "Functional Pattern of Different Lung Diseases for Computer-Assisted Diagnostic Procedures", *Prog. Resp. Res.*, **11**, 1979, 188–201.

[McClelland81] McClelland, J., and Rumelhart D., "An Interactive Activation Model of Context Effects in Letter Perception: Part 1. An Account of Basic Findings", *Psychological Review*, **88**, 1981, 375–407.

[Miller82] Miller, R., Pople, H. and Meyers, J., "Internist-1: An Experimental Computer-Based Diagnostic Consultant for General Internal Medicine", *New England Journal of Medicine*, **307**, 1982, 468–476.

[Minsky68] Minsky, M., *Semantic Information Processing*, MIT Press, Cambridge, Mass., 1968.

[Minsky75] Minsky, M., "A Framework for Representing Knowledge", in Winston, P. (Ed.) *The Psychology of Computer Vision*, McGraw-Hill, New York, 1975, 211–277.

[Mittal79] Mittal, S., Chandrasekaran, B., and Smith, J., "Overview of MDX – A System for Medical Diagnosis", *Proc. 3rd Annual Symposium on Computer Application in Medical Care, IEEE* Oct. 1979, 34–46.

[Mulsant88] Mulsant, B. and Servan-Schreiber, E., "A Connectionist Approach to the Diagnosis of Dementia", *Proc. Symp. Comp. Appl. in Medical Care, IEEE*, 1988, 245–250.

[Nau83] Nau, D., "Expert Computer Systems", *Computer, IEEE* **16**, 1983, 63–85.

[Nau84] Nau, D., and Reggia, J., "Relationship Between Deductive and Abductive Inference in Knowledge-Based Diagnostic Problem Solving", *Proc. First Intl. Workshop on Expert Database Systems*, Kerschberge, L. (ed.), Kiawah Island, SC, Oct, 1984, 500–509.

[Neapolitan87] Neapolitan, R., Georgakis, C., Evens, M., Kenevan, J., Jiwani, H., and Heir, D., "Using Set Covering and Uncertain Reasoning to Rank Explanations", *Proceedings of SCAMC*, Washington, DC, Nov., 1987. 213–219.

[Nilsson80] Nilsson, N., *Principles of Artificial Intelligence*, Tioga Publishing Company, 1980.

[Norusis75] Norusis, M., and Jacquez, J., "Diagnostic Model Based on Attribute Clusters – A Proposal and Comparisons", *Comp. and Biomed. Res.*, **8**, 1975, 173–188.

[O'Rorke88] O'Rorke, P. "Automated Abduction and Machine Learning", *Proc. AAAI Symposium on Explanation-Based Learning*, Stanford, CA. March 1988, 170–174.

[O'Rorke89] O'Rorke, P. Morris, S. and Schulenberg, D., "Theory Forma-
tion by Abduction: Initial Results of a Case Study Based on the
Chemical Revolution", *Proc. Sixth International Workshop on
Machine Learning*, 1989, in press.

[Pauker76] Pauker, S., Gorry, G., Kassirer, J., and Schwarz, M., "Towards
the Simulation of Clinical Cognition", *Am. J. Med.*, **60**, 1976, 981-
996.

[Pearl86a] Pearl, J., "Distributed Revision of Belief Commitment in
Multi-Hypotheses Interpretation", *Proc. the 2nd AAAI Workshop on
Uncertainty in Artificial Intelligence*, Philadelphia, PA., Aug. 1986,
201-209.

[Pearl86b] Pearl, J. "Fusion, Propagation, and Structuring in Belief Networks", *Artif. Intell.* **29**, 1986, 241-288.

[Pearl88] Pearl, J., *Probabilistic Reasoning in Intelligent Systems*, Morgan
Kaufmann, San Mateo, CA. 1988.

[Peirce31] Peirce, C., *Collected Papers of Charles Sanders Peirce*,
Hartshorne, C., Weiss, P., and Burks, A., (eds), Cambridge Press,
1931-1958, Vol. II, 272-607.

[Peirce55] Peirce, C., *Abduction and Induction*, Dover, 1955.

[Peng85] Peng, Y., *A Formalization of Parsimonious Covering and Probabilistic Reasoning in Abductive Diagnostic Inference*, Ph. D. Dissertation, Dept. of Comp. Sci., Univ. of Maryland, Dec. 1985.

[Peng86] Peng, Y., Reggia, J., "Plausibility of Diagnostic Hypotheses: The
Nature of Simplicity", *Proc. of National Conference on Artificial
Intelligence, AAAI*, 1986, 146-162

[Peng87a] Peng, Y., and Reggia, J., "A Probabilistic Causal Model for
Diagnostic Problem Solving. Part One: Integrating Symbolic Causal
Inference with Numeric Probabilistic Inference", *IEEE Trans. System,
Man and Cybernetics*, **17** (2), March 1987, 146-162.

[Peng87b] Peng, Y., and Reggia, J., "A Probabilistic Causal Model for
Diagnostic Problem Solving. Part Two: Diagnostic Strategy", *IEEE
Trans. Systems, Man and Cybernetics special issue for diagnosis*, **17**
(3), May 1987, 395-406.

[Peng87c] Peng, Y., and Reggia, J., "Diagnostic Problem-Solving with
Causal Chaining", *International Journal of Intelligent Systems*, **2**,
1987, 265-302.

[Peng89a] Peng, Y. and Reggia, J., "Comfort Measure for Diagnostic
Problem-Solving", *Information Sciences*, 1989, **48**, 149-184.

[Peng89b] Peng, Y. and Reggia, J., "A Connectionist Model for Diagnostic
Problem Solving", *IEEE Trans. Systems, Man and Cybernetics*, **19**
(2), March 1989, 285-298.

[Polya54] Polya, G., *Patterns of Plausible Inference*, Princeton University
Press, Princeton, NJ, 1954, chapter 13.

[Pople73] Pople, H., "On the Mechanization of Abductive Logic", *Proc. of International Joint Conference on Artificial Intelligence, IJCAI*, 1973, 147–152.

[Pople75] Pople, H., and Miller, R., "DIALOG: A Model of Diagnostic Logic for Internal Medicine", *Proc. of International Joint Conference on Artificial Intelligence, IJCAI*, 1975.

[Pople77] Pople, H., "The Formation of Composite Hypotheses in Diagnostic Problem–Solving – A Exercise in Synthetic Reasoning", *Proc. International Joint Conference on Artificial Intelligence, IJCAI*, 1977, 1030–1037.

[Pople82] Pople, H., "Heuristic Methods for Improving Structure on Ill–structured Problems: The Structuring of Medical Diagnostics", in Szolovits, P. (ed.) *Artificial Intelligence in Medicine*, 1982, 119–190.

[Pople85] Pople, H., "Evolution of an Expert System: from Internist to Caduceus", in DeLotto and Stefanelli (eds.), *Artificial Intelligence in Medicine*, 1985, 179–203.

[Punch86] Punch, W., Tanner, M., and Josephson, J. "Design Consideration for *Peirce*, A High–Level Language for Hypothesis Assembly", *Proc. Expert Systems in Government Symposium*, 1986, 279–281.

[Quillian68] Quillian, M., "Semantic Memory", in Minsky M. (Ed.) *Semantic Information Processing*, MIT Press, Cambridge, Mass, 1968, 227–270.

[Ramsey86] Ramsey, C., and Reggia, J., "A Comparative Analysis of Methods for Expert Systems", *Intl. J. Man–Machine Studies*, **24**, 1986, 475–499.

[Reggia78] Reggia, J., "A Production Rule System for Neurological Localization", *Proc. 5th Ann. Symp. Comp. Appl. Med. Care, IEEE*, 1978, 254–260.

[Reggia81] Reggia, J., *Knowledge–Based Decision Support System: Development Through KMS*, Dept. of Comp. Sci., Univ. of Maryland, Technical Report, TR–1121, Oct. 1981.

[Reggia82a] Reggia, J., "Computer–Assisted Medical Decision Making", in Schwartz (Ed.), *Applications of Computers in Medicine, IEEE*, 1982, 198–213.

[Reggia82b] Reggia, J. and Perricone, B., *KMS Manual*, Technical Report, TR–1136, Department of Computer Science, University of Maryland, College Park, Jan. 1982.

[Reggia83a] Reggia, J., Nau, D., and Wang, P., "Diagnostic Expert Systems Based on a Set Covering Model", *Intl. J. Man–Machine Studies*, Nov. 1983, 437–460.

[Reggia84a] Reggia, J., and Nau, D., "An Abductive Non–Monotonic Logic", *Proc. Workshop on Non–Monotonic Reasoning, AAAI*, Oct. 1984, 385–395.

[Reggia84b] Reggia, J. et al, "Computer–Aided Assessment of Transient Ischemic Attacks", *Arch Neurol*, **41**, Dec. 1984.

[Reggia85a] Reggia, J., Nau, D., Wang, P., and Peng, Y., "A Formal Model of Diagnostic Inference", *Information Sciences*, **37**, 1985, 227–285.

[Reggia85b] Reggia, J., "Abductive Inference", *Expert Systems in Government Symposiums*, Washington, DC, Oct. 1985.

[Reggia85c] Reggia, J., "Virtual Lateral Inhibition in Activation Model of Associative Memory", *Proc. of International Joint Conference on Artificial Intelligence, IJCAI*, 1985, 244–248.

[Reggia85d] Reggia, J., et al., "Answer Justification in Diagnostic Expert Systems", *IEEE Trans. on Biomed. Eng.*, **32**, no. 4, April 1985, 263–272.

[Reggia85e] Reggia, J. and Perricone, B., "Answer Justification in Medical Decision Support Systems Based on Bayesian Classification", *Comp. Biol. Med.*, **15**, 1985, 161–167.

[Reggia85f] Reggia, J., and Tuhrim, S., "An Overview of Methods for Computer–Assisted Medical Decision Making", in Reggia, J., and Tuhrim, S., (eds.), *Computer–Assisted Medical Decision Making*, Vol. 1, Springer–Verlag, NY, 1985b, 3–45.

[Reggia86] Reggia, J., and Berndt, R., "Modeling Reading Aloud and Its Relevance to Acquired Dyslexia", *Computer Methods and Programs in Biomedicine*, **22**, 1986, 13–19.

[Reggia87] Reggia, J., "Properties of a Competition–Based Activation Mechanism in Neuromimetic Network Models", *Proc. 1st Intl. Conf. on Neural Networks*, San Diego, June 1987, 313–138.

[Reggia89] Reggia, J. and Sutton, G. "Self–Processing Methods and Their Biomedical Implications", *Proc. IEEE*, **76**, 1988, 680–692.

[Reiter87] Reiter, R., "A Theory of Diagnosis from the First Principle", *Artif. Intell.* **32**, 1987, 57–95

[Richards77] Richards, B., and Goh, A., Computer Assistance in the treatment of Patients with Acid–Base and Electrolyte Disturbances", *MEDINFO-77*, IFIP, 1977, 407–410.

[Rogers79] Rogers, W., Ryack, B., and Moeller, G., "Computer–Aided Medical Diagnosis – Literature Review", *Intl. J. Biomed. Comp.*, **10**, 1979, 267–289.

[Rubin75] Rubin, A., "The Role of Hypotheses in Medical Diagnosis", *Proc. of International Joint Conference on Artificial Intelligence, IJCAI*, 1975, 856–862.

[Rumelhart82] Rumelhart D., and McClelland, J., "An Interactive Activation Model of Context Effects in Letter Perception: Part 2. The Contextual Enhancement Effect and Some Tests and Extension of the Model", *Psychological Review*, **89**, 1982, 60–94.

[Shafer76] Shafer, G., *A Mathematical Theory of Evidence*, Princeton University Press, Princeton, NJ, 1976.

[Shapiro77] Shapiro, A., "The Evaluation of Clinical Predictions", *New England Journal of Medicine*, **296**, 1977, 1509–1514.

[Shortliffe75] Shortliffe, E., and Buchanan, B., "A Model of Inexact Reasoning in Medicine", *Mathematical Bioscience*, **23**, 1975, 351–379.

[Shortliffe76] Shortliffe, E., *Computer–Based Medical Consultation: MYCIN*, Elesevier, 1976.

[Shortliffe79] Shortliffe, E., Buchanan, B., and Feigenbaum, E., "Knowledge Engineering for Medical Decision Making: A Review of Computer–Based Clinical Decision Aids", *Proc. IEEE*, **67**, 9, Sept. 1979, 1207–1226.

[Shortliffe81] Shortliffe, E., et al, "ONCOCIN: An Expert System for Oncology Protocol Management", *Proc. of International Joint Conference on Artificial Intelligence, IJCAI*, 1981, 876–881.

[Shubin82] Shubin, H., and Ulrich, J., "IDT: An Intelligent Diagnostic Tool", *Proc. National Conference on Artificial Intelligence, AAAI*, 1982, 290–295.

[SIGART85] "Report of the Workshop on Automated Explanation Production", *SIGART Newsletter*, **85**, July 1983, 7–13.

[Simmons87] Simmons, R. and Davis, R., "Generate, Test and Debug: Combining Associational Rules and Causal Models", *Proc. of International Joint Conference on Artificial Intelligence, IJCAI*, 1987, 1071–1078.

[Smith85] Smith, J., Svirbely, J., Evans, C., Strohm, O., Josephson, J., and Tanner, M., "RED: A Red–Cell Antibody Identification Expert System", *J. of Medical Systems*, **9**(3), 1985, 121–138.

[Swartout83] Swartout, W., "XPLAIN: A System for Creating and Explaining Expert Consulting Program", *Artificial Intelligence*, **21**, 1983, 285–325.

[Szolovits78] Szolovits, P., and Pauker, S., "Categorical and Probabilistic Reasoning in Medical Diagnosis", *Artificial Intelligence*, **2**, 1978, 115–144.

[Tagamets89] Tagamets, M., and Reggia, J., "A Data Flow Implementation of a Competition–Based Connectionist Model", *Journal of Parallel and Distributed Computing*, **6**, 1989, 704–714.

[Templeton67] Templton, A. et al, "Solitary Pulmonary Lesions", *Radiology*, **89**, 1967, 605–613.

[Thagard78] Thagard, P., "The Best Explanation – Criteria for Theory Choice", *Journal of Philosophy*, **75**, 1978, 76–92.

[Thagard89] Thagard, P., "Explanatory Coherence", *Behavioral and Brain Sciences*, 1989, in press.

[Torasso89] Torasso, P. and Console, L. *Diagnostic Problem Solving*, Van Nostrand Reinbold, NY. 1989.

[Touretzky85] Touretzky, D., and Hinton, G., "Symbols Among the Neurons", *Proceedings of the Ninth International Joint Conference on Artificial Intelligence*, 1985, 238–243.

[Touretzky86] Touretzky, D., "BoltzCONS: Reconciling Connectionism with the Recursive Nature of Stacks and Trees", *Proceedings of the Eighth Annual Conference of the Cognitive Science*, 1986, 522–530.

[Tversky74] Tversky, A., "Assessing Uncertainty", *J. Royal Statistical Society*, **B36**, 1974, 148–159.

[Van Melle] Van Melle, W. "A Domain Independent Production Rule System for Consultation Program", *Proc. of International Joint Conference on Artificial Intelligence*, *IJCAI*, Tokyo 1979, 923–925.

[Wald89] Wald, J., Farach, M., Tagamets, M. and Reggia, J., "Generating Plausible Diagnostic Hypotheses with Self Processing Causal Networks", *Journal of Experimental and Theoretical AI*, **1**, 1989, 91–112.

[Wang88] Wang, P., Seidman, S. and Reggia, J., "Analysis of Competition–Based Spreading Activation in Connectionist Models", *Intl. J. of Man–Machine Studies*, **28**, 1988, 77–97.

[Warner64] Warner, H., Toronto, A., and Veasy, L., "Experience with Bayes' Theorem for Computer Diagnosis of Congenital Heart Disease", *Anns. N.Y. Acad. Sci.*, **115**, 1964, p.558–567.

[Weiss78] Weiss, S. and Kulikowski, C., "Glaucoma Consultation by Computers", *Comp. Biol. Med.*, **8**, 1978, 25–40.

[Weiss84] Weiss, S. and Kulikowski, C., *A Practical Guide to Designing Expert Systems*, Rowman & Allanheld, 1984.

[Winograd73] Winograd, T., "A Procedural Model of Language Understanding", in Schank, R. and Colby, K. (Eds.) *Computer Models of Thought and Language*, San Francisco, CA. Freeman, 1973, 152–186.

[Yager85] Yager, R., "Explanatory Models in Expert Systems", *Intl. Journal of Man–Machine Studies*, **23**, 1985, 539–549.

[Zagoria83] Zagoria, R., and Reggia, J., "Transferability of Medical Decision Support Systems Based on Bayesian Classification", *Medical Decision Making*, **3**, 1983, 501–510.

Index

G. Rayna: *REDUCE. Software for Algebraic Computation.* IX, 329 pages, 1987

D.D. McDonald, L. Bolc (Eds.): *Natural Language Generation Systems.* XI, 389 pages, 84 figs. 1988

L. Bolc, M.J. Coombs (Eds.): *Expert System Applications.* IX, 471 pages, 84 figs., 1988

C.-H. Tzeng: *A Theory of Heuristic Information in Game-Tree Search.* X, 107 pages, 22 figs., 1988

H. Coelho, J.C. Cotta: *Prolog by Example. How to Learn, Teach, and Use It.* X. 382 pages, 68 figs., 1988

L. Kanal, V. Kumar (Eds.): *Search in Artificial Intelligence.* X, 482 pages, 67 figs., 1988

H. Abramson, V. Dahl: *Logic Grammars.* XIV, 234 pages, 40 figs. 1989

R. Hausser: *Computation of Language. An Essay on Syntax, Semantics, and Pragmatics in Natural Man-Machine Communication.* XVI, 425 pages, 1989

B. D'Ambrosio: *Qualitative Process Theory Using Linguistic Variables.* X, 156 pages, 22 figs., 1989

A. Kobsa, W. Wahlster (Eds.): *User Models in Dialog Systems.* XI, 471 pages, 113 figs., 1989

P. Besnard: *An Introduction to Default Logic.* XI, 208 pages, 1989

V. Kumar, P.S. Gopalakrishnan, L. Kanal (Eds.): *Parallel Algorithms for Machine Intelligence and Vision.* XII, 433 pages, 148 figs., 1990

Y. Peng, J.A. Reggia: *Abductive Inference Models for Diagnostic Problem-Solving.* XI, 304 pages, 25 figs., 1990